# The Romance of History

Spanish scholars were astounded at the publication of Prescott's work. How did a man in a remote country learn what was hidden in their dusty archives? How did he convey with such accurate detail the long-buried history of the Spanish invasion of the New World? The answer lies in Prescott's profound scholarly delving, his limitless patience, and his enduring artistry as a writer.

This classic, written more than a century ago, has yet to be surpassed. Though new facts have been uncovered through archaeological findings, they seem to justify Prescott's conclusions, some of which must have been arrived at through inspired intuition.

Here is a historical edifice, built stone on stone by a great scholar, capturing all the romance of a mysterious, resplendent civilization and its tragic conquest by a more ruthless race of men.

❧ ❧

*The waterjar on the back cover of this book depicts a human trophy head, made about fifteen hundred years before the Spanish Conquest. The drawing was made from a replica of the original jar. The illustrations in the book are by John Davis; the diagrams of architectural restorations by Emilio Harth-Terré; and the maps by Mario Guerra.*

# William H. Prescott

# History of
# THE CONQUEST
# OF PERU

---

## PARTLY ABRIDGED AND REVISED

---

THE CLASSIC STORY OF THE INCA EMPIRE AND ITS SUBJUGATION BY THE SPANIARDS, WITH AN INTRODUCTION, NEW NOTES AND A NEW SUMMARY OF THE CIVIL WARS AND SUBSEQUENT EVENTS BY THE DISTINGUISHED ARCHAEOLOGICAL HISTORIAN,

## Victor W. von Hagen

**MENTOR: ANCIENT CIVILIZATIONS**
Published by the New American Library

For Van Wyck Brooks,
*who brought William Prescott alive for this
generation in* The Flowering of New England,
*this new edition of* The Conquest of Peru
*is affectionately dedicated by the editor.*

LA MOLINA
LIMA, PERU

—V.W.v.H.

# Contents

# Illustrations

## Maps and Diagrams

# Introduction

*The Conquest of Peru,* by the very spaciousness of its subject and the interest of its narrative, belongs to historical literature. And *as* literature it is a small miracle. Few historical pieces such as this have withstood the test of time so well, and even less have such pioneer works withstood the assault of archaeological discoveries—and historians. Although in this last century they have unearthed a mass of documents unknown to Prescott, still they have succeeded only in adding illuminating details to his history.

Posterity well knows its business. It makes no exceptions. It confirms that which is solid, it reduces to dust that which is not; and that which is purely sonorous vanishes. Time has a mysterious and implacable sense of final conclusions. A work becomes a masterpiece only with the aid of time; and time, which is the measurer of all things, has made *The Conquest of Peru* into a masterpiece.

Prescott had the formula for writing a masterpiece: he wrote for himself. Since he did not have to write for his bread, he set his own theme and his own pace and so produced his masterwork under an inexorable fatality. ". . . My publishers," he wrote to a friend on June 27, 1847, "have today sent my Peruvian bantling into the world. . . ." With this droll understatement he told of the publication of The *History of the Conquest of Peru*—a book of 1,070 pages and one which had been particularly laborious: it had taken him precisely two years and nine months to finish it.

Yet greater than his book, there stands the man himself. He wrote under conditions which would have appalled most, and before he could begin his career he had to make a conquest of his own. So, as someone put it, Prescott's conquests were not two, but three: the third, and perhaps the greatest, was his own life.

William Prescott's personal drama began in 1811. It came out of a thrown crust of bread. As everyone of substance in Boston then did, Prescott entered Harvard College. At fifteen years of age he was preparing to read law and to echo the profession of his father, Judge Prescott. Anyone who saw the "charming, amusing son of the Judge, living in his ample house on Bedford Street" could then have given a précis of his future life. The Prescotts were among the earliest to arrive

William Hickling Prescott in his fiftieth year. The conquest of his own infirmity, the loss of an eye, made possible the first dramatic history of the Spanish conquest of America. (From George Ticknor, *Life of W. H. Prescott.* Philadelphia: J. B. Lippincott Company, 1863.)

from England; there they had been Puritans, had fought for Oliver Cromwell, and had then, twenty years later, migrated to New England.

As men of probity and responsibility, the Prescotts were soon selected to manage the affairs of the Colony of Massachusetts. Later, when the winds of doctrine welled up the storm of revolt, it was a Prescott, Colonel William Prescott, who was ordered to defend Bunker Hill overlooking Boston. There he commanded, on June 16, 1775, one of the earliest battles of the American Revolution.

As America grew, so did the Prescotts. Judge Prescott

moved to Salem, practiced law, and gained his fortune, later augmented by lucrative railway and manufacturing investments. It was in this same Salem, Massachusetts, three years before the death of Washington, that William Hickling Prescott was born, on May 4, 1796. Now the Prescotts, with the passage of time, by investment in selves and country, belonged, if anyone did, to the aristocracy of New England. They were trained from childhood to have a sense of dedication as Federalists and Unitarians; they had an inward consciousness of belonging. This was William Prescott's heritage. He was a proper Bostonian ". . . in its most attractive form," as Van Wyck Brooks said, ". . . a positivist, clear, full of romantic feeling, with scarcely a shred of intuition: William Prescott was a boy from first to last, a charming, virile and romantic boy with a scholar's conscience and an artist's genius. One might well ask for different things, but one could scarcely ask for anything better. . . ."

Prescott's life was changed from the accepted norm of a proper Bostonian by that crust of bread. While in his junior year at Harvard, the students one day, while eating in the Commons, turned the room into pandemonium by bombarding each other with food; in the midst of it Prescott, who turned at the call of his name, was struck by a crust of bread accurately thrown. It hit him in the open left eye, striking the unprotected pupil; it had the effect usually attending a brain concussion. When he recovered he was made instantly aware that he had lost the sight of his left eye.

The second war with England had come to a close in 1814, when Prescott, aged eighteen, was graduated from Harvard. Immediately he went into his "natural inheritance," beginning

The stylus used by Prescott. On this he composed his four histories of Spain in Spain and Spain in America. (From George Ticknor, *Life of W. H. Prescott.* Philadelphia: J. B. Lippincott Company, 1863.)

as a law clerk in his father's office. Within five months the concentration of his "good eye" on the small print of the law brought on a relapse—a traumatic rheumatism through head and neck which at times deprived him of the sight of the remaining eye. After that there was to be no more of Blackstone; he was to travel abroad for consultation with European specialists.

It was to be one of the rare times he left America; he went to the Azores, Italy, France, and England in search of a cure—but there was none. "I can hope for no remedy and few alleviations." Strong lights or colors affected him, and he could read only briefly. He returned to Boston, married in 1820 Susan Amory, daughter of one of the most affluent Boston families, and sired a brood of self-reliant children. During the same period he set about making a conquest of his infirmity.

At the age of twenty-five and known only to a few in Boston, Prescott set out to mold himself into a historian; first he taught himself the use of the noctograph, by means of which, with the aid of an ivory stylus guided by silver wires and pressing on a sheet of carbon paper, he wrote down his notes; he learned to use it in semi-darkness. A secretary was hired to read the books which he selected. He gave himself a year to learn French, another year for Spanish; he studied the great historical stylists—Bacon, Gibbon, Brown—read widely, and studied historical theory. Like Taine, he felt that literary criticism was one of the forms of history. Though it was one of the last of literary forms and perhaps would end in absorbing them all, still Prescott thought it had to be the guiding point in selecting and judging authors. Further in his preparations he attended the lectures of George Ticknor on Spanish history and joined a literary club. Then, to give his Pegasus wings, he began to write critical essays for the reviews; on one of these, "The Arabs in Spain," he spent seven months of agonized effort. Was blindness altogether bad? Had not poets from Homer to Milton proved that sightlessness was good for literary invention? Blindness increased the sensitivity, the ferreting out, the subtleties in research. "He made his ears do the work of his eyes"; he trained himself to memorize sentences, paragraphs, in fact whole chapters, before committing anything to paper.

Boston at first did not reconcile the gay young Prescott, who wore his learning lightly, with the works that he was producing. It is difficult for the public to believe that scholarship and youth can go together; it thinks that in order to know what is what, one must have studied a lifetime, and that deep reading is the business alone of old men.

Prescott sought his theme. It must be one that would be at once novel and grandiose. Now Spain had occupied American thought for some decades—the Peninsular War, the struggles in South America, all these brought it into focus as a possible choice. Spanish scholars were then performing their herculean labors in the Spanish archives so as to publish the documents of their golden age, but as yet no historiographer had assimilated all this greatness or written of it in a style that the epic demanded. Spain, then, was to be his theme. In 1827, after long preparation, Prescott began to lay down the broad outline for a history of Ferdinand and Isabella of Spain; ten years later the work appeared.

"Suddenly, in 1837," wrote Van Wyck Brooks in *The Flowering of New England*, ". . . a great work appeared, like a wonder of nature as it seemed to American readers—*The Reign of Ferdinand and Isabella*. It was a brilliant performance, as any child could see, and no scholar was ever to deny. . . . As a work of art, a great historical narrative, grounded at every point in historical fact, and with all the glow and color of Livy and Froissart, it was a magnificent success."

It was natural that, having succeeded in finding theme and style in a new form of history, he would go on—to the Spanish conquest.

Prescott had hardly begun when he heard that Washington Irving, the popular author of the *Life of Columbus* and himself a former minister to Spain, was contemplating a work on the conquest of Mexico. He wrote to say he would turn aside from the subject if Mr. Irving was committed to it, but Washington Irving, even though it had been a cherished theme for many years, gave him leave. Although Prescott handsomely acknowledged this in the book, Irving later, in a bitter aside, said, "But I doubt whether in giving him permission Mr. Prescott was aware that I also gave him my bread."

In 1838 Prescott found that his history of the conquest of Mexico would require a prodigious amount of research, for many of the contemporary accounts had never been published, but were hidden away in the official archives of Spain. At the beginning of the conquest and colonization of the New World, Hernán Cortés, Juan de Acosta, and Pedro de Cieza de León were permitted to pass the censors. But finally the exaggerated reports of Spanish cruelty as given out by Bishop de Las Casas

Prescott's house on Beacon Street in Boston.

slipped out from the King's Council—who met so as to revise their polity with "New Laws"—and were published abroad and used against Spain. Then the liberal attitude changed. Henceforth most of the literature which today is the fount and source of history was denied license and impounded by order of the king. Much of Spain's history lay unpublished for centuries; even as late as 1609 royal license was refused for the "Royal Commentaries" of Garcilasso de la Vega.

One cannot say of Prescott what contemporaries said of Molière, that

> Sa muse en campagne
> Vole dans mille auteurs les sottises d'Espagne . . .

for there was more research done by Prescott for one book than most authors put into twenty; enough diplomacy was involved, in gathering the material, to have founded a small republic. Prescott, having found that Arthur Middleton, a classmate at Harvard, was then minister to Spain, asked him to aid; through Middleton he found the German historian Friedrich Lembke, then working his way through the chaos of the archives. Lembke soon put to work a company-of scriveners copying manuscripts. Pascual de Gayangos, an authority on Spanish-Moorish history then resident in England, became Prescott's most indefatigable helper. Even though he was in strained financial circumstances, he refused to accept any emolument other than the actual costs involved; he searched the archives at Simancas and found there papers that no historian had ever seen—Philip II's own personal papers lying forgotten.

When the first 8,000 pages of copied manuscripts arrived, Prescott had them brought to his house on Beacon Street. There, in his book-lined study, he listened as his secretary read the beginnings of the history of the conquest from the documents. Every page of these manuscripts had to go through that process. If they were very important, he risked his good eye to read them himself; if not, they were read over and over, "some," he said, "a dozen times," so that he would be able to fix the material in his mind.

There was nothing dry-as-dust about Prescott. The odor of old books was not about him; he was virile and gallant, ". . . a first-rate human being . . ." in Van Wyck Brooks' opinion. As Prescott did not have to write for his bread, he had, in order to keep to schedule, to make bets with himself or with his secretary and even with his manservant Nathan so that he would finish a given task on time. Every morning

Prescott's library (stylus on desk and curtains arranged so that they could be pulled down to darken the room as he worked) in Boston. In this room *The Conquest of Peru* and *The Conquest of Mexico* were written. (From George Tickner, *Life of W. H. Prescott.* Philadelphia: J. B. Lippincott Company, 1863.)

in summer, and even in winter, he mounted his horse and galloped to Jamaica Plain, "to see," he said, "the sunrise on the hill." On the way he would compose over and over in his mind the sentences he would that day commit to paper. On one of these mornings, December 5, 1840, he started off the day by writing to Fanny Calderón de la Barca: "I am now setting about the conquest of Mexico."

Fanny was his "eyes and ears" in Mexico. She had married, at thirty-four, Angel Calderón de la Barca, a career diplomat, the first Spanish minister to Mexico since the Wars of Independence. Fanny, née Frances Erskine, who once assisted her mother in running a fashionable girls' school in Boston, was sprightly and observant and as Frances, Marquesa Calderón de la Barca, was to play an interesting part in Spanish history. She took to Mexico a daguerreotype camera which Prescott had purchased, and there she exposed pictures of the land and of the people; it is because of this, along with her own inimitable descriptions of people and places, that one "feels" Mexico in Prescott.

In three years it was done; *The Conquest of Mexico* was published in three volumes on December 6, 1843, by Harper & Brothers; it sold 5,000 copies in four months, 23,000 copies in three years. Angel Calderón de la Barca translated it into Spanish; it was published in France, England, and in Germany, where Humboldt ". . . never ceased to praise it."

Prescott's third great theme arose with a sort of inevitability; he found that the material he had collected for Mexico overlapped—and that he had not the need in his second *Conquest* to search for manuscript material. During the summer of 1844 he worked every evening by candlelight. During these months he taxed his "good eye" reading Pedro de Cieza, Garcilasso, Montesinos and other Peruvian historians, so that he could grasp all that related to Peru, its land, its fables, its antiquities. By August, 1844, he had found time to make eighty pages of notes, scrawling them as half-formed words on his noctograph. He advanced far enough to lay down the time for completion of *The Conquest of Peru,* "5–6 months for the introduction, another 8 months for the narrative of the conquest, etc. . . . Now I must really buckle on my harness for Pizarro."

On August 12, 1844, one year after *Mexico* was published, he wrote the first sentence of *Peru.* And with that he set off into the uncertain sea of Peruvian antiquities.

Prescott found it at once "most troublesome and disagreeable"—Peru was so far away and so little known, few modern critical books had been written about it, he had never seen it and never would. He found it maddening. He had written to Humboldt that he was engaged on Peru, "but I feel a great loss at the outset of your friendly hand to aid me . . . for although your great work *Vues des Cordilleres et Monuments . . . de l'Amerique* sheds much light on scattered points yet your own *Voyage* stops short of Peru. . . . I shall have to grope my way through the greater part of it without the master's hand, which in your New Spain led me so securely."

Tortured he was—and he groped his way through it in the semidarkness of his room trying to conjure up the Andes, what they must have been like and how the awesome canyons appeared which rent that world down into its very bowels. He walked scores of miles, said Van Wyck Brooks, from corner to corner of his study, "throwing out his elbow to feel the walls—until he wore away the plaster." Even then he could not yet "feel" the Andes as he had the bald mountains of Mexico, because he had no one to give him the sensuous feel of the land, no one like Fanny Calderón de la Barca who told him so much in her witty, sharp-edged letters from Mexico City. He felt that he could not quite encompass it— until the arrival of General Miller. "Among our visitors here," he wrote, "is General Miller. . . . He has given me many fine details relative to Peru and South America. He is a very fine fellow. . . ." And later: "General Miller of Peru is passing the winter here [in Boston]; *I see him often. . . .*" Prescott could have found no one better.

General William Miller had taken part in every important battle during the wars of South American independence, ranging from Argentina to Chile through Bolivia and Peru; he was in the first of those battles, and he was also destined to be in the last. Born in Kent, England, about the time of Prescott's birth, he served in the British army against Napoleon until the peace of 1815; he saw action with the British against Washington, D.C., took part in the British fiasco at New Orleans, retreated, was shipwrecked off Mobile, and later reached England. Even then he could not quite rid his nostrils of gunpowder, so he sailed to Buenos Aires in 1817 and there was brevetted as a captain in San Martín's army. He took part in all the important engagement in Chile; then, licking his wounds, he sailed toward Peru, where the patriot army was preparing to take on the strongest force Spain had ever concentrated in South America. In Peru, while attempting to fire Congreve rockets—the first time they were used in South America—he was blown up and lay for months in hellish torment. When he arose he had scars which he carried all the rest of his life. Slender, blue-eyed, with a lithe, lean body almost feminine in its delicacy, light hair worn in a sort of *en coup de vent,* his appearance belied his profession; he was a superb horseman, tireless and fearless. As commander of Simón Bolívar's cavalry, he was also chief of the guerrillas, who harassed the royalist troops. The itinerary of war carried him the length and breadth of Peru; he had fought in Moquegua, lodged in the Tambo de Vítor, collected "several thousands of oxen and mules grazing upon the lomas of Atiquipa"; he had ridden up and down the coast, over the Inca Highway (there was no other then) dozens of times; he had moved north of Lima to Huarmey "to look for saltpeter," then to Huambacho, where as a military man he noted "the extensive line of pre-Inca fortifications"; he rode along the great Chimú wall, which was unknown to the world until discovered by air survey in 1931, "that great wall, in many parts still entire . . . with its salient angles . . . that runs along the side of lofty mountains close to the sea at Santa. . . ." He went far beyond this up to the border with Ecuador, "to obtain the best mules, which are from Piura." In 1824, at the final stages of the war, he was made chief of staff of Simón Bolívar. He then trained and led his cavalry from the coast at Trujillo over the Andes to Lake Junín; there at that battle it was the charge of his cavalry which gave Bolívar his first military victory on Peruvian soil. Later in the same year—December 9, 1824—he was one of the generals who helped to bring independence with the decisive victory of Ayacucho. Nor did it end here. After a rest in England he was back again in Peru serving for five years the republic he had helped to create; his journals show that these travels brought him into many obscure and little-known Andean valleys, all of which held in one way or another remains of the empire of the Incas. General Miller, no mere military martinet, noted down what he saw, and collected material documents of Peru's past even while he commanded a host of engagements that seemed always to have to be fought. In 1834 he was created Gran Mariscal del Peru. After that he had ill luck: his fortunes were tied to the losing side within the republic; he was exiled from Peru, sailing on the H.M.B. *Sarang* on February 22, 1839. He took advantage then of the opportunity to go to Mexico and later to Boston, where, as Prescott noted, "among the visitors here is General Miller. . . ."

*The Conquest of Peru* owes much to General William Miller, for he often sat with Prescott, bent over maps explaining this feature or that of that variegated land—and it is strange that Prescott, who always so gallantly acknowledged aid, did not formally tell of General Miller in his *Peru.* After

Miller was appointed British consul in Honolulu, he carried on his correspondence with Prescott, who was then in the full stream of his narrative history of the rise and fall of the Inca empire. "Be pleased to bear in mind," he wrote on July 5, 1844, "that if you set to work in earnest upon the history of Peru and bring it down to the end of the eighteenth century, I possess most interesting and ample documents relative to the . . . revolution of Tupac Amaru that commenced at the latter end of 1780. . . . I procured the manuscript from a learned friar named Guzmán in Chile. . . . I drew up a rough sketch of . . . their contents which afterwards in 1835 I had an opportunity of enlarging and improving while at Cuzco. . . . I have also the will and testament of [Mancio Sierra] Ledesma, the last to die of Pizarro's companions. . . . I have other documents of that sort which I copied from the originals in the archives at Cuzco containing proofs of the most interesting historical facts. *I need not add that all I have is at your disposal.*"

Prescott was halfway through *Peru* when the agitation for war with Mexico began. He was so busy with his own *Conquest* that he had scarcely any time to give his attention to that being undertaken by his own country. "I take refuge," he wrote to a friend, "from these political squabbles among the Andes, where I am trying to dig a few grains of Peruvian gold." By September, 1844, Prescott had taken hold; he was writing up to twelve original pages every day. His first book, *Ferdinand and Isabella,* was a ten-year task—three and a half years' study before he wrote a single line, *Mexico* took him several years of research and a considerable time before he began to write, and then three years of actual writing. *Peru* was different; he was now master of his materials. He loved exactitude, and his accuracy was in itself a form of genius. Now his skill of documentation, his sense of selection, his ability to thread his way through claim and counterclaim, the freshness and freedom of description, gave, as Van Wyck Brooks observed, a new note: "its unity and proportion of structure, the quiet and modest authority of the apparatus, the lustre of the language, were new notes in American history writing."

*Peru* had not the simplicity of the drama that was *Mexico.* In the Aztec conquest there were beginning and end, the drama built up to the final siege of Mexico and then the dramatic fall of Tenochtitlan. *Peru* was not this; first there was Pizarro's long search for "Birú," the kingdom of gold, along the entire length of the tropical coast from Panamá to Ecuador, the confirmation of the reality of the Inca empire and the long

Fitful Head, outside of Boston, where on hot summer days Prescott worked on *The Conquest of Peru*. (From George Ticknor, *Life of W. H. Prescott*. Philadelphia: J. B. Lippincott Company, 1863.)

interval of preparation, then the capture of the Inca without battle within thirty minutes. After that the whole history remained indecisive, with battles scattered over the broad expanse of Peru. There followed the interminable civil wars between the conquistadors over the carcass of the empire. Prescott confessed that although he was "up to my elbows in Peruvian antiquities . . . and . . . amazingly well provided with paper ammunition for my campaign . . . still it was a brutal story," and he complained: "I can't make a *preux chevalier* out of Pizarro. Imagine! A hero who could not even write his own signature. . . ."

Prescott often composed on horseback. He liked to do this especially when he was describing a battle; he would gallop back and forth and imagine himself in the thick of it. Like those who are fully blind he had a prodigious memory, and on horseback he could often visualize a whole chapter within an hour and a half. He need then on his return only dictate this to his secretary (in 1844 it was John Foster Kirk). However, not all of it was dash and struggle; often Prescott had to work out as in a fugue of interlocking themes a description of those cultures which were dominant when the Spaniards arrived. When those moments occurred Prescott took off for Pepperell.

Overlooking the sea at Pepperell was a plain old salt-box farmhouse, which had been home to his ancestors for generations. In it Prescott felt added strength; there he raveled out the conflicting themes of the conquest. Under the shade of age-old oak trees he composed many of his more complicated chapters, walking back and forth dictating to the winds. "Fitful Head" at Nahant, another villa perched on a wild cliff, Prescott used when the heat was too intense in Boston. There, while composing in his mind, Prescott would walk around the shade of an old cherry tree which protected his sensitive eyes from the glare of the sea, "walking there every day," wrote Van Wyck Brooks, "until he had worn a path in the greensward. The traces of this path remained for years, worn by no foot but his. . . ."

By November 15, 1845, he could exult to a friend: "I have reeled off two volumes on *Peru,*" and to another, "I am within six months of completing *Peru*—I am now writing with my hands dripping with Pizarro blood. . . ."

He was nearing the end of the *Conquest of Peru.* He approached those chapters he liked best, the arrival of Pedro de La Gasca, who with the art of diplomacy—and one very short battle—was to seal the wounds of Peru, bleeding from ten years of internecine strife. He was near the end—and the La

Gasca papers which he urgently needed had not yet arrived from Spain. His friend Pascual de Gayangos, then in Spain, had disclosed that "a gentleman of Madrid owns the manuscripts relating to Bishop Pedro de La Gasca. . . . I have good reason to think that he will sell." But he was unsuccessful at Simancas: "here I have been for more than a month . . . in the Library of Simancas turning over papers like wind in the poop. . . . I find that one of the articles of the barbarous and stupid General Regulations forbids . . . one to copy or make extracts. . . ." For once Prescott lost patience and spoke of things which he had never heretofore mentioned: "It will be very hard if the Spanish authorities confuse me with those unfriendly writers who employ their pens to throw a cloud over the fame of their country; I believe I may say without vanity or exaggeration on this occasion that with the exception of Washington Irving I have done as much as any foreigner of the present day to exhibit Spain in a high and honorable point of view. . . . How absurd of them now I have amassed a large collection of documents to compel me to forego the work altogether or to undertake it under embarrassment. . . ."

Pascual de Gayangos persisted, and the papers were copied and sent. From Prescott he had a characteristic witty letter on September 28, 1845, beginning with a quotation from Ovid, ". . . the lost treasures, the papers of Pedro de La Gasca, are safe in Boston harbor." And with these in hand he moved up again to Pepperell, and there in the quiet stillness of the woods he began to set down the last chapters of *Peru.*

Delay now came from another source—it was his eyes again. "I have strained the nerve. . . . Heaven knows how, probably by manuscript digging. Ever since March 10 [1845] I have not read or written, in all, five minutes of my history nor ten minutes of anything else." The prescribed rest at Pepperell did him much good, for soon he was using his "good eye" a half-hour a day, then an hour, so that the notes were completed on La Gasca. In November, 1846, he wrote the last chapter of *Peru.* It was finished in a morning's gallop through the woods, which were then "shedding their multicolored leaves on his head." On December 6, 1846, he dictated the last page of the *History of the Conquest of Peru.*

It was while the book was being stereotyped under his supervision that he had doubts about its quality. It began to haunt him; he was worried about its reception, for he felt that *Peru* had neither the breadth nor the importance of his earlier works. Peru as theme was less unified than Mexico; Pizarro's conquest was short and dramatic—the rest was an anticlimax. He worried about presentation, about style: for rapid movement he had used short, staccato sentences; ornament was restricted to alliteration. In *"Ferdinand and Isabella* he had turned the thousands of sheets of ancient manuscripts into threads for a Gobelin tapestry"; he was now not so sure that his weaving of the tapestry of the rise and decline of Peru had this quality. He had not tried to dazzle the reader with the perpetual scintillation of a many-faceted style; he did not try to hide poor research by a thick frosting of dazzling sentences; he wrote an easy, laughing, limpid prose. All the while the proofs passed through the printers he worried and fretted. Yet once he had left his study he either forgot or dissimulated; people remember his walking "in the street with his rosy air, with his gay satin waistcoat, tall, graceful," and always with a light bantering air. If someone who knew asked about the progress of *Peru,* he passed it off lightly: "You see, I have been carrying on the conquest of Peru while our Government has been making the conquest of Mexico . . . but mine is the best of the two, since it cost only the shedding of ink . . . and if I get ever so little fame by it, that is better than the dirty superfluous acres which we shall get by the other. . . ."

George Bancroft, the celebrated historian, tried to put his anxiety at rest: "Our opinion is that *Peru* was more difficult than *Mexico,* but you have overcome the difficulties and it shows higher evidence of talent than the other. . . ." Gayangos, who had given so much help, absorbed the proofs with the greatest pleasure: "I have read it with as much gusto as if it were a novel and I never put it down until it was finished." Alexander von Humboldt added his praise to theirs; a friend wrote Prescott: "I had the pleasure of hearing many interesting and pleasant things from Humboldt's lips in praise of you; he begged me to hand this letter to you, he said a man like you does more for an honorable and noble intercourse of his nation with other states as well as for the good reception abroad of his fellow citizens than many a diplomatic transaction. . . ." When copies of *Peru* reached General Miller, now British consul in Honolulu, that old warrior who had coached Prescott on the geography of Peru wrote: ". . . your descriptions on the suspension bridges, the vestiges of ancient roads and all the scenery of the Andes, are, so far as my judgment goes—singularly graphic and correct."

On June 27, 1847, Harper & Brothers published *The History of the Conquest of Peru.* Unlike the others, which were three volumes, *Peru* was only two: "The Harpers have sent my bantling into the world three days since," he wrote, "so that it has hardly had time to make its voice heard. I think the public is somewhat relieved that I am only delivered of twins this time. . . ." But the "voice" was soon heard. Prescott made a very advantageous contract with his publishers; he sold the English rights at once, and Angel Calderón de la Barca, who had translated *Mexico,* said he would do the same with *Peru;* it seemed even more popular than the other. "Not a syllable have I heard," wrote George Bancroft from London, "but of unqualified praise, not a notice or a review but breathes the kindliest spirit of willing admiration. Look at the London papers! There is but one opinion; they speak without jealousy, you are the only American person, state or thing, that they commend without reserve."

The Spaniards, sensitive to age-long scurrilities, read it closely; they liked Prescott's impartiality and his masterly use of materials, and for a century no historian has equaled Prescott's popularity in Spain. Yet *The Conquest of Peru,* like *Mexico,* came upon them as a severe shock—that a half-blind American lawyer who had seen neither Spain, Mexico, nor Peru could have written this and that he had tapped their own unpublished material lying dust-covered in the Spanish archives. They knew, and Prescott acknowledged the fact, that he had not explored a *terra incognita.* The Spanish scholar Muñoz had gathered and published material with the idea of writing of Spain's explorations of the Americas; Navarrete too had begun to edit the unpublished material on Hispanic America. Still, no one there had the genius to gather on so vast a scale and to make out of the contradictory material a history such as this. The importance of Prescott was that he shamed Spain's scholars. His publications inspired them out of wounded national pride to look into their archives and publish what should have been published long ago. This may have been the secondary importance of Prescott, but it was almost as important as his publications.

*The History of the Conquest of Peru* still remains the standard authority on the over-all story of Peru and its conquest. Of course it has its limitations; he did not have that which we now have—an archaeological survey of all the other cultures which preceded the Inca. The specialist—that is, one who knows his own narrow corner in Peruvian archaeology— may find here and there things to cavil about—a date that is not correct, the acceptance as a fact of what is now known to be not a fact; still the over-all history remains as solid as it was built, for "the book had been planned like a battle and built as stoutly as a Salem clipper to sail through many enchanted minds for generations to come."

Prescott's account of the Inca social institutions is masterly, his survey on the administration of the Inca empire is most valid. Further, Prescott's treatment of the social and economic arrangement of the Inca empire, while broad, is still so accurate that later writers, even with the great assistance archaeology has provided, have only been able to modify and point up details.

As editor of this edition I indeed find it difficult to form a completely unprejudiced judgment of Prescott. I scarcely remember the time when I did not know him. He is one of my most youthful recollections; the images he drew for me set me off to ride in my imagination with the conquistadors. Prescott was with me when I explored Ecuador, the Galápagos, and the Amazon, and he was with me when for two years I covered all of Peru in search of the remains of the famed Inca highways; and now before me lies my old copy of the *Conquest*. Dog-eared and pencil-marked, it tells me how long I have known it, and my notes suggest how I checked him on the spot—wondering how one who had never been to Peru could still have been so exact in his description. As an explorer I have been over all the ground covered by the *Conquest* and as an historian I have had access to documents which he never saw. All of this can only confirm the solidity of his own work.

There was one black feature in the universal success of *The Conquest of Peru*. When Prescott worked as he did, he knew and doubtless made rough calculations of what that literary work would do to strain his remaining eye. He suffered greatly from pains which racked brain, head, and eye; most times he could not read at all, at other times he was completely blind. "Here I am," he wrote to Gayangos, "on my ocean rock at Nahant overlooking the wide waste of the Atlantic which rolls its dark billows under my window and dashes its spray over the piazza. As I look over this mighty breadth of water I think of the day when Columbus . . . ventured out . . . when the sons of Spain were so ready to launch forth on generous enterprise. . . . Now . . . my eyes are in a very poor condition . . . the vision . . . dim. . . ."

Prescott now knew. An oculist in New York had given him his life sentence. In the spring of 1850 he accepted his oculist's advice: he dropped the plans for his new book and used his eye only for "the casual purposes of life." With his secretary John Kirk he sailed to Europe. On his arrival in London, where he had many friends mostly as a result of long correspondence with them, he was instantly lionized: he was presented to the Duke of Wellington ("he certainly does not show the wear and tear of time and thought"); he was given a dinner by Sir Robert Peel; he made a tour of the country and the galleries; he was presented at Court to Queen Victoria, where he appeared in blue coat, white trousers begilded with buttons and metal, sword, gold lace ("and a whole hour with a lady of the court getting instructions for demeaning myself"). All this was climaxed by a doctorate of law bestowed on him by Oxford University. After that he made a brief tour of the continent; it was a continued round of triumph. However, he soon tired of it, "not that I do not enjoy the parties . . . but I am weary of the dissipation of time. . . . Moreover, it is hard work to make a *life* of pleasure. . . ."

Prescott returned to Boston. He was working again on the biography of Philip II, which he had started as early as 1849. "Last Thursday [July 26] began the composition of chapter first of Philip II." This time the work would run to four volumes. He had lost the use of his eyes; he scarcely ever read (his secretary did that); he never wrote except in his noctograph—it was dictation all the way. Despite interruptions, Prescott finished and published the first two volumes of *The Reign of Philip II* by 1855.

There had been warnings for some time: severe pains in neck and head, a return of the rheumatism, moments when he would go completely blind. On February 4, 1858, he had his first stroke; he gradually recovered and slowly went back to work on Volume III of his *Philip II*. He "continued to Philipize," as he called it, even though the pain of rheumatism was so great that he had to lie on the floor of his study to use his noctograph. "My spirits are always as high as my pulse . . . about 15 points above normal," he said. He could never quite rid himself of the thought of death: ". . . the gentleman in black always seems about now. . . ." One day he interrupted his dictation at a critical part of his book to say that he was very worried about being buried alive; he stipulated that once he had been pronounced dead, the great artery in his arm be opened and drained of blood, "so that there would be no chance of his being buried alive." Then, just as casually, he went back to dictating the life and wretched times of Philip of Spain.

Prescott always envied soldiers who died in harness; it somehow fitted their profession. He often said that when death came, like a soldier he too should like to die in battle. On one of the liveliest days of many years, he was pacing up and down dictating and in fine form. It was a battle scene, and he seemed himself to be leading the charge. He momentarily forgot a name, went to the door, and called his wife Susan out of the study to see if she could recall it. She did. He had just turned back to continue to dictate, saying "How came you to remember . . ." when— He stopped short, his mouth dropped slightly open, his blue eyes stared openly as if he had received a mortal wound in combat. And so he had. He fell, never regained consciousness, and, as he had wished, died in the literary harness which had been his life.

The date was January 28, 1859.

—Victor Wolfgang von Hagen

*Silvania*
*La Rinconada, La Molina*
*Lima, Peru*
*January 28, 1959*

# Preface

The most brilliant passages in the history of Spanish adventure in the New World are undoubtedly afforded by the conquests of Mexico and Peru, the two states which combined with the largest extent of empire a refined social polity and considerable progress in the arts of civilization. Indeed, so prominently do they stand out on the great canvas of history that the name of the one, notwithstanding the contrast they exhibit in their respective institutions, most naturally suggests that of the other; and when I sent to Spain to collect materials for an account of the Conquest of Mexico, I included in my researches those relating to the Conquest of Peru.

The large part of the documents, in both cases, was obtained from the same great repository—the archives of the Royal Academy of History at Madrid, a body specially entrusted with the preservation of whatever may serve to illustrate the Spanish colonial annals. The richest portion of its collection is probably that furnished by the papers of Muñoz. This eminent scholar, the historiographer of the Indies, employed nearly fifty years of his life in amassing materials for a history of Spanish discovery and conquest in America. For this, as he acted under the authority of the government, every facility was afforded him; and public offices and private depositories, in all the principal cities of the empire, both at home and throughout the wide extent of its colonial possessions, were freely opened to his inspection. The result was a magnificent collection of manuscripts, many of which he patiently transcribed with his own hand. But he did not live to reap the fruits of his persevering industry. The first volume of his work, relating to the voyages of Columbus, was scarcely finished when he died; and his manuscripts, at least that portion of them which have reference to Mexico and Peru, were destined to serve the uses of another, an inhabitant of that New World to which they related.

Another scholar, to whose literary stores I am largely indebted, is Don Martin Fernandez de Navarrete, late Director of the Royal Academy of History. Through the greater part of his long life he was employed in assembling original documents to illustrate the colonial annals. Many of these have been incorporated in his great work, *Coleccion de los Viages y Descubrimientos,* which, although far from being completed after the original plan of its author, is of inestimable service to the historian. In following down the track of discovery, Navarrete turned aside from the conquests of Mexico and Peru, to exhibit the voyages of his countrymen in the Indian seas. His manuscripts relating to the two former countries he courteously allowed to be copied for me. Some of them have since appeared in print, under the auspices of his learned coadjutors, Salvà and Baranda, associated with him in the Academy; but the documents placed in my hands formed a most important contribution to my materials for the present history.

The death of this illustrious man, which occurred sometime after the present work was begun, has left a void in his country not easy to be filled; for he was zealously devoted to letters, and few have done more to extend the knowledge of her colonial history. Far from an exclusive solicitude for his own literary projects, he was ever ready to extend his sympathy and assistance to those of others. His reputation as a scholar was enhanced by the higher qualities which he possessed as a man—by his benevolence, his simplicity of manners, and unsullied moral worth. My own obligations to him are large; for from the publication of my first historical work, down to the last week of his life, I have constantly received proofs from him of his hearty and most efficient interest in the prosecution of my historical labors; and I now the more willingly pay this well-merited tribute to his deserts, that it must be exempt from all suspicion of flattery.

In the list of those to whom I have been indebted for materials I must also include the name of M. Ternaux-Compans, so well known by his faithful and elegant French versions of the Muñoz manuscripts; and that of my friend Don Pascual de Gayangos, who, under the modest dress of translation, has furnished a most acute and learned commentary on Spanish-Arabian history, securing for himself the foremost rank in that difficult department of letters, which has been illuminated by the labors of a Masdeu, a Casiri, and a Conde.

To the materials derived from these sources I have added some manuscripts of an important character from the library of the Escorial. These, which chiefly relate to the ancient institutions of Peru, formed part of the splendid collection of Lord Kingsborough, which has unfortunately shared the lot of most literary collections, and been dispersed since the death of its noble author. For these I am indebted to that industrious bibliographer Mr. O. Rich, now resident in London. Lastly, I must not omit to mention my obligations, in another way, to my friend Charles Folsom, Esq., the learned librarian of the Boston Athenaeum, whose minute acquaintance with the grammatical structure and the true idiom of our English tongue has enabled me to correct many inaccuracies into which I had fallen in the composition both of this and of my former works.

From these different quarters I have accumulated a large amount of manuscripts, of the most various character and from the most authentic sources: royal grants and ordinances, instructions of the court, letters of the emperor to the great colonial officers, municipal records, personal diaries and memoranda, and a mass of private correspondence of the principal actors in this turbulent drama. Perhaps it was the turbulent state of the country which led to a more frequent correspondence between the government at home and the colonial officers. But, whatever be the cause, the collection of manuscript materials in reference to Peru is fuller and more complete than that which relates to Mexico; so that there is scarcely a nook or corner so obscure, in the path of the adventurer, that some light has not been thrown on it by the written correspondence of the period. The historian has rather had occasion to complain of the *embarras des richesses;* for in the multiplicity of contradictory testimony it is not always easy to detect the truth, as the multiplicity of cross-lights is apt to dazzle and bewilder the eye of the spectator.

The present History has been conducted on the same general plan with that of the Conquest of Mexico. In an introductory book I have endeavored to portray the institutions of the Incas, that the reader may be acquainted with the character and condition of that extraordinary race before he enters on the story of their subjugation. The remaining books are occupied with the narrative of the Conquest. And here the subject, it must be allowed, notwithstanding the opportunities it presents for the display of character, strange romantic incident, and picturesque scenery, does not afford so obvious advantages to the historian as the Conquest of Mexico. Indeed, few subjects can present a parallel with that, for the purposes either of the historian or the poet. The natural development of the story, there, is precisely what would be prescribed by the severest rules of art. The conquest of the country is the great end always in the view of the reader. From the first landing of the Spaniards on the soil, their subsequent adventures, their battles and negotiations, their ruinous retreat, their rally and final siege, all tend to this grand result, till the long series is closed by the downfall of the capital. In the march of events, all moves steadily forward to their consummation. It is a magnificent epic, in which the unity of interest is complete.

In *The Conquest of Peru,* the action, so far as it is founded on the subversion of the Incas, terminates long before the close of the narrative. The remaining portion is taken up with the fierce feuds of the Conquerors, which would seem, from their very nature, to be incapable of being gathered round a central point of interest. To secure this, we must look beyond the immediate overthrow of the Indian empire. The conquest of the natives is/but the first step, to be followed by the conquest of the Spaniards—the rebel Spaniards—themselves, till the supremacy of the crown is permanently established over the country. It is not till this period that the acquisition of this transatlantic empire can be said to be completed; and by fixing the eye on this remoter point the successive steps of the narrative will be found leading to one great result, and that unity of interest preserved which is scarcely less essential to historic than dramatic composition. How far this has been effected in the present work must be left to the judgment of the reader.

No history of the conquest of Peru, founded on original documents and aspiring to the credit of a classic composition, like the *Conquest of Mexico* by Solís, has been attempted, so far as I am aware, by the Spaniards. The English possess one of high value, from the pen of Robertson, whose masterly sketch occupies its due space in his great work on America. It has been my object to exhibit this same story in all its romantic details; not merely to portray the characteristic features of the Conquest, but to fill up the outline with the coloring of life, so as to present a minute and faithful picture of the times. For this purpose, I have, in the composition of the work, availed myself freely of my manuscript materials, allowed the actors to speak as much as possible for themselves, and especially made frequent use of their letters; for nowhere is the heart more likely to disclose itself than in the freedom of private correspondence. I have made liberal extracts from these authorities in the notes, both to sustain the text and to put in a printed form those productions of the eminent captains and statesmen of the time which are not very accessible to Spaniards themselves.

M. Amédée Pichot, in the Preface of the French translation of *The Conquest of Mexico,* infers from the plan of the composition that I must have carefully studied the writings of his countryman, M. de Barante. The acute critic does me but justice in supposing me familiar with the principles of that writer's historical theory, so ably developed in the Preface to his *Ducs de Bourgogne.* And I have had occasion to admire the skilful manner in which he illustrates this theory himself, by constructing out of the rude materials of a distant time a monument of genius that transports us at once into the midst of the Feudal Ages—and this without the incongruity which usually attaches to a modern-antique. In like manner I have attempted to seize the characteristic expression of a distant age, and to exhibit it in the freshness of life. But in an essential particular I have deviated from the plan of the French historian. I have suffered the scaffolding to remain after the building has been completed. In other words, I have shown to the reader the steps of the process by which I have come to my conclusions. Instead of requiring him to take my version of the story on trust, I have endeavored to give him a reason for my faith. By copious citations from the original authorities, and by such critical notices of them as would explain to him the influences to which they were subjected, I have endeavored to put him in a position for judging for himself, and thus for revising, and, if need be, reversing the judgments of the historian. He will at any rate, by this means, be enabled to estimate the difficulty of arriving at truth amidst the conflict of testimony; and he will learn to place little reliance on those writers who pronounce on the mysterious past with what Fontenelle calls "a frightful degree of certainty"—a spirit the most opposite to that of the true philosophy of history.

Yet it must be admitted that the chronicler who records the events of an earlier age has some obvious advantages in the store of manuscript materials at his command—the statements of friends, rivals, and enemies furnishing a wholesome counterpoise to each other—and also in the general course of events, as they actually occurred, affording the best commentary on the true motives of the parties. The actor, engaged in the heat of the strife, finds his view bounded by the circle around him, and his vision blinded by the smoke and dust of the conflict; while the spectator, whose eye ranges over the ground from a more distant and elevated point, though the individual objects may lose somewhat of their vividness, takes in at a glance all the operations of the field. Paradoxical as it may appear, truth founded on contemporary testimony would seem, after all, as likely to be attained by the writer of a later day as by contemporaries themselves.

Before closing these remarks, I may be permitted to add a few of a personal nature. In several foreign notices of my writings, the author has been said to be blind; and more than once I have had the credit of having lost my sight in the composition of my first history. When I have met with such erroneous accounts, I have hastened to correct them. But the present occasion affords me the best means of doing so; and I am the more desirous of this, as I fear some of my own remarks, in the prefaces to my former histories, have led to the mistake.

While at the University, I received my injury in one of my eyes, which deprived me of the sight of it. The other, soon after, was attacked by inflammation so severely that for some time I lost the sight of that also; and though it was subsequently restored, the organ was so much disordered as to remain permanently debilitated; while twice in my life, since, I have been deprived of the use of it for all purposes of reading and writing for several years together. It was during one of these periods that I received from Madrid the materials for the *History of Ferdinand and Isabella*, and in my disabled condition, with my transatlantic treasures lying around me, I was like one pining from hunger in the midst of abundance. In this state, I resolved to make the ear, if possible, do the work of the eye. I procured the services of a secretary, who read to me the various authorities; and in time I became so far familiar with the sounds of the different foreign languages (to some of which, indeed, I had been previously accustomed by a residence abroad) that I could comprehend his reading without much difficulty. As the reader proceeded, I dictated copious notes; and when these had swelled to a considerable amount they were read to me repeatedly, till I had mastered their contents sufficiently for the purposes of composition. The same notes furnished an easy means of reference to sustain the text.

Still another difficulty occurred, in the mechanical labor of writing, which I found a severe trial to the eye. This was remedied by means of a writing-case, such as is used by the blind, which enabled me to commit my thoughts to paper without the aid of sight, serving me equally well in the dark as in the light. The characters thus formed made a near approach to hieroglyphics; but my secretary became expert in the art of deciphering, and a fair copy—with a liberal allowance for unavoidable blunders—was transcribed for the use of the printer. I have described the process with more minuteness, as some curiosity has been repeatedly expressed in reference to my *modus operandi* under my privations, and the knowledge of it may be of some assistance to others in similar circumstances.

Though I was encouraged by the sensible progress of my work, it was necessarily slow. But in time the tendency to inflammation diminished, and the strength of the eye was confirmed more and more. It was at length so far restored that I could read for several hours of the day, though my labors in this way necessary terminated with the daylight. Nor could I ever dispense with the services of a secretary, or with the writing-case; for, contrary to the usual experience, I have found writing a severer trial to the eye than reading—a remark, however, which does not apply to the reading of manuscript; and to enable myself, therefore, to revise my composition more carefully, I caused a copy of the *History of Ferdinand and Isabella* to be printed for my own inspection before it was sent to the press for publication. Such as I have described was the improved state of my health during the preparation of the *Conquest of Mexico;* and, satisfied with being raised so nearly to a level with the rest of my species, I scarcely envied the superior good fortune of those who could prolong their studies into the evening and the later hours of the night.

But a change has again taken place during the last two years. The side of my eye has become gradually dimmed, while the sensibility of the nerve has been so far increased that for several weeks of the last year I have not opened a volume; and through the whole time I have not had the use of it, on an average, for more than an hour a day. Nor can I cheer myself with the delusive expectation that, impaired as the organ has become from having been tasked, probably, beyond its strength, it can ever renew its youth, or be of much service to me hereafter in my literary researches. Whether I shall have the heart to enter, as I had proposed, on a new and more extensive field of historical labor, with these impediments, I cannot say. Perhaps long habit, and a natural desire to follow up the career which I have so long pursued, may make this, in a manner, necessary, as my past experience has already proved that it is practicable.

From this statement—too long, I fear, for his patience—the reader who feels any curiosity about the matter will understand the real extent of my embarrassments in my historical pursuits. That they have not been very light will be readily admitted when it is considered that I have had but a limited use of my eye in its best state, and that much of the time I have been debarred from the use of it altogether. Yet the difficulties I have had to contend with are very far inferior to those which fall to the lot of a blind man. I know of no historian now alive who can claim the glory of having overcome such obstacles but the author of *La Conquête de l'Angleterre par les Normands,* who, to use his own touching and beautiful language, "has made himself the friend of darkness," and who, to a profound philosophy that require no light but that from within, unites a capacity for extensive and various research that might well demand the severest application of the student.

The remarks into which I have been led at such length will, I trust, not to be set down by the reader to an unworthy egotism, but to their true source, a desire to correct a misapprehension to which I may have unintentionally given rise myself, and which has gained me the credit with some—far from grateful to my feelings, since undeserved—of having surmounted the incalculable obstacles which lie in the path of the blind man.

*Boston, April 2, 1847*

# BOOK I

## INTRODUCTION

### View of the Civilization of the Incas

### ◁ CHAPTER ONE ▷

PHYSICAL ASPECT OF THE COUNTRY—SOURCES OF

PERUVIAN CIVILIZATION—EMPIRE OF THE

INCAS—ROYAL FAMILY—NOBILITY

Of the numerous nations which occupied the great American continent at the time of its discovery by the Europeans, the two most advanced in power and refinement were undoubtedly those of Mexico and Peru. But, though resembling one another in extent of civilization, they differed widely as to the nature of it; and the philosophical student of his species may feel a natural curiosity to trace the different steps by which these two nations strove to emerge from the state of barbarism and place themselves on a higher point in the scale of humanity. In a former work I have endeavored to exhibit the institutions and character of the ancient Mexicans, and the story of their conquest by the Spaniards. The present will be devoted to the Peruvians; and if their history shall be found to present less strange anomalies and striking contrasts than that of the Aztecs, it may interest us quite as much by the pleasing picture it offers of a well-regulated government and sober habits of industry under the patriarchal sway of the Incas.

The empire of Peru, at the period of the Spanish invasion,

stretched along the Pacific from about the second degree north to the thirty-seventh degree of south latitude; a line, also, which describes the western boundaries of the modern republics of Ecuador, Peru, Bolivia, and Chile. Its breadth cannot so easily be determined; for, though bounded everywhere by the great ocean on the west, towards the east it spread out, in many parts, considerably beyond the mountains, to the confines of barbarous states whose exact position cannot be determined, or whose names are effaced from the map of history. It is certain, however, that its breadth was altogether disproportioned to its length.

The topographical aspect of the country is very remarkable. A strip of land, rarely exceeding twenty leagues in width, runs along the coast, and is hemmed in through its whole extent by a colossal range of mountains, which, advancing from the Straits of Magellan, reaches its highest elevation—indeed, the highest on the American continent—about the seventeenth degree south, and, after crossing the line, gradually subsides into hills of inconsiderable magnitude, as it enters the Isthmus of Panamá. This is the famous Cordillera of the Andes, or "copper mountains," as termed by the natives, though they might with more reason have been called "mountains of gold." Arranged sometimes in a single line, though more frequently in two or three lines running parallel or obliquely to each other, they seem to the voyager on the ocean but one continuous chain; while the huge volcanoes, which to the inhabitants of the tableland look like solitary and independent masses, appear to him only like so many peaks of the same vast and magnificent range. So immense is the scale on which nature works in these regions that it is only when viewed from a great distance that the spectator can in any degree comprehend the relation of the several parts to the stupendous whole. Few of the works of nature, indeed, are calculated to produce impressions of higher sublimity than the aspect of this coast as it is gradually unfolded to the eye of the mariner sailing on the distant waters of the Pacific, where mountain is seen to rise above mountain, and Chimborazo, with its glorious canopy of snow, glittering far above the clouds, crowns the whole as with a celestial diadem.

The face of the country would appear to be peculiarly unfavorable to the purposes both of agriculture and of internal communication. The sandy strip along the coast, where rain rarely falls, is fed only by a few scanty streams, that furnish a remarkable contrast to the vast volumes of water which roll down the eastern sides of the Cordilleras into the Atlantic. The precipitous steeps of the sierra, with its splintered sides of porphyry and granite, and its higher regions wrapped in snows that never melt under the fierce sun of the equator, unless it be from the desolating action of its own volcanic fires, might seem equally unpropitious to the labors of the husbandman. And all communication between the parts of the long-extended territory might be thought to be precluded by the savage character of the region, broken up by precipices, furious torrents, and impassable *quebradas*—those hideous rents in the mountain chain, whose depths the eye of the terrified traveler, as he winds along his aerial pathway, vainly endeavors to fathom. Yet the industry, we might almost say the genius, of the Indian was sufficient to overcome all these impediments of nature.

By a judicious system of canals and subterraneous aqueducts, the waste places on the coast were refreshed by copious streams that clothed them in fertility and beauty. Terraces were raised upon the steep sides of the Cordillera; and as the different elevations had the effect of difference of latitude, they exhibited in regular gradation every variety of vegetable form, from the stimulated growth of the tropics to the temperate products of a northern clime, while flocks of *llamas* —the Peruvian sheep—wandered with their shepherds over the broad, snow-covered wastes on the crests of the sierra, which rose beyond the limits of cultivation. An industrious population settled along the lofty regions of the plateaus, and towns and hamlets, clustering amidst orchards and wide-spreading gardens, seemed suspended in the air far above the ordinary elevation of the clouds. Intercourse was maintained between these numerous settlements by means of the great roads which traversed the mountain-passes and opened an easy communication between the capital and the remotest extremities of the empire.

The source of this civilization is traced to the valley of Cuzco, the central region of Peru, as its name implies. The origin of the Peruvian empire, like the origin of all nations, except the very few which, like our own, have had the good fortune to date from a civilized period and people, is lost in the mists of fable, which, in fact, have settled as darkly round its history as round that of any nation, ancient or modern, in the Old World. According to the tradition most familiar to the European scholar, the time was when the ancient races of the continent were all plunged in deplorable barbarism; when they worshiped nearly every object in nature indiscriminately, made war their pastime, and feasted on the flesh of their slaughtered captives. The Sun, the great luminary and parent of mankind, taking compassion on their degraded condition, sent two of his children, Manco Capac and Mama Ocllo, to gather the natives into communities and teach them the arts of civilized life. The celestial pair, brother and sister, husband and wife, advanced along the high plains in the neighborhood of Lake Titicaca to about the sixteenth degree south. They bore with them a golden wedge, and were directed to take up their residence on the spot where the sacred emblem should without effort sink into the ground. They proceeded accordingly but a short distance, as far as the valley of Cuzco, the spot indicated by the performance of the miracle, since there the wedge speedily sank into the earth and disappeared forever. Here the children of the Sun established their residence, and soon entered upon their beneficent mission among the rude inhabitants of the country, Manco Capac teaching the men the arts of agriculture, and Mama Ocllo initiating her own sex in the mysteries of weaving and spinning. The simple people lent a willing ear to the messengers of Heaven, and, gathering together in considerable numbers, laid the foundations of the city of Cuzco. The same wise and benevolent maxims which regulated the conduct of the first Incas descended to their successors, and under their mild scepter a community gradually extended itself along the broad surface of the tableland, which asserted its superiority over the surrounding tribes. Such is the pleasing picture of the origin of the Peruvian monarchy, as portrayed by Garcilasso de la Vega, the descendant of the Incas, and through him made familiar to the European reader. [1]

But this tradition is only one of several current among the Peruvian Indians, and probably not the one most generally received. Another legend speaks of certain white and bearded men, who, advancing from the shores of Lake Titicaca, established an ascendency over the natives and imparted to them the blessings of civilization. It may remind us of the tradition existing among the Aztecs in respect to Quetzalcoatl, the good deity, who with a similar garb and aspect came up the great plateau from the east on a like benevolent mission to the natives. The analogy is the more remarkable as there is no trace of any communication with, or even knowledge of, each other to be found in the two nations.

The date usually assigned for these extraordinary events was about four hundred years before the coming of the Spaniards, or early in the twelfth century. But, however pleasing to the imagination, and however popular, the legend of Manco Capac, it requires but little reflection to show its improbability, even when divested of supernatural accompaniments. On the shores of Lake Titicaca extensive ruins exist at the present day, which the Peruvians themselves acknowledge to be of older date than the pretended advent of the Incas, and to have furnished them with the models of their architecture. The date of their appearance, indeed, is manifestly irreconcilable with their subsequent history. No account assigns to the Inca dynasty more than thirteen princes before the Conquest. But this number is altogether too small to have spread over four hundred years, and would not carry back the foundations of the monarchy, on any probable computation, beyond two centuries and a half—an antiquity not incredible in itself, and which, it may be remarked, does not precede by more than half a century the alleged foundation of the capital of Mexico. The fiction of Manco Capac and his sister-wife was devised, no doubt, at a later period, to gratify the vanity of the Peruvian monarchs, and to give additional sanction to their authority by deriving it from a celestial origin.

We may reasonably conclude that there existed in the country a race advanced in civilization before the time of the Incas, [2] and, in conformity with nearly every tradition, we may derive this race from the neighborhood of Lake Titicaca; a conclusion strongly confirmed by the imposing architectural remains which still endure, after the lapse of so many years, on its borders. Who this race were, and whence they came, may afford a tempting theme for inquiry to the speculative antiquarian. But it is a land of darkness that lies far beyond the domain of history.

The same mists that hang round the origin of the Incas continue to settle on their subsequent annals; and so imperfect were the records employed by the Peruvians, and so confused and contradictory their traditions, that the historian finds no firm footing on which to stand till within a century of the Spanish conquest. At first, the progress of the Peruvians seems to have been slow and almost imperceptible. By their wise and temperate policy they gradually won over the neighboring tribes to their dominion, as these latter became more and more convinced of the benefits of a just and well-regulated government. As they grew stronger, they were enabled to rely more directly on force; but, still advancing under cover of the same beneficent pretexts employed by their predecessors, they proclaimed peace and civilization at the point of the sword. The rude nations of the country, without any principle of cohesion among themselves, fell one after another before the victorious arm of the Incas. Yet it was not till the middle of the fifteenth century that the famous Topa Inca Yupanqui, grandfather of the monarch who occupied the throne at the coming of the Spaniards, led his armies across the terrible desert of Atacama and, penetrating to the southern region of Chili, fixed the permanent boundary of his dominions at the river Maule. His son, Huayna Capac, possessed of ambition and military talent fully equal to his father's, marched along the Cordillera towards the north, and, pushing his conquests across the equator, added the powerful kingdom of Quito to the empire of Peru. [3]

The ancient city of Cuzco, meanwhile, had been gradually advancing in wealth and population, till it had become the worthy metropolis of a great and flourishing monarchy. It stood in a beautiful valley on an elevated region of the plateau, which among the Alps would have been buried in eternal snows, but which within the tropics enjoyed a genial and salubrious temperature. Towards the north it was defended by a lofty eminence, a spur of the great Cordillera; and the city was traversed by a river, or rather a small stream, over which bridges of timber, covered with heavy slabs of stone, furnished an easy means of communication with the opposite banks. The streets were long and narrow, the houses low, and those of the poorer sort built of clay and reeds. But Cuzco was the royal residence, and was adorned with the ample dwellings of the great nobility; and the massy fragments still incorporated in many of the modern edifices bear testimony to the size and solidity of the ancient.

The health of the city was promoted by spacious openings and squares, in which a numerous population from the capital and the distant country assembled to celebrate the high festivals of their religion. For Cuzco was the "Holy City"; and the great temple of the Sun, to which pilgrims resorted from the farthest borders of the empire, was the most magnificent structure in the New World, and unsurpassed, probably, in the costliness of its decorations by any building in the Old.

Towards the north, on the sierra or rugged eminence already noticed, rose a strong fortress, the remains of which at the present day, by their vast size, excite the admiration of the traveler. [4] It was defended by a single wall of great thickness, and twelve hundred feet long on the side facing the city, where the precipitous character of the ground was of itself almost sufficient for its defense. On the other quarter, where the approaches were less difficult, it was protected by two other semicircular walls of the same length as the preceding. They were separated a considerable distance from one another and from the fortress; and the intervening ground was raised so that the walls afforded a breastwork for the troops stationed there in times of assault. The fortress consisted of three towers, detached from one another. One was appropriated to the Inca, and was garnished with the sumptuous decorations befitting a royal residence rather than a military post. The other two were held by the garrison, drawn from the Peruvian nobles, and commanded by an officer of the blood royal, for the position was of too great importance to be entrusted to inferior hands. The hill was excavated below the towers, and several subterraneous galleries communicated with the city and the palaces of the Inca.

The fortress, the walls, and the galleries were all built of stone, the heavy blocks of which were not laid in regular courses, but so disposed that the small ones might fill up the interstices between the great. They formed a sort of rustic work being rough-hewn except towards the edges, which were finely wrought; and though no cement was used, the several blocks were adjusted with so much exactness and united so closely that it was impossible to introduce even the blade of a knife between them. Many of these stones were of vast size, some of them being fully thirty-eight feet long, by eighteen broad, and six feet thick.

We are filled with astonishment when we consider that these enormous masses were hewn from their native bed and fashioned into shape by a people ignorant of the use of iron; that they were brought from quarries, from four to fifteen leagues distant, without the aid of beasts of burden; were transported across rivers and ravines, raised to their elevated position on the sierra, and finally adjusted there with the nicest accuracy, without the knowledge of tools and machinery familiar to the European. Twenty thousand men are said to have been employed on this great structure, and fifty years consumed in the building. However this may be, we see in it the workings of a despotism which had the lives and fortunes of its vassals at its absolute disposal, and which, however mild in its general character, esteemed these vassals, when employed in its service, as lightly as the brute animals for which they served as a substitute.

The fortress of Cuzco was but part of a system of fortifications established throughout their dominions by the Incas. This system formed a prominent feature in their military policy; but before entering on this latter it will be proper to give the reader some view of their civil institutions and scheme of government.

The scepter of the Incas, if we may credit their historian, descended in unbroken succession from father to son, through their whole dynasty. Whatever we may think of this, it appears probable that the right of inheritance might be claimed by the eldest son of the *Coya,* or lawful queen, as she was styled, to distinguish her from the host of concubines who shared the affections of the sovereign. The queen was further distinguished, at least in later reigns, by the circumstance of being selected from the sisters of the Inca, an arrangement which, however revolting to the ideas of civilized nations, was recommended to the Peruvians by its securing an heir to the crown of the pure heaven-born race, uncontaminated by any mixture of earthly mold.

In his early years, the royal offspring was entrusted to the care of the *amautas,* or "wise men," as the teachers of Peruvian science were called, who instructed him in such elements of knowledge as they possessed, and especially in the cumbrous ceremonial of their religion, in which he was to take a prominent part. Great care was also bestowed on his military education, of the last importance in a state which, with its professions of peace and good-will, was ever at war for the acquisition of empire.

In this military school he was educated with such of the Inca nobles as were nearly of his own age; for the sacred name of Inca—a fruitful source of obscurity in their annals—was applied indifferently to all who descended by the male line from the founder of the monarchy. At the age of sixteen the pupils underwent a public examination, previous to their admission to what may be called the order of chivalry. This examination was conducted by some of the oldest and most illustrious Incas. The candidates were required to show their prowess in the athletic exercises of the warrior; in wrestling and boxing, in running such long courses as fully tried their agility and strength, in severe fasts of several days' duration, and in mimic combats, which, although the weapons were blunted, were always attended with wounds, and sometimes with death. During this trial, which lasted thirty days, the royal neophyte fared no better than his comrades, sleeping on the bare ground, going unshod, and wearing a mean attire— a mode of life, it was supposed, which might tend to inspire him with more sympathy with the destitute. With all this show of impartiality, however, it will probably be doing no injustice to the judges to suppose that a politic discretion may have somewhat quickened their perceptions of the real merits of the heir apparent.

At the end of the appointed time, the candidates selected as worthy of the honors of their barbaric chivalry were presented to the sovereign, who condescended to take a principal part in the ceremony of inauguration. He began with a brief discourse, in which, after congratulating the young aspirants on the proficiency they had shown in martial exercises, he reminded them of the responsibilities attached to their birth and station, and, addressing them affectionately as "children of the Sun," he exhorted them to imitate their great progenitor in his glorious career of beneficence to mankind. The novices then drew near, and, kneeling one by one before the Inca, he pierced their ears with a golden bodkin; and this was suffered to remain there till an opening had been made large enough for the enormous pendants which were peculiar to their order, and which gave them, with the Spaniards, the name of *orejones*. This ornament was so massy in the ears of the sovereign that the cartilage was distended by it nearly to the shoulder, producing what seemed a monstrous deformity in the eyes of the Europeans, though, under the magical influence of fashion, it was regarded as a beauty by the natives.

When this operation was performed, one of the most venerable of the nobles dressed the feet of the candidates in the sandals worn by the order, which may remind us of the ceremony of buckling on the spurs of the Christian knight. They were then allowed to assume the girdle or sash around the loins, corresponding with the *toga virilis* of the Romans, and intimating that they had reached the season of manhood. Their heads were adorned with garlands of flowers, which, by their various colors, were emblematic of the clemency and goodness that should grace the character of every true warrior; and the leaves of an evergreen plant were mingled with the flowers, to show that these virtues should endure without end. The prince's head was further ornamented by a fillet, or tasseled fringe, of a yellow color, made of the fine threads of the vicuña wool, which encircled the forehead as the peculiar insignia of the heir apparent. The great body of the Inca nobility next made their appearance, and, beginning with those nearest of kin, knelt down before the prince and did him homage as successor to the crown. The whole assembly then moved to the great square of the capital, where songs and dances and other public festivities closed the important ceremonial of the *huaracu*.

The reader will be less surprised by the resemblance which this ceremonial bears to the inauguration of a Christian knight in the feudal ages, if he reflects that a similar analogy may be traced in the institutions of other people more or less civilized, and that it is natural that nations occupied with the one great business of war should mark the period when the preparatory education for it was ended, by similar characteristic ceremonies.

Having thus honorably passed through his ordeal, the heir apparent was deemed worthy to sit in the councils of his father, and was employed in offices of trust at home, or, more usually, sent on distant expeditions to practice in the field the lessons which he had hitherto studied only on the mimic theater of war. His first campaigns were conducted under the renowned commanders who had grown gray in the service of his father, until, advancing in years and experience, he was placed in command himself, like Huayna Capac, the last and most illustrious of his line, carried the banner of the rainbow, the armorial ensign of his house, far over the borders, among the remotest tribes of the plateau.

The government of Peru was a despotism, mild in its character, but in its form a pure and unmitigated despotism. The sovereign was placed at an immeasurable distance above his subjects. Even the proudest of the Inca nobility, claiming a descent from the same divine original as himself, could not venture into the royal presence unless barefoot, and bearing a light burden on his shoulders in token of homage. As the representative of the Sun, he stood at the head of the priesthood, and presided at the most important of the religious festivals. He raised armies, and usually commanded them in person. He imposed taxes, made laws, and provided for their execution by the appointment of judges, whom he removed at pleasure. He was the source from which everything flowed—all dignity, all power, all emolument. He was, in short, in the well-known phrase of the European despot, "himself the state."

The Inca asserted his claims as a superior being by assuming a pomp in his manner of living well calculated to impose on his people. His dress was of the finest wool of the vicuña, richly dyed, and ornamented with a profusion of gold and precious stones. Round his head was wreathed a turban of many-colored folds, called the *llautu*, with a tasseled fringe, like that worn by the prince, but of a scarlet color, while two feathers of a rare and curious bird, called the *corequenque*, placed upright in it, were the distinguishing insignia of royalty. The birds from which these feathers were obtained were found in a desert country among the mountains; and it was death to destroy or to take them, as they were reserved for the exclusive purpose of supplying the royal headgear. Every succeeding monarch was provided with a new pair of these plumes, and his credulous subjects fondly believed that only two individuals of the species had ever existed to furnish the simple ornament for the diadem of the Incas.

Although the Peruvian monarch was raised so far above the highest of his subjects, he condescended to mingle occasionally with them, and took great pains personally to inspect the condition of the humbler classes. He presided at some of the religious celebrations, and on these occasions entertained the great nobles at his table, when he complimented them, after the fashion of more civilized nations, by drinking the health of those whom he most delighted to honor.

But the most effectual means taken by the Incas for communicating with their people were their progresses through the empire. These were conducted, at intervals of several years, with great state and magnificence. The sedan, or litter, in which they traveled, richly emblazoned with gold and emeralds, was guarded by a numerous escort. The men who bore it on their shoulders were provided by two cities, specially appointed for the purpose. It was a post to be coveted by no one if, as is asserted, a fall was punished with death. They traveled with ease and expedition, halting at the tambos,[5] or inns, erected by government along the route, and occasionally at the royal palaces, which in the great towns afforded ample accommodations to the whole of the monarch's retinue. The noble roads which traversed the tableland were lined with people, who swept away the stones and stubble from their surface, strewing them with sweet-scented flowers, and vying with each other in carrying forward the baggage from one village to another. The monarch halted from time to time to listen to the grievances of his subjects or to settle some points which had been referred to his decision by the regular tribunals. As the princely train wound its way along the mountain passes, every place was thronged with spectators eager to catch a glimpse of their sovereign; and when he raised the curtains of his litter and showed himself to their eyes, the air was rent with acclamations as they invoked blessings on his head. Tradition long commemorated the spots at which he halted, and the simple people of the country held them in reverence as places consecrated by the presence of an Inca.

The royal palaces were on a magnificent scale and, far from being confined to the capital or a few principal towns, were scattered over all the provinces of their vast empire. [6] The buildings were low, but covered a wide extent of ground. Some of the apartments were spacious, but they were generally small, and had no communication with one another except that they opened into a common square or court. The walls were made of blocks of stone of various sizes, like those described in the fortress of Cuzco, rough-hewn but carefully wrought near the line of junction, which was scarcely visible to the eye. The roofs were of wood or rushes, which have perished under the rude touch of time, that has shown more

The plaza of Vilcashuaman. Situated in the Andes at an altitude of 11,000 feet, Vilcashuaman ("Sanctuary of the Hawk") was said by the Incas to be the center of their empire; that is, from Vilcas the distance to Quito was the same as the distance to Chile. It was the largest Inca administration center between Jauja and Cuzco. After being conquered by Inca Pachacuti about 1440, it was depopulated by war, and the Inca transplanted a whole population of 200,000 to replace the original inhabitants. The immense plaza of Vilcas could hold, the Spaniards said, 20,000 people; the ruins of the palace are as large as a whole square city block. The Sun Temple (the only one still intact throughout the whole Inca realm) was described by Pedro de Cieza de Len in 1548 as "made of very fine-fitting stones . . . two large doorways . . . approximately 30 stone steps . . . and on top of the temple where the Lord Inca sat to view the dances and festivals a seat hewn out of a single piece of stone . . . covered with gold plate." (1) The trapezoid-shaped plaza; (2) the Sun Temple of thirty-two steps; (3) the stone seat for the Lord Inca; (4) a truncated temple, with six-foot stone Inca niches around its sides; (5) the Inca palace (now the site of the Church of Vilcashuaman); (6) the high stone wall made with fitted stones in the best Inca manner; (7) the exit to the royal Inca road to Cuzco; (8) the road, which descends to the Vishcongo River and becomes the royal road to Quito.

respect for the walls of the edifices. The whole seems to have been characterized by solidity and strength, rather than by any attempt at architectural elegance.

But whatever want of elegance there may have been in the exterior of the imperial dwellings, it was amply compensated by the interior, in which all the opulence of the Peruvian princes was ostentatiously displayed. The sides of the apartments were thickly studded with gold and silver ornaments. Niches prepared in the walls were filled with images of animals and plants curiously wrought of the same costly materials; and even much of the domestic furniture, including the utensils devoted to the most ordinary menial services, displayed the like wanton magnificence! With these gorgeous decorations were mingled richly colored stuffs of the delicate manufacture of the Peruvian wool, which were of so beautiful a texture that the Spanish sovereigns, with all the luxuries of Europe and Asia at their command, did not disdain to use them. The royal household consisted of a throng of menials, supplied by the neighboring towns and villages, which, as in Mexico, were bound to furnish the monarch with fuel and other necessaries for the consumption of the palace.

But the favorite residence of the Incas was at Yucay, about four leagues distant from the capital. In this delicious valley, locked up within the friendly arms of the sierra, which sheltered it from the rude breezes of the east, and refreshed by gushing fountains and streams of running water, they built the most beautiful of their palaces. Here, when wearied with the dust and toil of the city, they loved to retreat and solace themselves with the society of their favorite concubines, wandering amidst groves and airy gardens that shed around their soft, intoxicating odors and lulled the senses to voluptuous repose. Here, too, they loved to indulge in the luxury of their baths, replenished by streams of crystal water which were conducted through subterraneous silver channels into basins of gold. The spacious gardens were stocked with numerous varieties of plants and flowers that grew without effort in this *temperate* region of the tropics, while parterres of a more extraordinary kind were planted by their side, glowing with the various forms of vegetable life skillfully imitated in gold and silver! Among them the Indian corn, the most beautiful of American grains, is particularly commemorated, and the curious workmanship is noticed with which the golden ear was half disclosed amidst the broad leaves of silver, and the light tassel of the same material that floated gracefully from its top. [7]

If this dazzling picture staggers the faith of the reader, he may reflect that the Peruvian mountains teemed with gold; that the natives understood the art of working the mines, to a considerable extent; that none of the ore, as we shall see hereafter, was converted into coin, and that the whole of it passed into the hands of the sovereign for his own exclusive benefit, whether for purposes of utility or ornament. Certain it is that no fact is better attested by the conquerors themselves, who had ample means of information, and no motive for misstatement. The Italian poets, in their gorgeous pictures of the gardens of Alcina and Morgana, came nearer the truth than they imagined.

Our surprise, however, may reasonably be excited when we consider that the wealth displayed by the Peruvian princes was only that which each had amassed individually for himself. He owed nothing to inheritance from his predecessors. On the decease of an Inca, his palaces were abandoned; all his treasures, except what were employed in his obsequies, his furniture and apparel, were suffered to remain as he left them, and his mansions, save one, were closed up forever. The new sovereign was to provide himself with everything new for his royal state. The reason for this was the popular belief that the soul of the departed monarch would return after a time to reanimate his body on earth; and they wished that he should find everything to which he had been used in life prepared for his reception.

When an Inca died, or, to use his own language, "was called home to the mansions of his father, the Sun," his obsequies were celebrated with great pomp and solemnity. The bowels were taken from the body and deposited in the temple of Tampu, about five leagues from the capital. A quantity of his plate and jewels was buried with them, and a number of his attendants and favorite concubines, amounting sometimes, it is said, to a thousand, were immolated on his tomb. Some of them showed the natural repugnance to the sacrifice occasionally manifested by the victims of a similar superstition in India. But these were probably the menials and more humble attendants; since the women have been known, in more than one instance, to lay violent hands on themselves, when restrained from testifying their fidelity by this act of conjugal martyrdom. This melancholy ceremony was followed by a general mourning throughout the empire. At stated intervals, for a year, the people assembled to renew the expressions of their sorrow; processions were made, displaying the banner of the departed monarch; bards and minstrels were appointed to chronicle his achievements, and their songs continued to be rehearsed at high festivals in the presence of the reigning monarch—thus stimulating the living by the glorious example of the dead.

The body of the deceased Inca was skillfully embalmed and removed to the great temple of the Sun at Cuzco. There the Peruvian sovereign, on entering the awful sanctuary, might behold the effigies of his royal ancestors, ranged in opposite files—the men on the right, and their queens on the left, of the great luminary which blazed in refulgent gold on the walls of the temple. The bodies, clothed in the princely attire which they had been accustomed to wear, were placed on chairs of gold, and sat with their heads inclined downward, their hands placidly crossed over their bosoms, their countenances exhibiting their natural dusky hue—less liable to change than the fresher coloring of a European complexion—and their hair of raven black, or silvered over with age, according to the period at which they died! It seemed like a company of solemn worshipers fixed in devotion, so true were the forms and lineaments to life. The Peruvians were as successful as the Egyptians in the miserable attempt to perpetuate the existence of the body beyond the limits assigned to it by nature.

They cherished a still stranger illusion in the attentions which they continued to pay to these insensible remains, as if they were instinct with life. One of the houses belonging to a deceased Inca was kept open and occupied by his guard and attendants, with all the state appropriate to royalty. On certain festivals, the revered bodies of the sovereigns were brought out with great ceremony into the public square of the capital. Invitations were sent by the captains of the guard of the respective Incas to the different nobles and officers of the court; and entertainments were provided in the names of their masters, which displayed all the profuse magnificence of their treasures—and "such a display," says an ancient chronicler, "was there in the great square of Cuzco, on this occasion, of gold and silver plate and jewels, as no other city in the world ever witnessed." The banquet was served by the menials of the respective households, and the guests partook of the melancholy cheer in the presence of the royal phantom with the same attention to the forms of courtly etiquette as if the living monarch had presided!

The nobility of Peru [8] consisted of two orders, the first and by far the most important of which was that of the Incas, who, boasting a common descent with their sovereign, lived, as it were, in the reflected light of his glory. As the Peruvian monarchs availed themselves of the right of polygamy to a very liberal extent, leaving behind them families of one or even two hundred children, the nobles of the blood royal, though comprehending only their descendants in the male line, came in the course of years to be very numerous. They were divided into different lineages, each of which traced its pedigree to a different member of the royal dynasty, though all terminated in the divine founder of the empire.

They were distinguished by many exclusive and very important privileges; they wore a peculiar dress, spoke a dialect, if we may believe the chronicler, peculiar to themselves, and had the choicest portion of the public domain assigned for their support. They lived, most of them, at court, near the person of the prince, sharing in his counsels, dining at his board, or supplied from his table. They alone were admissible to the great offices in the priesthood. They were invested with the command of armies and of distant garrisons, were placed over the provinces, and, in short, filled every station of high trust and emolument. Even the laws, severe in their general tenor, seem not to have been framed with reference to them; and the people, investing the whole order with a portion of the sacred character which belonged to the sovereign, held that an Inca noble was incapable of crime.

The other order of nobility was the *Curacas*, the caciques of the conquered nations, or their descendants. They were usually continued by the government in their places, though they were required to visit the capital occasionally, and to allow their sons to be educated there as the pledges of their loyalty. It is not easy to define the nature or extent of their privileges. They were possessed of more or less power, according to the extent of their patrimony and the number of their vassals. Their authority was usually transmitted from father to son, though sometimes the successor was chosen by the people. They did not occupy the highest posts of state, or those nearest the person of the sovereign, like the nobles of the blood. Their authority seems to have been usually local, and always in subordination to the territorial jurisdiction of the great provincial governors, who were taken from the Incas.

It was the Inca nobility, indeed, who constituted the real strength of the Peruvian monarchy. Attached to their prince by ties of consanguinity, they had common sympathies and, to a considerable extent, common interests with him. Distinguished by a peculiar dress and insignia, as well as by language and blood, from the rest of the community, they were never confounded with the other tribes and nations who were incorporated into the great Peruvian monarchy. After the lapse of centuries they still retained their individuality as a peculiar people. They were to the conquered races of the country what the Romans were to the barbarous hordes of the Empire, or the Normans to the ancient inhabitants of the British Isles. Clustering around the throne, they formed an invincible phalanx to shield it alike from secret conspiracy and open insurrection. Though living chiefly in the capital, they were also distributed throughout the country in all its high stations and strong military posts, thus establishing lines of communication with the court, which enabled the sovereign to act simultaneously and with effect on the most distant quarters of his empire. They possessed, moreover, an intellectual pre-eminence, which, no less than their station, gave them authority with the people. Indeed, it may be said to have been the principal foundation of their authority. The crania of the Inca race show a decided superiority over the other races of the land in intellectual power; and it cannot be denied that it was the fountain of that peculiar civilization and social polity which raised the Peruvian monarchy above every other state in South America. Whence this remarkable race came, and what was its early history, are among those mysteries that meet us so frequently in the annals of the New World, and which time and the antiquary have as yet done little to explain.

# ☙ CHAPTER TWO ☘

ORDERS OF THE STATE—PROVISIONS FOR JUSTICE—

DIVISION OF LANDS—REVENUES AND

REGISTERS—GREAT ROADS AND POSTS—

MILITARY TACTICS AND POLICY

If we are surprised at the peculiar and original features of what may be called the Peruvian aristocracy, we shall be still more so as we descend to the lower orders of the community and see the very artificial character of their institutions—as artificial as those of ancient Sparta, and, though in a different way, quite as repugnant to the essential principles of our nature. The institutions of Lycurgus, however, were designed for a petty state, while those of Peru, although originally intended for such, seemed, like the magic tent in the Arabian tale, to have an indefinite power of expansion, and were as well suited to the most flourishing condition of the empire as to its infant fortunes. In this remarkable accommodation to change of circumstances we see the proofs of a contrivance that argues no slight advance in civilization.

The name of Peru was not known to the natives. It was given by the Spaniards, and originated, it is said, in a misapprehension of the Indian name of "river." However this may be, it is certain that the natives had no other epithet by which to designate the large collection of tribes and nations who were assembled under the scepter of the Incas, than that of *Tawantinsuyu,* or "four quarters of the world." [9] This will not surprise a citizen of the United States, who has no other name by which to class himself among nations than what is borrowed from a quarter of the globe. The kingdom, conformably to its name, was divided into four parts, distinguished each by a separate title, and to each of which ran one of the four great roads that diverged from Cuzco, the capital or *navel* of the Peruvian monarchy. The city was in like manner divided into four quarters; and the various races which gathered there from the distant parts of the empire lived each in the quarter

Uquira, in the dry river valley of Asia, south of Lima—a typical coastal Inca administration center. The conquering Incas took over previously built centers, enlarged them, gave them an Inca character. Uquira lies close to the coastal Inca road as it turns from the well-watered valley of Mala across the dry desert wastes that lead to the Canete Valley. About Uquira were (and still are) numerous small farms as well as artificially terraced hills. The duty of the officials at this center (there are many such on the coast) was to see that the tribute tax was collected and sent on to larger areas. Temples, plazas for games, and living quarters of the administrators are part of this compact center.

nearest to its respective province. They all continued to wear their peculiar national costume, so that it was easy to determine their origin; and the same order and system of arrangement prevailed in the motley population of the capital as in the great provinces of the empire. The capital, in fact, was a miniature image of the empire.

The four great provinces were each placed under a viceroy or governor, who ruled over them with the assistance of one or more councils for the different departments. These viceroys resided, some portion of their time at least, in the capital, where they constituted a sort of council of state to the Inca. The nation at large was distributed into decades, or small bodies of ten; and every tenth man, or head of a decade, had supervision of the rest, being required to see that they enjoyed the rights and immunities to which they were entitled, to solicit aid in their behalf from government when necessary, and to bring offenders to justice. To this last they were stimulated by a law that imposed on them, in case of neglect, the same penalty that would have been incurred by the guilty party. With this law hanging over his head, the magistrate of Peru, we may well believe, did not often go to sleep on his post.

The people were still further divided into bodies of fifty, one hundred, five hundred, and a thousand, each with an officer having general supervision over those beneath, and the higher ones possessing, to a certain extent, authority in matters of police. Lastly, the whole empire was distributed into sections or departments of ten thousand inhabitants, with a governor over each, from the Inca nobility, who had control over the *curacas* and other territorial officers in the district. There were also regular tribunals of justice, consisting of magistrates in each of the towns or small communities, with jurisdiction over petty offenses, while those of a graver character were carried before superior judges, usually the governors or rulers of the districts. These judges all held their authority and received their support from the crown, by which they were appointed and removed at pleasure. They were obliged to determine every suit in five days from the time it was brought before them; and there was no appeal from one tribunal to another. Yet there were important provisions for the security of justice. A committee of visitors patrolled the kingdom at certain times to investigate the character and conduct of the magistrates; and any neglect or violation of duty was punished in the most exemplary manner. The inferior courts were also required to make monthly returns of their proceedings to the higher ones, and these made reports in like manner to the viceroys; so that the monarch, seated in the center of his dominions, could look abroad, as it were, to their most distant extremities, and review and rectify any abuses in the administration of the law.

The laws were few and exceedingly severe. They related almost wholly to criminal matters. Few other laws were needed by a people who had no money, little trade, and hardly anything that could be called fixed property. The crimes of theft, adultery, and murder were all capital, though it was wisely provided that some extenuating circumstances might be allowed to mitigate the punishment. Blasphemy against the Sun and malediction of the Inca—offenses, indeed, of the same complexion—were also punished with death. Removing landmarks, turning the water away from a neighbor's land into one's own, burning a house, were all severely punished. To burn a bridge was death. The Inca allowed no obstacle to those facilities of communication so essential to the maintenance of public order. A rebellious city or province was laid waste, and its inhabitants exterminated. Rebellion against the "Child of the Sun" was the greatest of all crimes.

The simplicity and severity of the Peruvian code may be thought to infer a state of society but little advanced, which had few of those complex interests and relations that grow up in a civilized community, and which had not proceeded far enough in the science of legislation to economize human suffering by proportioning penalties to crimes. But the Peruvian institutions must be regarded from a different point of view from that in which we study those of other nations. The laws emanated from the sovereign, and that sovereign held a divine commission and was possessed of a divine nature. To violate the law was not only to insult the majesty of the throne, but it was sacrilege. The slightest offense, viewed in this light, merited death; and the gravest could incur no heavier penalty. Yet in the infliction of their punishments they showed no unnecessary cruelty; and the sufferings of the victim were not prolonged by the ingenious torments so frequent among barbarous nations.

These legislative provisions may strike us as very defective, even as compared with those of the semi-civilized races of Anahuac, where a gradation of courts, moreover with the right of appeal, afforded a tolerable security for justice. But in a country like Peru, where few but criminal causes were known, the right of appeal was of less consequence. The law was simple, its application easy; and, where the judge was honest, the case was as likely to be determined correctly on the first hearing as on the second. The inspection of the board of visitors, and the monthly returns of the tribunals, afforded no slight guarantee for their integrity. The law which required a decision within five days would seem little suited to the complex and embarrassing litigation of a modern tribunal. But, in the simple questions submitted to the Peruvian judge, delay would have been useless; and the Spaniards, familiar with the evils growing out of long-protracted suits, where the successful litigant is too often a ruined man, are loud in their encomiums of this swift-handed and economical justice.

The fiscal regulations of the Incas, and the laws respecting property, are the most remarkable features in the Peruvian polity. The whole territory of the empire was divided into three parts, one for the Sun, another for the Inca, and the last for the people. Which of the three was the largest is doubtful. The proportions differed materially in different provinces. The distribution, indeed, was made on the same general principle as each new conquest was added to the monarchy; but the proportion varied according to the amount of population, and the greater or less amount of land consequently required for the support of the inhabitants.

The lands assigned to the Sun furnished a revenue to support the temples and maintain the costly ceremonial of the Peruvian worship and the multitudinous priesthood. Those reserved for the Inca went to support the royal state, as well as the numerous members of his household and his kindred, and supplied the various exigencies of government. The remainder of the lands was divided, *per capita*, in equal shares among the people. It was provided by law, as we shall see hereafter, that every Peruvian should marry at a certain age. When this event took place, the community or district in which he lived furnished him with a dwelling, which, as it was constructed of humble materials, was done at little cost. A lot of land was then assigned to him sufficient for his own maintenance and that of his wife. An additional portion was granted for every child, the amount allowed for a son being double of that for a daughter. The division of the soil was renewed every year, and the possessions of the tenant were increased or diminished according to the numbers in his family. The same arrangement was observed with reference to the curacas, except only that a domain was assigned to them corresponding with the superior dignity of their stations.

A more thorough and effectual agrarian law than this cannot be imagined. In other countries where such a law has been introduced, its operation, after a time, has given way to the natural order of events, and under the superior intelligence and thrift of some and the prodigality of others, the usual vicissitudes of fortune have been allowed to take their course and restore things to their natural inequality. Even the iron law of Lycurgus ceased to operate after a time, and melted away before spirit and luxury and avarice. The nearest approach to the Peruvian constitution was probably in Judea, where, on the recurrence of the great national jubilee, at the close of every half-century, estates reverted to their original proprietors. There was this important difference in Peru: that not only did the lease, if we may so call it, terminate with the year, but during that period the tenant had no power to alienate or to add to his possessions. The end of the brief term found him in precisely the same condition that he was in at the beginning. Such a state of things might be supposed to be fatal to anything like attachment to the soil, or to that desire of improving it which is natural to the permanent proprietor, and hardly less so to the holder of a long lease. But the practical operation of the law seems to have been otherwise; and it is probable that, under the influence of that love of order and aversion to change which marked the Peruvian institutions, each new partition of the soil usually confirmed the occupant in his possession, and the tenant for a year was converted into a proprietor for life.

The territory was cultivated wholly by the people. The lands belonging to the Sun were first attended to. They next tilled the lands of the old, of the sick, of the widow and the orphan, and of soldiers engaged in actual service; in short, of all that part of the community who, from bodily infirmity or any other cause, were unable to attend to their own concerns. The people were then allowed to work on their own ground, each man for himself, but with the general obligation to assist his neighbors when any circumstance—the burden of a young and numerous family, for example—might demand it. Lastly, they cultivated the lands of the Inca. This was done, with great ceremony, by the whole population in a body. At break of day they were summoned together by proclamation from some neighboring tower of eminence, and all the inhabitants of the district, men, women, and children, appeared dressed in their gayest apparel, bedecked with their little store of finery and ornaments, as if for some great jubilee. They went through the labors of the day with the same joyous spirit, chanting their popular ballads which commemorated the heroic deeds of the Incas, regulating their movements by the measure of the chant, and all mingling in the chorus, of which the word *hailli,* or "triumph," was usually the burden. These national airs had something soft and pleasing in their character, that recommended them to the Spaniards; and many a Peruvian song was set to music by them after the Conquest, and was listened to by the unfortunate natives with melancholy satisfaction, as it called up recollections of the past, when their days glided peacefully away under the scepter of the Incas.

A similar arrangement prevailed with respect to the different manufactures as to the agricultural products of the country. The flocks of llamas were appropriated exclusively to the Sun and to the Inca. Their number was immense. They were scattered over the different provinces, chiefly in the colder regions of the country, where they were entrusted to the care of experienced shepherds, who conducted them to different pastures according to the change of season. A large number was every year sent to the capital for the consumption of the court, and for the religious festivals and sacrifices. But these were only the males, as no female was allowed to be killed. The regulations for the care and breeding of these flocks were prescribed with the greatest minuteness, and with a sagacity which excited the admiration of the Spaniards, who were familiar with the management of the great migratory flocks of merinos in their own country.

At the appointed season they were all sheared, and the wool was deposited in the public magazines. It was then dealt out to each family in such quantities as sufficed for its wants, and was consigned to the female part of the household, who were well instructed in the business of spinning and weaving. When this labor was accomplished, and the family was provided with a coarse but warm covering, suited to the cold climate of the mountains—for in the lower country, cotton, furnished in like manner by the crown, took the place, to a certain extent, of wool—the people were required to labor for the Inca. The quantity of the cloth needed, as well as the peculiar kind and quality of the fabric, was first determined at Cuzco. The work was then apportioned among the different provinces. Officers appointed for the purpose superintended the distribution of the wool, so that the manufacture of the different articles should be entrusted to the most competent hands. They did not leave the matter here, but entered the dwellings, from time to time, and saw that the work was faithfully executed. This domestic inquisition was not confined to the labors for the Inca. It included, also, those for the several families; and care was taken that each household should employ the materials furnished for its own use in the manner that was intended, so that no one should be unprovided with necessary apparel. In this domestic labor all the female part of the establishment was expected to join. Occupation was found for all, from the child five years old to the aged matron not too infirm to hold a distaff. No one, at least none but the decrepit and the sick, was allowed to eat the bread of idleness in Peru. Idleness was a crime in the eye of the law, and, as such, severely punished; while industry was publicly commended and stimulated by rewards.

The like course was pursued with reference to the other requisitions of the government. All the mines in the kingdom belonged to the Inca. They were wrought exclusively for his benefit, by persons familiar with this service and selected from the districts where the mines were situated. Every Peruvian of the lower class was a husbandman, and, with the exception of those already specified, was expected to provide for his own support by the cultivation of his land. A small portion of the community, however, was instructed in mechanical arts—some of them of the more elegant kind, subservient to the purposes of luxury and ornament. The demand for these was chiefly limited to the sovereign and his court; but the labor of a larger number of hands was exacted for the execution of the great public works which covered the land. The nature and amount of the services required were all determined at Cuzco by commissioners well instructed in the resources of the country and in the character of the inhabitants of different provinces.

This information was obtained by an admirable regulation, which has scarcely a counterpart in the annals of a semi-civilized people. A register was kept of all the births and deaths throughout the country, and exact returns of the actual population were made to the government every year, by means of the *quipus,* a curious invention, which will be explained hereafter. [10] At certain intervals, also, a general survey of the country was made, exhibiting a complete view of the character of the soil, its fertility, the nature of its products, both agricultural and mineral—in short, of all that constituted the physical resources of the empire. Furnished with these statistical details, it was easy for the government, after determining the amount of requisitions, to distribute the work among the respective provinces best qualified to execute it. The task of apportioning the labor was assigned to the local authorities, and great care was taken that it should be done in such a manner that, while the most competent hands were selected, the weight should not fall disproportionately on any.

The different provinces of the country furnished persons peculiarly suited to different employments, which, as we shall see hereafter, usually descended from father to son. Thus, one district supplied those most skilled in working the mines, another the most curious workers in metals or in wood, and so on. The artisan was provided by government with the materials; and no one was required to give more than a stipulated portion of his time to the public service. He was then succeeded by another for the like term; and it should be observed that all who were engaged in the employment of the government—and the remark applies equally to agricultural labor—were maintained, for the time, at the public expense. By this constant rotation of labor it was intended that no one should be overburdened, and that each man should have time to provide for the demands of his own household. It was impossible—in the judgment of a high Spanish authority—to improve on the system of distribution, so carefully was it accommodated to the condition and comfort of the artisan. The security of the working classes seems to have been ever kept in view in the regulations of the government; and these were so discreetly arranged that the most wearing and unwholesome labors, as those of the mines, occasioned no detriment to the health of the laborer; a striking contrast to his subsequent condition under the Spanish rule.

A part of the agricultural produce and manufactures was transported to Cuzco, to minister to the immediate demands of the Inca and his court. But far the greater part was stored in magazines scattered over the different provinces. These spacious buildings, constructed of stone, were divided between

**"A part of the agricultural produce and manufactures was transported to Cuzco, to minister to the immediate demands of the Inca and his Court."**

the Sun and the Inca, though the greater share seems to have been appropriated by the monarch. By a wise regulation, any deficiency in the contributions of the Inca might be supplied from the granaries of the Sun. But such a necessity could rarely have happened; and the providence of the government usually left a large surplus in the royal depositories, which was removed to a third class of magazines, whose design was to supply the people in seasons of scarcity, and, occasionally, to furnish relief to individuals whom sickness or misfortune had reduced to poverty; thus in a manner justifying the assertion of a Castilian document, that a large portion of the revenues of the Inca found its way back again, through one channel or another, into the hands of the people. These magazines were found by the Spaniards, on their arrival, stored with all the various products and manufactures of the country—with maize, *coca, quinua,* woolen and cotton stuffs of the finest quality, with vases and utensils of gold, silver, and copper, in short, with every article of luxury or use within the compass of Peruvian skill. The magazines of grain, in particular, would frequently have sufficed for the consumption of the adjoining district for several years. An inventory of the various products of the country, and the quarters whence they were obtained, was every year taken by the royal officers, and recorded by the *quipucamayus* on their registers, with surprising regularity and precision. These registers were transmitted to the capital and submitted to the Inca, who could thus at a glance, as it were, embrace the whole results of the national industry and see how far they corresponded with the requisitions of the government.

Such are some of the most remarkable features of the Peruvian institutions relating to property, as delineated by writers who, however contradictory in the details, have a general conformity of outline. These institutions are certainly so remarkable that it is hardly credible they should ever have been enforced throughout a great empire, and for a long period of years. Yet we have the most unequivocal testimony to the fact from the Spaniards, who landed in Peru in time to witness their operation; some of whom, men of high judicial station and character, were commissioned by the government to make investigations into the state of the country under its ancient rulers.

The impositions on the Peruvian people seem to have been sufficiently heavy. On them rested the whole burden of maintaining not only their own order, but every other order in the state. The members of the royal house, the great nobles, even the public functionaries, and the numerous body of the priesthood, were all exempt from taxation. The whole duty of defraying the expenses of the government belonged to the people. Yet this was not materially different from the condition of things formerly existing in most parts of Europe, where the various privileged classes claimed exemption—not always with success, indeed—from bearing part of the public burdens. The great hardship in the case of the Peruvian was that he could not better his condition. His labors were for others rather than for himself. However industrious, he could not add a rood to his own possessions, nor advance himself one hair's breadth in the social scale. The great and universal motive to honest industry, that of bettering one's lot, was lost upon him. The great law of human progress was not for him. As he was born, so he was to die. Even his time he could not properly call his own. Without money, with little property of any kind, he paid his taxes in labor. No wonder that the government should have dealt with sloth as a crime. It was a crime against the state, and to be wasteful of time was, in a manner, to rob the exchequer. The Peruvian, laboring all his life for others, might be compared to the convict in a treadmill, going the same dull round of incessant toil, with the consciousness that, however profitable the results to the state, they were nothing to him.

But this is the dark side of the picture. If no man could become rich in Peru, no man could become poor. No spendthrift could waste his substance in riotous luxury. No adventurous schemer could impoverish his family by the spirit of speculation. The law was constantly directed to enforce a steady industry and a sober management of his affairs. No mendicant was tolerated in Peru. When a man was reduced by poverty or misfortune (it could hardly be by fault), the arm of the law was stretched out to minister relief; not the stinted relief of private charity, nor that which is doled out, drop by drop, as it were, from the frozen reservoirs of "the parish," but in generous measure, bringing no humiliation to the object of it, and placing him on a level with the rest of his countrymen.

No man could be rich, no man could be poor in Peru; but all might enjoy, and did enjoy, a competence. Ambition, avarice, the love of change, the morbid spirit of discontent, those passions which most agitate the minds of men, found no place in the bosom of the Peruvian. The very condition of his being seemed to be at war with change. He moved on in the same unbroken circle in which his fathers had moved before him and in which his children were to follow. It was the object of the Incas to infuse into their subjects a spirit of passive obedience and tranquillity—a perfect acquiescence in the established order of things. In this they fully succeeded. The Spaniards who first visited the country are emphatic in their testimony that no government could have been better suited to the genius of the people, and no people could have appeared more contented with their lot or more devoted to their government.

Those who may distrust the accounts of Peruvian industry will find their doubts removed on a visit to the country. The traveler still meets, especially in the central regions of the tableland, with memorials of the past, remains of temples, palaces, fortresses, terraced mountains, great military roads, aqueducts, and other public works, which, whatever degree of science they may display in their execution, astonish him by their number, the massive character of the materials, and the grandeur of the design. Among them perhaps the most remarkable are the great roads, the broken remains of which are still in sufficient preservation to attest their former magnificence. There were many of these roads, traversing different parts of the kingdom; but the most considerable were the two which extended from Quito to Cuzco and, again diverging from the capital, continued in a southerly direction towards Chile.

One of these roads passed over the grand plateau, and the other along the lowlands on the borders of the ocean. The former was much the more difficult achievement, from the character of the country. It was conducted over pathless sierras buried in snow; galleries were cut for leagues through the living rock; rivers were crossed by means of bridges that swung suspended in the air; precipices were scaled by stairways hewn out of the native bed; ravines of hideous depth were filled up with solid masonry: in short, all the difficulties that beset a wild and mountainous region, and which might appall the most courageous engineer of modern times, were encountered and successfully overcome. The length of the road, of which scattered fragments only remain, is variously estimated at from fifteen hundred to two thousand miles; and stone pillars, in the manner of European milestones, were erected at stated intervals of somewhat more than a league all along the route. Its breadth scarcely exceeded twenty feet. It was built of heavy flags of freestone and, in some parts at least, covered with a bituminous cement, which time has made harder than the stone itself. In some places, where the ravines had been filled up with masonry, the mountain torrents, wearing on it for ages, have gradually eaten a way through the base, and left the superincumbent mass—such is

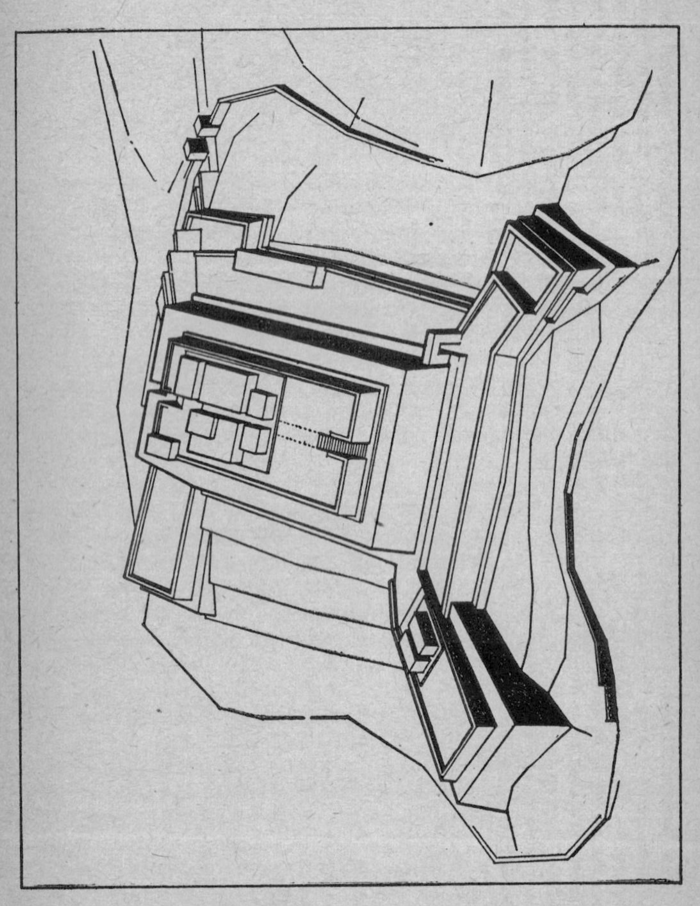

The coastal fortress of Paramonga. This is the best-preserved example of coastal fortifications. Half a mile from the sea, it rises terrace on terrace from the summit of an arid eminence. The Inca coastal road ran below it, and a perennial river was close by. It is presumed to have been built by the Chimu, the coastal empire with its capital at Chan Chan (Trujillo) as a defense against its southern enemies. The Incas took Paramonga after 1450. Hernando Pizarro, who visited it in February, 1533, described it as "a strong fort with seven encircling walls painted with many forms both inside and outside, with portals well built like those of Spain and two tigers painted at the principal doorways."

the cohesion of the materials—still spanning the valley like an arch! [11]

Over some of the boldest streams it was necessary to construct suspension bridges, as they are termed, made of the tough fibers of the maguey, or of the osier of the country, which has an extraordinary degree of tenacity and strength. These osiers were woven into cables of the thickness of a man's body. The huge ropes, then stretched across the water, were conducted through rings or holes cut in immense buttresses of stone raised on the opposite banks of the river, and there secured to heavy pieces of timber. Several of these enormous cables, bound together, formed a bridge, which, covered with planks, well secured and defended by a railing of the same osier materials on the sides, afforded a safe passage for the traveler. The length of this aerial bridge, sometimes exceeding two hundred feet, caused it, confined as it was only at the extremities, to dip with an alarming inclination towards the center, while the motion given to it by the passenger occasioned an oscillation still more frightful, as his eye wandered over the dark abyss of waters that foamed and tumbled many a fathom beneath. Yet these light and fragile fabrics were crossed without fear by the Peruvians, and are still retained by the Spaniards over those streams which, from the depth or impetuosity of the current, would seem impracticable for the usual modes of conveyance. The wider and more tranquil waters were crossed on *balsas*—a kind of raft still much used by the natives—to which sails were attached, furnishing the only instance of this higher kind of navigation among the American Indians.

The other great road of the Incas lay through the level country between the Andes and the ocean. It was constructed in a different manner, as demanded by the nature of the ground, which was for the most part low, and much of it sandy. The causeway was raised on a high embankment of earth, and defended on either side by a parapet or wall of clay; and trees and odoriferous shrubs were planted along the margin, regaling the sense of the traveler with their perfumes, and refreshing him by their shades, so grateful under the burning sky of the tropics. In the strips of sandy waste which occasionally intervened, where the light and volatile soil was incapable of sustaining a road, huge piles, many of them to be seen to this day, were driven into the ground to indicate the route to the traveler.

All along these highways caravansaries, or *tambos,* as they were called, were erected, at the distance of ten or twelve miles from each other, for the accommodation, more particularly, of the Inca and his suite and those who journeyed on the public business. There were few other travelers in Peru. Some of these buildings were on an extensive scale, consisting of a fortress, barracks, and other military works, surrounded by a parapet of stone and covering a large tract of ground. These were evidently destined for the accommodation of the imperial armies when on their march across the country. The care of the great roads was committed to the districts through which they passed, and under the Incas a large number of hands was constantly employed to keep them in repair. This was the more easily done in a country where the mode of traveling was altogether on foot, though the roads are said to have been so nicely constructed that a carriage might have rolled over them as securely as on any of the great roads of Europe. Still, in a region where the elements of fire and water are both actively at work in the business of destruction, they must, without constant supervision, have gradually gone to decay. Such has been their fate under the Spanish conquerors, who took no care to enforce the admirable system for their preservation adopted by the Incas. Yet the broken portions that still survive here and there, like the fragments of the great Roman roads scattered over Europe, bear evidence to their primitive grandeur, and have drawn forth the eulogium from a discriminating traveler, usually not too profuse in his panegyric, that "the roads of the Incas were among the most useful and stupendous works ever executed by man."

The system of communication through their dominions was still further improved by the Peruvian sovereigns by the introduction of posts, in the same manner as was done by the Aztecs. The Peruvian posts, however, established on all the great routes that conducted to the capital, were on a much more extended plan than those in Mexico. All along these routes, small buildings were erected, at the distance of less than five miles asunder, in each of which a number of runners, or *chasquis*, [12] as they were called, were stationed to carry forward the dispatches of government. These dispatches were either verbal or conveyed by means of *quipus*, and sometimes accompanied by a thread of the crimson fringe worn round the temples of the Inca, which was regarded with the same implicit deference as the signet ring of an Oriental despot.

The *chasquis* were dressed in a peculiar livery, intimating their profession. They were all trained to the employment, and selected for their speed and fidelity. As the distance each courier had to perform was small, and as he had ample time to refresh himself at the stations, they ran over the ground

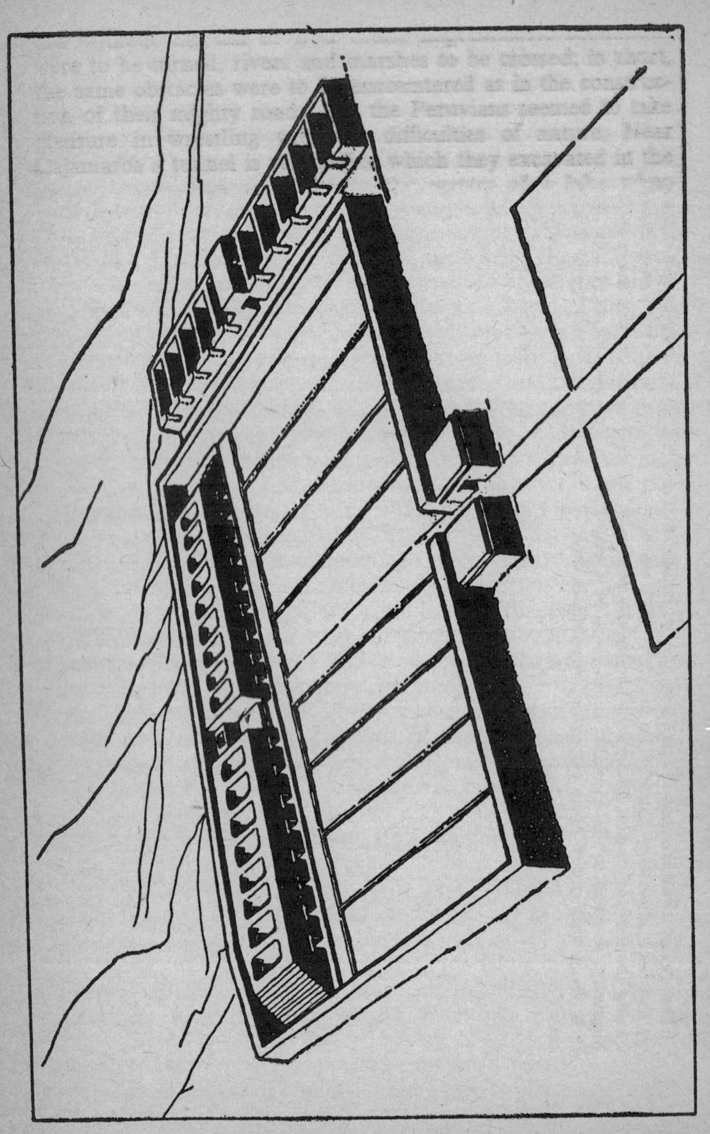

The great shellfish depot at Chala in southern coastal Peru; it was found almost intact by the Inca Highway Expedition in 1953. It is on one of the richest shellfish-gathering bays on the immediate coast, 300 meters from the sea and 100 meters from the main Inca coastal highway. A road leads directly from here to Cuzco, 170 miles up and east into the Andes. It is from this place that chasquis, running in relays, brought the Inca fresh fish from the sea.

with great swiftness, and messages were carried through the whole extent of the long routes at the rate of a hundred and fifty miles a day. The office of the *chasquis* was not limited to carrying dispatches. They frequently brought various articles for the use of the court; and in this way fish from the distant ocean, fruits, game, and different commodities from the hot regions on the coast were taken to the capital in good condition and served fresh at the royal table. It is remarkable that this important institution should have been known to both the Mexicans and the Peruvians without any correspondence with one another, and that it should have been found among two barbarian nations of the New World long before it was introduced among the civilized nations of Europe.

By these wise contrivances of the Incas, the most distant parts of the long-extended empire of Peru were brought into intimate relations with each other. And while the capitals of Christendom, but a few hundred miles apart, remained as far asunder as if seas had rolled between them, the great capitals Cuzco and Quito were placed by the highroads of the Incas in immediate correspondence. Intelligence from the numerous provinces was transmitted on the wings of the wind to the Peruvian metropolis, the great focus to which all the lines of communication converged. Not an insurrectionary movement could occur, not an invasion on the remotest frontier, before the tidings were conveyed to the capital, and the imperial armies were on their march across the magnificent roads of the country to suppress it. So admirable was the machinery contrived by the American despots for maintaining tranquillity throughout their dominions! It may remind us of the similar institutions of ancient Rome, when, under the Caesars, she was mistress of half the world.

A principal design of the great roads was to serve the purposes of military communication. It formed an important item of their military policy, which is quite as well worth studying as their municipal.

Notwithstanding the pacific professions of the Incas, and the pacific tendency, indeed, of their domestic institutions, they were constantly at war. It was by war that their paltry territory had been gradually enlarged to a powerful empire. When this was achieved, the capital, safe in its central position, was no longer shaken by these military movements, and the country enjoyed, in a great degree, the blessings of tranquillity and order. But, however tranquil at heart, there is not a reign upon record in which the nation was not engaged in war against the barbarous nations on the frontier. Religion furnished a plausible pretext for incessant aggression, and disguised the lust of conquest in the Incas, probably, from their own eyes, as well as from those of their subjects. Like the followers of Mahomet, bearing the sword in one hand and the Koran in the other, the Incas of Peru offered no alternative but the worship of the Sun or war.

It is true, their fanaticism—or their policy—showed itself in a milder form than was found in the descendants of the Prophet. Like the great luminary which they adored, they operated by gentleness, more potent than violence. They sought to soften the hearts of the rude tribes around them, and melt them by acts of condescension and kindness. Far from provoking hostilities, they allowed time for the salutary example of their own institutions to work its effect, trusting that their less civilized neighbors would submit to their scepter, from a conviction of the blessings it would secure to them. When this course failed, they employed other measures, but still of a pacific character, and endeavored by negotiation, by conciliatory treatment, and by presents to the leading men, to win them over to their dominion. In short, they practiced all the arts familiar to the most subtle politician of a civilized land to secure the acquisition of empire. When all these expedients failed, they prepared for war.

Their levies were drawn from all the different provinces; though from some, where the character of the people was particularly hardy, more than from others. It seems probable that every Peruvian who had reached a certain age might be called to bear arms. But the rotation of military service, and the regular drills, which took place twice or thrice in a month, of the inhabitants of every village, raised the soldiers generally above the rank of a raw militia. The Peruvian army, at first inconsiderable, came with the increase of population, in the latter days of the empire, to be very large, so that their monarchs could bring into the field, as contemporaries assure us, a force amounting to two hundred thousand men. They showed the same skill and respect for order in their military organization as in other things. The troops were divided into bodies corresponding with our battalions and companies, led by officers, that rose, in regular gradation, from the lowest subaltern to the Inca noble who was entrusted with the general command.

Their arms consisted of the usual weapons employed by nations, whether civilized or uncivilized, before the invention of powder—bows and arrows, lances, darts, a short kind of sword, a battle-ax or partisan, and slings, with which they were very expert. Their spears and arrows were tipped with copper or, more commonly, with bone, and the weapons of the Inca lords were frequently mounted with gold or silver.

The granary of "New Cuzco" (now called Inca Huasi), part of a complex Inca city located in the valley of Canete in southern Peru; it is at the bottom of a rainless mountain spur, close to the Canete River. In the middle of the fifteenth century the Incas under Topa Inca undertook a conquest of the coast. They were stopped by the stubborn defense of Chuquimancu, who held it by means of a large fortress built on top of a rugged stone outcrop in the center of the valley. The war dragged on for four years. The Inca decided to build a city twenty-five miles up the valley, to be modeled on his capital; he called it "New Cuzco." It is the largest Inca-built city on Peru's entire coast. In order to feed his troops, he ordered this immense storage chamber built to hold corn, beans, peppers, and all that was needed for a protracted siege. The storage chambers are without roofs, since there is normally no rainfall here. The greater length is 500 feet. (1) Brewery for *chicha*, the beverage made from corn; (2) principal administration center; (3) another part where *chicha* and other products were prepared for food; (4) llama stalls; (5) guardhouse and observation tower and living quarters; (6) areas for drying corn, peppers, beans, shellfish, etc.; (7) ceremonial center where rituals connected with harvesting were performed; (8) the cells, 8 feet square and 10 feet deep, for storing the harvests.

Their heads were protected by casques made either of wood or of the skins of wild animals, and sometimes richly decorated with metal and with precious stones, surmounted by the brilliant plumage of the tropical birds. These, of course, were the ornaments only of the higher orders. The great mass of the soldiery were dressed in the peculiar costume of their provinces, and their heads were wreathed with a sort of turban or roll of different-colored cloths that produced a gay and animating effect. Their defensive armor consisted of a shield or buckler and a close tunic of quilted cotton, in the same manner as with the Mexicans. Each company had its particular banner, and the imperial standard, high above all, displayed the glittering device of the rainbow—the armorial ensign of the Incas, intimating their claims as children of the skies.

By means of the thorough system of communication established in the country, a short time sufficed to draw the levies together from the most distant quarters. The army was put under the direction of some experienced chief, of the blood royal, or, more frequently, headed by the Inca in person. The march was rapidly performed, and with little fatigue to the soldier; for all along the great routes quarters were provided for him, at regular distances, where he could find ample accommodations. The country is still covered with the remains of military works, constructed of porphyry or granite, which tradition assures us were designed to lodge the Inca and his army.

At regular intervals, also, magazines were established, filled with grain, weapons, and the different munitions of war, with which the army was supplied on its march. It was the especial care of the government to see that these magazines, which were furnished from the stores of the Incas, were always well filled. When the Spaniards invaded the country, they supported their own armies for a long time on provisions found in them. The Peruvian soldier was forbidden to commit any trespass on the property of the inhabitants whose territory lay in the line of march. Any violation of this order was punished with death. The soldier was clothed and fed by the industry of the people, and the Incas rightly resolved that he should not repay this by violence. Far from being a tax on the labors of the husbandman, or even a burden on his hospitality, the imperial armies traversed the country, from one extremity to the other, with as little inconvenience to the inhabitants as would be created by a procession of peaceful burghers or a muster of holiday soldiers for a review.

From the moment war was proclaimed, the Peruvian monarch used all possible expedition in assembling his forces, that he might anticipate the movements of his enemies and prevent a combination with their allies. It was, however, from the neglect of such a principle of combination that the several nations of the country, who might have prevailed by confederated strength, fell one after another under the imperial yoke. Yet, once in the field, the Inca did not usually show any disposition to push his advantages to the utmost and urge his foe to extremity. In every stage of the war, he was open to propositions for peace; and, although he sought to reduce his enemies by carrying off their harvests and distressing them by famine, he allowed his troops to commit no unnecessary outrage on person or property. "We must spare our enemies," one of the Peruvian princes is quoted as saying, "or it will be our loss, since they and all that belongs to them must soon be ours." It was a wise maxim, and, like most other wise maxims, founded equally on benevolence and prudence. The Incas adopted the policy claimed for the Romans by their countryman, who tells us that they gained more by clemency to the vanquished than by their victories.

In the same considerate spirit, they were most careful to provide for the security and comfort of their own troops; and when a war was long protracted, or the climate proved unhealthy, they took care to relieve their men by frequent reinforcements, allowing the earlier recruits to return to their homes. But while thus economical of life, both in their own followers and in the enemy, they did not shrink from sterner measures when provoked by the ferocious or obstinate character of the resistance; and the Peruvian annals contain more than one of those sanguinary pages which cannot be pondered at the present day without a shudder. It should be added that the beneficent policy which I have been delineating as characteristic of the Incas did not belong to all, and that there was more than one of the royal line who displayed a full measure of the bold and unscrupulous spirit of the vulgar conqueror.

The first step of the government after the reduction of a country was to introduce there the worship of the Sun. Temples were erected and placed under the care of a numerous priesthood, who expounded to the conquered people the mysteries of their new faith, and dazzled them by the display of its rich and stately ceremonial. Yet the religion of the conquered was not treated with dishonor. The Sun was to be worshiped above all; but the images of their gods were removed to Cuzco and established in one of the temples, to hold their rank among the inferior deities of the Peruvian Pantheon. Here they remained as hostages, in some sort, for the conquered nation, which would be the less inclined to forsake its allegiance when by doing so it must leave its own gods in the hands of its enemies.

The Incas provided for the settlement of their new conquests by ordering a census to be taken of the population and a careful survey to be made of the country, ascertaining its products and the character and capacity of its soil. A division of the territory was then made on the same principle with that adopted throughout their own kingdom, and their respective portions were assigned to the Sun, the sovereign, and the people. The amount of the last was regulated by the amount of the population, but the share of each individual was uniformly the same. It may seem strange that any people should patiently have acquiesced in an arrangement which involved such a total surrender of property. But it was a conquered nation that did so, held in awe, on the least suspicion of meditated resistance, by army garrisons, which were established at various commanding points throughout the country. It is probable, too, that the Incas made no greater change than was essential to the new arrangement, and that they assigned estates, as far as possible, to their former proprietors. The curacas, in particular, were confirmed in their ancient authority; or, when it was found expedient to depose the existing curaca, his rightful heir was allowed to succeed him. Every respect was shown to the ancient usages and laws of the land, as far as was compatible with the fundamental institutions of the Incas. It must also be remembered that the conquered tribes were, many of them, too little advanced in civilization to possess that attachment to the soil which belongs to a cultivated nation. But, to whatever it be referred, it seems probable that the extraordinary institutions of the Incas were established with little opposition in the conquered territories.

Yet the Peruvian sovereigns did not trust altogether to this show of obedience in their new vassals; and, to secure it more effectually, they adopted some expedients too remarkable to be passed over in silence. Immediately after a recent conquest, the curacas and their families were removed for a time to Cuzco. Here they learned the language of the capital, became familiar with the manners and usages of the court, as well as with the general policy of the government, and experienced such marks of favor from the sovereign as would be most grateful to their feelings, and might attach them most warmly to his person. Under the influence of these sentiments, they were again sent to rule over their vassals, but still leaving their eldest sons in the capital, to remain there as a guarantee for their own fidelity, as well as to grace the court of the Inca.

Another expedient was of a bolder and more original character. This was nothing less than to revolutionize the language of the country. South America, like North America, had a great variety of dialects, or rather languages, having little affinity with one another. This circumstance occasioned great embarrassment to the government in the administration of the different provinces with whose idioms they were unacquainted. It was determined, therefore, to substitute one universal language, the Quechua,[13]—the language of the court, the capital, and the surrounding country—the richest and most comprehensive of the South American dialects. Teachers were provided in the towns and villages throughout the land, who were to give instruction to all, even the humblest classes; and it was intimated at the same time that no one should be raised to any office of dignity or profit who was unacquainted with this tongue. The curacas and other chiefs who attended at the capital became familiar with this dialect in their intercourse with the court, and, on their return home, set the example of conversing in it among themselves. This example was imitated by their followers, and the Quechua gradually became the language of elegance and fashion, in the same manner as the Norman French was affected by all those who aspired to any consideration in England after the Conquest. By this means, while each province retained its peculiar tongue, a beautiful medium of communication was introduced, which enabled the inhabitants of one part of the country to hold intercourse with every other, and the Inca and his deputies to communicate with all. This was the state of things on the arrival of the Spaniards. It must be admitted that history furnishes few examples of more absolute authority than such a revolution in the language of an empire at the bidding of a master.

Yet little less remarkable was another device of the Incas for securing the loyalty of their subjects. When any portion of the recent conquests showed a pertinacious spirit of disaffection, it was not uncommon to cause a part of the population, amounting, it might be, to ten thousand inhabitants or more, to remove to a distant quarter of the kingdom, occupied by ancient vassals of undoubted fidelity to the crown. A like number of these last was transplanted to the territory left vacant by the emigrants. By this exchange the population was composed of two distinct races, who regarded each other with an eye of jealousy, that served as an effectual check on any mutinous proceeding. In time, the influence of the well-affected prevailed, supported as they were by royal authority and by the silent working of the national institutions, to which the strange races became gradually accustomed. A spirit of loyalty sprang up by degrees in their bosoms, and before a generation had passed away the different tribes mingled in harmony together as members of the same community. Yet the different races continued to be distinguished by difference of dress; since, by the law of the land, every citizen was required to wear the costume of his native province. Neither could the colonist who had been thus unceremoniously transplanted return to his native district. For, by another law, it was forbidden to anyone to change his residence without license. He was settled for life. The Peruvian government prescribed to every man his local habitation, his sphere of action, nay, the very nature and quality of that action. He ceased to be a free agent; it might be almost said that it relieved him of personal responsibility.

In following out this singular arrangement, the Incas showed as much regard for the comfort and convenience of the colonist as was compatible with the execution of their design. They were careful that the *mitimaes,* as these emigrants were styled, should be removed to climates most congenial with their own. The inhabitants of the cold countries were not transplanted to the warm, nor the inhabitants of the warm countries to the cold. Even their habitual occupations were consulted, and the fisherman was settled in the neighborhood of the ocean or the great lakes, while such lands were assigned to the husbandman as were best adapted to the culture with which he was most familiar. And, as migration by many, perhaps by most, would be regarded as a calamity, the government was careful to show particular marks of favor to the *mitimaes,* and, by various privileges and immunities, to ameliorate their condition, and thus to reconcile them, if possible, to their lot.

The Peruvian institutions, though they may have been modified and matured under successive sovereigns, all bear the stamp of the same original—were all cast in the same mold. The empire, strengthening and enlarging at every successive epoch of its history, was in its latter days but the development, on a great scale, of what it was in miniature at its commencement, as the infant germ is said to contain within itself all the ramifications of the future monarch of the forest. Each succeeding Inca seemed desirous only to tread in the path and carry out the plans of his predecessor. Great enterprises, commenced under one, were continued by another, and completed by a third. Thus, while all acted on a regular plan, without any of the eccentric or retrograde movements which betray the agency of different individuals, the state seemed to be under the direction of a single hand, and steadily pursued, as if through one long reign, its greater career of civilization and of conquest.

The ultimate aim of its institutions was domestic quiet. But it seemed as if this were to be obtained only by foreign war. Tranquillity in the heart of the monarchy, and war on its borders, was the condition of Peru. By this war it gave occupation to a part of its people, and, by the reduction and civilization of its barbarous neighbors, gave security to all. Every Inca sovereign, however mild and benevolent in his domestic rule, was a warrior, and led his armies in person. Each successive reign extended still wider the boundaries of the empire. Year after year saw the victorious monarch return laden with spoils and followed by a throng of tributary chieftains to his capital. His reception there was a Roman triumph. The whole of its numerous population poured out to welcome him, dressed in the gay and picturesque costumes of the different provinces, with banners waving above their heads, and strewing branches and flowers along the path of the conqueror. The Inca, borne aloft in his golden chair on the shoulders of his nobles, moved in solemn procession, under the triumphal arches that were thrown across the way, to the great temple of the Sun. There, without attendants—for all but the monarch were excluded from the hallowed precincts—the victorious prince, stripped of his royal insignia, barefooted, and with all humility, approached the awful shrine and offered up sacrifice and thanksgiving to the glorious deity who presided over the fortunes of the Incas. This ceremony concluded, the whole population gave itself up to festivity; music, revelry, and dancing were heard in every quarter of the capital, and illuminations and bonfires commemorated the victorious campaign of the Inca and the accession of a new territory to his empire.

In this celebration we see much of the character of a religious festival. Indeed, the character of religion was impressed on all the Peruvian wars. The life of an Inca was one long crusade against the infidel, to spread wide the worship of the Sun, to reclaim the benighted nations from their brutish superstitions, and impart to them the blessings of a well-regulated government. This, in the favorite phrase of our day, was the mission of the Christian conqueror who invaded the empire of this same Indian potentate. Which of the two executed his mission most faithfully, history must decide.

Yet the Peruvian monarchs did not show a childish impatience in the acquisition of empire. They paused after a campaign, and allowed time for the settlement of one conquest before they undertook another, and in this interval occupied themselves with the quiet administration of their kingdom, and with the long progresses which brought them into nearer intercourse with their people. During this interval, also, their new vassals had begun to accommodate themselves to the strange institutions of their masters. They learned to appreciate the value of a government which raised them above the physical evils of a state of barbarism, secured them protection of person and a full participation in all the privileges enjoyed by their conquerors; and, as they became more familiar with the peculiar institutions of the country, habit, that second nature, attached them the more strongly to these institutions from their very peculiarity. Thus, by degrees, and without violence, arose the great fabric of the Peruvian empire, composed of numerous independent and even hostile tribes, yet, under the influence of a common religion, common language, and common government, knit together as one nation, animated by a spirit of love for its institutions, and devoted loyalty to its sovereign. What a contrast to the condition of the Aztec monarchy, on the neighboring continent, which, composed of the like heterogeneous materials, without any internal principle of cohesion, was only held together by the stern pressure, from without, of physical force! Why the Peruvian monarchy should have fared no better than its rival in its conflict with European civilization will appear in the following pages.

# ◊ CHAPTER THREE ◊

PERUVIAN RELIGION—DEITIES—GORGEOUS

TEMPLES—FESTIVALS—VIRGINS OF

THE SUN—MARRIAGE

It is a remarkable fact that many, if not most, of the rude tribes inhabiting the vast American continent, however disfigured their creeds may have been in other respects by a childish superstition, had attained to the sublime conception of one Great Spirit, the Creator of the Universe, who, immaterial in his own nature, was not to be dishonored by an attempt at visible representation, and who, pervading all space, was not to be circumscribed within the walls of a temple. Yet these elevated ideas, so far beyond the ordinary range of the untutored intellect, do not seem to have led to the practical consequences that might have been expected; and few of the American nations have shown much solicitude for the maintenance of a religious worship, or found in their faith a powerful spring of action.

But with progress in civilization ideas more akin to those of civilized communities were gradually unfolded; a liberal provision was made, and a separate order instituted, for the services of religion, which were conducted with a minute and magnificent ceremonial, that challenged comparison, in some respects, with that of the most polished nations of Christendom. This was the case with the nations inhabiting the table-land of North America, and with the natives of Bogotá, Quito, Peru, and the other elevated regions on the great southern continent. It was, above all, the case with the Peruvians, who claimed a divine original for the founders of their empire, whose laws all rested on a divine sanction, and whose domestic institutions and foreign wars were alike directed to preserve and propagate their faith. Religion was the basis of their polity, the very condition, as it were, of their social existence. The government of the Incas, in its essential principles, was a theocracy.

Yet, though religion entered so largely into the fabric and conduct of the political institutions of the people, their mythology, that is, the traditionary legends by which they affected to unfold the mysteries of the universe, was exceedingly mean and puerile. Scarce one of their traditions—except the beautiful one respecting the founders of their royal dynasty—is worthy of note, or throws much light on their own antiquities or the primitive history of man. Among the traditions of importance is one of the Deluge, which they held in common with so many of the nations in all parts of the globe, and which they related with some particulars that bear resemblance to a Mexican legend.

Their ideas in respect to a future state of being deserve more attention. They admitted the existence of the soul hereafter, and connected with this a belief in the resurrection of the body. They assigned two distinct places for the residence of the good and of the wicked, the latter of which they fixed in the center of the earth. The good, they supposed, were to pass a luxurious life of tranquillity and ease, which comprehended their highest notions of happiness. The wicked were to expiate their crimes by ages of wearisome labor. They associated with these ideas a belief in an evil principle of spirit, bearing the name of Cupay, whom they did not attempt to propitiate by sacrifices, and who seems to have been only a shadowy personification of sin, that exercised little influence over their conduct.

It was this belief in the resurrection of the body which led them to preserve the body with so much solicitude—by a simple process, however, that, unlike the elaborate embalming of the Egyptians, consisted in exposing it to the action of the cold, exceedingly dry, and highly rarefied atmosphere of the mountains. As they believed that the occupations in the future world would have great resemblance to those of the present, they buried with the deceased noble some of his apparel, his utensils, and frequently his treasures, and completed the gloomy ceremony by sacrificing his wives and favorite domestics, to bear him company and do him service in the happy regions beyond the clouds. Vast mounds of an irregular or, more frequently, oblong shape, penetrated by galleries running at right angles to each other, were raised over the dead, whose dried bodies or mummies have been found in considerable numbers, sometimes erect, but more often in the sitting posture common to the Indian tribes of both continents. Treasures of great value have also been occasionally drawn from these monumental deposits, and have stimulated speculators to repeated excavations with the hope of similar good fortune.

It was a lottery like that of searching after mines, but where the chances have proved still more against the adventurers.

The Peruvians, like so many other of the Indian races, acknowledged a Supreme Being, the Creator and Ruler of the Universe, whom they adored under the different names of Pachacamac and Viracocha. No temple was raised to this invisible Being, save one only in the valley which took its name from the deity himself, not far from the Spanish city of Lima. Even this temple had existed there before the country came under the sway of the Incas, and was the great resort of Indian pilgrims from remote parts of the land—a circumstance which suggests the idea that the worship of this Great Spirit, though countenanced, perhaps, by their accommodating policy, did not originate with the Peruvian princes.

The deity whose worship they especially inculcated, and which they never failed to establish wherever their banners were known to penetrate, was the Sun. It was he who, in a particular manner, presided over the destinies of man, gave light and warmth to the nations, and life to the vegetable world; whom they reverenced as the father of their royal dynasty, the founder of their empire; and whose temples rose in every city and almost every village throughout the land, while his altars smoked with burnt offerings—a form of sacrifice peculiar to the Peruvians, among the semi-civilized nations of the New World.

Besides the Sun, the Incas acknowledged various objects of worship in some way or other connected with this principal deity. Such was the Moon, his sister-wife; the Stars, revered as part of her heavenly train—though the fairest of them, Venus, known to the Peruvians by the name of Chasca, or the "youth with the long and curling locks," was adored as the page of the Sun, whom he attends so closely in his rising and in his setting. They dedicated temples also to the Thunder and Lightning in whom they recognized the Sun's dread ministers, and to the Rainbow, whom they worshiped as a beautiful emanation of their glorious deity.

In addition to these, the subjects of the Incas enrolled among their inferior deities many objects in nature, as the elements, the winds, the earth, the air, great mountains and rivers, which impressed them with ideas of sublimity and power, or were supposed in some way or other to exercise a mysterious influence over the destinies of man. They adopted also a notion, not unlike that professed by some of the schools of ancient philosophy, that everything on earth had its archetype or idea, its *mother,* as they emphatically styled it, which they held sacred, as, in some sort, its spiritual essence. But their system, far from being limited even to these multiplied objects of devotion, embraced within its ample folds the numerous deities of the conquered nations, whose images were transported to the capital, where the burdensome charges of their worship were defrayed by their respective provinces. It was a rare stroke of policy in the Incas, who could thus accommodate their religion to their interests.

But the worship of the Sun constituted the peculiar care of the Incas, and was the object of their lavish expenditure. The most ancient of the many temples dedicated to this divinity was in the island of Titicaca, whence the royal founders of the Peruvian line were said to have proceeded. From this circumstance, this sanctuary was held in peculiar veneration. Everything which belonged to it, even the broad fields of maize which surrounded the temple and formed part of its domain, imbibed a portion of its sanctity. The yearly produce was distributed among the different public magazines, in small quantities to each, as something that would sanctify the remainder of the store. Happy was the man who could secure even an ear of the blessed harvest for his own granary!

But the most renowned of the Peruvian temples, the pride of the capital, and the wonder of the empire, was at Cuzco, where, under the munificence of successive sovereigns, it had become so enriched that it received the name of *Curicancha*,[14] or "the Place of Gold." It consisted of a principal building and several chapels and inferior edifices, covering a large extent of ground in the heart of the city, and completely encompassed by a wall, which, with the edifices, was all constructed of stone. The work was of the kind already described in the other public buildings of the country, and was so finely executed that a Spaniard who saw it in its glory assures us he could call to mind only two edifices in Spain which, for their workmanship, were at all to be compared with it. Yet this substantial and, in some respects, magnificent structure was thatched with straw!

The interior of the temple was the most worthy of admiration. It was literally a mine of gold. On the western wall was emblazoned a representation of the deity, consisting of a human countenance looking forth from amidst innumerable rays of light, which emanated from it in every direction in the same manner as the Sun is often personified with us. The figure was engraved on a massive plate of gold of enormous dimensions, thickly powdered with emeralds and precious stones. It was so situated in front of the great eastern portal that the rays of the morning sun fell directly upon it at rising, lighting up the whole apartment with an effulgence that seemed more than natural, and which was reflected back from the golden ornaments with which the walls and ceiling were everywhere encrusted. Gold, in the figurative language of the people, was "the tears wept by the Sun," and every part of the interior of the temple glowed with burnished plates and studs of the precious metal. The cornices which surrounded the walls of the sanctuary were of the same costly material; and a broad belt or frieze of gold, let into the stonework, encompassed the whole exterior of the edifice.

Adjoining the principal structure were several chapels of smaller dimensions. One of them was consecrated to the Moon, the deity held next in reverence, as the mother of the Incas. Her effigy was delineated in the same manner as that of the Sun, on a vast plate that nearly covered one side of the apartment. But this plate, as well as all the decorations of the building, was of silver, as suited to the pale, silvery light of the beautiful planet. There were three other chapels, one of which was dedicated to the host of Stars, who formed the bright court of the Sister of the Sun; another was consecrated to his dread ministers of vengeance, the Thunder and the Lightning; and a third, to the Rainbow, whose many-colored arch spanned the walls of the edifice with hues almost as radiant as its own. There were, besides, several other buildings, or insulated apartments, for the accommodation of the numerous priests who officiated in the services of the temple.

All the plate, the ornaments, the utensils of every description, appropriated to the uses of religion, were of gold or silver. Twelve immense vases of the latter metal stood on the floor of the great saloon, filled with grain of the Indian corn; the censers for the perfumes, the ewers which held the water for sacrifice, the pipes which conducted it through subterranean channels into the buildings, the reservoirs that received it, even the agricultural implements used in the gardens of the temple, were all of the same rich materials. The gardens, like those described belonging to royal palaces, sparkled with flowers of gold and silver, and various imitations of the vegetable kingdom. Animals, also, were to be found there— among which the llama, with its golden fleece, was most conspicuous—executed in the same style, and with a degree of skill which, in this instance, probably, did not surpass the excellence of the material.

If the reader sees in this fairy picture only the romantic coloring of some fabulous *El Dorado*, he must recall what has been said before in reference to the palaces of the Incas, and consider that these "Houses of the Sun," as they were styled, were the common reservoir into which flowed all the streams of public and private benefaction throughout the empire. Some of the statements, through credulity, and others, in the desire of exciting admiration, may be greatly exaggerated; but in the coincidence of contemporary testimony it is not easy to determine the exact line which should mark the measure of our skepticism. Certain it is that the glowing picture I have given is warranted by those who saw these buildings in their pride, or shortly after they had been despoiled by the cupidity of their countrymen. Many of the costly articles were buried by the natives, or thrown into the waters of the rivers and the lakes; but enough remained to attest the unprecedented opulence of these religious establishments. Such things as were in their nature portable were speedily removed, to gratify the craving of the Conquerors, who even tore away the solid cornices and frieze of gold from the great temple, filling the vacant places with the cheaper, but—since it affords no temptation to avarice—more durable, material of plaster. Yet even thus shorn of their splendor the venerable edifices still presented an attraction to the spoiler, who found in their dilapidated walls an inexhaustible quarry for the erection of other buildings. On the very ground once crowned by the gorgeous Curicancha rose the stately church of St. Dominic, one of the most magnificent structures of the New World. Fields of maize and lucerne now bloom on the spot which glowed with the golden gardens of the temple; and the friar chants his orisons within the consecrated precincts once occupied by the Children of the Sun.

Besides the great temple of the Sun, there was a large number of inferior temples and religious houses in the Peruvian capital and its environs, amounting, as is stated, to three or four hundred. For Cuzco was a sanctified spot, venerated not only as the abode of the Incas, but of all those deities who presided over the motley nations of the empire. It was the city beloved of the Sun; where his worship was maintained in its splendor; "where every fountain, pathway, and wall," says an ancient chronicler, "was regarded as a holy mystery." And unfortunate was the Indian noble who, at some period or other of his life, had not made his pilgrimage to the Peruvian Mecca.

Other temples and religious dwellings were scattered over the provinces, and some of them constructed on a scale of magnificence that almost rivaled that of the metropolis. The attendants on these composed an army of themselves. The whole number of functionaries, including these of the sacerdotal order, who officiated at the Curicancha alone, was no less than four thousand.

At the head of all, both here and throughout the land, stood the great High Priest, or Villac Vmu, as he was called. He was second only to the Inca in dignity, and was usually chosen from his brothers or nearest kindred. He was appointed by the monarch, and held his office for life; and he, in turn, appointed to all the subordinate stations of his own order. This order was very numerous. Those members of it who officiated in the House of the Sun, in Cuzco, were taken exclusively from the sacred race of the Incas. The ministers in the provincial temples were drawn from the families of the curacas; but the office of high priest in each district was reserved for one of the blood royal. It was designed by this regulation to preserve the faith in its purity, and to guard against any departure from the stately ceremonial which it punctiliously prescribed.[15]

The sacerdotal order, though numerous, was not distinguished by any peculiar badge or costume from the rest of the nation. Neither was it the sole depository of the scanty science of the country, nor was it charged with the business of instruction, nor with those parochial duties, if they may so be called, which bring the priest in contact with the great body of the people, as was the case in Mexico. The cause of this peculiarity may probably be traced to the existence of a superior order, like that of the Inca nobles, whose sanctity of birth so far transcended all human appointments that they in a manner engrossed whatever there was of religious veneration in the people. They were, in fact, the holy order of the state. Doubtless any of them might, as very many of them did, take on themselves the sacerdotal functions; and their own insignia and peculiar privileges were too well understood to require any further badge to separate them from the people.

The duties of the priest were confined to ministration in the temple. Even here his attendance was not constant, as he was relieved after a stated interval by other brethren of his order, who succeeded one another in regular rotation. His science was limited to an acquaintance with the fasts and festivals of his religion and the appropriate ceremonies which distinguished them. This, however frivolous might be its character, was no easy acquisition; for the ritual of the Incas involved a routine of observances as complex and elaborate as ever distinguished that of any nation, whether pagan or Christian. Each month had its appropriate festival, or rather festivals. The four principal had reference to the Sun and commemorated the great periods of his annual progress, the solstices and equinoxes.

Perhaps the most magnificent of all the national solemnities was the feast of Inti Raymi, held at the period of the summer solstice, when the Sun, having touched the southern extremity of his course, retraced his path, as if to gladden the hearts of his chosen people by his presence. On this occasion the Indian nobles from the different quarters of the country thronged to the capital to take part in the great religious celebration.

For three days previous there was a general fast, and no fire was allowed to be lighted in the dwellings. When the appointed day arrived, the Inca and his court, followed by the whole population of the city, assembled at early dawn in the great square to greet the rising of the Sun. They were dressed in their gayest apparel, and the Indian lords vied with each other in the display of costly ornaments and jewels on their persons, while canopies of gaudy featherwork and richly tinted stuffs, borne by the attendants over their heads, gave to the great square, and the streets that emptied into it, the appearance of being spread over with one vast and magnificent awning. Eagerly they watched the coming of their deity, and no sooner did his first yellow rays strike the turrets and loftiest buildings of the capital than a shout of gratulation broke forth from the assembled multitude, accompanied by songs of triumph and the wild melody of barbaric instruments, that swelled louder and louder as his bright orb, rising above the mountain range towards the east, shone in full splendor on his votaries. After the usual ceremonies of adoration, a libation was offered to the great deity by the Inca, from a huge golden vase, filled with the fermented liquor of maize or of maguey, which, after the monarch had tasted it himself, he dispensed among his royal kindred. These ceremonies completed, the vast assembly was arranged in order of procession and took its way towards the Curicancha.

As they entered the street of the sacred edifice, all divested themselves of their sandals, except the Inca and his family, who did the same on passing through the portals of the temple, where none but these august personages were admitted. After a decent time spent in devotion, the sovereign, attended by his courtly train, again appeared, and preparations were made to commence the sacrifice. This, with the Peruvians, consisted of animals, grain, flowers, and sweet-scented gums—sometimes of human beings, on which occasions a child or beautiful maiden was usually selected as the victim. But such sacrifices were rare, being reserved to celebrate some great public event, as a coronation, the birth of a royal heir, or a great victory. They were never followed by those cannibal repasts familiar to the Mexicans and to many of the fierce tribes conquered by the Incas. Indeed, the conquests of these princes might well be deemed a blessing to the Indian nations, if it were only from their suppression of cannibalism, and the diminution, under their rule, of human sacrifices.

At the feast of Inti Raymi, the sacrifice usually offered was that of the llama; and the priest, after opening the body of his victim, sought in the appearances which it exhibited to read the lesson of the mysterious future. If the auguries were unpropitious, a second victim was slaughtered, in the hope of receiving some more comfortable assurance. The Peruvian augur might have learned a good lesson of the Roman—to consider every omen as favorable which served the interests of his country.

A fire was then kindled by means of a concave mirror of polished metal, which, collecting the rays of the Sun into a focus upon a quantity of dried cotton, speedily set it on fire. It was the expedient used on the like occasions in ancient Rome, at least under the reign of the pious Numa. When the sky was overcast, and the face of the good deity was hidden from his worshipers, which was esteemed a bad omen, fire was obtained by means of friction. The sacred flame was entrusted to the care of the Virgins of the Sun; and if, by any neglect, it was suffered to go out in the course of the year, the event was regarded as a calamity that boded some strange disaster to the monarchy. A burnt offering of the victims was then made on the altars of the deity. This sacrifice was but the prelude to the slaughter of a great number of llamas, part of the flocks of the Sun, which furnished a banquet not only for the Inca and his court, but for the people, who made amends at these festivals for the frugal fare to which they were usually condemned. A fine bread or cake, kneaded of maize flour by the fair hands of the Virgins of the Sun, was also placed on the royal board, where the Inca, presiding over the feast, pledged his great nobles in generous goblets of the fermented liquor of the country, and the long revelry of the day was closed at night by music and dancing. Dancing and drinking were the favorite pastimes of the Peruvians. These amusements continued for several days, though the sacrifices terminated on the first. Such was the great festival of Inti Raymi; and the recurrence of this and similar festivities gave relief to the monotonous routine of toil prescribed to the lower orders of the community.

In the distribution of bread and wine at this high festival, the orthodox Spaniards who first came into the country saw a striking resemblance to the Christian communion; as in the practice of confession and penance, which, in a most irregular form indeed, seems to have been used by the Peruvians, they discerned a coincidence with another of the sacraments of the Church. The good fathers were fond of tracing such coincidences, which they considered as the contrivance of Satan, who thus endeavored to delude his victims by counterfeiting the blessed rites of Christianity. Others, in a different vein, imagined that they saw in such analogies the evidence that some of the primitive teachers of the gospel, perhaps an apostle himself, had paid a visit to these distant regions and scattered over them the seeds of religious truth. But it seems hardly necessary to invoke the Prince of Darkness, or the intervention of the blessed saints, to account for coincidences which have existed in countries far removed from the light of Christianity, and in ages, indeed, when its light had not yet risen on the world. It is much more reasonable to refer such casual points of resemblance to the general constitution of man and the necessities of his moral nature.

Another singular analogy with Roman Catholic institutions is presented by the Virgins of the Sun, the "elect," as they were called, to whom I have already had occasion to refer. These were young maidens, dedicated to the service of the deity, who, at a tender age, were taken from their homes and introduced into convents, where they were placed under the care of certain elderly matrons, *mamaconas,* who had grown gray within their walls. Under these venerable guides the holy virgins were instructed in the nature of their religious duties. They were employed in spinning and embroidery, and, with the fine hair of the vicuña, wove the hangings for the temples, and the apparel for the Inca and his household. It was their duty, above all, to watch over the sacred fire obtained at the festival of Inti Raymi. From the moment they entered the establishment, they were cut off from all connection with the world, even with their own family and friends. No one but the Inca, and the Coya or queen, might enter the consecrated precincts. The greatest attention was paid to their morals, and visitors were sent every year to inspect the institutions and to report on the state of their discipline. Woe to the unhappy maiden who was detected in an intrigue! By the stern law of the Incas, she was to be buried alive, her lover was to be strangled, and the town or village to which he belonged was to be razed to the ground, and "sowed with stones," as if to efface every memorial of his existence. One is astonished to find so close a resemblance between the institutions of the American Indian, the ancient Roman, and the modern Catholic! Chastity and purity of life are virtues in women that would seem to be of equal estimation with the barbarian and with the civilized. Yet the ultimate destination of the inmates of the religious houses was materially different.

The great establishment at Cuzco consisted wholly of maidens of the royal blood, who amounted, it is said, to no less than fifteen hundred. The provincial convents were supplied from the daughters of the curacas and inferior nobles, and occasionally, where a girl was recommended by great personal attractions, from the lower classes of the people. The "Houses of the Virgins of the Sun" consisted of low ranges of stone buildings, covering a large extent of ground, surrounded by high walls, which excluded those within entirely from observation. They were provided with every accommodation for the fair inmates, and were embellished in the same sumptuous and costly manner as the palaces of the Incas, and the temples; for they received the particular care of the government, as an important part of the religious establishment.

Yet the career of all the inhabitants of these cloisters was not confined within their narrow walls. Though Virgins of the Sun, they were brides of the Inca, and at a marriageable age the most beautiful among them were selected for the honors of his bed, and transferred to the royal seraglio. The full complement of this amounted in time not only to hundreds, but thousands, who all found accommodations in his different palaces throughout the country. When the monarch was disposed to lessen the number of his establishment, the concubine with whose society he was willing to dispense returned, not to her former monastic residence, but to her own home; where, however humble might be her original condition, she was maintained in great state, and, far from being dishonored by the situation she had filled, was held in universal reverence as the Inca's bride.

The great nobles of Peru were allowed, like their sovereign, a plurality of wives. The people, generally, whether by law, or by necessity stronger than law, were more happily limited to one. Marriage was conducted in a manner that gave it quite as original a character as belonged to the other institutions of the country. On an appointed day of the year, all those of a marriageable age—which, having reference to their ability to take charge of a family, in the males was fixed at not less than twenty-four years, and in the women at eighteen or twenty—were called together in the great squares of their respective towns and villages throughout the empire. The Inca presided in person over the assembly of his own kindred, and, taking the hands of the different couples who were to be united, he placed them within each other, declaring the parties man and wife. The same was done by the curacas towards all persons of their own or inferior degree in their several districts. This was the simple form of marriage in Peru. No one was allowed to select a wife beyond the community to which he belonged, which generally comprehended all his own kindred; nor was any but the sovereign authorized to dispense with the law of nature—or, at least, the usual law of nations—so far as to marry his own sister. No marriage was esteemed valid without the consent of the parents; and the preference of the parties, it is said, was also to be consulted; though, considering the barriers imposed by the prescribed age of the candidates, this must have been within rather narrow and whimsical limits. A dwelling was got ready for the new-married pair at the charge of the district, and the prescribed portion of land assigned for their maintenance. The law of Peru provided for the future, as well as for the present. It left nothing to chance. The simple ceremony of marriage was followed by general festivities among the friends of the parties, which lasted several days; and as every wedding took place on the same day, and as there were few families who had not some one of their members or their kindred personally interested, there was one universal bridal jubilee throughout the empire.

The extraordinary regulations respecting marriage under the Incas are eminently characteristic of the genius of the government; which, far from limiting itself to matters of public concern, penetrated into the most private recesses of domestic life, allowing no man, however humble, to act for himself, even in those personal matters in which none but himself, or his family at most, might be supposed to be interested. No Peruvian was too low for the fostering vigilance of the government. None was so high that he was not made to feel his dependence upon it in every act of his life. His very existence as an individual was absorbed in that of the community. His hopes and his fears, his joys and his sorrows, the tenderest sympathies of his nature, which would most naturally shrink from observation, were all to be regulated by law. He was not allowed even to be happy in his own way. The government of the Incas was the mildest, but the most searching, of despotisms.

# ৫২ CHAPTER FOUR ৯৯

EDUCATION—QUIPUS—ASTRONOMY—AGRICULTURE—

AQUEDUCTS—GUANO—IMPORTANT ESCULENTS

"Science was not intended for the people, but for those of generous blood. Persons of low degree are only puffed up by it, and rendered vain and arrogant. Neither should such meddle with the affairs of government; for this would bring high offices into disrepute, and cause detriment to the state." Such was the favorite maxim, often repeated, of Tupac Inca Yupanqui, one of the most renowned of the Peruvian sovereigns. It may seem strange that such a maxim should ever have been proclaimed in the New World, where popular institutions have been established on a more extensive scale than was ever before witnessed; where government rests wholly on the people, and education—at least in the great northern division of the continent—is mainly directed to qualify the people for the duties of government. Yet this maxim was strictly conformable to the genius of the Peruvian monarchy, and may serve as a key to its habitual policy; since, while it watched with unwearied solicitude over its subjects, provided for their physical necessities, was mindful of their morals, and showed, throughout, the affectionate concern of a parent for his children, it yet regarded them only as children, who were never to emerge from the state of pupilage, to act or think for themselves, but whose whole duty was comprehended in the obligation of implicit obedience.

Such was the humiliating condition of the people under the Incas, while the numerous families of the blood royal enjoyed the benefit of all the light of education which the civilization of the country could afford, and long after the Conquest the spots continued to be pointed out where the seminaries had existed for their instruction. These were placed under the care of the *amautas,* or "wise men," who engrossed the scanty stock of science—if science it could be called—possessed by the Peruvians, and who were the sole teachers of youth. It was natural that the monarch should take a lively interest in the instruction of the young nobility, his own kindred. Several of the Peruvian princes are said to have built their palaces in the neighborhood of the schools, in order that they might the more easily visit them and listen to the lectures of the amautas, which they occasionally reinforced by a homily of their own. In these schools the royal pupils were instructed in all the different kinds of knowledge in which their teachers were versed, with especial reference to the stations they were to occupy in after life. They studied the laws and the principles of administering the government in which many of them were to take part. They were initiated in the peculiar rites of their religion most necessary to those who were to assume the sacerdotal functions. They learned also to emulate the achievements of their royal ancestors by listening to the chronicles compiled by the amautas. They were taught to speak their own dialect with purity and elegance; and they became acquainted with the mysterious science of the quipus, which supplied the Peruvians with the means of communicating their ideas to one another, and of transmitting them to future generations.

The quipu was a cord about two feet long, composed of different colored threads tightly twisted together, from which a quantity of smaller threads were suspended in the manner of a fringe. The threads were of different colors, and were tied into knots. The word *quipu*, indeed, signifies a *knot*. The colors denoted sensible objects; as, for instance, *white* represented *silver*, and *yellow*, *gold*. They sometimes also stood for

**"Officers were established in each of the districts who, under the title of quipucamayoc or 'keepers of the quipus,' were required to furnish the government with information."**

abstract ideas. Thus, *white* signified *peace,* and *red, war.* But the quipus were chiefly used for artificial purposes. The knots served instead of ciphers, and could be combined in such a manner as to represent numbers to any amount required. By means of these they went through their calculations with great rapidity, and the Spaniards who first visited the country bear testimony to their accuracy.

Officers were established in each of the districts, who, under the title of *quipucamayocs,* or "keepers of the quipus," were required to furnish the government with information on various important matters. One had charge of the revenues, reported on the quantity of raw material distributed among the laborers, the quality and quantity of the fabrics made from it, and the amount of stores, of various kinds, paid into the royal magazines. Another exhibited the register of births and deaths, the marriages, the number of those qualified to bear arms, and the like details in reference to the population of the kingdom. These returns were annually forwarded to the capital, where they were submitted to the inspection of officers acquainted with the art of deciphering these mystic records. The government was thus provided with a valuable means of statistical information, and the skeins of many-colored threads, collected and carefully preserved, constituted what might be called the national archives.

But, although the quipus sufficed for all the purposes of arithmetical computation demanded by the Peruvians, they were incompetent to represent the manifold ideas and images which are expressed by writing. Even here, however, the invention was not without its use. For, independently of the direct representation of simple objects, and even of abstract ideas, to a very limited extent, as above noticed, it afforded great help to the memory by way of association. The peculiar knot or color, in this way, suggested what it could not venture to represent; in the same manner—to borrow the homely illustration of an old writer—as the number of the Commandment calls to mind the Commandment itself. The quipus, thus used, might be regarded as the Peruvian system of mnemonics.

Annalists were appointed in each of the principal communities, whose business it was to record the most important events which occurred in them. Other functionaries of a higher character, usually the amautas, were instructed with the history of the empire, and were selected to chronicle the great deeds of the reigning Inca, or of his ancestors. The narrative, thus concocted, could be communicated only by oral tradition; but the quipus served the chronicler to arrange the incidents with method and to refresh his memory. The story, once treasured up in the mind, was indelibly impressed there by frequent repetition. It was repeated by the amauta to his pupils, and in this way history, conveyed partly by oral tradition and partly by arbitrary signs, was handed down from generation to generation, with sufficient discrepancy of details, but with a general conformity of outline to the truth.

The Peruvian quipus were, doubtless, a wretched substitute for that beautiful contrivance, the alphabet, which, employing a few simple characters as the representatives of sounds instead of ideas, is able to convey the most delicate shades of thought that ever passed through the mind of man. The Peruvian invention, indeed, was far below that of the hieroglyphics, even below the rude picture-writing of the Aztecs; for the latter art, however incompetent to convey abstract ideas, could depict sensible objects with tolerable accuracy. It is an evidence of the total ignorance in which the two nations remained of each other, that the Peruvians should have borrowed nothing of the hieroglyphical system of the Mexicans, and this, notwithstanding that the existence of the maguey plant, *agave*, in South America might have furnished them with the very material used by the Aztecs for the construction of their maps.

It is impossible to contemplate without interest the struggles made by different nations, as they emerge from barbarism, to supply themselves with some visible symbol of thought—that mysterious agency by which the mind of the individual may be put in communication with the minds of a whole community. The want of such a symbol is itself the greatest impediment to the progress of civilization. For what is it but to imprison the thought, which has the elements of immortality, within the bosom of its author, or of the small circle who come in contact with him, instead of sending it abroad to give light to thousands and to generations yet unborn! Not only is such a symbol an essential element of civilization, but it may be assumed as the very criterion of civilization; for the intellectual advancement of a people will keep pace pretty nearly with its facilities for intellectual communication.

Yet we must be careful not to underrate the real value of the Peruvian system, nor to suppose that the quipus were as awkward an instrument in the hand of a practiced native as they would be in ours. We know the effect of habit in all mechanical operations, and the Spaniards bear constant testimony to the adroitness and accuracy of the Peruvians in this. Their skill is not more surprising than the facility with which habit enables us to master the contents of a printed page, comprehending thousands of separate characters, by a single glance, as it were, though each character must require a distinct recognition by the eye, and that, too, without breaking the chain of thought in the reader's mind. We must not hold the invention of the quipus too lightly, when we reflect that they supplied the means of calculation demanded for the affairs of a great nation, and that, however insufficient, they afforded no little help to what aspired to the credit of literary composition.

The office of recording the national annals was not wholly confined to the amautas. It was assumed in part by the poets, who selected the most brilliant incidents for their songs or ballads, which were chanted at the royal festivals and at the table of the Inca. In this manner a body of traditional minstrelsy grew up, like the British and Spanish ballad poetry, by means of which the name of many a rude chieftain, that might have perished for want of a chronicler, has been borne down the tide of rustic melody to later generations.[16]

Yet history may be thought not to gain much by this alliance with poetry; for the domain of the poet extends over an ideal realm peopled with the shadowy forms of fancy, that bear little resemblance to the rude realities of life. The Peruvian annals may be deemed to show somewhat of the effects of this union, since there is a tinge of the marvelous spread over them down to the very latest period, which, like a mist before the reader's eye, makes it difficult to distinguish between fact and fiction.

The poet found a convenient instrument for his purposes in the beautiful Quechua dialect. We have already seen the extraordinary measures taken by the Incas for propagating their language throughout their empire. Thus naturalized in the remotest provinces, it became enriched by a variety of exotic words and idioms, which, under the influence of the court and of poetic culture, if I may so express myself, was gradually blended, like some finished mosaic made up of coarse and disjointed materials, into one harmonious whole. The Quechua became the most comprehensive and various, as well as the most elegant, of the South American dialects.

Besides the compositions already noticed, the Peruvians, it is said, showed some talent for theatrical exhibitions; not those barren pantomimes which, addressed simply to the eye, have formed the amusement of more than one rude nation. The Peruvian pieces aspired to the rank of dramatic compositions, sustained by character and dialogue, founded sometimes on themes of tragic interest, and at others on such as, from their light and social character, belong to comedy. Of the execution of these pieces we have no means of judging. It was probably rude enough, as befitted an unformed people. But, whatever may have been the execution, the mere conception of such an amusement is a proof of refinement that honorably distinguishes the Peruvian from the other American races, whose pastime was war, or the ferocious sports that reflect the image of it.

The intellectual character of the Peruvians, indeed, seems to have been marked rather by a tendency to refinement than by those hardier qualities which insure success in the severer walks of science. In these they were behind several of the semi-civilized nations of the New World. They had some acquaintance with geography, so far as related to their own empire, which was indeed extensive; and they constructed maps with lines raised on them to denote the boundaries and localities, on a similar principle with those formerly used by the blind. In astronomy they appear to have made but moderate proficiency. They divided the year into twelve lunar months, each of which, having its own name, was distinguished by its appropriate festival. They had, also, weeks, but of what length, whether of seven, nine, or ten days, is uncertain. As their lunar year would necessarily fall short of the true time, they rectified their calendar by solar observations made by means of a number of cylindrical columns raised on the high lands round Cuzco, which served them for taking azimuths; and by measuring their shadows they ascertained the exact times of the solstices. The period of the equinoxes they determined by the help of a solitary pillar, or gnomon, placed in the center of a circle, which was described in the area of the great temple and traversed by a diameter that was drawn from east to west. When the shadows were scarcely visible under the noontide rays of the sun, they said that "the god sat with all his light upon the column." Quito, which lay immediately under the equator, where the vertical rays of the Sun threw no shadow at noon, was held in especial veneration as the favored abode of the great deity. The period of the equinoxes was celebrated by public rejoicings. The pillar was crowned by the golden chair of the Sun, and both then, and at the solstices the columns were hung with garlands, and offerings of flowers and fruits were made, while high festival was kept throughout the empire. By these periods the Peruvians regulated their religious rites and ceremonial, and prescribed the nature of their agricultural labors. The year itself took its departure from the date of the winter solstice.

This meager account embraces nearly all that has come down to us of Peruvian astronomy. It may seem strange that a nation which had proceeded thus far in its observations should have gone no farther, and that, notwithstanding its general advance in civilization, it should in this science have fallen so far short not only of the Mexicans, but of the Muyscas inhabiting the same elevated regions of the great southern plateau with themselves. These latter regulated their calendar on the same general plan of cycles and periodical series as the Aztecs, approaching yet nearer to the system pursued by the people of Asia.

It might have been expected that the Incas, the boasted children of the Sun, would have made a particular study of the phenomena of the heavens, and have constructed a calendar on principles as scientific as that of their semi-civilized neighbors. One historian, indeed, assures us that they threw their years into cycles of ten, a hundred, and a thousand years, and that by these cycles they regulated their chronology. But this assertion—not improbable in itself—rests on a writer but little gifted with the spirit of criticism, and is counterbalanced by the silence of every higher and earlier authority, as well as by the absence of any monument, like those found among other American nations, to attest the existence of such a calendar. The inferiority of the Peruvians may be, perhaps, in part explained by the fact of their priesthood being drawn exclusively from the body of the Incas, a privileged order of nobility, who had no need, by the assumption of superior learning, to fence themselves round from the approaches of the vulgar. The little true science possessed by the Aztec priest supplied him with a key to unlock the mysteries of the heavens, and the false system of astrology which he built upon it gave him credit as a being who had something of divinity in his own nature. But the Inca noble was divine by birth. The illusory study of astrology, so captivating to the unenlightened mind, engaged no share of his attention. The only persons in Peru who claimed the power of reading the mysterious future were the diviners, men who, combining with their pretensions some skill in the healing art, resembled the conjurers found among many of the Indian tribes. But the office was held in little repute, except among the lower classes, and was abandoned to those whose age and infirmity disqualified them for the real business of life.

The Peruvians had knowledge of one or two constellations, and watched the motions of the planet Venus, to which, as we have seen, they dedicated altars. But their ignorance of the first principles of astronomical science is shown by their ideas of eclipses, which they supposed denoted some great derangement of the planet; and when the Moon labored under one of these mysterious infirmities they sounded their instruments, and filled the air with shouts and lamentations, to rouse her from her lethargy. Such puerile conceits as these form a striking contrast with the real knowledge of the Mexicans, as displayed in their hieroglyphical maps, in which the true cause of this phenomenon is plainly depicted.

But, if less successful in exploring the heavens, the Incas must be admitted to have surpassed every other American race in their dominion over the earth. Husbandry was pursued by them on principles that may be truly called scientific. It was the basis of their political institutions. Having no foreign commerce, it was agriculture that furnished them with the means of their internal exchanges, their subsistence, and their revenues. We have seen their remarkable provisions for distributing the land in equal shares among the people, while they required every man, except the privileged orders, to assist in its cultivation. The Inca himself did not disdain to set the example. On one of the great annual festivals he proceeded to the environs of Cuzco, attended by his court, and, in the presence of all the people turned up the earth with a golden plow—or an instrument that served as such—thus consecrating the occupation of the husbandman as one worthy to be followed by the Children of the Sun.

The patronage of the government did not stop with this cheap display of royal condescension, but was shown in the most efficient measures for facilitating the labors of the husbandman. Much of the country along the seacoast suffered from want of water, as little or no rain fell there, and the few streams, in their short and hurried course from the mountains, exerted only a very limited influence on the wide extent of territory. The soil, it is true, was for the most part sandy and sterile; but many places were capable of being reclaimed, and, indeed, needed only to be properly irrigated to be susceptible of extraordinary production. To these spots water was conveyed by means of canals and subterraneous aqueducts executed on a noble scale. They consisted of large slabs of freestone nicely fitted together without cement, and discharged a volume of water sufficient, by means of latent ducts or sluices, to moisten the lands in the lower level through which they passed. Some of these aqueducts were of great length. One that traversed the district of Conti-suyu measured between four and five hundred miles. They were brought from some elevated lake or natural reservoir in the heart of the mountains, and were fed at intervals by other basins which lay in their route along the slopes of the sierra. In this descent a passage was sometimes to be opened through rocks—and this without the aid of iron tools; impracticable mountains were to be turned, rivers and marshes to be crossed; in short, the same obstacles were to be encountered as in the construction of their mighty roads. But the Peruvians seemed to take pleasure in wrestling with the difficulties of nature. Near Cajamarca a tunnel is still visible which they excavated in the mountains to give an outlet to the waters of a lake when these rose to a height in the rainy seasons that threatened the country with inundation.

Most of these beneficent works of the Incas were suffered to go to decay by their Spanish conquerors. In some spots the waters are still left to flow in their silent, subterraneous channels, whose windings and whose sources have been alike unexplored. Others, though partially dilapidated, and closed up with rubbish and the rank vegetation of the soil, still betray their course by occasional patches of fertility. Such are the remains in the valley of Nasca, a fruitful spot that lies between long tracts of desert; where the ancient watercourses of the Incas, measuring four or five feet in depth by three in width, and formed of large blocks of uncemented masonry, are conducted from an unknown distance.

The greatest care was taken that every occupant of the land through which these streams passed should enjoy the benefit of them. The quantity of water allotted to each was prescribed by law; and royal overseers superintended the distribution and saw that it was faithfully applied to the irrigation of the ground.

The Peruvians showed a similar spirit of enterprise in their schemes for introducing cultivation into the mountainous parts of their domain. Many of the hills, though covered with a strong soil, were too precipitous to be tilled. These they cut into terraces, faced with rough stone, diminishing in regular gradation towards the summit; so that, while the lower strip, or *anden,* as it was called by the Spaniards, that belted round the base of the mountain, might comprehend hundreds of acres, the uppermost was only large enough to accommodate a few rows of Indian corn. Some of the eminences presented such a mass of solid rock, that after being hewn into terraces they were obliged to be covered deep with earth before they could serve the purpose of the husbandman. With such patient toil did the Peruvians combat the formidable obstacles presented by the face of their country! Without the use of the tools or the machinery familiar to the European, each individual could have done little; but acting in large masses, and under a common direction, they were enabled by indefatigable perseverance to achieve results to have attempted which might have filled even the European with dismay.

In the same spirit of economical husbandry which redeemed the rocky sierra from the curse of sterility, they dug below the arid soil of the valleys and sought for a stratum where some natural moisture might be found. These excavations, called by the Spaniards *hoyos,* or "pits," were made on a great scale, comprehending frequently more than an acre, sunk to the depth of fifteen or twenty feet, and fenced round within by a wall of *adobes,* or bricks baked in the sun. The bottom of the excavation, well prepared by a rich manure of the sardines— a small fish obtained in vast quantities along the coast—was planted with some kind of grain or vegetable.

The Peruvian farmers were well acquainted with the different kinds of manures, and made large use of them; a circumstance rare in the rich lands of the tropics, and probably not elsewhere practiced by the rude tribes of America. They made great use of *guano,* the valuable deposit of seafowl that has attracted so much attention of late from the agriculturists both of Europe and of our own country, and the stimulating and nutritious properties of which the Indians perfectly appreciated. This was found in such immense quantities on many of the little islands along the coast as to have the appearance of lofty hills, which, covered with a white saline incrustation, led the Conquerors to give them the name of the *sierra nevada,* or "snowy mountains."

The Incas took their usual precautions for securing the benefits of this important article to the husbandman. They assigned the small islands on the coast to the use of the respective districts which lay adjacent to them. When the island was large, it was distributed among several districts, and the boundaries for each were clearly defined. All encroachment on the rights of another was severely punished. And they secured the preservation of the fowl by penalties as stern as those by which the Norman tyrants of England protected their own game. No one was allowed to set foot on the island during the season for breeding, under pain of death; and to kill the birds at any time was punished in the like manner.

With this advancement in agricultural science, the Peruvians might be supposed to have had some knowledge of the plow, in such general use among the primitive nations of the Eastern continent. But they had neither the iron plowshare of the Old World, nor had they animals for draft which, indeed, were nowhere found in the New. The instrument which they used was a strong, sharp-pointed stake, traversed by a horizontal piece, ten or twelve inches from the point, on which the plowman might set his foot and force it into the ground. Six or eight strong men were attached by ropes to the stake, and dragged it forcibly along—pulling together, and keeping time as they moved by chanting their national songs, in which they were accompanied by the women who followed in their train, to break up the sods with their rakes. The mellow soil offered slight resistance; and the laborer, by long practice, acquired a dexterity which enabled him to turn up the ground to the requisite depth with astonishing facility. This substitute for the plow was but a clumsy contrivance; yet it is curious as the only specimen of the kind among the American aborigines, and was perhaps not much inferior to the wooden instrument introduced in its stead by the European conquerors.

It was frequently the policy of the Incas, after providing a deserted tract with the means for irrigation and thus fitting it for the labors of the husbandman, to transplant there a colony of *mitimaes*, who brought it under cultivation by raising the crops best suited to the soil. While the peculiar character and capacity of the lands were thus consulted, a means of exchange of the different products was afforded to the neighboring provinces, which, from the formation of the country, varied much more than usual within the same limits. To facilitate these agricultural exchanges, fairs were instituted, which took place three times a month in some of the most populous places, where, as money was unknown, a rude kind of commerce was kept up by the barter of their respective products. These fairs afforded so many holidays for the relaxation of the industrious laborer.

Such were the expedients adopted by the Incas for the im-

"The instrument which they used was a strong, sharp-pointed stake, traversed by a horizontal piece . . . on which the plowman might set his foot and force it into the ground."

provement of their territory; and, although imperfect, they must be allowed to show an acquaintance with the principles of agricultural science that gives them some claim to the rank of a civilized people. Under this patient and discriminating culture, every inch of good soil was tasked to its greatest power of production; while the most unpromising spots were compelled to contribute something to the subsistence of the people. Everywhere the land teemed with evidence of agricultural wealth, from the smiling valleys along the coast to the terraced steeps of the sierra, which, rising into pyramids of verdure, glowed with all the splendors of tropical vegetation.

The formation of the country was particularly favorable, as already remarked, to an infinite variety of products, not so much from its extent as from its various elevations, which, more remarkable even than those in Mexico, comprehend every degree of latitude from the equator to the polar regions. Yet, though the temperature changes in this region with the degree of elevation, it remains nearly the same in the same spots throughout the year; and the inhabitant feels none of those grateful vicissitudes of season which belong to the temperate latitudes of the globe. Thus, while the summer lies in full power on the burning regions of the palm and the cocoa tree that fringe the borders of the ocean, the broad surface of the tableland blooms with the freshness of perpetual spring, and the higher summits of the Cordilleras are white with everlasting winter.

The Peruvians turned this fixed variety of climate, if I may so say, to the best account, by cultivating the productions appropriate to each; and they particularly directed their attention to those which afforded the most nutriment to man. Thus, in the lower level were to be found the cassava tree and the banana, that bountiful plant, which seems to have relieved man from the primeval curse—if it were not rather a blessing—of toiling for his sustenance. As the banana faded from the landscape, a good substitute was found in the maize, the great agricultural staple of both the northern and southern divisions of the American continent, and which, after its exportation to the Old World, spread so rapidly there as to suggest the idea of its being indigenous to it. The Peruvians were well acquainted with the different modes of preparing this useful vegetable, though it seems they did not use it for bread, except at festivals; and they extracted a sort of honey from the stalk, and made an intoxicating liquor from the fermented grain, to which, like the Aztecs, they were immoderately addicted.

The temperate climate of the tableland furnished them with the cabuya, related to the agave, many of the extraordinary qualities of which they comprehended, though not its most important one of affording a material for paper. Tobacco, too, was among the products of this elevated region. Yet the Peruvians differed from every other Indian nation to whom it was known, by using it only for medicinal purposes, in the form of snuff. They may have found a substitute for its narcotic qualities in the coca (*Erythroxylum Peruvianum*) or *cuca*,[17] as it was called by the natives. This is a shrub which grows to the height of a man. The leaves when gathered are dried in the sun, and, being mixed with a little lime, form a preparation for chewing, much like the betel leaf of the East. With a small supply of this cuca in his pouch, and a handful of roasted maize, the Peruvian Indian of our time performs his wearisome journeys day after day without fatigue, or at least without complaint. Even food the most invigorating is less grateful to him than his loved narcotic. Under the Incas, it is said to have been exclusively reserved for the noble orders. If so, the people gained one luxury by the Conquest; and after that period it was so extensively used by them that this article constituted a most important item of the colonial revenue of Spain. Yet, with the soothing charms of an opiate, this weed, so much vaunted by the natives, when used to excess, is said to be attended with all the mischievous effects of habitual intoxication.

Higher up on the slopes of the Cordilleras, beyond the limits of the maize and of the *quinoa*—a grain bearing some resemblance to rice, and largely cultivated by the Indians—was to be found the potato, the introduction of which into Europe has made an era in the history of agriculture. Whether indigenous to Peru, or imported from the neighboring country of Chile, it formed the great staple of the more elevated plains, under the Incas, and its culture was continued to a height in the equatorial regions which reached many thousand feet above the limits of perpetual snow in the temperate latitudes of Europe. Wild specimens of the vegetable might be seen still higher, springing up spontaneously amidst the stunted shrubs that clothed the lofty sides of the Cordilleras, till these gradually subsided into the mosses and the short yellow grass, *pajonal*, which, like a golden carpet, was unrolled around the base of the mighty cones, that rose far into the regions of eternal silence, covered with the snows of centuries.

# ☙ CHAPTER FIVE ❧

## LLAMAS—GREAT HUNTS—MANUFACTURES—

## MECHANICAL SKILL—ARCHITECTURE—

## CONCLUDING REFLECTIONS

A nation which had made such progress in agriculture might be reasonably expected to have made also some proficiency in the mechanical arts—especially when, as in the case of the Peruvians, their agricultural economy demanded in itself no inconsiderable degree of mechanical skill. Among most nations, progress in manufactures has been found to have an intimate connection with the progress of husbandry. Both arts are directed to the same great object of supplying the necessaries, the comforts, or, in a more refined condition of society, the luxuries, of life; and when the one is brought to a perfection that infers a certain advance in civilization, the other must naturally find a corresponding development under the increasing demands and capacities of such a state. The subjects of the Incas, in their patient and tranquil devotion to the more humble occupations of industry which bound them to their native soil, bore greater resemblance to the Oriental nations, as the Hindus and Chinese, than they bore to the members of the great Anglo-Saxon family, whose hardy temper has driven them to seek their fortunes on the stormy ocean and to open a commerce with the most distant regions of the globe. The Peruvians, though lining a lone extent of seacoast, had no foreign commerce.

They had peculiar advantages for domestic manufacture in a material incomparably superior to anything possessed by the other races of the Western continent. They found a good substitute for linen in a fabric which, like the Aztecs, they knew how to weave from the tough thread of the maguey. Cotton grew luxuriantly on the low, sultry level of the coast, and furnished them with a clothing suitable to the milder latitudes of the country. But from the llama and the kindred species they obtained a fleece adapted to the colder climate of the tableland, "more estimable," to quote the language of a well-informed writer, "than the down of the Canadian beaver, the fleece of the *brebis des Calmoucks,* or of the Syrian goat."

Of the four varieties, the llama, the one most familiarly known, is the least valuable on account of its wool. It is chiefly employed as a beast of burden, for which, although it is somewhat larger than any of the other varieties, its diminutive size and strength would seem to disqualify it. It carries a load of little more than a hundred pounds, and cannot travel above three or four leagues in a day. But all this is compensated by the little care and cost required for its management and its maintenance. It picks up an easy subsistence from the moss and stunted herbage that grow scantily along the withered sides and the steeps of the Cordilleras. The structure of its stomach, like that of the camel, is such as to enable it to dispense with any supply of water for weeks, nay, months together. Its spongy hoof, armed with a claw or pointed talon to enable it to take secure hold on the ice, never requires to be shod; and the load laid upon its back rests securely in its bed of wool, without the aid of girth or saddle. The llamas moved in troops of five hundred or even a thousand, and thus, though each individual carries but little, the aggregate is considerable. The whole caravan travels on at its regular pace, passing the night in the open air without suffering from the coldest temperature, and marching in perfect order and in obedience to the voice of the driver. It is only when overloaded that the spirited little animal refuses to stir, and neither blows nor caresses can induce him to rise from the ground. He is as sturdy in asserting his rights on this occasion as he is usually docile and unresisting.

The employment of domestic animals distinguished the Peruvians from the other races of the New World. This economy of human labor by the substitution of the brute is an important element of civilization, inferior only to what is gained by the substitution of machinery for both. Yet the ancient Peruvians seem to have made much less account of it than their Spanish conquerors, and to have valued the llama, in common with the other animals of that genus, chiefly for its fleece. Immense herds of these "large cattle," as they were called, and of the "smaller cattle," or *alpacas,* were held by the government, as already noticed, and placed under the direction of shepherds, who conducted them from one quarter of the country to another, according to the changes of the season. These migrations were regulated with all the precision with which the code of the *mesta* determined the migrations of the vast merino flocks in Spain; and the Conquerors, when they landed in Peru, were amazed at finding a race of animals so similar to their own in properties and habits, and under the control of a system of legislation which might seem to have been imported from their native land.

But the richest store of wool was obtained, not from these domesticated animals, but from the two other species, the *huanacos* and the *vicuñas,*[18] which roamed in native freedom over the frozen ranges of the Cordilleras; where not unfrequently they might be seen scaling the snow-covered peaks which no living thing inhabits save the condor, the huge bird of the Andes, whose broad pinions bear him up in the atmosphere to the height of more than twenty thousand feet above the level of the sea. In these rugged pastures, "the flock without a fold" finds sufficient sustenance in the *ychu*, a species of grass which is found scattered all along the great ridge of the Cordilleras, from the equator to the southern limits of Patagonia. And as these limits define the territory traversed by the Peruvian sheep, which rarely, if ever, venture north of the line, it seems not improbable that this mysterious little plant is so important to their existence that the absence of it is the principal reason why they have not penetrated to the northern latitudes of Quito and New Granada.

But, although thus roaming without a master over the boundless wastes of the Cordilleras, the Peruvian peasant was never allowed to hunt these wild animals, which were protected by laws as severe as were the sleek herds that grazed on the more cultivated slopes of the plateau. The wild game of the forest and the mountain was as much the property of the government as if it had been enclosed within a park or penned within a fold. It was only on stated occasions, at the great hunts which took place once a year, under the personal superintendence of the Inca or his principal officers, that the game was allowed to be taken. These hunts were not repeated in the same quarter of the country oftener than once in four years, that time might be allowed for the waste occasioned by them to be replenished. At the appointed time, all those living in the district and its neighborhood, to the number, it might be, of fifty or sixty thousand men, were distributed round, so as to form a cordon of immense extent, that should embrace the whole country which was to be hunted over. The men were armed with long poles and spears, with which they beat up game of every description lurking in the woods, the valleys, and the mountains, killing the beasts of prey without mercy, and driving the others, consisting chiefly of the deer of the country, and the huanacos and vi-

"The Peruvians showed great skill in the manufacture of different articles for the royal household from . . . wool. It was wrought into shawls, robes . . . carpets, coverlets, and hangings."

cuñas, towards the center of the wide-extended circle; until, as this gradually contracted, the timid inhabitants of the forests were concentrated on some spacious plain, where the eye of the hunter might range freely over his victims, who found no place for shelter or escape.

The male deer and some of the coarser kind of the Peruvian sheep were slaughtered; their skins were reserved for the various useful manufactures to which they are ordinarily applied, and their flesh, cut into thin slices, was distributed among the people, who converted it into *charqui,* the dried meat of the country, which constituted then the sole, as it has since the principal, animal food of the lower classes of Peru.

But nearly the whole of the sheep, amounting usually to thirty or forty thousand, or even a larger number, after being carefully sheared, were suffered to escape and regain their solitary haunts among the mountains. The wool thus collected was deposited in the royal magazines, whence, in due time, it was dealt out to the people. The coarser quality was worked up into garments for their own use, and the finer for the Inca; for none but an Inca noble could wear the fine fabric of the vicuña.

The Peruvians showed great skill in the manufacture of different articles for the royal household from this delicate material, which, under the name of *vigonia* wool, is now familiar to the looms of Europe. It was wrought into shawls, robes, and other articles of dress for the monarch, and into carpets, coverlets, and hangings for the imperial palaces and the temples. The cloth was finished on both sides alike; the delicacy of the texture was such as to give it the luster of silk; and the brilliancy of the dyes excited the admiration and the envy of the European artisan. The Peruvians produced also an article of great strength and durability by mixing the hair of animals with wool; and they were expert in the beautiful featherwork, which they held of less account than the Mexicans, from the superior quality of the materials for other fabrics which they had at their command.

The natives showed a skill in other mechanical arts similar to that displayed by their manufactures of cloth. Every man in Peru was expected to be acquainted with the various handicrafts essential to domestic comfort. No long apprenticeship was required for this, where the wants were so few as among the simple peasantry of the Incas. But, if this were all, it would imply but a very moderate advancement in the arts. There were certain individuals, however, carefully trained to those occupations which minister to the demands of the more opulent classes of society. These occupations, like every other calling and office in Peru, always descended from father to son. The division of castes, in this particular, was as precise as that which existed in Egypt or Hindustan. If this arrangement be unfavorable to originality, or to the development of the peculiar talent of the individual, it at least conduces to an easy and finished execution, by familiarizing the artist with the practice of his art from childhood.

The royal magazines and the *huacas* or tombs of the Incas have been found to contain many specimens of curious and elaborate workmanship. Among these are vases of gold and silver, bracelets, collars, and other ornaments for the person; utensils of every description, some of fine clay, and many more of copper; mirrors, of a hard, polished stone or burnished silver, with a great variety of other articles made frequently on a whimsical pattern, evincing quite as much ingenuity as taste or inventive talent. The character of the Peruvian mind led to imitation, in fact, rather than invention, to delicacy and minuteness of finish, rather than to boldness or beauty of design.

That they should have accomplished these difficult works with such tools as they possessed is truly wonderful. It was comparatively easy to cast and even to sculpture metallic substances, both of which they did with consummate skill. But that they should have shown the like facility in cutting the hardest substances, as emeralds and other precious stones, is not so easy to explain. Emeralds they obtained in considerable quantity from the barren district of Atacames, and this inflexible material seems to have been almost as ductile in the hands of the Peruvian artist as if it had been made of clay. Yet the natives were unacquainted with the use of iron, though the soil was largely impregnated with it. The tools used were of stone, or more frequently of copper. But the material on which they relied for the execution of their most difficult tasks was formed by combining a very small portion of tin with copper. This composition gave a hardness to the metal which seems to have been little inferior to that of steel. With the aid of it, not only did the Peruvian artisan hew into shape porphyry and granite, but by his patient industry accomplished works which the European would not have ventured to undertake. Among the remains of the monuments of Cannar may be seen movable rings in the muzzles of animals, all nicely sculptured of one entire block of granite. It is worthy of remark that the Egyptians, the Mexicans, and the Peruvians, in their progress towards civilization, should never have detected the use of iron, which lay around them in abundance, and that they should each, without any knowledge of the other, have found a substitute for it in such a curious composition of metals as gave to their tools almost the temper of steel; a secret that has been lost—or, to speak more correctly, has never been discovered—by the civilized European.

I have already spoken of the large quantity of gold and silver wrought into various articles of elegance and utility for the Incas; though the amount was inconsiderable, in comparison with what could have been afforded by the mineral riches of the land, and with what has since been obtained by the more sagacious and unscrupulous cupidity of the white man. Gold was gathered by the Incas from the deposits of the streams. They extracted the ore also in considerable quantities from the valley of Curimayo, northeast of Caxamarca, as well as from other places; and the silver mines of Porco, in particular, yielded them considerable returns. Yet they did not attempt to penetrate into the bowels of the earth by sinking a shaft, but simply excavated a cavern in the steep sides of the mountain, or, at most, opened a horizontal vein of moderate depth. They were equally deficient in the knowledge of the best means of detaching the precious metal from the dross with which it was united, and had no idea of the virtues of quicksilver—a mineral not rare in Peru—as an amalgam to effect this decomposition. Their method of smelting the ore was by means of furnaces built in elevated and exposed situations, where they might be fanned by the strong breezes of the mountains. The subjects of the Incas, in short, with all their patient perseverance, did little more than penetrate below the crust, the outer rind, as it were, formed over those golden caverns which lie hidden in the dark depths of the Andes. Yet what they gleaned from the surface was more than adequate for all their demands. For they were not a commercial people, and had no knowledge of money. In this they differed from the ancient Mexicans, who had an established currency of a determinate value. In one respect, however, they were superior to their American rivals, since they made use of weights to determine the quantity of their commodities, a thing wholly unknown to the Aztecs. The fact is ascertained by the discovery of silver balances, adjusted with perfect accuracy, in some of the tombs of the Incas.

But the surest test of the civilization of a people—at least, as sure as any—afforded by mechanical art is to be found in their architecture, which presents so noble a field for the display of the grand and the beautiful, and which at the same time is so intimately connected with the essential comforts of life. There is no object on which the resources of the wealthy are more freely lavished, or which calls out more effectually the inventive talent of the artist. The painter and the sculptor may display their individual genius in creations of surpassing excellence, but it is the great monuments of architectural taste and magnificence that are stamped in a peculiar manner by the genius of the nation. The Greek, the Egyptian, the Saracen, the Gothic—what a key do their respective styles afford to the character and condition of the people! The monuments of China, of Hindustan, and of Central America are all indicative of an immature period, in which the imagination has not been disciplined by study, and which, therefore, in its best results, betrays only the ill-regulated aspirations after the beautiful that belong to a semicivilized people.

The Peruvian architecture, bearing also the general characteristics of an imperfect state of refinement, had still its peculiar character; and so uniform was that character that the edifices throughout the country seem all to have been cast in the same mold. They were usually built of porphyry or granite; not infrequently of brick. This, which was formed into blocks or squares of much larger dimensions than our brick, was made of a tenacious earth mixed up with reeds or tough grass, and acquired a degree of hardness with age that made it insensible alike to the storms and the more trying sun of the tropics. The walls were of great thickness, but low, seldom reaching to more than twelve or fourteen feet in height. It is rare to meet with accounts of a building that rose to a second story.

The apartments had no communication with one another, but usually opened into a court; and, as they were unprovided with windows, or apertures that served for them, the only light from without must have been admitted by the doorways. These were made with the sides approaching each other towards the top, so that the lintel was considerably narrower than the threshold, a peculiarity, also, in Egyptian architecture. The roofs have, for the most part, disappeared with time. Some few survive in the less ambitious edifices, of a singular bell-shape, and made of a composition of earth and pebbles. They are supposed, however, to have been generally formed of more perishable materials, of wood or straw. It is certain that some of the most considerable stone buildings were thatched with straw. Many seem to have been constructed without the aid of cement; and writers have contended that the Peruvians were unacquainted with the use of mortar, or cement of any kind. But a close, tenacious mold, mixed with lime, may be discovered filling up the interstices of the granite in some buildings; and in others, where the well-fitted blocks leave no room for this coarser material, the eye of the antiquary has detected a fine bituminous glue, as hard as the rock itself.

The greatest simplicity is observed in the construction of the buildings, which are usually free from outward ornament; though in some the huge stones are shaped into a convex form with great regularity, and adjusted with such nice precision to one another that it would be impossible, but for the flutings, to determine the line of junction. In others the stone is rough, as it was taken from the quarry, in the most irregular forms, with the edges nicely wrought and fitted to each other. There is no appearance of columns or of arches; though there is some contradiction as to the latter point. But it is not to be doubted that, although they may have made some approach to this mode of construction by the greater or less inclination of the walls, the Peruvian architects were wholly unacquainted with the true principle of the circular arch reposing on its keystone.

The architecture of the Incas is characterized, says an eminent traveler, "by simplicity, symmetry, and solidity." It may seem unphilosophical to condemn the peculiar fashion of a nation as indicating want of taste, because its standard of taste differs from our own. Yet there is an incongruity in the composition of the Peruvian buildings which argues a very imperfect acquaintance with the first principles of architecture. While they put together their bulky masses of porphyry and granite with the nicest art, they were incapable of mortising their timbers, and, in their ignorance of iron, knew no better way of holding the beams together than tying them with thongs of maguey. In the same incongruous spirit, the building that was thatched with straw and unilluminated by a window was glowing with tapestries of gold and silver! These are the inconsistencies of a rude people, among whom the arts are but partially developed. It might not be difficult to find examples of like inconsistency in the architecture and domestic arrangements of our Anglo-Saxon and, at a still later period, of our Norman ancestors.

Yet the buildings of the Incas were accommodated to the character of the climate, and were well fitted to resist those terrible convulsions which belong to the land of volcanoes. The wisdom of their plan is attested by the number which still survive, while the more modern constructions of the Conquerors have been buried in ruins. The hand of the Conquerors, indeed, has fallen heavily on these venerable monuments, and, in their blind and superstitious search for hidden treasure, has caused infinitely more ruin than time or the earthquake. Yet enough of these monuments still remains to invite the researchers of the antiquary. Those only in the most conspicuous situations have been hitherto examined. But, by the testimony of travelers, many more are to be found in the less frequented parts of the country; and we may hope they will one day call forth a kindred spirit of enterprise to that which has so successfully explored the mysterious recesses of Central America and Yucatán.

I cannot close this analysis of the Peruvian institutions without a few reflections on their general character and tendency, which, if they involve some repetition of previous remarks, may, I trust, be excused, from my desire to leave a correct and consistent impression on the reader. In this survey we cannot but be struck with the total dissimilarity between these institutions and those of the Aztecs,[19]—the other great nation which led in the march of civilization on this Western continent, and whose empire in the northern portion of it was as conspicuous as that of the Incas in the south. Both nations came on the plateau and commenced their career of conquest at dates, it may be, not far removed from each other. And it is worthy of notice that, in America, the elevated region along the crests of the great mountain range should have been the chosen seat of civilization in both hemispheres.

Very different was the policy pursued by the two races in their military career. The Aztecs, animated by the most ferocious spirit, carried on a war of extermination, signalizing their triumphs by the sacrifice of hecatombs of captives; while the Incas, although they pursued the game of conquest with equal pertinacity, preferred a milder policy, substituting negotiation and intrigue for violence, and dealt with their antagonists so that their future resources should not be crippled, and that they should come as friends, not as foes, into the bosom of the empire.[20]

Their policy towards the conquered forms a contrast no less striking to that pursued by the Aztecs. The Mexican vassals were ground by excessive imposts and military conscriptions. No regard was had to their welfare, and the only limit to oppression was the power of endurance. They were overawed by fortresses and armed garrisons, and were made to feel every hour that they were not part and parcel of the nation, but held only in subjugation as a conquered people. The Incas, on the other hand, admitted their new subjects at once to all the rights enjoyed by the rest of the community; and, though they made them conform to the established laws and usages of the empire, they watched over their personal security and comfort with a sort of parental solicitude. The motley population, thus bound together by common interest, was animated by a common feeling of loyalty, which gave greater strength and stability to the empire as it became more and more widely extended; while the various tribes who successively came under the Mexican scepter, being held together only by the pressure of external force, were ready to fall asunder the moment that that force was withdrawn. The policy of the two nations displayed the principle of fear as contrasted with the principle of love.

The characteristic features of their religious systems had as little resemblance to each other. The whole Aztec pantheon partook more or less of the sanguinary spirit of the terrible war-god who presided over it, and their frivolous ceremonial almost always terminated with human sacrifice and cannibal orgies. But the rites of the Peruvians were of a more innocent cast, as they tended to a more spiritual worship. For the worship of the Creator is most nearly approached by that of the heavenly bodies, which, as they revolve in their bright orbits, seem to be the most glorious symbols of His beneficence and power.

In the minuter mechanical arts, both showed considerable skill; but in the construction of important public works, of roads, aqueducts, canals, and in agriculture in all its details, the Peruvians were much superior. Strange that they should have fallen so far below their rivals in their efforts after a higher intellectual culture, in astronomical science more especially, and in the art of communicating thought by visible symbols. When we consider the greater refinement of the Incas, their inferiority to the Aztecs in these particulars can be explained only by the fact that the latter in all probability were indebted for their science to the race who preceded them in the land—that shadowy race whose origin and whose end are alike veiled from the eye of the inquirer, but who possibly may have sought a refuge from the ferocious invaders in those regions of Central America, the architectural remains of which now supply us with the most pleasing monuments of Indian civilization. It is with this more polished race, to whom the Peruvians seem to have borne some resemblance in their mental and moral organization, that they should be compared. Had the empire of the Incas been permitted to extend itself with the rapid strides with which it was advancing at the period of the Spanish conquest, the two races might have come into conflict, or perhaps into alliance, with one another.

The Mexicans and Peruvians, so different in the character of their peculiar civilization, were, it seems probable, ignorant of each other's existence; and it may appear singular that, during the simultaneous continuance of their empires, some of the seeds of science and of art which pass so imperceptibly from one people to another should not have found their way across the interval which separated the two nations. They furnish an interesting example for the opposite directions which the human mind may take in its struggle to emerge from darkness into the light of civilization.

A closer resemblance—as I have more than once taken occasion to notice—may be found between the Peruvian institutions and some of the despotic governments of Eastern Asia; those governments where despotism appears in its more mitigated form, and the whole people, under the patriarchal sway of the sovereign, seem to be gathered together like the members of one vast family. Such were the Chinese, for example, whom the Peruvians resembled in their implicit obedience to authority, their mild yet somewhat stubborn temper, their solicitude for forms, their reverence for ancient usage, their skill in the minuter manufactures, their imitative rather than inventive cast of mind, and their invincible patience, which serves instead of a more adventurous spirit for the execution of difficult undertakings.

A still closer analogy may be found with the natives of Hindustan in their division into castes, their worship of the heavenly bodies and the elements of nature, and their acquaintance with the scientific principles of husbandry. To the ancient Egyptians, also, they bore considerable resemblance in the same particulars, as well as in those ideas of a future existence which led them to attach so much importance to the permanent preservation of the body.

But we shall look in vain in the history of the East for a parallel to the absolute control exercised by the Incas over their subjects. In the East, this was founded on physical power —on the external resources of the government. The authority of the Inca might be compared with that of the Pope in the day of his might, when Christendom trembled at the thunders of the Vatican, and the successor of St. Peter set his foot on the necks of princes. But the authority of the Pope was founded on opinion. His temporal power was nothing. The empire of the Incas rested on both. It was a theocracy more potent in its operation than that of the Jews; for, though the sanction of the law might be as great among the latter, the law was expounded by a human lawgiver, the servant and representative of Divinity. But the Inca was both the lawgiver and the law. He was not merely the representative of Divinity, or, like the Pope, its vicegerent, but he was Divinity itself. The violation of his ordinance was sacrilege. Never was there a scheme of government enforced by such terrible sanctions, or which bore so oppressively on the subjects of it. For it reached not only to the visible acts, but to the private conduct, the words, the very thoughts, of its vassals.

It added not a little to the efficacy of the government that below the sovereign there was an order of hereditary nobles of the same divine original with himself, who, placed far below himself, were still immeasurably above the rest of the community, not merely by descent, but, as it would seem, by their intellectual nature. These were the exclusive depositaries of power, and as their long hereditary training made them familiar with their vocation and secured them implicit deference from the multitude, they became the prompt and well-practiced agents for carrying out the executive measures of the administration. All that occurred throughout the wide extent of his empire—such was the perfect system of communication—passed in review, as it were, before the eyes of the monarch, and a thousand hands, armed with irresistible authority, stood ready in every quarter to do his bidding. Was it not, as we have said, the most oppressive, though the mildest, of despotisms?

It was the mildest, from the very circumstance that the transcendent rank of the sovereign, and the humble, nay, superstitious, devotion to his will, made it superfluous to assert this will by acts of violence or rigor. The great mass of the people may have appeared to his eyes as but little removed above the condition of the brute, formed to minister to his pleasures. But from their very helplessness he regarded them with feelings of commiseration, like those which a kind master might feel for the poor animals committed to his charge, or—to do justice to the beneficent character attributed to many of the Incas—that a parent might feel for his young and impotent offspring. The laws were carefully directed to their preservation and personal comfort. The people were not allowed to be employed on works pernicious to their health, nor to pine —a sad contrast to their subsequent destiny—under the imposition of tasks too heavy for their powers. They were never made the victims of public or private extortion; and a benevolent forecast watched carefully over their necessities, and provided for their relief in seasons of infirmity and for their sustenance in health. The government of the Incas, however arbitrary in form, was in its spirit truly patriarchal.

Yet in this there was nothing cheering to the dignity of human nature. What the people had was conceded as a boon, not as a right. When a nation was brought under the scepter of the Incas, it resigned every personal right, even the rights dearest to humanity. Under this extraordinary polity, a people advanced in many of the social refinements, well skilled in manufactures and agriculture, were unacquainted, as we have seen, with money. They had nothing that deserved to be called property. They could follow no craft, could engage in no labor, no amusement, but such as was especially provided by law. They could not change their residence or their dress without a license from the government. They could not even exercise the freedom which is conceded to the most abject in other countries—that of selecting their own wives. The imperative spirit of despotism would not allow them to be happy or miserable in any way but that established by law. The power of free agency—the inestimable and inborn right of every human being—was annihilated in Peru.

The astonishing mechanism of the Peruvian polity could have resulted only from the combined authority of opinion and positive power in the ruler to an extent unprecedented in the history of man. Yet that it should have so successfully gone into operation, and so long endured, in opposition to the taste, the prejudices, and the very principles of our nature, is a strong proof of a generally wise and temperate administration of the government.

The policy habitually pursued by the Incas for the *prevention* of evils that might have disturbed the order of things is well exemplified in their provisions against poverty and idleness. In these they rightly discerned the two great causes of disaffection in a populous community. The industry of the people was secured not only by their compulsory occupations at home, but by their employment on those great public works which covered every part of the country, and which still bear testimony in their decay to their primitive grandeur. Yet it may well astonish us to find that the natural difficulty of these undertakings, sufficiently great in itself, considering the imperfection of their tools and machinery, was inconceivably enhanced by the politic contrivance of the government. The royal edifices of Quito, we are assured by the Spanish conquerors, were constructed of huge masses of stone, many of which were carried all the way along the mountain roads from Cuzco, a distance of several hundred leagues. The great square of the capital was filled to a considerable depth with mold brought with incredible labor up the steep slopes of the Cordilleras from the distant shores of the Pacific Ocean. Labor was regarded not only as a means, but as an end, by the Peruvian law.

With their manifold provisions against poverty the reader

has already been made acquainted. They were so perfect that in their wide extent of territory—much of it smitten with the curse of barrenness—no man, however humble, suffered for the want of food and clothing. Famine, so common a scourge in every other American nation, so common at that period in every country of civilized Europe, was an evil unknown in the dominions of the Incas.

The most enlightened of the Spaniards who first visited Peru, struck with the general appearance of plenty and prosperity, and with the astonishing order with which everything throughout the country was regulated, are loud in their expressions of admiration. No better government, in their opinion, could have been devised for the people. Contented with their condition, and free from vice, to borrow the language of an eminent authority of that early day, the mild and docile character of the Peruvians would have well fitted them to receive the teachings of Christianity, had the love of conversion, instead of gold, animated the breasts of the Conquerors. And a philosopher of a later time, warmed by the contemplation of the picture—which his own fancy had colored —of public prosperity and private happiness under the rule of the Incas, pronounces "the *moral* man in Peru far superior to the European."

Yet such results are scarcely reconcilable with the theory of the government I have attempted to analyze. Where there is no free agency there can be no morality. Were there is no temptation there can be little claim to virtue. Where the routine is rigorously prescribed by law, the law, and not the man, must have the credit of the conduct. If that government is the best which is felt the least, which encroaches on the natural liberty of the subject only so far as is essential to civil subordination, then of all governments devised by man the Peruvian has the least real claim to our admiration.

It is not easy to comprehend the genius and the full import of institutions so opposite to those of our own free republic, where every man, however humble his condition, may aspire to the highest honors of the state—may select his own career and carve out his fortune in his own way; where the light of knowledge, instead of being concentrated on a chosen few, is shed abroad like the light of day, and suffered to fall equally on the poor and the rich; where the collision of man with man wakens a generous emulation that calls out latent talent and tasks the energies to the utmost; where consciousness of independence gives a feeling of self-reliance unknown to the timid subjects of a despotism; where, in short, the government is made for man—not as in Peru, where man seemed to be made only for the government. The New World is the theater on which these two political systems, so opposite in their character, have been carried into operation. The empire of the Incas has passed away and left no trace. The other great experiment is still going on—the experiment which is to solve the problem, so long contested in the Old World, of the capacity of man for self-government. Alas for humanity if it should fail!

The testimony of the Spanish conquerors is not uniform in respect to the favorable influence exerted by the Peruvian institutions on the character of the people. Drinking and dancing are said to have been the pleasures to which they were immoderately addicted. Like the slaves and serfs in other lands, whose position excluded them from more serious and ennobling occupations, they found a substitute in frivolous or sensual indulgence. Lazy, luxurious, and licentious are the epithets bestowed on them by one of those who saw them at the Conquest, but whose pen was not too friendly to the Indian. Yet the spirit of independence could hardly be strong in a people who had no interest in the soil, no personal rights to defend; and the facility with which they yielded to the Spanish invader—after every allowance for their comparative inferiority—argues a deplorable destitution of that patriotic feeling which holds life as little in comparison with freedom.

But we must not judge too hardly of the unfortunate native because he quailed before the civilization of the European. We must not be insensible to the really great results that were achieved by the government of the Incas. We must not forget that under their rule the meanest of the people enjoyed a far greater degree of personal comfort, at least a greater exemption from physical suffering, than was possessed by similar classes in other nations on the American continent—greater, probably, than was possessed by these classes in most of the countries of feudal Europe. Under their scepter the higher orders of the state had made advances in many of the arts that belong to a cultivated community. The foundations of a regular government were laid, which, in an age of rapine, secured to its subjects the inestimable blessings of tranquillity and safety. By the well-sustained policy of the Incas, the rude tribes of the forests were gradually drawn from their fastnesses and gathered within the folds of civilization; and of these materials was constructed a flourishing and populous empire, such as was to be found in no other quarter of the American continent. The defects of this government were those of overrefinement in legislation—the last defects to have been looked for, certainly, in the American aborigines.

# BOOK II

## Discovery of Peru

## ❧ CHAPTER ONE ❧

ANCIENT AND MODERN SCIENCE—ART OF

NAVIGATION—MARITIME DISCOVERY—SPIRIT

OF THE SPANIARDS—POSSESSIONS

IN THE NEW WORLD—RUMORS

CONCERNING PERU

Whatever difference of opinion may exist as to the comparative merit of the ancients and the moderns in the arts, in poetry, eloquence, and all that depends on imagination, there can be no doubt that in science the moderns have eminently the advantage. It could not be otherwise. In the early ages of the world, as in the early period of life, there was the freshness of a morning existence, when the gloss of novelty was on everything that met the eye; when the senses, not blunted by familiarity, were more keenly alive to the beautiful, and the mind, under the influence of a healthy and natural taste, was not perverted by philosophical theory; when the simple was necessarily connected with the beautiful, and the epicurean intellect, sated by repetition, had not begun to seek for stimulants in the fantastic and capricious. The realms of fancy were all untraveled, and its fairest flowers had not been gathered, nor its beauties despoiled, by the rude touch of those who affected to cultivate them. The wing of genius was not bound to the earth by the cold and conventional rules of criticism, but was permitted to take its flight far and wide over the broad expanse of creation.

But with science it was otherwise. No genius could suffice for the creation of facts—hardly for their detection. They were to be gathered in by painful industry; to be collected from careful observation and experiment. Genius, indeed, might arrange and combine these facts into new forms, and elicit from their combinations new and important inferences, and in this process might almost rival in originality the creations of the poet and the artist. But if the processes of science are necessarily slow, they are sure. There is no retrograde movement in her domain. Arts may fade, the Muse become dumb, a moral lethargy may lock up the faculties of a nation, the nation itself may pass away and leave only the memory of its existence, but the stories of science it has garnered up will endure forever. As other nations come upon the stage, and new forms of civilization arise, the monuments of art and of imagination, productions of an older time, will lie as an obstacle in the path of improvement. They cannot be built upon; they occupy the ground which the new aspirant for immortality would cover. The whole work is to be gone over again, and other forms of beauty—whether higher or lower in the scale of merit, unlike the past—may arise to take a place by their side. But, in science, every stone that has been laid remains as the foundation for another. The coming generation takes up the work where the preceding left it. There is no retrograde movement. The individual nation may recede, but science still advances. Every step that has been gained makes the ascent easier for those who come after. Every step carries the patient inquirer after truth higher and higher towards heaven, and unfolds to him, as he rises, a wide horizon, and new and more magnificent views of the universe.

Geography partook of the embarrassments which belonged to every other department of science in the primitive ages of the world. The knowledge of the earth could come only from an extended commerce; and commerce is founded on artificial wants or an enlightened curiosity, hardly compatible with the earlier condition of society. In the infancy of nations, the different tribes, occupied with their domestic feuds, found few occasions to wander beyond the mountain chain or broad stream that formed the natural boundary of their domains. The Phoenicians, it is true, are said to have sailed beyond the Pillars of Hercules, and to have launched out on the great western ocean. But the adventures of these ancient voyagers belong to the mythic legends of antiquity, and ascend far beyond the domain of authentic record.

The Greeks, quick and adventurous, skilled in mechanical art, had many of the qualities of successful navigators, and within the limits of their little inland sea ranged fearlessly and freely. But the conquests of Alexander did more to extend the limits of geographical science, and opened an acquaintance with the remote countries of the East. Yet the march of the conqueror is slow in comparison with the movements of the unencumbered traveler. The Romans were still less enterprising than the Greeks, were less commercial in their character. The contributions to geographical knowledge grew with the slow acquisitions of empire. But their system was centralizing in its tendency; and, instead of taking an outward direction and looking abroad for discovery, every part of the vast imperial domain turned towards the capital as its head and central point of attraction. The Roman conqueror pursued his path by land, not by sea. But the water is the great highway between nations, the true element for the discoverer. The Romans were not a maritime people. At the close of their empire, geographical science could hardly be said to extend farther than to an acquaintance with Europe—and this not its freemen; and the petty republics on the Mediterranean and Africa; while they had no other conception of a world beyond the Western waters than was to be gathered from the fortunate prediction of the poet.

Then followed the Middle Ages; the dark ages, as they are called, though in their darkness were matured those seeds of knowledge which, in fulness of time, were to spring up into new and more glorious forms of civilization. The organization of society became more favorable to geographical science. Instead of one overgrown, lethargic empire, oppressing everything by its colossal weight, Europe was broken up into various independent communities, many of which, adopting liberal forms of government, felt all the impulses natural to freemen; and the petty republics on the Mediterranean and the Baltic sent forth their swarms of seamen in a profitable commerce, that knit together the different countries scattered along the great European waters.

But the improvements which took place in the art of navigation, the more accurate measurement of time, and, above all, the discovery of the polarity of the magnet, greatly advanced the cause of geographical knowledge. Instead of creeping timidly along the coast, or limiting his expeditions to the narrow basins of inland waters, the voyager might now spread his sails boldly on the deep, secure of a guide to direct his bark unerringly across the illimitable waste. The consciousness of this power led thought to travel in a new direction; and the mariner began to look with earnestness for another path to the Indian spice islands than that by which the Eastern caravans had traversed the continent of Asia. The nations on whom the spirit of enterprise at this crisis naturally descended were Spain and Portugal, placed as they were on the outposts of the European continent, commanding the great theater of future discovery.

Both countries felt the responsibility of their new position. The crown of Portugal was constant in its efforts, through the fifteenth century, to find a passage round the southern point of Africa into the Indian Ocean; though so timid was the navigation that every fresh headland became a formidable barrier, and it was not till the latter part of the century that the adventurous Díaz passed quite round the Stormy Cape, as he termed it, but which John the Second, with happier augury, called the Cape of Good Hope. But, before Vasco da Gama had availed himself of this discovery to spread his sails in the Indian seas, Spain entered on her glorious career and sent Columbus across the Western waters.

The object of the great navigator was still the discovery of a route to India, but by the west instead of the east. He had no expectation of meeting with a continent in his way, and, after repeated voyages, he remained in his original error, dying, as is well known, in the conviction that it was the eastern shore of Asia which he had reached. It was the same object which directed the nautical enterprises of those who followed in the Admiral's track; and the discovery of a strait into the Indian Ocean was the burden of every order from the government, and the design of many an expedition to different points of the new continent, which seemed to stretch its leviathan length along from one pole to the other. The discovery of an Indian passage is the true key to the maritime movements of the fifteenth and the first half of the sixteenth century. It was the great leading idea that gave its peculiar character to the enterprise of the age.

It is not easy at this time to comprehend the impulse given to Europe by the discovery of America. It was not the gradual acquisition of some border territory, a province or a kingdom that had been gained, but a new world that was now thrown open to the European. The races of animals, the mineral treasures, the vegetable forms, and the varied aspects of nature, man in the different phases of civilization, filled the mind with entirely new sets of ideas, that changed the habitual current of thought and stimulated it to indefinite conjecture. The eagerness to explore the wonderful secrets of the new hemisphere became so active that the principal cities of Spain were, in a manner, depopulated, as emigrants thronged one after another to take their chance upon the deep. It was a world of romance that was thrown open; for, whatever might be the luck of the adventurer, his reports on his return were tinged with a coloring of romance that stimulated still higher the sensitive fancies of his countrymen and nourished the chimerical sentiments of an age of chivalry. They listened with attentive ears to tales of Amazons which seemed to realize the classic legends of antiquity, to stories of Patagonian giants, to flaming pictures of an *El Dorado* where the sands sparkled with gems and golden pebbles as large as birds' eggs were dragged in nets out of the rivers.

Yet that the adventurers were no impostors, but dupes, too easy dupes, of their own credulous fancies, is shown by the extravagant character of their enterprises; by expeditions in search of the magical Fountain of Health, of the golden Temple of Doboyba, of the golden sepulchers of Sinu; for gold was ever floating before their distempered vision, and the name of *Castilla del Oro*, Golden Castile, the most unhealthy and unprofitable region of the Isthmus, held out a bright promise to the unfortunate settler, who too frequently, instead of gold, found there only his grave.

In this realm of enchantment, all the accessories served to maintain the illusion. The simple natives, with their defenseless bodies and rude weapons, were no match for the European warrior armed to the teeth in mail. The odds were as great as those found in any legend of chivalry, where the lance of the good knight overturned hundreds at a touch. The perils that lay in the discoverer's path, and the sufferings he had to sustain, were scarcely inferior to those that beset the knight-errant. Hunger and thirst and fatigue, the deadly effluvia of the morass with its swarms of venomous insects, the cold of mountain snows, and the scorching sun of the tropics, these were the lot of every cavalier who came to seek his fortunes in the New World. It was the reality of romance. The life of the Spanish adventurer was one chapter more—and not the least remarkable—in the chronicles of knight-errantry.

The character of the warrior took on somewhat of the exaggerated coloring shed over his exploits. Proud and vainglorious, swelled with lofty anticipations of his destiny and an invincible confidence in his own resources, no danger could appall and no toil could tire him. The greater the danger, indeed, the higher the charm; for his soul revealed in excitement, and the enterprise without peril wanted that spur of romance which was necessary to rouse his energies into action. Yet in the motives of action meaner influences were strangely mingled with the loftier, the temporal with the spiritual. Gold was the incentive and the recompense, and in the pursuit of it his inflexible nature rarely hesitated as to the means. His courage was sullied with cruelty, the cruelty that flowed equally—strange as it may seem—from his avarice and his religion; religion as it was understood in that age, the religion of the Crusader. It was the convenient cloak for a multitude of sins, which covered them even from himself. The Castilian, too proud for hypocrisy, committed more cruelties in the name of religion than were ever practiced by the pagan idolater or the fanatical Moslem. The burning of the infidel was a sacrifice acceptable to Heaven, and the conversion of those who survived amply atoned for the foulest offences. It is a melancholy and mortifying consideration that the most uncompromising spirit of intolerance—the spirit of the Inquisitor at home, and of the Crusader abroad—should have emanated from a religion which preached peace upon earth and good will towards man!

What a contrast did these children of Southern Europe present to the Anglo-Saxon races who scattered themselves along the great northern division of the Western Hemisphere! For the principle of action with these latter was not avarice, nor the most specious pretext of proselytism; but independence—independence religious and political. To secure this, they were content to earn a bare subsistence by a life of frugality and toil. They asked nothing from the soil but the reasonable returns of their own labor. No golden visions threw a deceitful halo around their path and beckoned them onwards through seas of blood to the subversion of an unoffending dynasty. They were content with the slow but steady progress of their social polity. They patiently endured the privations of the wilderness, watering the tree of liberty with their tears and with the sweat of their brow, till it took deep root in the land and sent up its branches high towards the heavens; while the communities of the neighboring continent, shooting up into the sudden splendors of a tropical vegetation, exhibited, even in their prime, the sure symptoms of decay.

It would seem to have been especially ordered by Providence that the discovery of the two great divisions of the American hemisphere should fall to the two races best fitted to conquer and colonize them. Thus, the northern section was consigned to the Anglo-Saxon race, whose orderly, industrious habits found an ample field for development under its colder skies and on its more rugged soil; while the southern portion, with its rich tropical products and treasures of mineral wealth, held out the most attractive bait to invite the enterprise of the Spaniard. How different might have been the result if the bark of Columbus had taken a more northerly direction, as he at one time meditated, and landed its band of adventurers on the shores of what is now Protestant America!

Under the pressure of that spirit of nautical enterprise which filled the maritime communities of Europe in the sixteenth century, the whole extent of the mighty continent, from Labrador to Terra del Fuego, was explored in less than thirty years after its discovery; and in 1521 the Portuguese Magellan, sailing under the Spanish flag, solved the problem of the strait, and found a westerly way to the long-sought Spice Islands of India—greatly to the astonishment of the Portuguese, who, sailing from the opposite direction, there met their rivals, face to face, at the antipodes. But while the whole eastern coast of the American continent had been explored, and the central portion of it colonized—even after the brilliant achievement of the Mexican conquest—the veil was not yet raised that hung over the golden shores of the Pacific.

Floating rumors had reached the Spaniards, from time to time, of countries in the far west, teeming with the metal they so much coveted; but the first distinct notice of Peru was about the year 1511, when Vasco Nuñez de Balboa, the discoverer of the Southern Sea, was weighing some gold which he had collected from the natives. A young barbarian chieftain, who was present, struck the scales with his fist, and, scattering the glittering metal around the apartment, exclaimed, "If this is what you prize so much that you are willing to leave your distant homes and risk even life itself for it, I can tell you of a land where they eat and drink out of golden vessels, and gold is as cheap as iron is with you." [21] It was not long after this startling intelligence that Balboa achieved the formidable adventure of scaling the mountain rampart of the isthmus which divides the two mighty oceans from each other; when, armed with sword and buckler, he rushed into the waters of the Pacific, and cried out, in the true chivalrous vein, that "he claimed this unknown sea, with all that it contained, for the King of Castile, and that he would make good the claim against all, Christian or infidel, who dared to gainsay it"! All the broad continent and sunny isles washed by the waters of the Southern Ocean! Little did the bold cavalier comprehend the full import of his magnificent vaunt.

On this spot he received more explicit tidings of the Peruvian empire, heard proofs recounted of its civilization, and was shown drawings of the llama, which, to the European eye, seemed a species of the Arabian camel. But, although he steered his caravel for these golden realms, and even pushed his discoveries some twenty leagues south of the Gulf of St. Michael, the adventure was not reserved for him. The illustrious discoverer was doomed to fall a victim of that miserable jealousy with which a little spirit regards the achievements of a great one.

The Spanish colonial domain was broken up into a number of petty governments, which were dispensed sometimes to court favorites, though, as the duties of the post, at this early period, were of an arduous nature, they were more frequently reserved for men of some practical talent and enterprise. Columbus, by virtue of his original contract with the crown, had jurisdiction over the territories discovered by himself, embracing some of the principal islands, and a few places on the continent. This jurisdiction differed from that of other functionaries, inasmuch as it was hereditary; a privilege found in the end too considerable for a subject, and commuted, therefore, for a title and a pension. These colonial governments were multiplied with the increase of empire, and by the year 1524, the period at which our narrative properly commences, were scattered over the islands, along the Isthmus of Darien, the broad tract of Terra Firma, and the recent conquests in Mexico. Some of these governments were of no great extent; others, like that of Mexico, were of the dimensions of a kingdom; and most had an indefinite range for discovery assigned to them in their immediate neighborhood, by which each of the petty potentates might enlarge his territorial sway and enrich his followers and himself. This politic arrangement best served the ends of the crown, by affording a perpetual incentive to the spirit of enterprise. Thus living on their own little domains at a long distance from the mother country, these military rulers held a sort of viceregal sway, and too frequently exercised it in the most oppressive and tyrannical manner—oppressive to the native, and tyrannical towards their own followers. It was the natural consequence when men originally low in station, and unprepared by education for office, were suddenly called to the possession of a brief, but in its nature irresponsible, authority. It was not till after some sad experience of these results that measures were taken to hold these petty tyrants in check by means of regular tribunals, or Royal Audiences, as they were termed, which, composed of men of character and learning, might interpose the arm of the law, or at least the voice of remonstrance, for the protection of both colonist and native.

Among the colonial governors who were indebted for their situation to their rank at home was Don Pedro Arias de Avila, or Pedrarias, as usually called. He was married to a daughter of Doña Beatriz de Bobadilla, the celebrated Marchioness of Moya, best known as the friend of Isabella the Catholic. He was a man of some military experience and considerable energy of character. But, as it proved, he was of a malignant temper; and the base qualities which might have passed unnoticed in the obscurity of private life were made conspicuous, and perhaps created in some measure, by sudden elevation to power; as the sunshine, which operates kindly on a generous soil and stimulates it to production, calls forth from the unwholesome marsh only foul and pestilent vapors. This man was placed over the territory of *Castilla del Oro*, the ground selected by Nuñez de Balboa for the theater of his discoveries. Success drew on this latter the jealousy of his superior, for it was crime enough in the eyes of Pedrarias to deserve too well. The tragical history of this cavalier belongs to a period somewhat earlier than that with which we are to be occupied. It has been traced by abler hands than mine, and, though brief, forms one of the most brilliant passages in the annals of the American conquerors.

But, though Pedrarias was willing to cut short the glorious career of his rival, he was not insensible to the important consequences of his discoveries. He saw at once the unsuitableness of Darien for prosecuting expeditions on the Pacific, and, conformably to the original suggestion of Balboa, in 1519 he caused his rising capital to be transferred from the shores of the Atlantic to the ancient site of Panamá, some distance east of the present city of that name. This most unhealthy spot, the cemetery of many an unfortunate colonist, was favorably situated for the great object of maritime enterprise; and the port, from its central position, afforded the best point of departure for expeditions, whether to the north or south, along the wide range of undiscovered coast that lined the Southern Ocean. Yet in this new and more favorable position several years were suffered to elapse before the course of discovery took the direction of Peru. This was turned exclusively towards the north, or rather west, in obedience to the orders of the government, which had ever at heart the detection of a strait, that, as was supposed, must intersect some part or other of the long extended Isthmus. Armament after armament was fitted out with this chimerical object; and Pedrarias saw his domain extending every year farther and farther without deriving any considerable advantage from his acquisitions. Veragua, Costa Rica, Nicaragua, were successively occupied; and his brave cavaliers forced a way across forest and mountains and warlike tribes of savages, till, at Honduras, they came in collision with the companions of Cortés, the Conquerors of Mexico, who had descended from the great northern plateau on the regions of Central America, and thus completed the survey of this wild and mysterious land.

It was not till 1522 that a regular expedition was dispatched in the direction south of Panamá, under the conduct of Pascual de Andagoya, a cavalier of much distinction in the colony. But that officer penetrated only to the Puerto de Piñas, the limit of Balboa's discoveries, when the bad state of his health compelled him to re-embark and abandon his enterprise at its commencement.

Yet the floating rumors of the wealth and civilization of a mighty nation at the south were continually reaching the ears and kindling the dreamy imaginations of the colonists; and it may seem astonishing that an expedition in that direction should have been so long deferred. But the exact position and distance of this fairy realm were matter of conjecture. The long tract of intervening country was occupied by rude and warlike races; and the little experience which the Spanish navigators had already had of the neighboring coast and its inhabitants, and still more, the tempestuous character of the seas—for their expeditions had taken place at the most unpropitious season of the year—enhanced the apparent difficulties of the undertaking and made even their stout hearts shrink from it.

Such was the state of feeling in the little community of Panamá for several years after its foundation. Meanwhile, the dazzling conquest of Mexico gave a new impulse to the ardor of discovery, and in 1524 three men were found in the colony in whom the spirit of adventure triumphed over every consideration of difficulty and danger that obstructed the prosecution of the enterprise. One among them was selected as fitted by his character to conduct it to a successful issue. That man was Francisco Pizarro; and as he held the same conspicuous post in the conquest of Peru that was occupied by Cortés in that of Mexico, it will be necessary to take a brief review of his early history.

## ⚜ CHAPTER TWO ⚜

FRANCISCO PIZARRO—HIS EARLY HISTORY—

FIRST EXPEDITION TO THE SOUTH—

DISTRESSES OF THE VOYAGERS—

SHARP ENCOUNTERS—RETURN

TO PANAMÁ—ALMAGRO'S EXPEDITION

Francisco Pizarro was born at Trujillo, a city of Estremadura, in Spain. The period of his birth is uncertain; but probably it was not far from 1471. He was an illegitimate child, and that his parents should not have taken pains to perpetuate the date of his birth is not surprising. Few care to make a particular record of their transgressions. His father, Gonzalo Pizarro, was a colonel of infantry, and served with some distinction in the Italian campaigns under the Great Captain, and afterwards in the wars of Navarre. His mother, named Francisca Gonzales, was a person of humble condition in the town of Trujillo.

But little is told of Francisco's early years, and that little not always deserving of credit. According to some, he was deserted by both his parents, and left as a foundling at the door of one of the principal churches of the city. It is even said that he would have perished, had he not been nursed by a sow. This is a more discreditable fountain of supply than that assigned to the infant Romulus. The early history of men who have made their names famous by deeds in after life, like the early history of nations, affords a fruitful field for invention.[22]

It seems certain that the young Pizarro received little care from either of his parents, and was suffered to grow up as nature dictated. He was neither taught to read nor write, and his principal occupation was that of a swineherd. But this torpid way of life did not suit the stirring spirit of Pizarro, as he grew older, and listened to the tales, widely circulated and so captivating to a youthful fancy, of the New World. He shared in the popular enthusiasm, and availed himself of a favorable moment to abandon his ignoble charge and escape to Seville, the port where the Spanish adventurers embarked to seek their fortunes in the West. Few of them could have turned their backs on their native land with less cause for regret than Pizarro.

In what year this important change in his destiny took place we are not informed. The first we hear of him in the New World is at the island of Hispaniola, in 1510, where he took part in the expedition to Uraba in Terra Firma, under Alonso de Ojeda, a cavalier whose character and achievements find no parallel but in the pages of Cervantes. Hernando Cortés, whose mother was a Pizarro, and related, it is said, to the father of Francis, was then in St. Domingo, and prepared to accompany Ojeda's expedition, but was prevented by a temporary lameness. Had he gone, the fall of the Aztec empire might have been postponed for some time longer, and the scepter of Montezuma have descended in peace to his posterity. Pizarro shared in the disastrous fortunes of Ojeda's colony, and by his discretion obtained so far the confidence of his commander as to be left in charge of the settlement when the latter returned for supplies to the islands. The lieutenant continued at his perilous post for nearly two months, waiting deliberately until death should have thinned off the colony sufficiently to allow the miserable remnant to be embarked in the single small vessel that remained to it.

After this, we find him associated with Balboa, the discoverer of the Pacific, and co-operating with him in establishing the settlement at Darien. He had the glory of accompanying this gallant cavalier in his terrible march across the mountains, and of being among the first Europeans, therefore, whose eyes were greeted with the long-promised vision of the Southern Ocean.

After the untimely death of his commander, Pizarro attached himself to the fortunes of Pedrarias, and was employed by that governor in several military expeditions, which, if they afforded nothing else, gave him the requisite training for the perils and privations that lay in the path of the future Conqueror of Peru.

In 1515 he was selected, with another cavalier, named Morales, to cross the Isthmus and traffic with the natives on the shores of the Pacific. And there, while engaged in collecting his booty of gold and pearls from the neighboring islands, as his eye ranged along the shadowy line of coast till it faded in the distance, his imagination may have been first fired with the idea of, one day, attempting the conquest of the mysterious regions beyond the mountains. On the removal of the seat of government across the Isthmus of Panamá, Pizarro accompanied Pedrarias, and his name became conspicuous among the cavaliers who extended the line of conquest to the north over the martial tribes of Veragua. But all these expeditions, whatever glory they may have brought him, were productive of very little gold, and at the age of fifty the captain Pizarro found himself in possession only of a tract of unhealthy land in the neighborhood of the capital, and of such *repartimientos* of the natives as were deemed suited to his military services. The New World was a lottery, where the great prizes were so few that the odds were much against the player; yet in the game he was content to stake health, fortune, and, too often, his fair fame.

Such was Pizarro's situation when, in 1522, Andagoya returned from his unfinished enterprise to the south of Panamá, bringing back with him more copious accounts than any hitherto received of the opulence and grandeur of the countries that lay beyond. It was at this time, too, that the splendid achievements of Cortés made their impression on the public mind and gave a new impulse to the spirit of adventure. The southern expeditions became a common topic of speculation among the colonists of Panamá. But the region of gold, as it lay behind the mighty curtain of the Cordilleras, was still veiled in obscurity. No idea could be formed of its actual distance; and the hardships and difficulties encountered by the few navigators who had sailed in that direction gave a gloomy character to the undertaking, which had hitherto deterred the most daring from embarking in it. There is no evidence that Pizarro showed any particular alacrity in the cause. Nor were his own funds such as to warrant any expectation of success without great assistance from others. He found this in two individuals of the colony, who took too important a part in the subsequent transactions not to be particularly noticed.

One of them, Diego de Almagro, was a soldier of fortune, somewhat older, it seems probable, than Pizarro; though little is known of his birth, and even the place of it is disputed. It is supposed to have been the town of Almagro in New Castile, whence his own name, for want of a better source, was derived; for, like Pizarro, he was a foundling. Few particulars are known of him till the present period of our history; for he was one of those whom the working of turbulent times first throws upon the surface—less fortunate, perhaps, than if left in their original obscurity. In his military career, Almagro had earned the reputation of a gallant soldier. He was frank and liberal in his disposition, somewhat hasty and ungovernable in his passions, but, like men of a sanguine temperament, after the first sallies had passed away, not difficult to be appeased. He had, in short, the good qualities and the defects incident to an honest nature not improved by the discipline of early education or self-control.

The other member of the confederacy was Hernando de Luque, a Spanish ecclesiastic, who exercised the functions of vicar at Panamá, and had formerly filled the office of schoolmaster in the Cathedral of Darien. He seems to have been a man of singular prudence and knowledge of the world, and by his respectable qualities had acquired considerable influence in the little community to which he belonged, as well as the control of funds, which made his co-operation essential to the success of the present enterprise.

It was arranged among the three associates that the two cavaliers should contribute their little stock towards defraying the expenses of the armament, but by far the greater part of the funds was to be furnished by Luque. Pizarro was to take command of the expedition, and the business of victualing and equipping the vessels was assigned to Almagro. The associates found no difficulty in obtaining the consent of the governor to their undertaking. After the return of Andagoya, he had projected another expedition, but the officer to whom it was to be entrusted died. Why he did not prosecute his original purpose, and commit the affair to an experienced captain like Pizarro, does not appear. He was probably not displeased that the burden of the enterprise should be borne by others so long as a good share of the profits went into his own coffers. This he did not overlook in his stipulations.

Thus fortified with the funds of Luque and the consent of the governor, Almagro was not slow to make preparations for the voyage. Two small vessels were purchased, the larger of which had been originally built by Balboa for himself, with a view to this same expedition. Since his death, it had lain dismantled in the harbor of Panamá. It was now refitted as well as circumstances would permit, and put in order for sea, while the stores and provisions were got on board with an alacrity which did more credit, as the event proved, to Almagro's zeal than to his forecast.

There was more difficulty in obtaining the necessary complement of hands; for a general feeling of distrust had gathered round expeditions in this direction, which could not readily be overcome. But there were many idle hangers-on in the colony, who had come out to mend their fortunes, and were willing to take their chance of doing so, however desperate. From such materials as these, Almagro assembled a body of somewhat more than a hundred men; and, everything being ready, Pizarro assumed the command, and, weighing anchor, took his departure from the little port of Panamá about the middle of November, 1524. Almagro was to follow in a second vessel of inferior size, as soon as it could be fitted out.

The time of year was the most unsuitable that could have been selected for the voyage; for it was the rainy season, when the navigation to the south, impeded by contrary winds, is made doubly dangerous by the tempests that sweep over the coast. But this was not understood by the adventurers. After touching at the Isle of Pearls, the frequent resort of navi-

"The land spread out into a vast swamp, where the heavy rains had settled in pools of stagnant water. . . . This dismal morass was fringed with woods, through whose thick and tangled undergrowth they found it difficult to penetrate."

gators, at a few leagues' distance from Panamá, Pizarro held his way across the Gulf of St. Michael, and steered almost due south for the Puerto de Piñas, a headland in the province of Biruquete, which marked the limit of Andagoya's voyage. Before his departure, Pizarro had obtained all the information which he could derive from that officer in respect to the country, and the route he was to follow. But the cavalier's own experience had been too limited to enable him to be of much assistance.

Doubling the Puerto de Piñas, the little vessel entered the river Birú, the misapplication of which name is supposed by some to have given rise to that of the empire of the Incas.

After sailing up this stream for a couple of leagues, Pizarro came to anchor, and, disembarking his whole force except the sailors, proceeded at the head of it to explore the country. The land spread out into a vast swamp, where the heavy rains had settled in pools of stagnant water, and the muddy soil afforded no footing to the traveler. This dismal morass was fringed with woods, through whose thick and tangled undergrowth they found it difficult to penetrate; and, emerging from them, they came out on a hilly country, so rough and rocky in its character that their feet were cut to the bone, and the weary soldier, encumbered with his heavy mail or thick-padded doublet of cotton, found it difficult to drag one foot after the other. The heat at times was oppressive; and, fainting with toil and famished for want of food, they sank down on the earth from mere exhaustion. Such was the ominous commencement of the expedition to Peru.

Pizarro, however, did not lose heart. He endeavored to revive the spirits of his men, and besought them not to be discouraged by difficulties which a brave heart would be sure to overcome, reminding them of the golden prize which awaited those who persevered. Yet it was obvious that nothing was to be gained by remaining longer in this desolate region. Returning to their vessel, therefore, it was suffered to drop down the river and proceed along its southern course on the great ocean.

After coasting a few leagues, Pizarro anchored off a place not very inviting in its appearance, where he took in a supply of wood and water. Then, stretching more towards the open sea, he held on in the same direction towards the south. But in this he was baffled by a succession of heavy tempests, accompanied with such tremendous peals of thunder and floods of rain as are found only in the terrible storms of the tropics. The sea was lashed into fury, and, swelling into mountain billows, threatened every moment to overwhelm the crazy little bark, which opened at every seam. For ten days the unfortunate voyagers were tossed about by the pitiless elements, and it was only by incessant exertions—the exertions of despair—that they preserved the ship from foundering. To add to their calamities, their provisions began to fail, and they were short of water, of which they had been furnished only with a small number of casks; for Almagro had counted on their recruiting their scanty supplies, from time to time, from the shore. Their meat was wholly consumed, and they were reduced to the wretched allowance of two ears of Indian corn a day for each man.

Thus harassed by hunger and the elements, the battered

voyagers were too happy to retrace their course and regain the port where they had last taken in supplies of wood and water. Yet nothing could be more unpromising than the aspect of the country. It had the same character of low, swampy soil that distinguished the former landing place; while thick-matted forests, of a depth which the eye could not penetrate, stretched along the coast to an interminable length. It was in vain that the wearied Spaniards endeavored to thread the mazes of this tangled thicket, where the creepers and flowering vines, that shoot up luxuriant in a hot and humid atmosphere, had twined themselves round the huge trunks of the forest trees and made a network that could be opened only with the axe. The rain, in the meantime, rarely slackened, and the ground, strewed with leaves and saturated with moisture, seemed to slip away beneath their feet.

Nothing could be more dreary and disheartening than the aspect of these funereal forests, where the exhalations from the overcharged surface of the ground poisoned the air, and seemed to allow no life, except that, indeed, of myriads of insects, whose enamelled wings glanced to and fro, like sparks of fire, in every opening of the woods. Even the brute creation appeared instinctively to have shunned the fatal spot, and neither beast nor bird of any description was seen by the wanderers. Silence reigned unbroken in the heart of these dismal solitudes; at least, the only sounds that could be heard were the splashing of the raindrops on the leaves, and the tread of the forlorn adventurers.

Entirely discouraged by the aspect of the country, the Spaniards began to comprehend that they had gained nothing by changing their quarters from sea to shore, and they felt the most serious apprehensions of perishing from famine in a region which afforded nothing but such unwholesome berries as they could pick here and there in the woods. They loudly complained of their hard lot, accusing their commander as the author of all their troubles, and as deluding them with promises of a fairyland, which seemed to recede in proportion as they advanced. It was of no use, they said, to contend against fate, and it was better to take their chance of regaining the port of Panamá in time to save their lives, than to wait where they were to die of hunger.

But Pizarro was prepared to encounter much greater evils than these before returning to Panamá, bankrupt in credit, an object of derision as a vainglorious dreamer who had persuaded others to embark in an adventure which he had not the courage to carry through himself. The present was his only chance. The return would be ruin. He used every argument, therefore, that mortified pride or avarice could suggest to turn his followers from their purpose; represented to them that these were the troubles that necessarily lay in the path of the discoverer, and called to mind the brilliant successes of their countrymen in other quarters, and the repeated reports which they had themselves received of the rich regions along this coast, of which it required only courage and constancy on their parts to become the masters. Yet, as their present exigencies were pressing, he resolved to send back the vessel to the Isle of Pearls, to lay in a fresh stock of provisions for his company, which might enable them to go forward with renewed confidence. The distance was not great, and in a few days they would all be relieved from their perilous position. The officer detached on this service was named Montenegro; and, taking with him nearly half the company, after receiving Pizarro's directions, he instantly weighed anchor and steered for the Isle of Pearls.

On the departure of his vessel, the Spanish commander made an attempt to explore the country and see if some Indian settlement might not be found, where he could procure refreshments for his followers. But his efforts were in vain, and no trace was visible of a human dwelling; though in the dense and impenetrable foliage of the equatorial regions the distance of a few rods might suffice to screen a city from observation. The only means of nourishment left to the unfortunate adventurers were such shellfish as they occasionally picked up on the shore, or the bitter buds of the palm tree, and such berries and unsavory herbs as grew wild in the woods. Some of these were so poisonous that the bodies of those who ate them swelled up and were tormented with racking pains. Others, preferring famine to this miserable diet, pined away from weakness and actually died of starvation. Yet their resolute leader strove to maintain his own cheerfulness and to keep up the drooping spirits of his men. He freely shared with them his scanty stock of provisions, was unwearied in his endeavors to procure them sustenance, tended the sick, and ordered barracks to be constructed for their accommodation, which might at least shelter them from the drenching storms of the season. By this ready sympathy with his followers in their sufferings he obtained an ascendency over their rough natures which the assertion of authority, at least in the present extremity, could never have secured to him.

Day after day, week after week, had now passed away, and no tidings were heard of the vessel that was to bring relief to the wanderers. In vain did they strain their eyes over the distant waters to catch a glimpse of their coming friends. Not a speck was to be seen in the blue distance, where the canoe of the savage dared not venture, and the sail of the white man was not yet spread. Those who had borne up bravely at first now gave way to despondency, as they felt themselves abandoned by their countrymen on this desolate shore. They pined under that sad feeling which "maketh the heart sick." More than twenty of the little band had already died, and the survivors seemed to be rapidly following.

At this crisis reports were brought to Pizarro of a light having been seen through a distant opening in the woods. He hailed the tidings with eagerness, as intimating the existence of some settlement in the neighborhood, and, putting himself at the head of a small party, went in the direction pointed out, to reconnoiter. He was not disappointed, and, after extricating himself from a dense wilderness of underbrush and foliage, he emerged into an open space, where a small Indian village was planted. The timid inhabitants, on the sudden apparition of the strangers, quitted their huts in dismay; and the famished Spaniards, rushing in, eagerly made themselves masters of their contents. These consisted of different articles of food, chiefly maize and cocoa nuts. The supply, though small, was too seasonable not to fill them with rapture.

The astonished natives made no attempt at resistance. But, gathering more confidence as no violence was offered to their persons, they drew nearer the white men and inquired, "Why they did not stay at home and till their own lands, instead of roaming about to rob others who had never harmed them?" Whatever may have been their opinion as to the question of right, the Spaniards, no doubt, felt then that it would have been wiser to do so. But the savages wore about their persons gold ornaments of some size, though of clumsy workmanship. This furnished the best reply to their demand. It was the golden bait which lured the Spanish adventurer to forsake his pleasant home for the trials of the wilderness. From the Indians Pizarro gathered a confirmation of the reports he had so often received of a rich country lying farther south; and at the distance of ten days' journey across the mountains, they told him, there dwelt a mighty monarch whose dominions had been invaded by another still more powerful, the child of the Sun. It may have been the invasion of Quito that was meant, by the valiant Inca Huayna Capac, which took place some years previous to Pizarro's expedition.

At length, after the expiration of more than six weeks, the Spaniards beheld with delight the return of the wandering bark that had borne away their comrades, and Montenegro sailed into port with an ample supply of provisions for his famishing countrymen. Great was his horror at the aspect presented by the latter, their wild and haggard countenances and wasted frames—so wasted by hunger and disease that their old companions found it difficult to recognize them. Montenegro accounted for his delay by incessant headwinds and bad weather; and he himself had also a doleful tale to tell of the distress to which he and his crew had been reduced by hunger on their passage to the Isle of Pearls. It is minute incidents like these with which we have been occupied that enable one to comprehend the extremity of suffering to which the Spanish adventurer was subjected in the prosecution of his great work of discovery.

Revived by the substantial nourishment to which they had so long been strangers, the Spanish cavaliers, with the buoyancy that belongs to men of a hazardous and roving life, forgot their past distresses in their eagerness to prosecute their enterprise. Re-embarking, therefore, on board his vessel, Pizarro bade adieu to the scene of so much suffering, which he branded with the appropriate name of *Puerto de la Hambre*, the Port of Famine, and again opened his sails to a favorable breeze that bore him onwards towards the south.

Had he struck boldly out into the deep, instead of hugging the inhospitable shore, where he had hitherto found so little to recompense him, he might have spared himself the repetition of wearisome and unprofitable adventures, and reached by a shorter route the point of his destination. But the Spanish mariner groped his way along these unknown coasts, landing at every convenient headland, as if fearful lest some fruitful region or precious mine might be overlooked should a single break occur in the line of survey. Yet it should be remembered that, though the true point of Pizarro's destination is obvious to us, familiar with the topography of these countries, he was wandering in the dark, feeling his way along inch by inch, as it were, without chart to guide him, without knowledge of the seas or of the bearings of the coast, and even with no better defined idea of the object at which he aimed than that of a land, teeming with gold, that lay somewhere at the south! It was a hunt after an *El Dorado*, on information scarcely more circumstantial or authentic than that which furnished the basis of so many chimerical enterprises in this land of wonders. Success only, the best argument with the multitude, redeemed the expeditions of Pizarro from a similar imputation of extravagance.

Holding on his southerly course under the lee of the shore, Pizarro, after a short run, found himself abreast of an open reach of country, or at least one less encumbered with wood, which rose by a gradual swell as it receded from the coast. He landed with a small body of men, and, advancing a short distance into the interior, fell in with an Indian hamlet. It was abandoned by the inhabitants, who on the approach of the invaders had betaken themselves to the mountains; and the Spaniards, entering their deserted dwellings, found there a good store of maize and other articles of food, and rude ornaments of gold of considerable value. Food was not more necessary for their bodies than was the sight of gold, from time to time, to stimulate their appetite for adventure. One spectacle, however, chilled their blood with horror. This was a sight of human flesh, which they found roasting before the fire, as the barbarians had left it, preparatory to their obscene repast. The Spaniards, conceiving that they had fallen in with a tribe of Caribs, the only race in that part of the New World known to be cannibals, retreated precipitately to their vessel. They were not steeled by sad familiarity with the spectacle, like the Conquerors of Mexico.

The weather, which had been favorable, now set in tempestuous, with heavy squalls, accompanied by incessant thunder and lightning, and the rain, as usual in these tropical tempests, descended not so much in drops as in unbroken sheets of water. The Spaniards, however, preferred to take their chance on the raging element rather than remain at the scene of such brutal abominations. But the fury of the storm gradually subsided, and the little vessel held on her way along the coast, till, coming abreast of a bold point of land named by Pizarro Punta Quemada, he gave orders to anchor. The margin of the shore was fringed with a deep belt of mangrove trees, the long roots of which, interlacing one another, formed a kind of submarine latticework that made the place difficult of approach. Several avenues, opening through this tangled thicket, led Pizarro to conclude that the country must be inhabited, and he disembarked, with the greater part of his force, to explore the interior.

He had not penetrated more than a league when he found his conjecture verified by the sight of an Indian town, of larger size than those he had hitherto seen, occupying the brow of an eminence, and well defended by palisades. The inhabitants, as usual, had fled, but left in their dwellings a good supply of provisions and some gold trinkets, which the Spaniards made no difficulty of appropriating to themselves. Pizarro's flimsy bark had been strained by the heavy gales it had of late encountered, so that it was unsafe to prosecute the voyage farther without more thorough repairs than could be given to her on this desolate coast. He accordingly determined to send her back with a few hands to be careened at Panamá, and meanwhile to establish his quarters in his present position, which was so favorable to defense. But first he dispatched a small party under Montenegro to reconnoiter the country, and, if possible, to open a communication with the natives.

The latter were a warlike race. They had left their habitations in order to place their wives and children in safety. But they had kept an eye on the movements of the invaders, and when they saw their forces divided they resolved to fall upon each body singly before it could communicate with the other. So soon, therefore, as Montenegro had penetrated through the defiles of the lofty hills which shoot out like spurs of the Cordilleras along this part of the coast, the Indian warriors, springing from their ambush, sent off a cloud of arrows and other missiles that darkened the air, while they made the forest ring with their shrill war whoop. The Spaniards, astonished at the appearance of the savages, with their naked bodies gaudily painted, and brandishing their weapons as they glanced among the trees and straggling underbrush that choked up the defile, were taken by surprise and thrown for a moment into disarray. Three of their number were killed and several wounded. Yet, speedily rallying, they returned the discharge of the assailants with their crossbows—for Pizarro's troops do not seem to have been provided with muskets on this expedition—and then, gallantly charging the enemy, sword in hand, succeeded in driving them back into the fastnesses of the mountains. But it only led them to shift their operations to another quarter and make an assault on Pizarro before he could be relieved by his lieutenant.

Availing themselves of their superior knowledge of the passes, they reached that commander's quarters long before Montenegro, who had commenced a countermarch in the same direction; and, issuing from the woods, the bold savages saluted the Spanish garrison with a tempest of darts and arrows, some of which found their way through the joints of the harness and the quilted mail of the cavaliers. But Pizarro was too well-practiced a soldier to be off his guard. Calling his men about him, he resolved not to abide the assault tamely in the works, but to sally out and meet the enemy on their own ground. The barbarians, who had advanced near the defenses, fell back as the Spaniards burst forth with their valiant leader at their head. But, soon returning with admirable ferocity to the charge, they singled out Pizarro, whom by his bold bearing and air of authority they easily recognized as the chief, and, hurling at him a storm of missiles, wounded him, in spite of his armor, in no less than seven places.

Driven back by the fury of the assault directed against his own person, the Spanish commander retreated down the slope of the hill, still defending himself as he could with sword and buckler, when his foot slipped, and he fell. The enemy set up a fierce yell of triumph, and some of the boldest sprang forward to dispatch him. But Pizarro was on his feet in an instant, and, striking down two of the foremost with his strong arm, held the rest at bay till his soldiers could come to the rescue. The barbarians, struck with admiration at his valor, began to falter, when Montenegro, luckily coming on the ground at the moment and falling on their rear, completed their confusion; and abandoning the field, they made the best of their way into the recesses of the mountains. The ground was covered with their slain; but the victory was dearly purchased by the death of two more Spaniards and a long list of wounded.

A council of war was then called. The position had lost its charm in the eyes of the Spaniards, who had met here with the first resistance they had yet experienced on their expedition. It was necessary to place the wounded in some secure spot, where their injuries could be attended to. Yet it was not safe to proceed farther, in the crippled state of their vessel. On the whole, it was decided to return and report their proceedings to the governor; and though the magnficent hopes of the adventurers had not been realized, Pizarro trusted that enough had been done to vindicate the importance of the enterprise and to secure the countenance of Pedrarias for the further prosecution of it.

Yet Pizarro could not make up his mind to present himself, in the present state of the undertaking, before the governor. He determined, therefore, to be set on shore with the principal part of his company at Chicama, a place on the mainland, at a short distance west of Panamá. From this place, which he reached without any further accident, he dispatched the vessel, and in it his treasurer, Nicolas de Ribera, with the gold he had collected, and with instructions to lay before the governor a full account of his discoveries and the result of the expedition.

While these events were passing, Pizarro's associate, Almagro, had been busily employed in fitting out another vessel for the expedition at the port of Panamá. It was not till long after his friend's departure that he was prepared to follow him. With the assistance of Luque, he at length succeeded in equipping a small caravel and embarking a body of between sixty and seventy adventurers, mostly of the lowest order of the colonists. He steered in the track of his comrade, with the intention of overtaking him as soon as possible. By a signal previously concerted of notching the trees, he was able to identify the spots visited by Pizarro—Puerto de Piñas, Puerto de la Hambre, Pueblo Quemado—touching successively at every point of the coast explored by his countrymen, though in a much shorter time. At the last-mentioned place he was received by the fierce natives with the same hostile demonstrations as Pizarro, though in the present encounter the Indians did not venture beyond their defenses. But the hot blood of Almagro was so exasperated by this check that he assaulted the place and carried it sword in hand, setting fire to the outworks and dwellings, and driving the wretched inhabitants into the forests.

His victory cost him dear. A wound from a javelin on the head caused an inflammation in one of his eyes, which, after great anguish, ended in the loss of it. Yet the intrepid adventurer did not hesitate to pursue his voyage, and, after touching at several places on the coast, some of which rewarded him with a considerable booty in gold, he reached the mouth of the Rio de San Juan, about the fourth degree of north latitude. He was struck with the beauty of the stream, and with the cultivation on its borders, which were sprinkled with Indian cottages showing some skill in their construction, and altogether intimating a higher civilization than anything he had yet seen.

Still his mind was filled with anxiety for the fate of Pizarro and his followers. No trace of them had been found on the coast for a long time, and it was evident they must have foundered at sea or made their way back to Panamá. This last he deemed most probable; as the vessel might have past him unnoticed under the cover of the night or of the dense fogs that sometimes hang over the coast.

Impressed with this belief, he felt no heart to continue his voyage of discovery, for which, indeed, his single bark, with its small complement of men, was altogether inadequate. He proposed, therefore, to return without delay. On his way he touched at the Isle of Pearls, and there learned the result of his friend's expedition and the place of his present residence. He directed his course at once to Chicama, where the two cavaliers soon had the satisfaction of embracing each other and recounting their several exploits and escapes. Almagro returned even better freighted with gold than his confederate, and at every step of his progress he had collected fresh confirmation of the existence of some great and opulent empire in the South. The confidence of the two friends was much strengthened by their discoveries; and they unhesitatingly pledged themselves to one another to die rather than abandon the enterprise.

The best means of obtaining the levies requisite for so formidable an undertaking—more formidable, as it now appeared to them, than before—were made the subject of long and serious discussion. It was at length decided that Pizarro should remain in his present quarters, inconvenient and even unwholesome as they were rendered by the humidity of the climate and the pestilent swarms of insects that filled the atmosphere. Almagro would pass over to Panamá, lay the case before the governor, and secure, if possible, his good will towards the prosecution of the enterprise. If no obstacle were thrown in their way from this quarter, they might hope, with the assistance of Luque, to raise the necessary supplies; while the results of the recent expedition were sufficiently encouraging to draw adventurers to their standard in a community which had a craving for excitement that gave even danger a charm, and which held life cheap in comparison with gold.

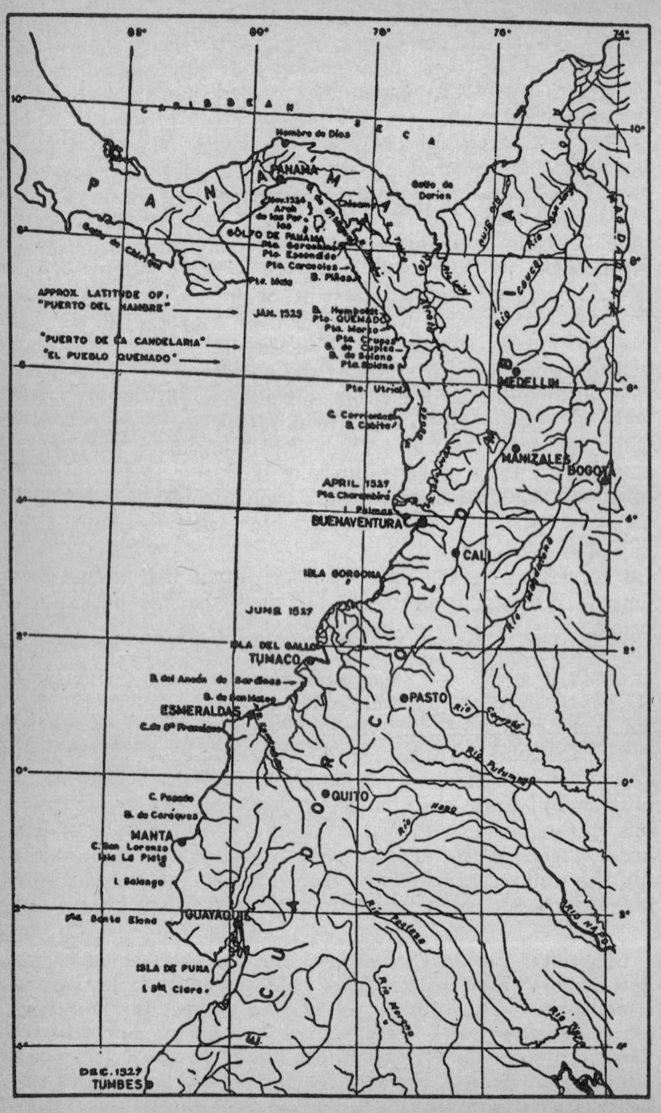

CARIBBEAN SEA
PANAMÁ
Nombre de Dios
Golfo de Darien
Chicamá
Nov. 1534
Arch. de las Perlas
GOLFO DE PANAMÁ
Pta. Garachiné
Pto. Escondido
Pta. Caracoles
B. Piñas
Pto. Mala
JAN. 1529
B. Humboldt
Pto. QUEMADO
Pta. Marzo
Pta. Cruces
G. de Cupica
B. de Solano
Pta. Solano
Pto. Utria
C. Corrientes
B. Cabita
APPROX. LATITUDE OF:
"PUERTO DEL HAMBRE"
"PUERTO DE LA CANDELARIA"
"EL PUEBLO QUEMADO"
Rio Atrato
Rio Cauca
Rio San Juan
MAGDALENA
MEDELLIN
MANIZALES
BOGOTA
APRIL 1527
Pta. Charambirá
I. Palmas
BUENAVENTURA
CALI
ISLA GORGONA
JUNE 1527
ISLA DEL GALLO
TUMACO
B. del Ancón de Sardinas
B. de San Mateo
ESMERALDAS
C. de S. Francisco
PASTO
Rio Caquetá
Rio Putumayo
C. Pasado
B. de Caráquez
MANTA
C. San Lorenzo
Isla La Plata
I. Salango
QUITO
Rio Napo
Pta. Santa Elena
GUAYAQUIL
Rio Pastaza
Rio Napo
ISLA DE PUNA
I. Sta. Clara
Rio Morona
Rio Tigre
Rio Nana
DEC. 1527
TUMBES

# ❧ CHAPTER THREE ❧

THE FAMOUS CONTRACT—SECOND EXPEDITION—RUIZ

EXPLORES THE COAST—PIZARRO'S SUFFERINGS

IN THE FORESTS—ARRIVAL OF NEW RECRUITS—

FRESH DISCOVERIES AND DISASTERS—

PIZARRO ON THE ISLE OF GALLO

## (1526–1527)

On his arrival at Panamá, Almagro found that events had taken a turn less favorable to his views than he had anticipated. Pedrarias, the governor, was preparing to lead an expedition in person against a rebellious officer in Nicaragua; and his temper, naturally not the most amiable, was still further soured by this defection of his lieutenant and the necessity it imposed on him of a long and perilous march. When, therefore, Almagro appeared before him with the request that he might be permitted to raise further levies to prosecute his enterprise, the governor received him with obvious dissatisfaction, listened coldly to the narrative of his losses, turned an incredulous ear to his magnificent promises for the future, and bluntly demanded an account of the lives which had been sacrificed by Pizarro's obstinacy, but

**(Opposite) The Spanish explorations in search of the "Kingdom of Peru" between the years 1522 and 1531. The names of rivers, ports, and towns shown are the present-day names of places identified with those visited by Pizarro. Approximate dates are given for his expeditions along the coast up to the discovery of Tumbes, the outpost of the Inca Empire. (After Robert Cushman Murphy, "The Earliest Spanish Advance Southward from Panama along the West Coast of South America," *Hispanic American Historical Review*, XXI:1, February, 1941.)**

which, had they been spared, might have stood him in good stead in his present expedition to Nicaragua. He positively declined to countenance the rash schemes of the two adventurers any longer, and the conquest of Peru would have been crushed in the bud, but for the efficient interposition of the remaining associate, Fernando de Luque.

This sagacious ecclesiastic had received a very different impression from Almagro's narrative from that which had been made on the mind of the irritable governor. The actual results of the enterprise in gold and silver thus far, indeed, had been small—forming a mortifying contrast to the magnitude of their expectations. But in another point of view they were of the last importance; since the intelligence which the adventurers had gained at every successive stage of their progress confirmed, in the strongest manner, the previous accounts, received from Andagoya and others, of a rich Indian empire at the south, which might repay the trouble of conquering it as well as Mexico had repaid the enterprise of Cortés. Fully entering, therefore, into the feelings of his military associates, he used all his influence with the governor to incline him to a more favorable view of Almagro's petition; and no one in the little community of Panamá exercised greater influence over the councils of the executive than Father Luque, for which he was indebted no less to his discretion and acknowledged sagacity than to his professional station.

But while Pedrarias, overcome by the arguments or importunity of the churchman, yielded a reluctant assent to the application, he took care to testify his displeasure with Pizarro, on whom he particularly charged the loss of his followers, by naming Almagro as his equal in command in the proposed expedition. This mortification sank deep into Pizarro's mind. He suspected his comrade, with what reason does not appear, of soliciting this boon from the governor. A temporary coldness arose between them, which subsided, in outward show at least, on Pizarro's reflecting that it was better to have this authority conferred on a friend than on a stranger, perhaps an enemy. But the seeds of permanent distrust were left in his bosom, and lay waiting for the due season to ripen into a fruitful harvest of discord.

Pedrarias had been originally interested in the enterprise, at least so far as to stipulate for a share of the gains, though he had not contributed, as it appears, a single ducat towards the expenses. He was at length, however, induced to relinquish all right to a share of the contingent profits. But in his manner of doing so he showed a mercenary spirit better becoming a petty trader than a high officer of the crown. He stipulated that the associates should secure to him the sum of one thousand *pesos de oro* in requital of his good will, and they eagerly closed with his proposal, rather than be encumbered with his pretensions. For so paltry a consideration did he resign his portion of the rich spoil of the Incas! But the governor was not gifted with the eye of a prophet. His avarice was of that short-sighted kind which defeats itself. He had sacrificed the chivalrous Balboa just as that officer was opening to him the conquest of Peru, and he would now have quenched the spirit of enterprise, that was taking the same direction, in Pizarro and his associates.

Not long after this, in the following year, he was succeeded in his government by Don Pedro de los Rios, a cavalier of Cordova. It was the policy of the Castilian crown to allow no one of the great colonial officers to occupy the same station so long as to render himself formidable by his authority. It had, moreover, many particular causes of disgust with Pedrarias. The functionary sent out to succeed him was fortified with ample instructions for the good of the colony and especially of the natives whose religious conversion was urged as a capital object, and whose personal freedom was unequivocally asserted, as loyal vassals of the crown. It is but justice to the Spanish government to admit that its provisions were generally guided by a humane and considerate policy, which was as regularly frustrated by the cupidity of the colonist and the capricious cruelty of the conqueror. The few remaining years of Pedrarias were spent in petty squabbles, both of a personal and official nature; for he was still continued in office, though in one of less consideration than that which he had hitherto filled. He survived but a few years, leaving behind him a reputation not to be envied, of one who united a pusillanimous spirit with uncontrollable passions, but who displayed, notwithstanding, a certain energy of character, or, to speak more correctly, an impetuosity of purpose, which might have led to good results had it taken a right direction. Unfortunately, his lack of discretion was such that the direction he took was rarely of service to his country or to himself.

Having settled their difficulties with the governor, and obtained his sanction to their enterprise, the confederates lost no time in making the requisite preparations for it. Their first step was to execute the memorable contract which served as the basis of their future arrangements; and, as Pizarro's name appears in this, it seems probable that that chief had crossed over to Panamá so soon as the favorable disposition of Pedrarias had been secured. The instrument, after invoking in the most solemn manner the names of the Holy Trinity and our Lady the Blessed Virgin, sets forth that whereas the parties have full authority to discover and subdue the countries and provinces lying south of the Gulf, belonging to the empire of Peru, and as Fernando de Luque had advanced the funds for the enterprise in bars of gold of the value of twenty thousand *pesos,* they mutually bind themselves to divide equally among them the whole of the conquered territory. This stipulation is reiterated over and over again, particularly with reference to Luque, who, it is declared, is to be entitled to one-third of all lands, *repartimientos,* treasures of every kind, gold, silver, and precious stones—to one-third even of all vassals, rents, and emoluments arising from such grants as may be conferred by the crown on either of his military associates, to be held for his own use, or for that of his heirs, assigns, or legal representatives.

The two captains solemnly engage to devote themselves exclusively to the present undertaking until it is accomplished; and in case of failure in their part of the covenant they pledge themselves to reimburse Luque for his advances, for which all the property they possess shall be held responsible, and this declaration is to be a sufficient warrant for the execution of judgment against them, in the same manner as if it had proceeded from the decree of a court of justice.

The commanders, Pizarro and Almagro, made oath, in the name of God and the Holy Evangelists, sacredly to keep this covenant, swearing it on the missal, on which they traced with their own hands the sacred emblem of the cross. To give still greater efficacy to the compact, Father Luque administered the sacrament to the parties, dividing the consecrated wafer into three portions, of which each one of them partook; while the bystanders, says an historian, were affected to tears by this spectacle of the solemn ceremonial with which these men voluntarily devoted themselves to a sacrifice that seemed little short of insanity.

The instrument, which was dated March 10, 1526, was subscribed by Luque, and attested by three respectable citizens of Panamá, one of whom signed on behalf of Pizarro, and the other for Almagro; since neither of these parties, according to the avowal of the instrument, was able to subscribe his own name.

Such was the singular compact by which three obscure individuals coolly carved out and partitioned among themselves an empire of whose extent, power, and resources, of whose situation, of whose existence even, they had no sure or precise knowledge. The positive and unhesitating manner in which they speak of the grandeur of this empire, of its stores of wealth, so conformable to the event, but of which they could have really known so little, forms a striking contrast with the general skepticism and indifference manifested by nearly every other person, high and low, in the community of Panamá.

The religious tone of the instrument is not the least remarkable feature in it, especially when we contrast this with the relentless policy pursued by the very men who were parties to it in their conquest of the country. "In the name of the Prince of Peace," says the illustrious historian of America, "they ratified a contract of which plunder and bloodshed were the objects." The reflection seems reasonable. Yet, in criticizing what is done, as well as what is written, we must take into account the spirit of the times. The invocation of Heaven was natural, where the object of the undertaking was in part a religious one. Religion entered more or less into the theory, at least, of the Spanish conquests in the New World. That motives of a baser sort mingled largely with these higher ones, and in different proportions according to the character of the individual, no one will deny. And few are they that have proposed to themselves a long career of action without the intermixture of some vulgar personal motive— fame, honors, or emolument. Yet that religion furnishes a key to the American crusades, however rudely they may have been conducted, is evident from the history of their origin; from the sanction openly given to them by the Head of the Church; from the throng of self-devoted missionaries who followed in the track of the conquerors to garner up the rich harvest of souls; from the reiterated instructions of the crown, the great object of which was the conversion of the natives; from those superstitious acts of the iron-hearted soldiery themselves, which, however they may be set down to fanaticism, were clearly too much in earnest to leave any ground for the charge of hypocrisy. It was indeed a fiery cross that was borne over the devoted land, scathing and consuming it in its terrible progress; but it was still the cross, the sign of man's salvation, the only sign by which generations and generations yet unborn were to be rescued from eternal perdition.

It is a remarkable fact, which has hitherto escaped the notice of the historian, that Luque was not the real party to this contract. He represented another, who placed in his hands the funds required for the undertaking. This appears from an instrument signed by Luque himself, and certified before the same notary that prepared the original contract. The instrument declares that the whole sum of twenty thousand *pesos* advanced for the expedition was furnished by the Licentiate Gaspar de Espinosa, then at Panamá; that the vicar acted only as his agent and by his authority; and that, in consequence, the said Espinosa and no other was entitled to a third of all the profits and acquisitions resulting from the conquest of Peru. This instrument, attested by three persons, one of them the same who had witnessed the original contract, was dated on the 6th of August, 1531. The Licentiate Espinosa was a respectable functionary, who had filled the office of principal alcalde in Darien, and since taken a conspicuous part in the conquest and settlement of Tierra Firme. He enjoyed much consideration for his personal character and station; and it is remarkable that so little should be known of the manner in which the covenant so solemnly made was executed in reference to him. As in the case of Columbus, it is probable that the unexpected magnitude of the results was such as to prevent a faithful adherence to the original stipulation; and yet, from the same consideration, one can hardly doubt that the twenty thousand *pesos* of the bold speculator must have brought him a magnificent return. Nor did the worthy vicar of Panamá, as the history will show hereafter, go without his reward.

Having completed these preliminary arrangements, the three associates lost no time in making preparations for the voyage. Two vessels were purchased, larger and in every way better than those employed on the former occasion. Stores were laid in, as experience dictated, on a larger scale than before, and proclamation was made of "an expedition to Peru." But the call was not readily answered by the skeptical citizens of Panamá. Of nearly two hundred men who had embarked on the former cruise, not more than three-fourths now remained. This dismal mortality, and the emaciated, poverty-stricken aspect of the survivors, spoke more eloquently than the braggart promises and magnificent prospects held out by the adventurers. Still, there were men in the community of such desperate circumstances that any change seemed like a chance of bettering their condition. Most of the former company also, strange to say, felt more pleased to follow up the adventure to the end than to abandon it as they saw the light of a better day dawning upon them. From these sources the two captains succeeded in mustering about one hundred and sixty men, making altogether a very inadequate force for the conquest of an empire. A few horses were also purchased, and a better supply of ammunition and military stores than before, though still on a very limited scale. Considering their funds, the only way of accounting for this must be by the difficulty of obtaining supplies at Panamá, which, recently founded, and on the remote coast of the Pacific, could be approached only by crossing the rugged barrier of mountains, which made the transportation of bulky articles extremely difficult. Even such scanty stock of materials as it possessed was probably laid under heavy contribution, at the present juncture, by the governor's preparations for his own expedition to the north.

Thus indifferently provided, the two captains, each in his own vessel, again took their departure from Panamá, under the direction of Bartholomew Ruiz,[23] a sagacious and resolute pilot, well experienced in the navigation of the Southern Ocean. He was a native of Moguer, in Andalusia, that little nursery of nautical enterprise, which furnished so many seamen for the first voyages of Columbus. Without touching at the intervening points of the coast, which offered no attraction to the voyagers, they stood farther out to sea, steering direct for the Rio de San Juan, the utmost limit reached by Almagro. The season was better selected than on the former occasion, and they were borne along by favorable breezes to the place of their destination, which they reached without accident in a few days. Entering the mouth of the river, they saw the banks well lined with Indian habitations; and Pizarro, disembarking at the head of a party of soldiers, succeeded in surprising a small village and carrying off a considerable booty of gold ornaments found in the dwellings, together with a few of the natives.

Flushed with their success, the two chiefs were confident that the sight of the rich spoil so speedily obtained could not fail to draw adventurers to their standard in Panamá; and as they felt more than ever the necessity of a stronger force to cope with the thickening population of the country which they were now to penetrate, it was decided that Almagro should return with the treasure and beat up for reinforcements, while the pilot Ruiz, in the other vessel, should reconnoiter the country towards the south and obtain such information as might determine their future movements. Pizarro, with the rest of the force, would remain in the neighborhood of the river, as he was assured by the Indian prisoners that not far off in the interior was an open reach of country, where he and his men could find comfortable quarters. This arrangement was instantly put in execution. We will first accompany the intrepid pilot in his cruise towards the south.

Coasting along the great continent, with his canvas still

"As he drew near, he found it was a large vessel, or rather raft, called *balsa* by the natives, consisting of a number of huge timbers of a light, porous wood, tightly lashed together, with a frail flooring of reeds raised on them by way of deck. Two masts or sturdy poles . . . sustained a large squaresail of cotton."

spread to favorable winds, the first place at which Ruiz cast anchor was off the little island of Gallo, about two degrees north. The inhabitants, who were not numerous, were prepared to give him a hostile reception; for tidings of the invaders had preceded them along the country, and even reached this insulated spot. As the object of Ruiz was to explore, not to conquer, he did not care to entangle himself in hostilities with the natives: so, changing his purpose of landing, he weighed anchor, and ran down the coast as far as what is now called the bay of San Mateo. The country, which, as he advanced, continued to exhibit evidence of a better culture as well as of a more dense population than the parts hitherto seen, was crowded, along the shores, with spectators, who gave no signs of fear or hostility. They stood gazing on the vessel of the white men as it glided smoothly into the crystal waters of the bay, fancying it, says an old writer, some mysterious being descended from the skies.

Without staying long enough on this friendly coast to undeceive the simple people, Ruiz, standing off shore, struck out into the deep sea; but he had not sailed far in that direction when he was surprised by the sight of a vessel, seeming in the distance like a caravel of considerable size, traversed by a large sail that carried it sluggishly over the water. The old navigator was not a little perplexed by this phenomenon, as he was confident no European bark could have been before him in these latitudes, and no Indian nation yet discovered, not even the civilized Mexicans, was acquainted with the use of sails in navigation. As he drew near, he found it was a large vessel, or rather raft, called *balsa* [24] by the natives, consisting of a number of huge timbers of a light, porous wood, tightly lashed together, with a frail flooring of reeds raised on them by way of deck. Two masts or sturdy poles, erected in the middle of the vessel, sustained a large square sail of cotton, while a rude kind of rudder and a movable keel made of plank inserted between the logs enabled the mariner to give a direction to the floating fabric, which held on its course without the aid of oar or paddle. The simple architecture of this craft was sufficient for the purposes of the natives, and indeed has continued to answer them to the present day; for the *balsa,* surmounted by small thatched huts or cabins, still supplies the most commodious means for the transportation of passengers and luggage on the streams and along the shores of this part of the South American continent.

On coming alongside, Ruiz found several Indians, both men and women, on board, some with rich ornaments on their persons, besides several articles wrought with considerable skill in gold and silver, which they were carrying for purposes of traffic to the different places along the coast. But what most attracted his attention was the woollen cloth of which some of their dresses were made. It was of a fine texture, delicately embroidered with figures of birds and flowers, and dyed in brilliant colors. He also observed in the boat a pair of balances made to weigh the precious metals. His astonishment at these proofs of ingenuity and civilization, so much higher than anything he had ever seen in the country, was heightened by the intelligence which he collected from some of these Indians. Two of them had come from Tumbes, a Peruvian port, some degrees to the south; and they gave him to understand that in their neighborhood the fields were covered with large flocks of the animals from which the wool was obtained, and that gold and silver were almost as common as wood in the palaces of their monarch. The Spaniards listened greedily to reports which harmonized so well with their fond desires. Though half distrusting the exaggeration, Ruiz resolved to detain some of the Indians, including the natives of Tumbes, that they might repeat the wondrous tale to his commander, and at the same time, by learning the Castilian, might hereafter serve as interpreters with their countrymen. The rest of the party he suffered to proceed without further interruption on their voyage. Then, holding on his course, the prudent pilot, without touching at any other point of the coast, advanced as far as the Punta de Pasado, about half a degree south, having the glory of being the first European who, sailing in this direction on the Pacific, had crossed the equinoctial line. This was the limit of his discoveries; on reaching which he tacked about, and, standing away to the north, succeeded, after an absence of several weeks, in regaining the spot where he had left Pizarro and his comrades.

It was high time; for the spirits of that little band had been sorely tried by the perils they had encountered. On the departure of his vessels, Pizarro marched into the interior, in the hope of finding the pleasant champaign country which had been promised him by the natives. But at every step the forests seemed to grow denser and darker, and the trees towered to a height such as he had never seen, even in these fruitful regions, where Nature works on so gigantic a scale. Hill continued to rise above hill, as he advanced, rolling onward, as it were, by successive waves to join that colossal barrier of the Andes, whose frosty sides, far away above the clouds, spread out like a curtain of burnished silver, that seemed to connect the heavens with the earth.

On crossing these woody eminences, the forlorn adventurers would plunge into ravines of frightful depth, where the exhalations of a humid soil steamed up amidst the incense of sweet-scented flowers, which shone through the deep gloom in every conceivable variety of color. Birds, especially of the parrot tribe, mocked this fantastic variety of nature with tints as brilliant as those of the vegetable world. Monkeys chattered in crowds above their heads, and made grimaces likes the fiendish spirits of these solitudes; while hideous reptiles, engendered in the slimy depths of the pools, gathered round the footsteps of the wanderers. Here was seen the gigantic boa, coiling his unwieldy folds about the trees, so as hardly to be distinguished from their trunks, till he was ready to dart upon his prey; and alligators lay basking on the borders of the streams, or, gliding under the waters, seized their incautious victim before he was aware of their approach. Many of the Spaniards perished miserably in this way, and others were waylaid by the natives, who kept a jealous eye on their movements and availed themselves of every opportunity to take them at advantage. Fourteen of Pizarro's men were cut off at once in a canoe which had stranded on the bank of a stream.

Famine came in addition to other troubles, and it was with difficulty that they found the means of sustaining life on the scanty fare of the forest—occasionally the potato, as it grew without cultivation, or the wild cocoanut, or, on the shore, the salt and bitter fruit of the mangrove; though the shore was less tolerable than the forest, from the swarms of mosquitoes which compelled the wretched adventurers to bury their bodies up to their very faces in the sand. In this extremity of suffering, they thought only of return; and all schemes of avarice and ambition—except with Pizarro and a few dauntless spirits—were exchanged for the one craving desire to return to Panamá.

It was at this crisis that the pilot Ruiz returned with the report of his brilliant discoveries; and, not long after, Almagro sailed into port with his vessel laden with provisions and a considerable reinforcement of volunteers. The voyage of that commander had been prosperous. When he arrived at Panamá, he found the government in the hands of Don Pedro de los Rios; and he came to anchor in the harbor, unwilling to trust himself on shore till he had obtained from Father Luque some account of the dispositions of the executive. These were sufficiently favorable; for the new governor had particular instructions fully to carry out the arrangements made by his predecessor with the associates. On learning of Almagro's arrival, he came down to the port to welcome him, professing his willingness to afford every facility for the execution of his designs. Fortunately, just before this period a small body of military adventurers had come to Panamá from the mother country, burning with desire to make their fortunes in the New World. They caught much more eagerly than the old and wary colonists at the golden bait held out to them; and with their addition, and that of a few supernumerary stragglers who hung about the town, Almagro found himself at the head of a reinforcement of at least eighty men, with which, having laid in a fresh supply of stores, he again set sail for the Rio de San Juan.

The arrival of the new recruits all eager to follow up the expedition, the comfortable change in their circumstances produced by an ample supply of provisions, and the glowing pictures of the wealth that awaited them in the south, all had their effect on the dejected spirits of Pizarro's followers. Their late toils and privations were speedily forgotten, and, with the buoyant and variable feelings incident to a free-booter's life, they now called as eagerly on their commander to go forward in the voyage as they had before called on him to abandon it. Availing themselves of the renewed spirit of enterprise, the captains embarked on board their vessels, and, under the guidance of the veteran pilot, steered in the same track he had lately pursued.

But the favorable season for a southern course, which in these latitudes lasts but a few months in the year, had been suffered to escape. The breezes blew steadily towards the north, and a strong current, not far from shore, set in the same direction. The winds frequently rose into tempests, and the unfortunate voyagers were tossed about, for many days, in the boiling surges, amidst the most awful storms of thunder and lightning, until at length they found a secure haven in the island of Gallo, already visited by Ruiz. As they were now too strong in numbers to apprehend an assault, the crews landed, and, experiencing no molestation from the natives, they continued on the island for a fortnight, refitting their damaged vessels, and recruiting themselves after the fatigues of the ocean. Then, resuming their voyage, the captains stood towards the south until they reached the bay of San Mateo. As they advanced along the coast, they were struck, as Ruiz had been before, with the evidences of a higher civilization constantly exhibited in the general aspect of the country and its inhabitants. The hand of cultivation was visible in every quarter. The natural appearance of the coast, too, had something in it more inviting; for instead of the eternal labyrinth of mangrove trees, with their complicated root snarled into

**"The men and women displayed many ornaments of gold and precious stones about their persons."**

formidable coils under the water, as if to waylay and entangle the voyager, the low margin of the sea was covered with a stately growth of ebony, and with a species of mahogany, and other hard woods that take the most brilliant and variegated polish. The sandalwood, and many balsamic trees of unknown names, scattered their sweet odors far and wide, not in an atmosphere tainted with vegetable corruption, but on the pure breezes of the ocean, bearing health as well as fragrance on their wings. Broad patches of cultivated land intervened, disclosing hillsides covered with the yellow maize and the potato, or checkered, in the lower levels, with blooming plantations of cacao.

The villages became more numerous; and, as the vessels rode at anchor off the port of Atacames, the Spaniards saw before them a town of two thousand houses or more, laid out into streets, with a numerous population clustering around it in the suburbs. The men and women displayed many ornaments of gold and precious stones about their persons, which may seem strange, considering that the Peruvian Incas claimed a monopoly of jewels for themselves and the nobles on whom they condescended to bestow them. But, although the Spaniards had now reached the outer limits of the Peruvian empire, it was not Peru, but Quito, and that portion of it but recently brought under the scepter of the Incas, where the ancient usages of the people could hardly have been effaced under the oppressive system of the American despots.

The adjacent country was, moreover, particularly rich in gold, which, collected from the washings of the streams, still forms one of the staple products of Barbacoas. Here, too, was the fair River of Emeralds, so called from the quarries of the beautiful gem on its borders, from which the Indian monarchs enriched their treasury.

The Spaniards gazed with delight on these undeniable evidences of wealth, and saw in the careful cultivation of the soil a comfortable assurance that they had at length reached the land which had so long been seen in brilliant, though distant, perspective before them. But here again they were doomed to be disappointed by the warlike spirit of the people, who, conscious of their own strength, showed no disposition to quail before the invaders. On the contrary, several of their canoes shot out, loaded with warriors, who, displaying a gold mask as their ensign, hovered round the vessels with looks of defiance, and, when pursued, easily took shelter under the lee of the land.

A more formidable body mustered along the shore, to the number, according to the Spanish accounts, of at least ten thousand warriors, eager, apparently, to come to close action with the invaders. Nor could Pizarro, who had landed with a party of his men in the hope of a conference with the natives, wholly prevent hostilities; and it might have gone hard with the Spaniards, hotly pressed by their resolute enemy so superior in numbers, but for a ludicrous accident reported by the historians as happening to one of the cavaliers. This was a fall from his horse, which so astonished the barbarians, who were not prepared for this division of what seemed one and the same being into two, that, filled with consternation, they fell back, and left a way open for the Christians to regain their vessels!

A council of war was now called. It was evident that the forces of the Spaniards were unequal to a contest with so numerous and well-appointed a body of natives; and even if they should prevail here, they could have no hope of stemming the torrent which must rise against them in their progress —for the country was becoming more and more thickly settled, and towns and hamlets started into view at every new headland which they doubled. It was better, in the opinion of some—the faint-hearted—to abandon the enterprise at once, as beyond their strength. But Almagro took a different view of the affair. "To go home," he said, "with nothing done, would be ruin, as well as disgrace. There was scarcely one but had left creditors at Panamá, who looked for payment to the fruits of this expedition. To go home now would be to deliver themselves at once into their hands. It would be to go to prison. Better to roam a freeman, though in the wilderness, than to lie bound with fetters in the dungeons of Panamá. The only course for them," he concluded, "was the one lately pursued. Pizarro might find some more commodious place where he could remain with part of the force while he himself went back for recruits to Panamá. The story they had now to tell of the riches of the land, as they had seen them with their own eyes, would put their expedition in a very different light, and could not fail to draw to their banner as many volunteers as they needed."

But this recommendation, however judicious, was not altogether to the taste of the latter commander, who did not relish the part, which constantly fell to him, of remaining behind in the swamps and forests of this wild country. "It is all very well," he said to Almagro, "for you, who pass your time pleasantly enough, careering to and fro in your vessel, or snugly sheltered in the land of plenty at Panamá; but it is quite another matter for those who stay behind to droop and die of hunger in the wilderness." To this Almagro retorted with some heat, professing his own willingness to take charge of the brave men who would remain with him, if Pizarro declined it. The controversy assuming a more angry and menacing tone, from words they would have soon come to blows, as both, laying their hands on their swords, were preparing to rush on each other, when the treasurer Ribera, aided by the pilot Ruiz, succeeded in pacifying them. It required but little effort on the part of these cooler counselors to convince the cavaliers of the folly of a conduct which must at once terminate the expedition in a manner little creditable to its projectors, A reconciliation consequently took place, sufficient, at least in outward show, to allow the two commanders to act together in concert. Almagro's plan was then adopted; and it only remained to find out the most secure and convenient spot for Pizarro's quarters.

Several days were passed in touching at different parts of the coast, as they retraced their course; but everywhere the natives appeared to have caught the alarm, and assumed a menacing, and from their numbers a formidable, aspect. The more northerly region, with its unwholesome fens and forests, where nature wages a war even more relentless than man, was not to be thought of. In this perplexity, they decided on the little island of Gallo,[25] as being, on the whole, from its distance from the shore, and from the scantiness of its population, the most eligible spot for them in their forlorn and destitute condition.

But no sooner was the resolution of the two captains made known than a feeling of discontent broke forth among their followers, especially those who were to remain with Pizarro on the island. "What!" they exclaimed, "were they to be dragged to that obscure spot to die by hunger? The whole expedition had been a cheat and a failure, from beginning to end. The golden countries, so much vaunted, had seemed to fly before them as they advanced; and the little gold they had been fortunate enough to glean had all been sent back to Panamá to entice other fools to follow their example. What had they got in return for all their sufferings? The only treasures they could boast were their bows and arrows, and they were now to be left to die on this dreary island, without so much as a rood of consevrated ground to lay their bones in!"

In this exasperated state of feeling, several of the soldiers wrote back to their friends, informing them of their deplorable condition, and complaining of the cold-blooded manner in which they were to be sacrificed to the obstinate cupidity of their leaders. But the latter were wary enough to anticipate this movement, and Almagro defeated it by seizing all the letters in the vessels, and thus cutting off at once the means of communication with their friends at home. Yet this act of unscrupulous violence, like most other similar acts, fell short of its purpose; for a soldier named Sarabia had the ingenuity to evade it by introducing a letter into a ball of cotton, which was to be taken to Panamá as a specimen of the products of the country and presented to the governor's lady.

The letter, which was signed by several of the disaffected soldiery besides the writer, painted in gloomy colors the miseries of their condition, accused the two commanders of being the authors of this, and called on the authorities at Panamá to interfere by sending a vessel to take them from the desolate spot while some of them might still be found surviving the horrors of their confinement. The epistle concluded with a stanza, in which the two leaders were stigmatized as partners in a slaughterhouse—one being employed to drive in the cattle for the other to butcher. The verses, which had a currency in their day among the colonists to which they were certainly not entitled by their poetical merits, may be thus rendered into corresponding doggerel:

> "Look out, Señor Governor,
>     For the drover while he's near;
>     Since he goes home to get the sheep
>     For the butcher, who stays here."

# CHAPTER FOUR



Not long after Almagro's departure, Pizarro sent off the remaining vessel, under the pretext of its being put in repair at Panamá. It probably relieved him of a part of his followers, whose mutinous spirit made them an obstacle rather than a help in his forlorn condition, and with whom he was the more willing to part from the difficulty of finding subsistence on the barren spot which he now occupied.

Great was the dismay occasioned by the return of Almagro and his followers in the little community of Panamá; for the letter surreptitiously conveyed in the ball of cotton fell into the hands for which it was intended, and the contents soon got abroad, with the usual quantity of exaggeration. The haggard and dejected mien of the adventurers of itself told a tale sufficiently disheartening, and it was soon generally believed that the few ill-fated survivors of the expedition were detained against their will by Pizarro, to end their days with their disappointed leader on his desolate island.

Pedro de los Rios, the governor, was so much incensed at the result of the expedition, and the waste of life it had occasioned to the colony, that he turned a deaf ear to all the applications of Luque and Almagro for further countenance in the affair; he derided their sanguine anticipations of the future, and finally resolved to send an officer to the isle of Gallo, with orders to bring back every Spaniard whom he should find still living in that dreary abode. Two vessels were immediately dispatched for the purpose, and placed under charge of a cavalier named Tafur, a native of Cordova.

Meanwhile, Pizarro and his followers were experiencing all the miseries which might have been expected from the character of the barren spot on which they were imprisoned. They were, indeed, relieved from all apprehensions of the natives, since these had quitted the island on its occupation by the white men; but they had to endure the pains of hunger even in a greater degree than they had formerly experienced in the wild woods of the neighboring continent. Their principal food was crabs and such shellfish as they could scantily pick up along the shores. Incessant storms of thunder and lightning, for it was the rainy season, swept over the island, and drenched them with a perpetual flood. Thus, half naked, and pining with famine, there were few in that little company who did not feel the spirit of enterprise quenched within them, or who looked for any happier termination of their difficulties than that afforded by a return to Panamá. The appearance of Tafur, therefore, with his two vessels, well stored with provisions, was greeted with all the rapture that the crew of a sinking wreck might feel on the arrival of some unexpected succor; and the only thought, after satisfying the immediate cravings of hunger, was to embark and leave the detested isle for ever.

But by the same vessel letters came to Pizarro from his two confederates, Luque and Almagro, beseeching him not to despair in his present extremity, but to hold fast to his original purpose. To return under the present circumstances would be to seal the fate of the expedition; and they solemnly engaged, if he would remain firm at his post, to furnish him in a short time with the necessary means for going forward.

A ray of hope was enough for the courageous spirit of Pizarro. It does not appear that he himself had entertained, at any time, thoughts of returning. If he had, these words of encouragement entirely banished them from his bosom, and he prepared to stand the fortune of the cast on which he had so desperately ventured. He knew, however, that solicitations or remonstrances would avail little with the companions of his enterprise; and he probably did not care to win over the more timid spirits who, by perpetually looking back, would only be a clog on his future movements. He announced his own purpose, however, in a laconic but decided manner, characteristic of a man more accustomed to act than to talk, and well calculated to make an impression on his rough followers.

Drawing his sword, he traced a line with it on the sand from east to west. Then, turning towards the south, "Friends and comrades!" he said, "on that side are toil, hunger, nakedness, the drenching storm, desertion, and death; on this side, ease and pleasure. There lies Peru with its riches; here, Panamá and its poverty. Choose, each man, what best becomes a brave Castilian. For my part, I go to the south." So saying, he stepped across the line. He was followed by the brave pilot Ruiz; next by Pedro de Candia, a cavalier, born, as his name imports, in one of the isles of Greece. Eleven others successively crossed the line, thus intimating their willingness to abide the fortunes of their leader, for good or for evil. Fame, to quote the enthusiastic language of an ancient chronicler, has commemorated the names of this little band, "who thus, in the face of difficulties unexampled in history, with death rather than riches for their reward, preferred it all to abandoning their honor, and stood firm by their leader as an example of loyalty to future ages."

But the act excited no such admiration in the mind of Tafur, who looked on it as one of gross disobedience to the commands of the governor, and as little better than madness, involving the certain destruction of the parties engaged in it. He refused to give any sanction to it himself by leaving one of his vessels with the adventurers to prosecute their voyage, and it was with great difficulty that he could be persuaded even to allow them a part of the stores which he had brought for their support. This had no influence on their determination, and the little party, bidding adieu to their returning comrades, remained unshaken in their purpose of abiding the fortunes of their commander.

There is something striking to the imagination in the spectacle of these few brave spirits thus consecrating themselves to a daring enterprise, which seemed as far above their strength as any recorded in the fabulous annals of knight-errantry. A handful of men, without food, without clothing, almost without arms, without knowledge of the land to which they were bound, without vessel to transport them, were here left on a lonely rock in the ocean with the avowed purpose of carrying on a crusade against a powerful empire, staking their lives on its success. What is there in the legends of chivalry that surpasses it? This was the crisis of Pizarro's fate. There are moments in the lives of men, which, as they are seized or neglected, decide their future destiny. Had

Pizarro faltered from his strong purpose, and yielded to the occasion, now so temptingly presented, for extricating himself and his broken band from their desperate position, his name would have been buried with his fortunes, and the conquest of Peru would have been left for other and more successful adventurers. But his constancy was equal to the occasion, and his conduct here proved him competent to the perilous post he had assumed, and inspired others with a confidence in him which was the best assurance of success.

In the vessel that bore back Tafur and those who seceded from the expedition the pilot Ruiz was also permitted to return, in order to co-operate with Luque and Almagro in their application for further succor.

Not long after the departure of the ships, it was decided by Pizarro to abandon his present quarters, which had little to recommend them, and which, he reflected, might now be exposed to annoyance from the original inhabitants, should they take courage and return on learning the diminished number of the white men. The Spaniards, therefore, by his orders, constructed a rude boat or raft, on which they succeeded in transporting themselves to the little island of Gorgona, twenty-five leagues to the north of their present residence. It lay about five leagues from the continent, and was uninhabited. It had some advantages over the isle of Gallo; for it stood higher above the sea, and was partially covered with wood, which afforded shelter to a species of pheasant, and the hare or rabbit of the country, so that the Spaniards, with their crossbows, were enabled to procure a tolerable supply of game. Cool streams that issued from the living rock furnished abundance of water, though the drenching rains that fell without intermission left them in no danger of perishing by thirst. From this annoyance they found some protection in the rude huts which they constructed; though here, as in their former residence, they suffered from the no less intolerable annoyance of venomous insects, which multiplied and swarmed in the exhalations of the rank and stimulated soil. In this dreary abode Pizarro omitted no means by which to sustain the drooping spirits of his men. Morning prayers were duly said, and the evening hymn to the Virgin was regularly chanted; the festivals of the Church were carefully commemorated, and every means taken by their commander to give a kind of religious character to his enterprise, and to inspire his rough followers with a confidence in the protection of Heaven, that might support them in their perilous circumstances.

In these uncomfortable quarters, their chief employment was to keep watch on the melancholy ocean, that they might hail the first signal of the anticipated succor. But many a tedious month passed away, and no sign of it appeared. All around was the same wide waste of waters, except to the eastward, where the frozen crest of the Andes, touched with the ardent sun of the equator, glowed like a ridge of fire along the whole extent of the great continent. Every speck in the distant horizon was carefully noticed, and the drifting timber or masses of sea weed, heaving to and fro on the bosom of the waters, was converted by their imaginations into the promised vessel; till, sinking under successive disappointments, hope gradually gave way to doubt, and doubt settled into despair.

Meanwhile the vessel of Tafur had reached the port of Panamá. The tidings which she brought of the inflexible obstinacy of Pizarro and his followers filled the governor with indignation. He could look on it in no other light than as an act of suicide, and steadily refused to send further assistance to men who were obstinately bent on their own destruction. Yet Luque and Almagro were true to their engagements. They represented to the governor that, if the conduct of their comrade was rash, it was at least in the service of the crown and in prosecuting the great work of discovery. Rios had been instructed, on his taking the government, to aid Pizarro in the enterprise; and to desert him now would be to throw away the remaining chance of success, and to incur the responsibility of his death and that of the brave men who adhered to him. These remonstrances, at length, so far operated on the mind of that functionary that he reluctantly consented that a vessel should be sent to the island of Gorgona, but with no more hands than were necessary to work her, and with positive instructions to Pizarro to return in six months and report himself at Panamá, whatever might be the future results of his expedition.

Having thus secured the sanction of the executive, the two associates lost no time in fitting out a small vessel with stores and a supply of arms and ammunition, and dispatched it to the island. The unfortunate tenants of this little wilderness, who had now occupied it for seven months, hardly dared to trust their senses when they descried the white sails of the friendly bark coming over the waters. And although, when the vessel anchored off the shore, Pizarro was disappointed to find that it brought no additional recruits for the enterprise, yet he greeted it with joy, as affording the means of solving the great problem of the existence of the rich southern empire, and of thus opening the way for its future conquest. Two of his men were so ill that it was determined to leave them in the care of some of the friendly Indians who had continued with him through the whole of his sojourn, and to call for them on his return. Taking with him the rest of his hardy followers and the natives of Tumbes, he embarked, and, speedily weighing anchor, bade adieu to the "Hell," as it was called by the Spaniards, which had been the scene of so much suffering and such undaunted resolution.

Every heart was now elated with hope, as they found themselves once more on the waters, under the guidance of the good pilot Ruiz, who, obeying the directions of the Indians, proposed to steer for the land of Tumbes, which would bring them at once into the golden empire of the Incas—the El Dorado of which they had been so long in pursuit. Passing by the dreary isle of Gallo, which they had such good cause to remember, they stood farther out to sea until they made Point Atacames, near which they had landed on their previous voyage. They did not touch at any part of the coast, but steadily held on their way, though considerably impeded by the currents, as well as by the wind, which blew with little variation from the south. Fortunately, the wind was light, and, as the weather was favorable, their voyage, though slow, was not uncomfortable. In a few days they came in sight of Point Pasado, the limit of the pilot's former navigation; and, crossing the line, the little bark entered upon those unknown seas which had never been plowed by European keel before. The coast, they observed, gradually declined from its former bold and rugged character, gently sloping towards the shore, and spreading out into sandy plains, relieved here and there by patches of uncommon richness and beauty; while the white cottages of the natives glistening along the margin of the sea, and the smoke that rose among the distant hills, intimated the increasing population of the country.

At length, after the lapse of twenty days from their departure from the island, the adventurous vessel rounded the point of St. Helena and glided smoothly into the waters of the beautiful gulf of Guayaquil. The country was here studded along the shore with towns and villages, though the mighty chain of the Cordilleras, sweeping up abruptly from the coast, left but a narrow strip of emerald verdure through which numerous rivulets, spreading fertility around them, wound their way to the sea.

The voyagers were now abreast of some of the most stupendous heights of this magnificent range; Chimborazo, with its broad round summit, towering like the dome of the Andes, and Cotopaxi, with its dazzling cone of silvery white, that knows no change except from the action of its own volcanic fires; for this mountain is the most terrible of the American volcanoes, and was in formidable activity at no great distance from the period of our narrative. Well pleased with the signs of civilization that opened on them at every league of their progress, the Spaniards at length came to anchor, off the island of Santa Clara, lying at the entrance of the bay of Tumbes.

The place was uninhabited, but was recognized by the Indians on board as occasionally resorted to by the warlike people of the neighboring island of Puná [26] for purposes of sacrifice and worship. The Spaniards found on the spot a few bits of gold rudely wrought into various shapes, and probably designed as offerings to the Indian deity. Their hearts were cheered, as the natives assured them they would see abundance of the same precious metal in their own city of Tumbes.

The following morning they stood across the bay for this place. As they drew near, they beheld a town of considerable size, with many of the buildings apparently of stone and plaster, situated in the bosom of a fruitful meadow, which seemed to have been redeemed from the sterility of the surrounding country by careful and minute irrigation. When at some distance from shore, Pizarro saw standing towards him several large balsas, which were found to be filled with warriors going on an expedition against the island of Puná. Running alongside of the Indian flotilla, he invited some of the chiefs to come on board of his vessel. The Peruvians gazed with wonder on every object which met their eyes, and especially on their own countrymen, whom they had little expected to meet there. The latter informed them in what manner they had fallen into the hands of the strangers, whom they described as a wonderful race of beings, that had come thither for no harm, but solely to be made acquainted with the country and its inhabitants. This account was confirmed by the Spanish commander, who persuaded the Indians to return in their balsas and report what they had learned to their townsmen, requesting them at the same time to provide his vessel with refreshments, as it was his desire to enter into friendly intercourse with the natives.

The people of Tumbes were gathered along the shore, and were gazing with unutterable amazement on the floating castle, which, now having dropped anchor, rode lazily at its moorings in their bay. They eagerly listened to the accounts of their countrymen, and instantly reported the affair to the *curaca* or ruler of the district, who, conceiving that the strangers must be beings of a superior order, prepared at once to comply with their request. It was not long before several balsas were seen steering for the vessel, laden with bananas, plantains, yucca, Indian corn, sweet potatoes, pineapples, cocoanuts,[27] and other rich products of the bountiful vale of Tumbes. Game and fish, also, were added, with a number of llamas, of which Pizarro had seen the rude drawings belonging to Balboa, but of which till now he had met with no living specimen. He examined this curious animal, the Peruvian sheep—or, as the Spaniards called it, the "little camel" of the Indians—with much interest, greatly admiring the mixture of wool and hair which supplied the natives with the materials for their fabrics.

At that time there happened to be at Tumbes an Inca noble, or *orejon*—for so, as I have already noticed, men of his rank were called by the Spaniards, from the huge ornaments of gold attached to their ears. He expressed great curiosity to see the wonderful strangers, and had, accordingly, come out with the balsas for the purpose. It was easy to perceive, from the superior quality of his dress, as well as from the deference paid to him by the others, that he was a person of consideration; and Pizarro received him with marked distinction. He showed him the different parts of the ship, explaining to him the uses of whatever engaged his attention, and answering his numerous queries, as well as he could, by means of the Indian interpreters. The Peruvian chief was especially desirous of knowing whence and why Pizarro and his followers had come to these shores. The Spanish captain replied that he was the vassal of a great prince, the greatest and most powerful in the world, and that he had come to this country to assert his master's *lawful supremacy* over it. He had further come to rescue the inhabitants from the darkness of unbelief in which they were now wandering. They worshiped an evil spirit, who would sink their souls into everlasting perdition; and he would give them the knowledge of the true and only God, Jesus Christ, since to believe in Him was eternal salvation.

The Indian prince listened with deep attention and apparent wonder, but answered nothing. It may be that neither he nor his interpreters had any very distinct ideas of the doctrines thus abruptly revealed to them. It may be that he did not believe there was any other potentate on earth greater than the Inca; none, at least, who had a better right to rule over his dominions. And it is very possible he was not disposed to admit that the great luminary whom he worshiped was inferior to the God of the Spaniards. But whatever may have passed in the untutored mind of the barbarian, he did not give vent to it, but maintained a discreet silence, without any attempt to controvert or to convince his Christian antagonist.

He remained on board the vessel till the hour of dinner, of which he partook with the Spaniards, expressing his satisfaction at the strange dishes, and especially pleased with the wine, which he pronounced far superior to the fermented liquors of his own country. On taking leave, he courteously pressed the Spaniards to visit Tumbes, and Pizarro dismissed him with the present, among other things, of an iron hatchet, which had greatly excited his admiration; for the use of iron, as we have seen, was as little known to the Peruvians as to the Mexicans.

On the day following, the Spanish captain sent one of his own men, named Alonso de Molina, on shore, accompanied by a Negro who had come in the vessel from Panamá, together with a present for the curaca of some swine and poultry, neither of which was indigenous to the New World. Towards evening his emissary returned with a fresh supply of fruits and vegetables, that the friendly people sent to the vessel. Molina had a wondrous tale to tell. On landing, he was surrounded by the natives, who expressed the greatest astonishment at his dress, his fair complexion, and his long beard. The women, especially, manifested great curiosity in respect to him, and Molina seemed to be entirely won by their charms and captivating manners. He probably intimated

**"On landing, Molina was surrounded by the natives, who expressed the greatest astonishment at his dress, his fair complexion, and his long beard."**

his satisfaction by his demeanor, since they urged him to stay among them, promising in that case to provide him with a beautiful wife.

Their surprise was equally great at the complexion of his sable companion. They could not believe it was natural, and tried to rub off the imaginary dye with their hands. As the African bore all this with characteristic good humor, displaying at the same time his rows of ivory teeth, they were prodigiously delighted. The animals were no less above their comprehension; and when the cock crew, the simple people clapped their hands and inquired what he was saying. Their

"Pedro de Candia, the Greek cavalier . . . was sent on shore, dressed in complete mail . . . with his sword by his side and his arquebuse on his shoulder."

intellects were so bewildered by sights so novel that they seemed incapable of distinguishing between man and brute.

Molina was then escorted to the residence of the curaca, whom he found living in much state, with porters stationed at his doors, and with a quantity of gold and silver vessels, from which he was served. He was then taken to different parts of the Indian city, and saw a fortress built of rough stone, and, though low, spreading over a large extent of ground. Near this was a temple; and the Spaniard's description of its decorations, blazing with gold and silver, seemed so extravagant that Pizarro, distrusting his whole account, resolved to send a more discreet and trustworthy emissary on the following day.

The person selected was Pedro de Candia,[28] the Greek cavalier mentioned as one of the first who intimated his intention to share the fortunes of his commander. He was sent on shore, dressed in complete mail, as became a good knight, with his sword by his side, and his arquebus on his shoulder. The Indians were even more dazzled by his appearance than by Molina's, as the sun fell brightly on his polished armor and glanced from his military weapons. They had heard much of the formidable arquebus from their townsmen who had come in the vessel, and they besought Candia "to let it speak to them." He accordingly set up a wooden board as a target, and, taking deliberate aim, fired off the musket. The flash of the powder and the startling report of the piece, as the board, struck by the ball, was shivered into splinters, filled the natives with dismay. Some fell on the ground, covering their faces with their hands, and others approached the cavalier with feelings of awe, which were gradually dispelled by the assurance they received from the smiling expression of his countenance.

They then showed him the same hospitable attentions which they had paid to Molina; and his description of the marvels of the place, on his return, fell nothing short of his predecessor's. The fortress, which was surrounded by a triple row of wall, was strongly garrisoned. The temple he described as literally tapestried with plates of gold and silver. Adjoining this structure was a sort of convent appropriated to the Inca's destined brides, who manifested great curiosity to see him. Whether this was gratified is not clear; but Candia described the gardens of the convent, which he entered, as glowing with imitations of fruits and vegetables all in pure gold and silver. He had seen a number of artisans at work, whose sole business seemed to be to furnish these gorgeous decorations for the religious houses.

The reports of the cavalier may have been somewhat over-colored. It was natural that men coming from the dreary wilderness in which they had been buried the last six months should have been vividly impressed by the tokens of civilization which met them on the Peruvian coast. But Tumbes was a favorite city of the Peruvian princes. It was the most important place on the northern borders of the empire, contiguous to the recent acquisition of Quito. The great Topa Inca had established a strong fortress there, and peopled it with a colony of *mitimaes*. The temple, and the house occupied by the Virgins of the Sun, had been erected by Huayna

Capac, and were liberally endowed by that Inca, after the sumptuous fashion of the religious establishments of Peru. The town was well supplied with water by numerous aqueducts; and the fruitful valley in which it was embosomed, and the ocean which bathed its shores, supplied ample means of subsistence to a considerable population. But the cupidity of the Spaniards, after the Conquest, was not slow in despoiling the place of its glories; and the site of its proud towers and temples, in less than half a century after that fatal period, was to be traced only by the huge mass of ruins that encumbered the ground.[29]

The Spaniards were nearly mad with joy, says an old writer, at receiving these brilliant tidings of the Peruvian city. All their fond dreams were now to be realized, and they had at length reached the realm which had so long flitted in visionary splendor before them. Pizarro expressed his gratitude to heaven for having crowned his labors with so glorious a result; but he bitterly lamented the hard fate which, by depriving him of his followers, denied him, at such a moment, the means of availing himself of his success. Yet he had no cause for lamentation; and the devout Catholic saw in this very circumstance a providential interposition which prevented the attempt at conquest while such attempts would have been premature. Peru was not yet torn asunder by the dissensions of rival candidates for the throne; and, united and strong under the scepter of a warlike monarch, she might well have bid defiance to all the forces that Pizarro could muster. "It was manifestly the work of Heaven," exclaims a devout son of the Church, "that the natives of the country should have received him in so kind and loving a spirit as best fitted to facilitate the conquest; for it was the Lord's hand which led him and his followers to this remote region for the extension of the holy faith, and for the salvation of souls."

Having now collected all the information essential to his object, Pizarro, after taking leave of the natives of Tumbes and promising a speedy return, weighed anchor, and again turned his prow towards the south. Still keeping as near as possible to the coast, that no place of importance might escape his observation, he passed Cape Blanco, and, after sailing about a degree and a half, made the port of Payta. The inhabitants, who had notice of his approach, came out in their balsas to get sight of the wonderful strangers, bringing with them stores of fruits, fish, and vegetables, with the same hospitable spirit shown by their countrymen at Tumbes.

After staying here a short time, and interchanging presents

**"Everywhere Pizarro was received with the same spirit of generous hospitality; the natives coming out in their balsas to welcome him, laden with their little cargoes of fruits and vegetables."**

of trifling value with the natives, Pizarro continued his cruise; and sailing by the sandy plains of Sechura for an extent of near a hundred miles, he doubled the Punta de Aguja, and swept down the coast as it fell off towards the east, still carried forward by light and somewhat variable breezes. The weather now became unfavorable, and the voyagers encountered a succession of heavy gales, which drove them some distance out to sea and tossed them about for many days. But they did not lose sight of the mighty ranges of the Andes, which, as they proceeded towards the south, were still seen, at nearly the same distance from the shore, rolling onwards, peak after peak, with their stupendous surges of ice, like some vast ocean that had been suddenly arrested and frozen up in the midst of its wild and tumultuous career. With this landmark always in view, the navigator had little need of star or compass to guide his bark on her course.

As soon as the tempest had subsided, Pizarro stood in again for the continent, touching at the principal points as he coasted along. Everywhere he was received with the same spirit of generous hospitality, the natives coming out in their balsas to welcome him, laden with their little cargoes of fruits and vegetables, of all the luscious varieties that grow in the *tierra caliente*. All were eager to have a glimpse of the strangers, the "Children of the Sun," as the Spaniards began already to be called, from their fair complexions, brilliant armor, and the thunderbolts which they bore in their hands. The most favorable reports, too, had preceded them, of the urbanity and gentleness of their manners, thus unlocking the hearts of the simple natives and disposing them to confidence and kindness. The iron-hearted soldier had not yet disclosed the darker side of his character. He was too weak to do so. The hour of conquest had not yet come.

In every place Pizarro received the same accounts of a powerful monarch who ruled over the land, and held his court on the mountain plains of the interior, where his capital was depicted as blazing with gold and silver, and displaying all the profusion of an Oriental satrap. The Spaniards, except at Tumbes, seem to have met with little of the precious metals among the natives on the coast. More than one writer asserts that they did not covet them, or at least, by Pizarro's orders, affected not to do so. He would not have them betray their appetite for gold, and actually refused gifts when they were proffered! It is more probable that they saw little display of wealth, except in the embellishments of the temples and other sacred buildings, which they did not dare to violate. The precious metals, reserved for the uses of religion and for persons of high degree, were not likely to abound in the remote towns and hamlets on the coast.

Yet the Spaniards met with sufficient evidence of general civilization and power to convince them that there was much foundation for the reports of the natives. Repeatedly they saw structures of stone and plaster, occasionally showing architectural skill in the execution, if not elegance of design. Wherever they cast anchor, they beheld green patches of cultivated country redeemed from the sterility of nature and blooming with the variegated vegetation of the tropics; while a refined system of irrigation, by means of aqueducts and canals, seemed to be spread like a network over the surface of the country, making even the desert to blossom as the rose. At many places where they landed they saw the great road of the Incas, which traversed the seacoast, often, indeed, lost in the volatile sands, where no road could be maintained, but rising into a broad and substantial causeway as it emerged on a firmer soil. Such a provision for internal communication was in itself no slight monument of power and civilization.

Still beating to the south, Pizarro passed the site of the future flourishing city of Trujillo, founded by himself some years later, and pressed on till he rode off the port of Santa. It stood on the banks of a broad and beautiful stream; but the surrounding country was so exceedingly arid that it was frequently selected for the preservation of their mummies. So numerous, indeed, were the Indian *huacas* that the place might rather be called the abode of the dead than of the living.[30]

Having reached this point, about the ninth degree of southern latitude, Pizarro's followers besought him not to prosecute the voyage farther. Enough and more than enough had been done, they said, to prove the existence and actual position of the great Indian empire of which they had so long been in search. Yet, with their slender force, they had no power to profit by the discovery. All that remained, therefore, was to return and report the success of their enterprise to the governor at Panamá. Pizarro acquiesced in the reasonableness of this demand. He had now penetrated nine degrees farther than any former navigator in these southern seas, and instead of the blight which, up to this hour, had seemed to hang over his fortunes, he could now return in triumph to his countrymen. Without hesitation, therefore, he prepared to retrace his course, and stood again towards the north.

On his way he touched at several places where he had before landed. At one of these, called by the Spaniards Santa Cruz, he had been invited on shore by an Indian woman of rank, and had promised to visit her on his return. No sooner did his vessel cast anchor off the village where she lived, than she came on board, followed by a numerous train of attendants. Pizarro received her with every mark of respect, and on her departure presented her with some trinkets which had a real value in the eyes of an Indian princess. She urged the Spanish commander and his companions to return the visit, engaging to send a number of hostages on board as security for their good treatment. Pizarro assured her that the frank confidence she had shown towards them proved that this was unnecessary. Yet no sooner did he put off in his boat, the following day, to go on shore, than several of the principal persons in the place came alongside of the ship to be received as hostages during the absence of the Spaniards— a singular proof of consideration for the sensitive apprehensions of her guests.

Pizarro found that preparations had been made for his reception in a style of simple hospitality that evinced some degree of taste. Arbors were formed of luxuriant and widespreading branches, interwoven with fragrant flowers and shrubs that diffused a delicious perfume through the air. A banquet was provided, teeming with viands prepared in the style of the Peruvian cookery, and with fruits and vegetables of tempting hue and luscious to the taste, though their names and nature were unknown to the Spaniards. After the collation was ended, the guests were entertained with music and dancing by a troop of young men and maidens simply attired, who exhibited in their favorite national amusement all the agility and grace which the supple limbs of the Peruvian Indians so well qualified them to display. Before his departure, Pizarro stated to his kind host the motives of his visit to the country, in the same manner as he had done on other occasions, and he concluded by unfurling the royal banner of Castile, which he had brought on shore, requesting her and her attendants to raise it in token of their allegiance to his sovereign. This they did with great good humor, laughing all the while, says the chronicler, and making it clear that they had a very imperfect conception of the serious nature of the ceremony. Pizarro was contented with this outward display of loyalty, and returned to his vessel well satisfied with the entertainment he had received, and meditating, it may be, on the best mode of repaying it, hereafter, by the subjugation and conversion of the country.

The Spanish commander did not omit to touch also at Tumbes on his homeward voyage. Here some of his followers, won by the comfortable aspect of the place and the manners of the people, intimated a wish to remain, conceiving, no doubt, that it would be better to live where they would be persons of consequence than to return to an obscure condition in the community of Panamá. One of these men was Alonso de Molina, the same who had first gone on shore at this place and been captivated by the charms of the Indian beauties. Pizarro complied with their wishes, thinking it would not be amiss to find, on his return, some of his own followers who would be instructed in the language and usage of the natives. He was also allowed to carry back in his vessel two or three Peruvians, for the similar purpose of instructing them in the Castilian. One of them, a youth named by the Spaniards Felipillo, plays a part of some importance in the history of subsequent events.

On leaving Tumbes the adventurers steered directly for Panamá, touching only, on their way, at the ill-fated island of

Gorgona, to take on board their two companions who were left there too ill to proceed with them. One had died; and, receiving the other, Pizarro and his gallant little band continued their voyage, and, after an absence of at least eighteen months, found themselves once more safely riding at anchor in the harbor of Panamá.

The sensation caused by their arrival was great, as might have been expected. For there were few, even among the most sanguine of their friends, who did not imagine that they had long since paid for their temerity, and fallen victims to the climate or the natives, or miserably perished in a watery grave. Their joy was proportionably great, therefore, as they saw the wanderers now returned, not only in health and safety, but with certain tidings of the fair countries which had so long eluded their grasp. It was a moment of proud satisfaction to the three associates, who, in spite of obloquy, derision, and every impediment which the distrust of friends or the coldness of government could throw in their way, had persevered in their great enterprise until they had established the truth of what had been so generally denounced as a chimera. It is the misfortune of those daring spirits who conceive an idea too vast for their own generation to comprehend, or, at least, to attempt to carry out, that they pass for visionary dreamers. Such had been the fate of Luque and his associates. The existence of a rich Indian empire at the south, which in their minds, dwelling long on the same idea and alive to all the arguments in its favor, had risen to the certainty of conviction, had been derided by the rest of their countrymen as a mere *mirage* of the fancy, which, on nearer approach, would melt into air; while the projectors who staked their fortunes on the adventure were denounced as madmen. But their hour of triumph, their slow and hard-earned triumph, had now arrived.

Yet the governor, Pedro de los Rios, did not seem, even at this moment, to be possessed with a conviction of the magnitude of the discovery—or perhaps he was discouraged by its very magnitude. When the associates now with more confidence applied to him for patronage in an undertaking too vast for their individual resources, he coldly replied, "He had no desire to build up other states at the expense of his own; nor would he be led to throw away more lives than had already been sacrificed by the cheap display of gold and silver toys and a few llamas!"

Sorely disheartened by this repulse from the only quarter whence effectual aid could be expected, the confederates, without funds, and with credit nearly exhausted by their past efforts, were perplexed in the extreme. Yet to stop now—

what was it but to abandon the rich mine which their own industry and perseverance had laid open, for others to work at pleasure? In this extremity the fruitful mind of Luque suggested the only expedient by which they could hope for success. This was to apply to the crown itself. No one was so much interested in the result of the expedition. It was for the government, indeed, that discoveries were to be made, that the country was to be conquered. The government alone was competent to provide the requisite means, and was likely to take a much broader and more liberal view of the matter than a petty colonial officer.

But who was there qualified to take charge of this delicate mission? Luque was chained by his professional duties to Panamá; and his associates, unlettered soldiers, were much better fitted for the business of the camp than of the court. Almagro, blunt, though somewhat swelling and ostentatious in his address, with a diminutive stature and a countenance naturally plain, now much disfigured by the loss of an eye, was not so well qualified for the mission as his companion in arms, who, possessing a good person and altogether a commanding presence, was plausible, and, with all his defects of education, could, where deeply interested, be even eloquent in discourse. The ecclesiastic, however, suggested that the negotiation should be committed to the Licentiate Corral, a respectable functionary, then about to return on some public business to the mother country. But to this Almagro strongly objected. No one, he said, could conduct the affair so well as the party interested in it. He had a high opinion of Pizarro's prudence, his discernment of character, and his cool, deliberate policy. He knew enough of his comrade to have confidence that his presence of mind would not desert him even in the new, and therefore embarrassing, circumstances in which he would be placed at court. No one, he said, could tell the story of their adventures with such effect as the man who had been the chief actor in them. No one could so well paint the unparalleled sufferings and sacrifices which they had encountered; no one could tell so forcibly what had been done, what yet remained to do, and what assistance would be necessary to carry it into execution. He concluded, with characteristic frankness, by strongly urging his confederate to undertake the mission.

Pizarro felt the force of Almagro's reasoning and, though with undisguised reluctance, acquiesced in a measure which was less to his taste than an expedition to the wilderness. But Luque came into the arrangement with more difficulty. "God grant, my children," exclaimed the ecclesiastic, "that one of you may not defraud the other of his blessing!" Pizarro engaged to consult the interests of his associates equally with his own. But Luque, it is clear, did not trust Pizarro.

There was some difficulty in raising the funds necessary for putting the envoy in condition to make a suitable appearance at court; so low had the credit of the confederates fallen, and so little confidence was yet placed in the result of their splendid discoveries. Fifteen hundred ducats were at length raised; and Pizarro, in the spring of 1528, bade adieu to Panamá, accompanied by Pedro de Candia. He took with him, also, some of the natives, as well as two or three llamas, various nice fabrics of cloth, with many ornaments and vases of gold and silver, as specimens of the civilization of the country, and vouchers for his wonderful story.

# BOOK III

## Conquest of Peru

### ❧ CHAPTER ONE ☙

PIZARRO'S RECEPTION AT COURT—HIS CAPITULATION
WITH THE CROWN—HE VISITS HIS BIRTHPLACE—
RETURNS TO THE NEW WORLD—DIFFICULTIES
WITH ALMAGRO—HIS THIRD EXPEDITION—
ADVENTURES ON THE COAST—
BATTLES IN THE ISLE OF PUNÁ

(1528–1531)

Pizarro and his officer, having crossed the Isthmus, embarked at Nombre de Dios for the old country, and, after a good passage, reached Seville early in the summer of 1528. There happened to be at that time in port a person well known in the history of Spanish adventure as the Bachelor Enciso. He had taken an active part in the colonization of Tierra Firme, and had a pecuniary claim against the early colonists of Darien, of whom Pizarro was one. Immediately on the landing of the latter, he was seized by Enciso's orders and held in custody for the debt. Pizarro, who had fled from his native land as a forlorn and houseless adventurer, after an absence of more than twenty years, passed, most of them, in unprecedented toil and suffering, now found himself on his return the inmate of a prison. Such was the commencement of those brilliant fortunes which, as he had trusted, awaited him at home. The circumstance excited general indignation; and no sooner was the court advised of his arrival in the country and the great purpose of his mission than orders were sent for his release, with permission to proceed at once on his journey.

Pizarro found the emperor at Toledo, which he was soon to quit in order to embark for Italy. Spain was not the favorable residence of Charles the Fifth in the earlier part of his reign. He was now at that period of it when he was enjoying the full flush of his triumphs over his gallant rival of France, whom he had defeated and taken prisoner at the great battle of Pavia; and the victor was at this moment preparing to pass into Italy to receive the imperial crown from the hands of the Roman Pontiff. Elated by his successes and his elevation to the German throne, Charles made little account of his hereditary kingdom, as his ambition found so splendid a career thrown open to it on the wide field of European politics. He had hitherto received too inconsiderable returns from his transatlantic possessions to give them the attention they deserved. But, as the recent acquisition of Mexico and the brilliant anticipation in respect to the southern continent were pressed upon his notice, he felt their importance as likely to afford him the means of prosecuting his ambitious and most expensive enterprises.

Pizarro, therefore, who had now come to satisfy the royal eyes, by visible proofs, of the truth of the golden rumors which from time to time had reached Castile, was graciously received by the emperor. Charles examined the various objects which his officer exhibited to him with great attention. He was particularly interested by the appearance of the llama, so remarkable as the only beast of burden yet known on the new continent; and the fine fabrics of woolen cloth which were made from its shaggy sides gave it a much higher value, in the eyes of the sagacious monarch, than what it possessed as an animal for domestic labor. But the specimens of gold and silver manufacture, and the wonderful tale which Pizarro had to tell of the abundance of the precious metals, must have satisfied even the cravings of royal cupidity.

Pizarro, far from being embarrassed by the novelty of his situation, maintained his usual self-possession, and showed that decorum and even dignity in his address which belong to the Castilian. He spoke in a simple and respectful style, but with the earnestness and natural eloquence of one who had been an actor in the scenes he described, and who was conscious that the impression he made on his audience was to decide his future destiny. All listened with eagerness to the account of his strange adventures by sea and land, his wanderings in the forests, or in the dismal and pestilent swamps on the seacoast, without food, almost without raiment, with feet torn and bleeding at every step, with his few companions becoming still fewer by disease and death, and yet pressing on with unconquerable spirit to extend the empire of Castile and the name and power of her sovereign; but when he painted his lonely condition on the desolate island, abandoned by the government at home, deserted by all but a handful of devoted followers, his royal auditor, though not easily moved, was affected to tears. On his departure from Toledo, Charles commended the affairs of his vassal in the most favorable terms to the consideration of the Council of the Indies.

There was at this time another man at court, who had come there on a similar errand from the New World, but whose splendid achievements had already won for him a name that threw the rising reputation of Pizarro comparatively into the shade. This man was Hernando Cortés, the Conqueror of Mexico. He had come home to lay an empire at the feet of his sovereign, and to demand in return the redress of his wrongs and the recompense of his great services. He was at the close of his career, as Pizarro was at the commencement of his; the Conqueror of the North and of the South; the two men appointed by Providence to overturn the most potent of the Indian dynasties, and to open the golden gates by which the treasures of the New World were to pass into the coffers of Spain.

Notwithstanding the emperor's recommendation, the business of Pizarro went forward at the tardy pace with which affairs are usually conducted in the court of Castile. He found his limited means gradually sinking under the expenses incurred by his present situation, and he represented that unless some measures were speedily taken in reference to his suit, however favorable they might be in the end, he should be in no condition to profit by them. The queen, accordingly, who had charge of the business, on her husband's departure, expedited the affair, and on the twenty-sixth of July, 1529, she executed the memorable *Capitulation* which defined the powers and privileges of Pizarro.

The instrument secured to that chief the right of discovery and conquest in the province of Peru, or New Castile—as the country was then called, in the same manner as Mexico had received the name of New Spain—for the distance of two hundred leagues south of Santiago. He was to receive the titles and rank of Governor and Captain-General of the province, together with those of Adelantado and Alguacil Mayor, for life; and he was to have a salary of seven hundred and twenty-five thousand maravedis,[31] with the obligation of maintaining certain officers and military retainers, corresponding with the dignity of his station. He was to have the right to erect certain fortresses, with the absolute government of them; to assign *encomiendas* of Indians, under the limitations prescribed by law; and, in fine, to exercise nearly all the prerogatives incident to the authority of a viceroy.

His associate, Almagro, was declared commander of the fortress of Tumbes, with an annual rent of three hundred thousand maravedis, and with the further rank and privileges of an hidalgo. The Reverend Father Luque received the reward for his services in the bishopric of Tumbes, and he was also declared Protector of the Indians of Peru. He was to enjoy the yearly stipend of a thousand ducats—to be derived, like the other salaries and gratuities in this instrument, from the revenues of the conquered territory.

Nor were the subordinate actors in the expedition forgotten. Ruiz received the title of Grand Pilot of the Southern Ocean, with a liberal provision; Candia was placed at the head of the artillery; and the remaining eleven companions on the desolate island were created hidalgos and cavalleros, and raised to certain municipal dignities—in prospect.

Several provisions of a liberal tenor were also made, to encourage emigration to the country. The new settlers were to be exempted from some of the most onerous but customary taxes, as the *alcabala,* or to be subject to them only in a mitigated form. The tax on the precious metals drawn from mines was to be reduced, at first, to one-tenth, instead of the fifth imposed on the same metals when obtained by barter or by rapine.

It was expressly enjoined on Pizarro to observe the existing regulations for the good government and protection of the natives; and he was required to carry out with him a specified number of ecclesiastics, with whom he was to take counsel in the conquest of the country, and whose efforts were to be dedicated to the service and conversion of the Indians; while lawyers and attorneys, on the other hand, whose presence was considered as boding ill to the harmony of the new settlements, were strictly prohibited from setting foot in them.

Pizarro, on his part, was bound, in six months from the date of the instrument, to raise a force, well equipped for the service, of two hundred and fifty men, of whom one hundred might be drawn from the colonies; and the government engaged to furnish some trifling assistance in the purchase of artillery and military stores. Finally, he was to be prepared, in six months after his return to Panamá, to leave that port and embark on his expedition.

Such are some of the principal provisions of this Capitulation, by which the Castilian government, with the sagacious policy which it usually pursued on the like occasions, stimulated the ambitious hopes of the adventurer by high-sounding titles and liberal promises of reward contingent on his success, but took care to stake nothing itself on the issue of the enterprise. It was careful to reap the fruits of his toil, but not to pay the cost of them.

A circumstance that could not fail to be remarked in these provisions was the manner in which the high and lucrative posts were accumulated on Pizarro, to the exclusion of Almagro, who, if he had not taken as conspicuous a part in personal toil and exposure, had at least divided with him the original burden of the enterprise, and, by his labors in another direction, had contributed quite as essentially to its success. Almagro had willingly conceded the post of honor to his confederate; but it had been stipulated, on Pizarro's departure for Spain, that, while he solicited the office of Governor and Captain-General for himself, he should secure that of Adelantado for his companion. In like manner, he had engaged to apply for the see of Tumbes for the vicar of Panamá, and the office of Alguacil Mayor for the pilot Ruiz. The bishopric took the direction that was concerted, for the soldier could scarcely claim that miter of the prelate; but the other offices, instead of their appropriate distribution, were all concentrated in himself. Yet it was in reference to his application for his friends that Pizarro had promised on his departure to deal fairly and honorably by them all.

It is stated by the military chronicler, Pedro Pizarro, that his kinsman did, in fact, urge the suit strongly in behalf of Almagro, but that he was refused by the government, on the ground that offices of such paramount importance could not be committed to different individuals. The ill effects of such an arrangement had been long since felt in more than one of the Indian colonies, where it had led to rivalry and fatal collision. Pizarro, therefore, finding his remonstrances unheeded, had no alternative but to combine the offices in his own person, or to see the expedition fall to the ground. This explanation of the affair has not received the sanction of other contemporary historians. The apprehensions expressed by Luque, at the time of Pizarro's assuming the mission, of some such result as actually occurred, founded, doubtless, on a knowledge of his associate's character, may warrant us in distrusting the alleged vindication of his conduct; and our distrust will not be diminished by familiarity with his subsequent career. Pizarro's virtue was not of a kind to withstand temptation—though of a much weaker sort than that now thrown in his path.

The fortunate cavalier was also honored with the habit of Santiago; and he was authorized to make an important innovation in his family escutcheon—for by the father's side he might claim his armorial bearings. The black eagle and the two pillars emblazoned on the royal arms were incorporated with those of the Pizarros; and an Indian city, with a vessel in the distance on the waters, and the llama of Peru, revealed the theater and the character of his exploits; while the legend announced that "under the auspices of Charles, and by the industry, the genius, and the resources of Pizarro, the country had been discovered and reduced to tranquillity" —thus modestly intimating both the past and prospective services of the Conqueror.

These arrangements having been thus completed to Pizarro's satisfaction, he left Toledo for Trujillo, his native place, in Estremadura, where he thought he should be most likely to meet with adherents for his new enterprise, and where it doubtless gratified his vanity to display himself in the palmy, or at least promising, state of his present circumstances. If vanity be ever pardonable, it is certainly in a man who, born in an obscure station in life, without family, interest, or friends to back him, has carved out his own fortunes in the world, and, by his own resources, triumphed over all the obstacles which nature and accident had thrown in his way. Such was the condition of Pizarro as he now revisited the place of his nativity, where he had hitherto been known only as a poor outcast, without a home to shelter, a father to own him, or a friend to lean upon. But he now found both friends and followers, and some who were eager to claim kindred with him and take part in his future fortunes. Among these were four brothers. Three of them, like himself, were illegitimate—one of whom, named Francisco Martin de Alcántara, was related to him by the mother's side; the other two, named Gonzalo and Juan Pizarro, were descended from the father. "They were all poor, and proud as they were poor," says Oviedo, who had seen them; "and their eagerness for gain was in proportion to their poverty."

The remaining and eldest brother, named Hernando, was a legitimate son—"legitimate," continues the same caustic authority, "by his pride, as well as by his birth." His features were plain, even disagreeably so; but his figure was good. He was large of stature, and, like his brother Francisco, had on the whole an imposing presence. In his character he combined some of the worst defects incident to the Castilian. He was jealous in the extreme; impatient, not merely of affront, but of the least slight, and implacable in his resentment. He was decisive in his measures, and unscrupulous in their execution. No touch of pity had power to arrest his arm. His arrogance was such that he was constantly wounding the self-love of those with whom he acted; thus begetting an ill-will which unnecessarily multiplied obstacles in his path. In this he differed from his brother Francisco, whose plausible manners smoothed away difficulties and conciliated confidence and co-operation in his enterprises. Unfortunately, the evil counsels of Hernando exercised an influence over his brother which more than compensated the advantages derived from his singular capacity for business.

Notwithstanding the general interest which Pizarro's adventures excited in his country, that chief did not find it easy to comply with the provisions of the Capitulation in respect to the amount of his levies. Those who were most astonished by his narrative were not always most inclined to take part in his fortunes. They shrank from the unparalleled hardships which lay in the path of the adventurer in that direction; and they listened with visible distrust to the gorgeous pictures of the golden temples and gardens of Tumbes, which they looked upon as indebted in some degree, at least, to the coloring of his fancy, with the obvious purpose of attracting followers to his banner. It is even said that Pizarro would have found it difficult to raise the necessary funds, but for the seasonable aid of Cortés, a native of Estremadura like himself, his companion in arms in early days, and, according to report, his kinsman. No one was in a better condition to hold out a helping hand to a brother adventurer, and probably no one felt greater sympathy in Pizarro's fortunes, or greater confidence in his eventual success, than the man who had so lately trod the same career with renown.

The six months allowed by the Capitulation had elapsed, and Pizarro had assembled somewhat less than his stipulated complement of men, with which he was preparing to embark in a little squadron of three vessels at Seville; but before they were wholly ready he received intelligence that officers of the Council of the Indies proposed to inquire into the condition of the vessels and ascertain how far the requisitions had been complied with.

Without loss of time, therefore, Pizarro, afraid, if the facts were known, that his enterprise might be nipped in the bud, slipped his cables, and, crossing the bar of San Lucar, in January, 1530, stood for the isle of Gomera—one of the Canaries—where he ordered his brother Hernando, who had charge of the remaining vessels, to meet him.

Scarcely had he gone, before the officers arrived to institute the search. But when they objected the deficiency of men, they were easily—perhaps willingly—deceived by the pretext that the remainder had gone forward in the vessel with Pizarro. At all events, no further obstacles were thrown in Hernando's way, and he was permitted, with the rest of the squadron, to join his brother, according to agreement, at Gomera.

After a prosperous voyage, the adventurers reached the northern coast of the great southern continent, and anchored off the port of Santa Marta. Here they received such discouraging reports of the countries to which they were bound, of forests teeming with insects and venomous serpents, of huge alligators that swarmed on the banks of the streams, and of hardships and perils such as their own fears had never painted, that several of Pizarro's men deserted, and their leader, thinking it no longer safe to abide in such treacherous quarters, set sail at once for Nombre de Dios.

Soon after his arrival there, he was met by his two associates, Luque and Almagro, who had crossed the mountains for the purpose of hearing from his own lips the precise import of the Capitulation with the crown. Great, as might have been expected, was Almagro's discontent at learning the result of what he regarded as the perfidious machinations of his associate. "Is it thus," he exclaimed, "that you have dealt with the friend who shared equally with you in the trials, the dangers, and the cost of the enterprise, and this, notwithstanding your solemn engagements on your departure to provi‹ for his interests as faithfully as your own? How could you allow me to be thus dishonored in the eyes of the world by so paltry a compensation, which seems to estimate my services as nothing in comparison with your own?"

Pizarro, in reply, assured his companion that he had faithfully urged his suit, but that the government refused to confide powers which entrenched so closely on one another to different hands. He had no alternative but to accept all himself or to decline all; and he endeavored to mitigate Almagro's displeasure by representing that the country was large enough for the ambition of both, and that the powers conferred on himself were, in fact, conferred on Almagro, since all that he had would ever be at his friend's disposal, as if it were his own. But these honeyed words did not satisfy the injured party; and the two captains soon after returned to Panamá with feelings of estrangement, if not hostility, towards one another, which did not augur well for their enterprise.

Still, Almagro was of a generous temper, and might have been appeased by the politic concessions of his rival, but for the interference of Hernando Pizarro, who, from the first hour of their meeting, showed little respect for the veteran, which, indeed, the diminutive person of the latter was not calculated to inspire, and who now regarded him with particular aversion as an impediment to the career of his brother.

Almagro's friends—and his frank and liberal manners had secured him many—were no less disgusted than himself with the overbearing conduct of this new ally. They loudly complained that it was quite enough to suffer from the perfidy of Pizarro, without being exposed to the insults of his family, who had now come over with him to fatten on the spoils of conquest which belonged to their leader. The rupture soon proceeded to such a length that Almagro avowed his intention to prosecute the expedition without further co-operation with his partner, and actually entered into negotiations for

**"On St. John the Evangelist's day, the banners of the company and the royal standard were consecrated in the cathedral church of Panama; a sermon was preached . . . and the sacrament administered to every soldier."**

the purchase of vessels for that object. But Luque, and the Licentiate Espinosa, who had fortunately come over at that time from St. Domingo, now interposed to repair a breach which must end in the ruin of the enterprise, and the probable destruction of those most interested in its success. By their mediation, a show of reconciliation was at length effected between the parties, on Pizarro's assurance that he would relinquish the dignity of Adelantado in favor of his rival, and petition the emperor to confirm him in the possession of it—an assurance, it may be remarked, not easy to reconcile with his former assertion in respect to the avowed policy of the crown in bestowing this office. He was, moreover, to apply for a distinct government for his associate, so soon as he had become master of the country assigned to himself, and was to solicit no office for either of his own brothers until Almagro had been first provided for. Lastly, the former contract in regard to the division of the spoil into three equal shares between the three original associates was confirmed in the most explicit manner. The reconciliation thus effected among the parties answered the temporary purpose of enabling them to go forward in concert in the expedition. But it was only a thin scar that had healed over the wound, which, deep and rankling within, waited only fresh cause of irritation to break out with a virulence more fatal than ever.

No time was now lost in preparing for the voyage. It found little encouragement, however, among the colonists of Panamá, who were too familiar with the sufferings on the former expeditions to care to undertake another, even with the rich bribe that was held out to allure them. A few of the old company were content to follow out the adventure to its close; and some additional stragglers were collected from the province of Nicaragua—a shoot, it may be remarked, from the colony of Panamá. But Pizarro made slender additions to the force brought over with him from Spain, though this body was in better condition, and, in respect to arms, ammunition, and equipment generally, was on a much better footing, than his former levies. The whole number did not exceed one hundred and eighty men, with twenty-seven horses for the cavalry. He had provided himself with three vessels, two of them of a good size, to take the place of those which he had been compelled to leave on the opposite side of the Isthmus at Nombre de Dios; an armament small for the conquest of an empire, and far short of that prescribed by the Capitulation with the crown. With this the intrepid chief proposed to commence operations, trusting to his own successes, and the exertions of Almagro, who was to remain behind for the present to muster reinforcements.

On St. John the Evangelist's day, the banners of the company and the royal standard were consecrated in the cathedral church of Panamá; a sermon was preached before the little army by Fray Juan de Vargas, one of the Dominicans selected by the government for the Peruvian mission; and mass was performed, and the sacrament administered to every soldier previous to his engaging in the crusade against the infidel. Having thus solemnly invoked the blessing of Heaven on the enterprise, Pizarro and his followers went on board their vessels, which rode at anchor in the Bay of Panamá, and early in January, 1531, sallied forth on his third and last expedition for the conquest of Peru.

It was his intention to steer direct for Tumbes, which held out so magnificent a show of treasure on his former voyage. But headwinds and currents, as usual, baffled his purpose, and after a run of thirteen days, much shorter than the period formerly required for the same distance, his little squadron came to anchor in the Bay of St. Matthew, about one degree north; and Pizarro, after consulting with his officers, resolved to disembark his forces and advance along the coast, while the vessels held their course at a convenient distance from the shore.

The march of the troops was severe and painful in the extreme; for the road was constantly intersected by streams, which, swollen by the winter rains, widened at their mouths into spacious estuaries. Pizarro, who had some previous knowledge of the country, acted as guide as well as commander of the expedition. He was ever ready to give aid where it was needed, encouraging his followers to ford or swim the torrents as they best could, and cheering the desponding by his own buoyant and courageous spirit.

At length they reached a thick-settled hamlet, or rather town, in the province of Coaque. The Spaniards rushed on the place, and the inhabitants, without offering resistance, fled in terror to the neighboring forests, leaving their effects—of much greater value than had been anticipated—in the hands of the invaders. "We fell on them, sword in hand," says one of the Conquerors, with some *naïveté;* "for if we had advised the Indians of our approach, we should never have found there such store of gold and precious stones." The natives, however, according to another authority, stayed voluntarily; "for, as they had done no harm to the white men, they flattered themselves none would be offered to them, but that there would be only an interchange of good offices with the strangers"—an expectation founded, it may be, on the good character which the Spaniards had established for themselves on their preceding visit, but one in which the simple people now found themselves most unpleasantly deceived.

Rushing into the deserted dwellings, the invaders found there, besides stuffs of various kinds, and food most welcome in their famished condition, a large quantity of gold and silver wrought into clumsy ornaments, together with many precious stones; for this was the region of the *esmeraldas,* or emeralds, where the valuable gem was most abundant. One of these jewels, that fell into the hands of Pizarro in this neighborhood, was as large as a pigeon's egg. Unluckily, his rude followers did not know the value of their prize; and they broke many of them in pieces by pounding them with hammers.[32] They were led to this extraordinary proceeding, it is said, by one of the Dominican missionaries, Fray Reginaldo de Pedraza, who assured them that this was the way to prove the true emerald, which could not be broken. It was observed that the good father did not subject his own jewels to this wise experiment; but as the stones, in consequence of it, fell in value, being regarded merely as colored glass, he carried back a considerable store of them to Panamá.

The gold and silver ornaments rifled from the dwellings were brought together and deposited in a common heap when a fifth was deducted for the crown, and Pizarro distributed the remainder in due proportions among the officers and privates of his company. This was the usage invariably observed on the like occasions throughout the Conquest. The invaders had embarked in a common adventure. Their interest was common, and to have allowed everyone to plunder on his own account would only have led to insubordination and perpetual broils. All were required, therefore, on pain of death, to contribute whatever they obtained, whether by bargain or by rapine, to the general stock; and all were too much interested in the execution of the penalty to allow the unhappy culprit who violated the law any chance of escape.

Pizarro, with his usual policy, sent back to Panamá a large quantity of the gold, no less than twenty thousand *castellanos* in value, in the belief that the sight of so much treasure, thus speedily acquired, would settle the doubts of the wavering and decide them on joining his banner. He judged right. As one of the Conquerors piously expresses it, "It pleased the Lord that we should fall in with the town of Coaque, that the riches of the land might find credit with the people, and that they should flock to it."

Pizarro, having refreshed his men, continued his march

along the coast, but no longer accompanied by the vessels, which had returned for recruits to Panamá. The road, as he advanced, was checkered with strips of sandy waste, which, drifted about by the winds, blinded the soldiers, and afforded only treacherous footing for man and beast. The glare was intense; and the rays of a vertical sun beat fiercely on the iron mail and the thick quilted doublets of cotton, till the fainting troops were almost suffocated with the heat. To add to their distresses, a strange epidemic broke out in the little army. It took the form of ulcers, or rather hideous warts of great size, which covered the body, and when lanced, as was the case with some, discharged such a quantity of blood as proved fatal to the sufferer. Several died of this frightful disorder, which was so sudden in its attack, and attended with such prostration of strength, that those who lay down well at night were unable to lift their hands to their heads in the morning. The epidemic, which made its first appearance during this invasion, and which did not long survive it, spread over the country, sparing neither native nor white man. It was one of those plagues from the vial of wrath, which the destroying angel, who follows in the path of the conqueror, pours out on the devoted nations.

The Spaniards rarely experienced on their march either resistance or annoyance from the inhabitants, who, instructed by the example of Coaque, fled with their effects into the woods and neighboring mountains. No one came out to welcome the strangers and offer the rites of hospitality, as on their last visit to the land. For the white men were no longer regarded as good beings that had come from heaven, but as ruthless destroyers, who, invulnerable to the assaults of the Indians, were borne along on the backs of fierce animals, swifter than the wind, with weapons in their hands that scattered fire and desolation as they went. Such were the stories now circulated of the invaders, which, preceding them everywhere on their march, closed the hearts, if not the doors, of the natives against them. Exhausted by the fatigue of travel and by disease, and grievously disappointed at the poverty of the land, which now offered no compensation for their toils, the soldiers of Pizarro cursed the hour in which they had enlisted under his standard, and the men of Nicaragua in particular, says the old chronicler, calling to mind their pleasant quarters in their luxurious land, sighed only to return to their Mahometan paradise.

At this juncture the army was gladdened by the sight of a vessel from Panamá, which brought some supplies, together with the royal treasurer, the *veedor* or inspector, the comptroller, and other high officers appointed by the crown to attend the expedition. They had been left in Spain by Pizarro, in consequence of his abrupt departure from the country; and the Council of the Indies, on learning the circumstances, had sent instructions to Panamá to prevent the sailing of his squadron from that port. But the Spanish government, with more wisdom, countermanded the order, only requiring the functionaries to quicken their own departure and take their place without loss of time in the expedition.

The Spaniards in their march along the coast had now advanced as far as Puerto Viejo. Here they were soon after joined by another small reinforcement of about thirty men, under an officer named Benalcazar, who subsequently rose to high distinction in this service. Many of the followers of Pizarro would now have halted at this spot and established a colony there. But the chief thought more of conquering than of colonizing, at least for the present; and he proposed, as his first step, to get possession of Tumbes, which he regarded as the gate of the Peruvian empire. Continuing his march, therefore, to the shores of what is now called the Gulf of Guayaquil, he arrived off the little island of Puná, lying at no great distance from the Bay of Tumbes. This island, he thought, would afford him a convenient place to encamp until he was prepared to make his descent on the Indian city.

The dispositions of the islanders seemed to favor his purpose. He had not been long in their neighborhood before a deputation of the natives, with their cacique at their head, crossed over in their balsas to the mainland to welcome the Spaniards to their residence. But the Indian interpreters of Tumbes, who had returned with Pizarro from Spain and continued with the camp, put their master on his guard against the meditated treachery of the islanders, whom they accused of designing to destroy the Spaniards by cutting the ropes that held together the floats and leaving those upon them to perish in the waters. Yet the cacique, when charged by Pizarro with this perfidious scheme, denied it with such an air of conscious innocence that the Spanish commander trusted himself and his followers, without further hesitation, to his conveyance, and was transported in safety to the shores of Puná.

Here he was received in a hospitable manner, and his troops were provided with comfortable quarters. Well satisfied with his present position, Pizarro resolved to occupy it until the violence of the rainy season was past, when the arrival of the reinforcements he expected would put him in better condition for marching into the country of the Inca.

"Maddened . . . the people of Puna sprang to arms, and threw themselves at once, with fearful yells . . . on the Spanish camp."

The island, which lies in the mouth of the river of Guayaquil, and is about eight leagues in length by four in breadth at the widest part, was at that time partially covered with a noble growth of timber. But a large portion of it was subjected to cultivation, and bloomed with plantations of cacao, of the sweet potato, and the different products of a tropical clime, evincing agricultural knowledge as well as industry in the population. They were a warlike race, but had received from their Peruvian foes the appellation of "perfidious." It was the brand fastened by the Roman historians on their Carthaginian enemies—with perhaps no better reason. The bold and independent islanders opposed a stubborn resistance to the arms of the Incas; and, though they had finally yielded, they had been ever since at feud, and often in deadly hostility with their neighbors of Tumbes.

The latter no sooner heard of Pizarro's arrival on the island than, trusting probably to their former friendly relations with him, they came over in some numbers to the Spanish quarters. The presence of their detested rivals was by no means grateful to the jealous inhabitants of Puná, and the prolonged residence of the white men on their island could not be otherwise than burdensome. In their outward demeanor they still maintained the same show of amity; but Pizarro's interpreters again put him on his guard against the proverbial perfidy of their hosts. With his suspicions thus aroused, the Spanish commander was informed that a number of the chiefs had met together to deliberate on a plan of insurrection. Not caring to wait for the springing of the mine, he surrounded the place of meeting with his soldiers and made prisoners of the suspected chieftains. According to one authority, they confessed their guilt. This is by no means certain. Nor is it certain that they meditated an insurrection. Yet the fact is not improbable in itself, though it derives little additional probability from the assertion of the hostile interpreters. It is certain, however, that Pizarro was satisfied of the existence of a conspiracy; and without further hesitation, he abandoned his wretched prisoners, ten or twelve in number, to the tender mercies of their rivals of Tumbes, who instantly massacred them before his eyes.

Maddened by this outrage, the people of Puná sprang to arms, and threw themselves at once, with fearful yells and the wildest menaces of despair, on the Spanish camp. The odds of numbers were greatly in their favor, for they mustered several thousand warriors. But the more decisive odds of arms and discipline were on the side of their antagonists; and, as the Indians rushed forward in a confused mass to the assault, the Castilians coolly received them on their long pikes or swept them down by the volleys of their musketry. Their ill-protected bodies were easily cut to pieces by the sharp sword of the Spaniard; and Hernando Pizarro, putting himself at the head of the cavalry, charged boldly into the midst, and scattered them far and wide over the field, until, panic-struck by the terrible array of steel-clad horsemen and the stunning reports and the flash of firearms, the fugitives sought shelter in the depths of their forests. Yet the victory was owing, in some degree, at least—if we may credit the Conquerors—to the interposition of Heaven; for St. Michael and his legions were seen high in the air above the combatants, contending with the arch-enemy of man and cheering on the Christians by their example!

Not more than three or four Spaniards fell in the fight; but many were wounded, and among them Hernando Pizarro, who received a severe injury in the leg from a javelin. Nor did the war end here; for the implacable islanders, taking advantage of the cover of night, or of any remissness on the part of the invaders, were ever ready to steal out of their fastnesses and spring on their enemy's camp, while, by cutting off his straggling parties and destroying his provisions, they kept him in perpetual alarm.

In this uncomfortable situation, the Spanish commander was gladdened by the appearance of two vessels off the island. They brought a reinforcement consisting of a hundred volunteers, besides horses for the cavalry. It was commanded by Hernando de Soto, a captain afterwards famous as the discoverer of the Mississippi, which still rolls its majestic current over the place of his burial—a fitting monument for his remains, as it is of his renown.

This reinforcement was most welcome to Pizarro, who had been long discontented with his position on an island, where he found nothing to compensate the life of unintermitting hostility which he was compelled to lead. With these recruits he felt himself in sufficient strength to cross over to the continent and resume military operations on the proper theater for discovery and conquest. From the Indians of Tumbes he learned that the country had been for some time distracted by a civil war between two sons of the late monarch, competitors for the throne. This intelligence he regarded as of the utmost importance, for he remembered the use which Cortés had made of similar dissensions among the tribes of Anahuac. Indeed, Pizarro seems to have had the example of his great predecessor before his eyes on more occasions than this. But he fell far short of his model; for, notwithstanding the restraint he sometimes put upon himself, his coarser nature and more ferocious temper often betrayed him into acts more repugnant to sound policy, which would never have been countenanced by the Conqueror of Mexico.

# ↩ CHAPTER TWO ↪

PERU AT THE TIME OF THE CONQUEST—REIGN

OF HUAYNA CAPAC—THE INCA BROTHERS—

CONTEST FOR THE EMPIRE—TRIUMPH

AND CRUELTIES OF ATAHUALLPA

Before accompanying the march of Pizarro and his followers into the country of the Incas, it is necessary to make the reader acquainted with the critical situation of the kingdom at that time. For the Spaniards arrived just at the consummation of an important revolution—a crisis most favorable to their views of conquest, and one, indeed, but for which the conquest, with such a handful of soldiers, could never have been achieved.

In the latter part of the fifteenth century died Topa Inca, one of the most renowned of the "Children of the Sun," who, carrying the Peruvian arms across the burning sands of Atacama, penetrated to the remote borders of Chile, while in the opposite direction he enlarged the limits of the empire by the acquisition of the southern provinces of Quito. The war in this quarter was conducted by his son Huayna Capac, who succeeded his father on the throne, and fully equaled him in military daring and in capacity for government.

Under this prince, the whole of the powerful state of Quito, which rivaled that of Peru itself in wealth and refinement, was brought under the scepter of the Incas, whose empire received by this conquest the most important accession yet made to it since the foundation of the dynasty of Manco Capac. The remaining days of the victorious monarch were passed in reducing the independent tribes on the remote limits of his territory, and, still more, in cementing his conquests by the introduction of the Peruvian polity. He was actively engaged in completing the great works of his father, especially the high roads which led from Quito to the capital. He perfected the establishment of posts, took great pains to introduce the Quechua dialect throughout the empire, promoted a better system of agriculture, and in fine, encouraged the different branches of domestic industry and the various enlightened plans of his predecessors for the improvement of his people. Under his sway, the Peruvian monarchy reached its most palmy state; and under both him and his illustrious father it was advancing with such rapid strides in the march of civilization as would soon have carried it to a level with the more refined despotisms of Asia, furnishing the world, perhaps, with higher evidence of the capabilities of the American Indian than is elsewhere to be found on the great Western continent. But other and gloomier destinies were in reserve for the Indian races.

The first arrival of the white men on the South American shores of the Pacific was about ten years before the death of Huayna Capac, when Balboa crossed the Gulf of St. Michael and obtained the first clear report of the empire of the Incas. Whether tidings of these adventurers reached the Indian monarch's ear is doubtful. There is no doubt, however, that he obtained the news of the first expedition under Pizarro and Almagro, when the latter commander penetrated as far as the Rio de San Juan, about the fourth degree north. The accounts which he received made a strong impression on the

"Topa Inca . . . carrying the Peruvian arms across the burning sands of Atacama, penetrated to the remote borders of Chile."

mind of Huayna Capac. He discerned in the formidable prowess and weapons of the invaders proofs of a civilization far superior to that of his own people. He intimated his apprehension that they would return, and that at some day, not far distant perhaps, the throne of the Incas might be shaken by these strangers endowed with such incomprehensible powers. To the vulgar eye it was a little speck on the verge of the horizon; but that of the sagacious monarch seemed to descry in it the dark thundercloud that was to spread wider and wider till it burst in fury on his nation.

There is some ground for believing thus much. But other accounts, which have obtained a popular currency, not content with this, connect the first tidings of the white men with predictions long extant in the country, and with supernatural appearances which filled the hearts of the whole nation with dismay. Comets were seen flaming athwart the heavens. Earthquakes shook the land; the moon was girdled with rings of fire of many colors; a thunderbolt fell on one of the royal palaces and consumed it to ashes; and an eagle, chased by several hawks, was seen, screaming in the air, to hover above the great square of Cuzco, when, pierced by the talons of his tormentors, the king of birds fell lifeless in the presence of many of the Inca nobles, who read in this an augury of their own destruction. Huayna Capac himself, calling his great officers around him, as he found he was drawing near his end, announced the subversion of his empire by the race of white and bearded strangers, as the consummation predicted by the oracles after the reign of the twelfth Inca, and he enjoined it on his vassals not to resist the decrees of Heaven, but to yield obedience to its messengers.

Such is the report of the impressions made by the appearance of the Spaniards in the country, reminding one of the similar feelings of superstitious terror occasioned by their appearance in Mexico. But the traditions of the latter land rest on much higher authority than those of the Peruvians, which, unsupported by contemporary testimony, rest almost wholly on the naked assertion of one of their own nation, who thought to find, doubtless, in the inevitable decrees of Heaven, the best apology for the supineness of his countrymen.

It is not improbable that rumors of the advent of a strange and mysterious race should have spread gradually among the Indian tribes along the great tableland of the Cordilleras, and should have shaken the hearts of the stoutest warriors with feelings of undefined dread, as of some impending calamity. In this state of mind, it was natural that physical convulsions, to which that volcanic country is peculiarly subject, should have made an unwonted impression on their minds, and that the phenomena which might have been regarded only as extraordinary in the usual seasons of political security, should now be interpreted by the superstitious soothsayer as the handwriting on the heavens, by which the God of the Incas proclaimed the approaching downfall of their empire.

Huayna Capac had, as usual with the Peruvian princes, a multitude of concubines, by whom he left a numerous posterity. The heir to the crown, the son of his lawful wife and sister, was named Huascar. At the period of the history at which we are now arrived, he was about thirty years of age. Next to the heir apparent, by another wife, a cousin of the monarch's, came Manco II, a young prince who will occupy an important place in our subsequent story. But the best-beloved of the Inca's children was Atahuallpa. His mother was the daughter of the last *Scyri* of Quito, who had died of grief, it was said, not long after the subversion of his kingdom by Huayna Capac. The princess was beautiful, and the Inca, whether to gratify his passion, or, as the Peruvians say, willing to make amends for the ruin of her parents, received her among his concubines. The historians of Quito assert that she was his lawful wife; but this dignity, according to the usages of the empire, was reserved for maidens of the Inca blood.

The latter years of Huayna Capac were passed in his new kingdom of Quito. Atahuallpa was accordingly brought up under his own eye, accompanied him, while in his tender years, in his campaigns, slept in the same tent with his royal father, and ate from the same plate. The vivacity of the boy, his courage and generous nature, won the affections of the old monarch to such a degree that he resolved to depart from the established usages of the realm and divide his empire between him and his elder brother Huascar. On his deathbed he called the great officers of the crown around him, and declared it to be his will that the ancient kingdom of Quito should pass to Atahuallpa, who might be considered as having a natural claim on it, as the dominion of his ancestors. The rest of the empire he settled on Huascar; and he enjoined it on the two brothers to acquiesce in this arrangement and to live in amity with each other. This was the last act of the heroic monarch; doutbless the most impolitic of his whole life. With his dying breath he subverted the fundamental laws of the empire; and while he recommended harmony between the successors to his authority, he left in this very division of it the seeds of inevitable discord.

His death took place, as seems probable, at the close of 1525, not quite seven years before Pizarro's arrival at Puná.[33]

The tidings of his decease spread sorrow and consternation throughout the land; for, though stern and even inexorable to the rebel and the long-resisting foe, he was a brave and magnanimous monarch, and legislated with the enlarged views of a prince who regarded every part of his dominions as equally his concern. The people of Quito, flattered by the proofs which he had given of preference for them by his permanent residence in that country and his embellishment of their capital, manifested unfeigned sorrow at his loss; and his subjects at Cuzco, proud of the glory which his arms and his abilities had secured for his native land, held him in no less admiration; while the more thoughtful and the more timid, in both countries, looked with apprehension to the future, when the scepter of the vast empire, instead of being swayed by an old and experienced hand, was to be consigned to rival princes, naturally jealous of one another, and, from their age, necessarily exposed to the unwholesome influence of crafty and ambitious counselors. The people testified their regret by the unwonted honors paid to the memory of the deceased Inca. His heart was retained in Quito, and his body, embalmed after the fashion of the country, was transported to Cuzco, to take its place in the great temple of the Sun, by the side of the remains of his royal ancestors. His obsequies were celebrated with sanguinary splendor in both the capitals of his far-extended empire; and several thousands of the imperial concubines, with numerous pages and officers of the palace, are said to have proved their sorrow, or their superstition, by offering up their own lives, that they might accompany their departed lord to the bright mansions of the Sun.

For nearly five years after the death of Huayna Capac, the royal brothers reigned, each over his allotted portion of the empire, without distrust of one another, or, at least, without collision.[34] It seemed as if the wish of their father was to be completely realized, and that the two states were to maintain their respective integrity and independence as much as if they had never been united into one. But with the manifold causes for jealousy and discontent, and the swarms of courtly sycophants who would find their account in fomenting these feelings, it was easy to see that this tranquil state of things could not long endure. Nor would it have endured so long, but for the more gentle temper of Huascar, the only party who had ground for complaint. He was four or five years older than his brother, and was possessed of courage not to be doubted; but he was a prince of a generous and easy nature, and perhaps, if left to himself, might have acquiesced in an arrangement which, however unpalatable, was the will of his

"Huascar . . . was four or five years older than his brother . . . ; he was a prince of generous and easy nature."

deified father. But Atahuallpa was of a different temper. War-like, ambitious, and daring, he was constantly engaged in enterprises for the enlargement of his own territory; though his crafty policy was scrupulous not to aim at extending his acquisitions in the direction of his royal brother. His restless spirit, however, excited some alarm at the court of Cuzco, and Huascar at length sent an envoy to Atahuallpa, to remonstrate with him on his ambitious enterprises, and to require him to render him homage for his kingdom of Quito.

This is one statement. Other accounts pretend that the immediate cause of rapture was a claim instituted by Huascar for the territory of Tomebamba, held by his brother as part of his patrimonial inheritance. It matters little what was the ostensible ground of collision between persons placed by circumstances in so false a position in regard to one another that

**"The liberal manners of the young Atahuallpa had endeared him to the soldiers. . . . These troops were the flower of the great army of the Inca."**

collision must, at some time or other, inevitably occur.

The commencement, and, indeed, the whole course, of hostilities which soon broke out between the rival brothers are stated with irreconcilable and, considering the period was so near to that of the Spanish invasion, with unaccountable discrepancy. By some it is said that in Atahuallpa's first encounter with the troops of Cuzco he was defeated and made prisoner near Tomebamba, a favorite residence of his father, in the ancient territory of Quito and in the district of Cañaris. From this disaster he recovered by a fortunate escape from confinement, when, regaining his capital, he soon found himself at the head of a numerous army, led by the most able and experienced captains in the empire. The liberal manners of the young Atahuallpa had endeared him to the soldiers, with whom, as we have seen, he served more than one campaign in his father's lifetime. These troops were the flower of the great army of the Inca, and some of them had grown gray in his long military career, which had left them at the north, where they readily transferred their allegiance to the young sovereign of Quito. They were commanded by two officers of great consideration, both possessed of large experience in military affairs and high in the confidence of the late Inca. One of them was named Quizquiz; the other, who was the maternal uncle of Atahuallpa, was called Calicuchima.

With these practiced warriors to guide him, the young monarch put himself at the head of his martial array and directed his march towards the south. He had not advanced farther than Ambato, about sixty miles distant from his capital, when he fell in with a numerous host which had been sent against him by his brother, under the command of a distinguished chieftain, of the Inca family. A bloody battle followed, which lasted the greater part of the day; and the theater of combat was the skirts of the mighty Chimborazo.

The battle ended favorably for Atahuallpa, and the Peruvians were routed with great slaughter and the loss of their commander. The prince of Quito availed himself of his advantage to push forward his march until he arrived before the gates of Tomebamba, which city, as well as the whole district of Cañaris, though an ancient dependency of Quito, had sided with his rival in the contest. Entering the captive city like a conqueror, he put the inhabitants to the sword, and razed it with all its stately edifices, some of which had been reared by his own father, to the ground. He carried on the same war of extermination as he marched through the offending district of Cañaris. In some places, it is said, bands of children, as well as older persons, were sent out, in melancholy procession, with green branches in their hands, to deprecate his wrath; but the vindictive conqueror, deaf to their entreaties, laid the country waste with fire and sword, sparing no man capable of bearing arms who fell into his hands.

The fate of Cañaris struck terror into the hearts of his enemies, and one place after another opened its gates to the victor, who held on his triumphant march towards the Peruvian capital. His arms experienced a temporary check before the island of Puná, whose bold warriors maintained the cause of his brother. After some days lost before this place, Atahuallpa left the contest to their old enemies, the people of Tumbes, who had early given in their adhesion to him, while he resumed his march and advanced as far as Cajamarca, about seven degrees south. Here he halted with a detachment of the army, sending forward the main body under the command of his two generals, with orders to move straight upon Cuzco. He preferred not to trust himself farther in the enemy's country, where a defeat might be fatal. By establishing his quarters at Cajamarca, he would be able to support his generals in case of a reverse, or, at worst, to secure his retreat on Quito until he was again in condition to renew hostilities.

The two commanders, advancing by rapid marches, at length crossed the Apurimac River, and arrived within a short distance of the Peruvian capital. Meanwhile, Huascar had not been idle. On receiving tidings of the discomfiture of his army at Ambato, he made every exertion to raise levies throughout the country. By the advice, it is said, of his priests —the most incompetent advisers in times of danger—he chose to await the approach of the enemy in his own capital; and it was not till the latter had arrived within a few leagues of Cuzco that the Inca, taking counsel of the same ghostly monitors, sailed forth to give him battle.

The two armies met on the plains of Quepaipa, in the neighborhood of the Indian metropolis. Their numbers are stated with the usual discrepancy; but Atahuallpa's troops had considerably the advantage in discipline and experience, for many of Huascar's levies had been drawn hastily together from the surrounding country. Both fought, however, with the desperation of men who felt that everything was at stake. It was no longer a contest for a province, but for the possession of an empire. Atahuallpa's troops, flushed with recent success, fought with the confidence of those who relied on their superior prowess; while the loyal vassals of the Inca displayed all the self-devotion of men who held their own lives cheap in the service of their master.

The fight raged with the greatest obstinacy from sunrise to sunset; and the ground was covered with heaps of the dying and the dead, whose bones lay bleaching on the battlefield long after the conquest by the Spaniards. At length, fortune declared in favor of Atahuallpa, or, rather, the usual result of superior discipline and military practice followed. The ranks of the Inca were thrown into irretrievable disorder, and gave way in all directions. The conquerors followed close on the heels of the flying. Huascar himself, among the latter, endeavored to make his escape with about a thousand men who remained round his person. But the royal fugitive was discovered before he had left the field; his little party was enveloped by clouds of the enemy, and nearly every one of the devoted band perished in defense of their Inca. Huascar was made prisoner, and the victorious chiefs marched at once on his capital, which they occupied in the name of their sovereign.

These events occurred in the spring of 1532, a few months before the landing of the Spaniards. The tidings of the success of his arms and the capture of his unfortunate brother reached Atahuallpa at Cajamarca. He instantly gave orders that Huascar should be treated with the respect due to his rank, but that he should be removed to the strong fortress of Jauja and held there in strict confinement. His orders did not stop here—if we are to believe the accounts of Garcilasso de la Vega, himself of the Inca race, and by his mother's side nephew of the great Huayna Capac.

According to this authority, Atahuallpa invited the Inca nobles throughout the country to assemble at Cuzco, in order to deliberate on the best means of partitioning the empire between him and his brother. When they had met in the capital, they were surrounded by the soldiery of Quito and butchered without mercy. The motive of this perfidious act was to exterminate the whole of the royal family, who might each one of them show a better title to the crown than the illegitimate Atahuallpa. But the massacre did not end here. The illegitimate offspring, like himself, half-brothers of the monster, all, in short, who had any of the Inca blood in their veins, were involved in it; and with an appetite for carnage unparalleled in the annals of the Roman Empire or of the French Republic, Atahuallpa ordered all the females of the blood royal, his aunts, nieces, and cousins, to be put to death, and that, too, with the most refined and lingering tortures. To give greater zest to his revenge, many of the executions took place in the presence of Huascar himself, who was thus compelled to witness the butchery of his own wives and sisters, while, in the extremity of anguish, they in vain called on him to protect them!

Such is the tale told by the historian of the Incas, and received by him, as he assures us, from his mother and uncle, who, being children at the time, were so fortunate as to be among the few that escaped the massacre of their house. And such is the account repeated by many a Castilian writer since, without any symptom of distrust. But a tissue of unprovoked atrocities like these is too repugnant to the principles of human nature—and, indeed, to common sense—to warrant our belief in them on ordinary testimony.

The annals of semicivilized nations unhappily show that there have been instances of similar attempts to extinguish the whole of a noxious race which had become the object of a tyrant's jealousy; though such an attempt is about as chimerical as it would be to extirpate any particular species of plant the seeds of which had been borne on every wind over the country. But if the attempt to exterminate the Inca race was actually made by Atahuallpa, how comes it that so many of the pure descendants of the blood royal—nearly six hundred in number—are admitted by the historian to have been in existence seventy years after the imputed massacre? Why was the massacre, instead of being limited to the legitimate members of the royal stock, who could show a better title to the crown than the usurper, extended to all, however remotely or in whatever way connected with the race? Why were aged women and young maidens involved in the proscription, and why were they subjected to such refined and superfluous tortures, when it is obvious that beings so impotent could have done nothing to provoke the jealousy of the tyrant? Why, when so many were sacrificed from some vague apprehension of distant danger, was his rival Huascar, together with his younger brother Manco Capac, the two men from whom the conqueror had most to fear, suffered to live? Why, in short, is the wonderful tale not recorded by others before the time of Garcilasso, and nearer by half a century to the events themselves?

That Atahuallpa may have been guilty of excesses, and abused the rights of conquest by some gratuitous acts of cruelty, may be readily believed; for no one who calls to mind his treatment of the Cañaris—which his own apologists do not affect to deny—will doubt that he had a full measure of the vindictive temper which belongs to

> "Those souls of fire, and Children of the Sun,
>     With whom revenge was virtue."

But there is a wide difference between this and the monstrous and most unprovoked atrocities imputed to him, implying a diabolical nature not to be admitted on the evidence of an Indian partisan, the sworn foe of his house, and repeated by Castilian chroniclers, who may naturally seek, by blazoning the enormities of Atahuallpa, to find some apology for the cruelty of their countrymen towards him.

The news of the great victory was borne on the wings of the wind to Cajamarca; and loud and long was the rejoicing, not only in the camp of Atahuallpa, but in the town and surrounding country; for all now came in, eager to offer their congratulations to the victor and do him homage. The prince of Quito no longer hesitated to assume the scarlet *borla,* the diadem of the Incas. His triumph was complete. He had beaten his enemies on their own ground, had taken their capital, had set his foot on the neck of his rival, and won for himself the ancient scepter of the Children of the Sun. But the hour of triumph was destined to be that of his deepest humiliation. Atahuallpa was not one of those to whom, in the language of the Grecian bard, "the gods are willing to reveal themselves." He had not read the handwriting on the heavens. The small speck which the clear-sighted eye of his father had discerned on the distant verge of the horizon, though little noticed by Atahuallpa, intent on the deadly strife with his biother, had now risen high towards the zenith, spreading wider and wider, till it wrapped the skies in darkness and was ready to burst in thunders on the devoted nation.

# CHAPTER THREE



## (1532)

We left the Spaniards at the island of Puná, preparing to make their descent on the neighboring continent at Tumbes. This port was but a few leagues distant, and Pizarro, with the greater part of his followers, passed over in the ships, while a few others were to transport the commander's baggage and the military stores on some of the Indian balsas. One of the latter vessels which first touched the shores was surrounded, and three persons who were on the raft were carried off by the natives to the adjacent woods and then massacred. The Indians then got possession of another of the balsas, containing Pizarro's wardrobe; but as the men who defended it raised loud cries for help, they reached the ears of Hernando Pizarro, who, with a small body of horse, had effected a landing some way farther down the shore. A broad tract of miry ground, overflowed at high water, lay between him and the party thus rudely assailed by the natives. The tide was out, and the bottom was soft and dangerous. With little regard to the danger, however, the bold cavalier spurred his horse into the slimy depths, and, followed by his men, with the mud up to their saddle-girths, plunged forward into the midst of the marauders, who, terrified by the strange apparition of the horsemen, fled precipitately, without show of fight, to the neighboring forests.

This conduct of the natives of Tumbes is not easy to be explained, considering the friendly relations maintained with the Spaniards on their preceding visit, and lately renewed in the island of Puná. But Pizarro was still more astonished, on entering their town, to find it not only deserted, but, with the exception of a few buildings, entirely demolished. Four or five of the most substantial private dwellings, the great temple, and the fortress—and these greatly damaged, and wholly despoiled of their interior decorations—alone survived to mark the site of the city and attest its former splendor. The scene of desolation filled the conquerors with dismay; for even the raw recruits, who had never visited the coast before, had heard the marvelous stories of the golden treasures of Tumbes, and they had confidently looked forward to them as an easy spoil after all their fatigues. But the gold of Peru seemed only like a deceitful phantom, which, after beckoning them on through toil and danger, vanished the moment they attempted to grasp it. Pizarro dispatched a small body of troops in pursuit of the fugitives; and, after some slight skirmishing, they got possession of several of the natives, and among them, as it chanced, the curaca of the place. When brought before the Spanish commander, he exonerated himself from any share in the violence offered to the white men, saying that it was done by a lawless party of his people, without his knowledge at the time; and he expressed his willingness to deliver them up to punishment, if they could be detected. He explained the dilapidated condition of the town by the long wars carried on with the fierce tribes of Puná, who had at length succeeded in getting possession of the place and driving the inhabitants into the neighboring woods and mountains. The Inca, to whose cause they were attached, was too much occupied with his own feuds to protect them against their enemies.

Whether Pizarro gave any credit to the cacique's exculpation of himself may be doubted. He dissembled his suspicions, however, and as the Indian lord promised obedience in his own name and that of his vassals, the Spanish general consented to take no further notice of the affair. He seems now to have felt for the first time, in its full force, that it was his policy to gain the good will of the people among whom he had thrown himself in the face of such tremendous odds. It was, perhaps, the excesses of which his men had been guilty in the earlier stages of the expedition that had shaken the confidence of the people of Tumbes and incited them to this treacherous retaliation.

Pizarro inquired of the natives, who now, under promise

of impunity, came into the camp, what had become of his two followers that remained with them in the former expedition. The answers they gave were obscure and contradictory. Some said they had died of an epidemic; others, that they had perished in the war with Puná; and others intimated that they had lost their lives in consequence of some outrage attempted on the Indian women. It was impossible to arrive at the truth. The last account was not the least probable. But, whatever might be the cause, there was no doubt they had both perished.

This intelligence spread an additional gloom over the Spaniards, which was not dispelled by the flaming pictures now given by the natives of the riches of the land, and of the state and magnificence of the monarch in his distant capital among the mountains. Nor did they credit the authenticity of a scroll of paper which Pizarro had obtained from an Indian to whom it had been delivered by one of the white men left in the country. "Know, whoever you may be," said the writing, "that may chance to set foot in this country, that it contains more gold and silver than there is iron in Biscay." This paper, when shown to the soldiers, excited only their ridicule as a device of their captain to keep alive their chimerical hopes.

Pizarro now saw that it was not politic to protract his stay in his present quarters, where a spirit of disaffection would soon creep into the ranks of his followers unless their spirits were stimulated by novelty or a life of incessant action. Yet he felt deeply anxious to obtain more particulars than he had hitherto gathered of the actual condition of the Peruvian empire, of its strength and resources, of the monarch who ruled over it, and of his present situation. He was also desirous, before taking any decisive step for penetrating the country, to seek out some commodious place for a settlement, which might afford him the means of a regular communication with the colonies, and a place of strength, on which he himself might retreat in case of disaster.

He decided, therefore, to leave part of his company at Tumbes including those who, from the state of their health, were least able to take the field, and with the remainder to make an excursion into the interior and reconnoiter the land, before deciding on any plan of operations. He set out early in May, 1532, and, keeping along the more level regions himself, sent a small detachment under the command of Hernando de Soto to explore the skirts of the vast sierra.

He maintained a rigid discipline on the march, commanding his soldiers to abstain from all acts of violence, and pun-

"The natives, as Pizarro marched through the thick-settled hamlets . . . between the Cordilleras and the ocean, welcomed him, providing good quarters for his troops."

ishing disobedience in the most prompt and resolute manner. The natives rarely offered resistance. When they did so, they were soon reduced, and Pizarro, far from adopting vindictive measures, was open to the first demonstrations of submission. By this lenient and liberal policy he soon acquired a name among the inhabitants which effaced the unfavorable impressions made of him in the earlier part of the campaign. The natives, as he marched through the thick-settled hamlets which sprinkled the level regions between the Cordilleras and the ocean, welcomed him with rustic hospitality, providing good quarters for his troops, and abundant supplies, which cost but little in the prolific soil of the *tierra caliente*. Everywhere Pizarro made proclamation that he came in the name of the Holy Vicar of God and of the sovereign of Spain, requiring the obedience of the inhabitants as true children of the Church and vassals of his lord and master. And as the simple people made no opposition to a formula of which they could not comprehend a syllable, they were admitted as good subjects of the crown of Castile, and their act of homage—or what was readily interpreted as such—was duly recorded and attested by the notary.

At the expiration of some three or four weeks spent in reconnoitering the country, Pizarro came to the conclusion that the most eligible site for his new settlement was in the rich valley of Tangarara, thirty leagues south of Tumbes, traversed by more than one stream that opens a communication with the ocean. To this spot, accordingly, he ordered the men left at Tumbes to repair at once in their vessels; and no sooner had they arrived than busy preparations were made for building up the town in a manner suited to the wants of the colony. Timber was procured from the neighboring woods, stones were dragged from their quarries, and edifices gradually rose, some of which made pretensions of strength, if not of elegance. Among them were a church, a magazine for public stores, a hall of justice, and a fortress. A municipal government was organized, consisting of regidores, alcaldes, and the usual civic functionaries. The adjacent territory was parceled out among the residents, and each colonist had a certain number of the natives allotted to assist him in his labors; for, as Pizarro's secretary remarks, "it being evident that the colonists could not support themselves without the services of the Indians, the ecclesiastics and the leaders of the expedition all agreed that a *repartimiento* of the natives would serve the cause of religion, and tend greatly to their spiritual welfare, since they would thus have the opportunity of being initiated in the true faith."

Having made these arrangements with such conscientious regard to the welfare of the benighted heathen, Pizarro gave his infant city the name of San Miguel, in acknowledgment of the service rendered him by that saint in his battles with the Indians of Puná. The site originally occupied by the settlement was afterwards found to be so unhealthy that it was abandoned for another on the banks of the beautiful Piura. The town is still of some note for its manufactures, though dwindled from its ancient importance; but the name of San Miguel de Piura, which it bears, still commemorates the foundation of the first European colony in the empire of the Incas.

Before quitting the new settlement, Pizarro caused the gold and silver ornaments which he had obtained in different parts of the country to be melted down into one mass, and a fifth to be deducted for the crown. The remainder, which belonged to the troops, he persuaded them to relinquish for the present, under the assurance of being repaid from the first spoils that fell into their hands. With these funds, and other articles collected in the course of the campaign, he sent back the vessels to Panamá. The gold was applied to paying off the shipowners and those who had furnished the stores for the expedition. That he should so easily have persuaded his men to resign present possessions for a future contingency is proof that the spirit of enterprise was renewed in their bosoms in all its former vigor, and that they looked forward with the same buoyant confidence to the results.

In his late tour of observation the Spanish commander had gathered much important intelligence in regard to the state of the kingdom. He had ascertained the result of the struggle between the Inca brothers, and that the victor now lay with his army encamped at the distance of only ten or twelve days' journey from San Miguel. The accounts he heard of the opulence and power of that monarch, and of his great southern capital, perfectly corresponded with the general rumors before received, and contained, therefore, something to stagger the confidence, as well as to stimulate the cupidity, of the invaders.

Pizarro would gladly have seen his little army strengthened by reinforcements, however small the amount, and on that account postponed his departure for several weeks. But no reinforcement arrived; and as he received no further tidings from his associates, he judged that longer delay would probably be attended with evils greater than those to be encountered on the march; that discontents would inevitably spring up in a life of inaction, and the strength and spirits of the soldier sink under the enervating influence of a tropical climate. Yet the force at his command, amounting to less than two hundred soldiers in all, after reserving fifty for the protection of the new settlement, seemed but a small one for the conquest of an empire. He might, indeed, instead of marching against the Inca, take a southerly direction towards the rich capital of Cuzco. But this would only be to postpone the hour of reckoning. For in what quarter of the empire could he hope to set his foot, where the arm of its master would not reach him? By such a course, moreover, he would show his own distrust of himself. He would shake that opinion of his invincible prowess which he had hitherto endeavored to impress on the natives, and which constituted a great secret of his strength; which, in short, held sterner sway over the mind than the display of numbers and mere physical force. Worse than all, such a course would impair the confidence of his troops in themselves and their reliance on himself. This would be to palsy the arm of enterprise at once. It was not to be thought of.

But, while Pizarro decided to march into the interior, it is doubtful whether he had formed any more definite plan of action. We have no means of knowing his intentions, at this distance of time, otherwise than as they are shown by his actions. Unfortunately, he could not write, and he has left no record, like the inestimable Commentaries of Cortés, to enlighten us as to his motives. His secretary and some of his companions in arms have recited his actions in detail; but the motives which led to them they were not always so competent to disclose.

It is possible that the Spanish general, even so early as the period of his residence at San Miguel, may have meditated some daring stroke, some effective *coup-de-main*, which, like that of Cortés when he carried off the Aztec monarch to his quarters, might strike terror into the hearts of the people and at once decide the fortunes of the day. It is more probable, however, that he now only proposed to present himself before the Inca as the peaceful representative of a brother monarch, and by these friendly demonstrations disarm any feeling of hostility, or even of suspicion. When once in communication with the Indian prince, he could regulate his future course by circumstances.

On the 24th of September, 1532, five months after landing at Tumbes, Pizarro marched out at the head of his little body of adventurers from the gates of San Miguel, having enjoined it on the colonists to treat their Indian vassals with humanity, and to conduct themselves in such a manner as would secure the good will of the surrounding tribes. Their own existence, and with it the safety of the army and the success of the undertaking, depended on this course. In the place were to remain the royal treasurer, the *veedor* or inspector of metals, and other officers of the crown; and the command of the garrison was entrusted to the *contador*, Antonio Navarro. Then, putting himself at the head of his troops, the chief struck boldly into the heart of the country in the direction where, as he was informed, lay the camp of the Inca. It was a daring enterprise, thus to venture with a handful of followers into the heart of a powerful empire, to present himself face to face before the Indian monarch in his own camp, encompassed by the flower of his victorious army! Pizarro had already experienced more than once the difficulty of maintaining his ground against the rude tribes of the north, so much inferior in strength and numbers to the warlike legions of Peru. But the hazard of the game, as I have already more than once had occasion to remark, constituted its great charm with the Spaniard. The brilliant achievements of his countrymen, on the like occasions, with means so inadequate, inspired him with confidence in his own good star, and this confidence was one source of his success. Had he faltered for a moment, had he stopped to calculate chances, he must inevitably have failed; for the odds were too great to be combated by sober reason. They were only to be met triumphantly by the spirit of the knight-errant.

After crossing the smooth waters of the Piura, the little army continued to advance over a level district intersected by streams that descended from the neighboring Cordilleras. The face of the country was shagged over with forests of gigantic growth, and occasionally traversed by ridges of barren land, that seemed like shoots of the adjacent Andes, breaking up the surface of the region into little sequestered valleys of singular loveliness. The soil, though rarely watered by the rains of heaven, was naturally rich, and wherever it was refreshed with moisture, as on the margins of the streams, it was enameled with the brightest verdure. The industry of the inhabitants, moreover, had turned these streams to the best account, and canals and aqueducts were soon crossing the low lands in all directions, and spreading over the country like a vast network, diffusing fertility and beauty around them. The air was scented with the sweet odors of flowers, and everywhere the eye was refreshed by the sight of orchards laden with unknown fruits, and of fields waving with yellow grain and rich in luscious vegetables of every description that teem in the sunny clime of the equator. The Spaniards were among a people who had carried the refinements of husbandry to a greater extent than any yet found on the American continent; and, as they journeyed through this paradise of plenty, their condition formed a pleasing contrast to what they had before endured in the dreary wilderness of the mangroves.

Everywhere, too, they were received with confiding hospitality by the simple people; for which they were no doubt indebted, in a great measure, to their own inoffensive deportment. Every Spaniard seemed to be aware that his only chance of success lay in conciliating the good opinion of the inhabitants among whom he had so recklessly cast his fortunes. In most of the hamlets, and in every place of considerable size, some fortress was to be found, or royal caravansary, destined for the Inca on his progresses, the ample halls of which furnished abundant accommodations for the Spaniards; who were thus provided with quarters along their route at the charge of the very government which they were preparing to overturn.

On the fifth day after leaving San Miguel, Pizarro halted in one of these delicious valleys, to give his troops repose and to make a more complete inspection of them. Their number amounted in all to one hundred and seventy-seven, of which sixty-seven were cavalry. He mustered only three arquebusiers in his whole company, and a few crossbow-men, altogether not exceeding twenty. The troops were tolerably well equipped, and in good condition. But the watchful eye of their commander noticed with uneasiness that, notwithstanding the general heartiness in the cause manifested by his followers, there were some among them whose countenances lowered with discontent, and who, although they did not give vent to it in open murmurs, were far from moving with their wonted alacrity. He was aware that if this spirit became contagious it would be the ruin of the enterprise; and he thought it best to exterminate the gangrene at once, and at whatever cost, than to wait until it had infected the whole system. He came to an extraordinary resolution.

Calling his men together, he told them that "a crisis had now arrived in their affairs, which it demanded all their courage to meet. No man should think of going forward in the expedition who could not do so with his whole heart, or who had the least misgiving as to its success. If any repented of his share in it, it was not too late to turn back. San Miguel was but poorly garrisoned, and he should be glad to see it in greater strength. Those who chose might return to this place, and they should be entitled to the same proportion of lands and Indian vassals as the present residents. With the rest, were they few or many, who chose to take their chances with him, he should pursue the adventure to the end."

It was certainly a remarkable proposal for a commander who was ignorant of the amount of disaffection in his ranks, and who could not safely spare a single man from his force, already far too feeble for the undertaking. Yet, by insisting on the wants of the little colony of San Miguel, he afforded a decent pretext for the secession of the malcontents, and swept away the barrier of shame which might have still held them in the camp. Notwithstanding the fair opening thus afforded, there were but few, nine in all, who availed themselves of the general's permission. Four of these belonged to the infantry, and five to the horse. The rest loudly declared their resolve to go forward with their brave leader; and if there were some whose voices were faint amidst the general acclamation, they at least relinquished the right of complaining hereafter, since they had voluntarily rejected the permission to return. This stroke of policy in their sagacious captain was attended with the best effects. He had winnowed out the few grains of discontent which, if left to themselves, might have fermented in secret till the whole mass had swelled into mutiny. Cortés had compelled his men to go forward heartily in his enterprise by burning their vessels, and thus cutting off the only means of retreat. Pizarro, on the other hand, threw open the gates to the disaffected, and facilitated their departure. Both judged right, under their peculiar circumstances, and both were perfectly successful.

Feeling himself strengthened, instead of weakened, by his loss, Pizarro now resumed his march, and on the second day arrived before a place called Zaran,[35] situated in a fruitful valley among the mountains. Some of the inhabitants had been drawn off to swell the levies of Atahuallpa. The Spaniards had repeated experience on their march of the oppressive exactions of the Inca, who had almost depopulated some of the valleys to obtain reinforcements for his army. The curaca of the Indian town where Pizarro now arrived received him with kindness and hospitality, and the troops were quartered as usual in one of the royal *tambos* or caravansaries, which were found in all the principal places.

Yet the Spaniards saw no signs of their approach to the royal encampment, though more time had already elapsed than was originally allowed for reaching it. Shortly before entering Zaran, Pizarro had heard that a Peruvian garrison was established in a place called Caxas, lying among the hills, at no great distance from his present quarters. He immediately dispatched a small party under Hernando de Soto in that direction, to reconnoiter the ground, and bring him intelligence of the actual state of things, at Zaran, where he would halt until his officer's return.[36]

Day after day passed on, and a week had elapsed before tidings were received of his companions, and Pizarro was becoming seriously alarmed for their fate, when on the eighth morning Soto appeared, bringing with him an envoy from the Inca himself. He was a person of rank, and was attended by several followers of inferior condition. He had met the Spaniards at Caxas, and now accompanied them on their return, to deliver his sovereign's message, with a present to the Spanish commander. The present consisted of two fountains, made of stone, in the form of fortresses; some fine stuffs of woolen embroidered with gold and silver; and a quantity of goose flesh, dried and seasoned in a peculiar manner, and much used as a perfume, in a pulverized state, by the Peruvian nobles. The Indian ambassador came charged also with his master's greeting to the strangers, whom Atahuallpa welcomed to his country and invited to visit him in his camp among the mountains.

Pizarro well understood that the Inca's object in this diplomatic visit was less to do him courtesy than to inform himself of the strength and condition of the invaders. But he was well pleased with the embassy, and dissembled his consciousness of its real purpose. He caused the Peruvian to be entertained in the best manner the camp could afford, and paid him the respect, says one of the Conquerors, due to the ambassador of so great a monarch. Pizarro urged him to prolong his visit for some days, which the Indian envoy declined, but made the most of his time while there, by gleaning all the information he could in respect to the use of every strange article which he saw, as well as the object of the white men's visit to the land, and the quarter whence they came.

The Spanish captain satisfied his curiosity in all these particulars. The intercourse with the natives, it may be here remarked, was maintained by means of two of the youths who had accompanied the Conquerors on their return home from their preceding voyage. They had been taken by Pizarro to Spain, and as much pains had been bestowed on teaching them the Castilian, they now filled the office of interpreters, and opened an easy communication with their countrymen. It was of inestimable service: and well did the Spanish commander reap the fruits of his forecast.

On the departure of the Peruvian messenger, Pizarro presented him with a cap of crimson cloth, some cheap but showy ornaments of glass, and other toys, which he had brought for the purpose from Castile. He charged the envoy to tell his master that the Spaniards came from a powerful prince who dwelt far beyond the waters; that they had heard much of the fame of Atahuallpa's victories, and were come to pay their respects to him, and to offer their services by aiding him with their arms against his enemies; and he might be assured they would not halt on the road longer than was necessary, before presenting themselves before him.

Pizarro now received from Soto a full account of his late expedition. That chief, on entering Caxas, found the inhabitants mustered in hostile array, as if to dispute his passage. But the cavalier soon convinced them of his pacific intentions, and, laying aside their menacing attitude, they received the Spaniards with the same courtesy which had been shown them in most places on their march.

Here Soto found one of the royal officers, employed in collecting the tribute for the government. From this functionary he learned that the Inca was quartered with a large army at Cajamarca, a place of considerable size on the other side of the Cordillera, where he was enjoying the luxury of the warm baths, supplied by natural springs, for which it was then famous, as it is at the present day. The cavalier gathered also much important information in regard to the resources and the general policy of government, the state maintained by the Inca, and the stern severity with which obedience to the law was everywhere enforced. He had some opportunity of observing this for himself, as, on entering the village, he saw several Indians hanging dead by their heels, having been executed for some violence offered to the Virgins of the Sun, of whom there was a convent in the neighborhood.

From Caxas, De Soto had passed to the adjacent town of Ghuancabamba, much larger, more populous, and better built than the preceding. The houses, instead of being made of clay baked in the sun, were many of them constructed of solid stone, so nicely put together that it was impossible to detect the line of junction. A river which passed through the town was traversed by a bridge, and the highroad of the Incas which crossed this district was far superior to that which the Spaniards had seen on the seaboard. It was raised in many places, like a causeway, paved with heavy stone flags, and bordered by trees that afforded a grateful shade to the passenger, while streams of water were conducted through aqueducts along the sides to slake his thirst. At certain distances, also, they noticed small houses, which, they were told, were for the accommodation of the traveler, who might thus pass without inconvenience from one end of the kingdom to the other. In another quarter they beheld one of those magazines destined for the army, filled with grain and with articles of clothing; and at the entrance of the town was a stone building, occupied by a public officer, whose business it was to collect the tolls or duties on various commodities brought into the place or carried out of it. These accounts of De Soto not only confirmed all that the Spaniards had heard of the Indian empire, but greatly raised their ideas of its resources and domestic policy. They might well have shaken the confidence of hearts less courageous.

Pizarro, before leaving his present quarters, dispatched a messenger to San Miguel with particulars of his movements, sending at the same time the articles received from the Inca, as well as those obtained at different places on the route. The skill shown in the execution of some of these fabrics sent to Castile excited great admiration there. The fine woolen cloths, especially with their rich embroidery, were pronounced equal to textures of silk, from which it was not easy to distinguish them. The material was probably the delicate wool of the vicuña, none of which had then been seen in Europe.

Pizarro, having now acquainted himself with the most direct route to Cajamarca—the Cajamarca of the present day—resumed his march, taking a direction nearly south. The first place of any size at which he halted was Motupe, pleasantly situated in a fruitful valley, among hills of no great elevation, which cluster round the base of the Cordilleras. The place was deserted by its curaca, who, with three hundred of its warriors, had gone to join the standard of their Inca. Here the general, notwithstanding his avowed purpose to push forward without delay, halted four days. The tardiness of his movements can be explained only by the hope which he may have still entertained of being joined by further reinforcements before crossing the Cordilleras. None such appeared, however; and, advancing across a country in which tracts of sandy plain were occasionally relieved by a broad expanse of verdant meadow, watered by natural streams and still more abundantly by those brought through artificial channels, the troops at length arrived at the borders of a river. It was broad and deep, and the rapidity of the current opposed more than ordinary difficulty to the passage. Pizarro, apprehensive lest this might be disputed by the natives on the opposite bank, ordered his brother Hernando to cross over with a small detachment under cover of night and secure a safe landing for the rest of the troops. At break of day Pizarro made preparations for his own passage, by hewing timber in the neighboring woods and constructing a sort of floating bridge, on which before nightfall the whole company passed in safety, the horses swimming, being led by the bridle. It was a day of severe labor, and Pizarro took his own share in it freely, like a common soldier, having ever a word of encouragement to say to his followers.

On reaching the opposite side, they learned from their comrades that the people of the country, instead of offering resistance, had fled in dismay. One of them, having been taken and brought before Hernando Pizarro, refused to answer the questions put to him respecting the Inca and his army; till, being put to the torture, he stated that Atahuallpa was encamped, with his whole force, in three separate divisions, occupying the high grounds and plains of Cajamarca. He further stated that the Inca was aware of the approach of the white men and of their small number, and that he was purposely decoying them into his own quarters, that he might have them more completely in his power.

This account, when reported by Hernando to his brother, caused the latter much anxiety. As the timidity of the peasantry, however, gradually wore off, some of them mingled with the troops, and among them the curaca or principal person of the village. He had himself visited the royal camp, and he informed the general that Atahuallpa lay at the strong town of Huamachuco, twenty leagues or more south of Cajamarca, with an army of at least fifty thousand men.

These contradictory statements greatly perplexed the chieftain, and he proposed to one of the Indians who had borne him company during a great part of the march to go as a spy into the Inca's quarters and bring him intelligence of his actual position, and, as far as he could learn them, of his intentions towards the Spaniards. But the man declined this dangerous service, though he professed his willingness to go as an authorized messenger of the Spanish commander.

Pizarro acquiesced in this proposal, and instructed his envoy to assure the Inca that he was advancing with all convenient speed to meet him. He was to acquaint the monarch with the uniformly considerate conduct of the Spaniards towards his subjects in their progress through the land, and to assure him that they were now coming in full confidence of finding in him the same amicable feelings towards themselves. The emissary was particularly instructed to observe if the strong passes on the road were defended, or if any preparations of a hostile character were to be discerned. This last intelligence he was to communicate to the general by means of two or three nimble-footed attendants who were to accompany him on his mission.

Having taken this precaution, the wary commander again resumed his march, and at the end of three days reached the base of the mountain rampart behind which lay the ancient town of Cajamarca. Before him rose the stupendous Andes, rock piled upon rock, their skirts below dark with evergreen forests, varied here and there by treated patches of cultivated garden, with the peasant's cottage clinging to their shaggy sides, and their crests of snow glittering high in the heavens —presenting altogether such a wild chaos of magnificence and beauty as no other mountain scenery in the world can show. Across this tremendous rampart, through a labyrinth of passes easily capable of defense by a handful of men against an army, the troops were now to march. To the right ran a broad and level road, with its border of friendly shades, and wide enough for two carriages to pass abreast. It was one of the great routes leading to Cuzco, and seemed by its pleasant and easy access to invite the wayworn soldier to choose it in preference to the dangerous mountain defiles. Many were accordingly of opinion that the army should take this course and abandon the original destination to Cajamarca. But such was not the decision of Pizarro.

The Spaniards had everywhere proclaimed their purpose, he said, to visit the Inca in his camp. This purpose had been communicated to the Inca himself. To take an opposite direction now would only be to draw on them the imputation of cowardice, and to incur Atahuallpa's contempt. No alternative remained but to march straight across the sierra to his quarters. "Let every one of you," said the bold cavalier, "take heart and go forward like a good soldier, nothing daunted by the smallness of your numbers. For in the greatest extremity God ever fights for his own; and doubt not He will humble the pride of the heathen, and bring him to the knowledge of the true faith, the great end and object of the Conquest."

Pizarro, like Cortés, possessed a good share of that frank and manly eloquence which touches the heart of the soldier more than the parade of rhetoric or the finest flow of elocution. He was a soldier himself, and partook in all the feelings of the soldier, his joys, his hopes, and his disappointments. He was not raised by rank and education above sympathy with the humblest of his followers. Every chord in their bosoms vibrated with the same pulsations as his own, and the conviction of this gave him a mastery over them. "Lead on," they shouted, as he finished his brief but animating address, "lead on wherever you think best. We will follow with good will, and you shall see that we can do our duty in the cause of God and the King!" There was no longer hesitation. All thoughts were now bent on the instant passage of the Cordilleras.

# ❧ CHAPTER FOUR ❧

SEVERE PASSAGE OF THE ANDES—EMBASSIES FROM

ATAHUALLPA—THE SPANIARDS REACH

CAJAMARCA—EMBASSY TO THE INCA—INTERVIEW

WITH THE INCA—DESPONDENCY OF

THE SPANIARDS

## (1532)

That night Pizarro held a council of his principal officers, and it was determined that he should lead the advance, consisting of forty horse and sixty foot, and reconnoiter the ground; while the rest of the company, under his brother Hernando, should occupy their present position till they received further orders.

At early dawn the Spanish general and his detachment were under arms and prepared to breast the difficulties of the sierra. These proved even greater than had been foreseen. The path had been conducted in the most judicious manner round the rugged and precipitous sides of the mountains, so as best to avoid the natural impediments presented by the ground. But it was necessarily so steep, in many places, that the cavalry were obliged to dismount, and, scrambling up as they could, to lead their horses by the bridle. In many places, too, where some huge crag or eminence overhung the road, this was driven to the very verge of the precipice; and the traveler was compelled to wind along the narrow ledge of rock, scarcely wide enough for his single steed, where a mis-step would precipitate him hundreds, nay, thousands of feet into the dreadful abyss! The wild passes of the sierra, prac-ticable for the half-naked Indian, and even for the sure and circumspect mule—an animal that seems to have been cre-ated for the roads of the Cordilleras—were formidable to the man-at-arms encumbered with his panoply of mail. The tremendous fissures or *quebradas,* so frightful in this mountain chain, yawned open, as if the Andes had been split asunder by some terrible convulsion, showing a broad expanse of the primitive rock on their sides, partially mantled over with the spontaneous vegetation of ages; while their obscure depths furnished a channel for the torrents, that, rising in the heart of the sierra, worked their way gradually into light and spread over the savannas and green valleys of the *tierra caliente* on their way to the great ocean.

Many of these passes afforded obvious points of defense; and the Spaniards, as they entered the rocky defiles, looked with apprehension lest they might rouse some foe from his ambush. This apprehension was heightened as, at the summit of a steep and narrow gorge, in which they were engaged, they beheld a strong work, rising like a fortress, and frowning, as it were, in gloomy defiance on the invaders. As they drew near this building, which was of solid stone, commanding an angle of the road, they almost expected to see the dusky forms of the warriors rise over the battlements, and to receive their tempest of missiles on their bucklers; for it was in so strong a position that a few resolute men might easily have held there an army at bay. But they had the satisfaction to find the place untenanted, and their spirits were greatly raised by the conviction that the Indian monarch did not intend to dispute their passage, when it would have been easy to do so with success.

Pizarro now sent orders to his brother to follow without delay, and, after refreshing his men, continued his toilsome ascent, and before nightfall reached an eminence crowned by another fortress, of even greater strength than the preceding. It was built of solid masonry, the lower part excavated from the living rock, and the whole work executed with skill not inferior to that of the European architect.

Here Pizarro took up his quarters for the night. Without waiting for the arrival of the rear, on the following morning he resumed his march, leading still deeper into the intricate gorges of the sierra. The climate had gradually changed, and the men and horses, especially the latter, suffered severely from the cold, so long accustomed as they had been to the sultry climate of the tropics. The vegetation also had changed its character; and the magnificent timber which covered the lower level of the country had gradually given way to the funereal forest of pine, and, as they rose still higher, to the stunted growth of numberless Alpine plants, whose hardy natures found a congenial temperature in the icy atmosphere of the more elevated regions. These dreary solitudes seemed to be nearly abandoned by the brute creation as well as by man.

The light-footed vicuña, roaming in its native state, might be sometimes seen looking down from some airy cliff, where the foot of the hunter dared not venture. But instead of the feathered tribes whose gay plumage sparkled in the deep glooms of the tropical forests, the adventurers now beheld only the great bird of the Andes, the loathsome condor, which, sailing high above the clouds, followed with doleful cries in the track of the army, as if guided by instinct in the path of blood and carnage.

At length they reached the crest of the Cordillera, where it spreads out into a bold and bleak expanse, with scarcely a vestige of vegetation, except what is afforded by the *pajonal*, a dried yellow grass, which, as it is seen from below, encircling the base of the snow-covered peaks, looks, with its brilliant straw-color lighted up in the rays of an ardent sun, like a setting of gold round pinnacles of burnished silver. The land was sterile, as usual in mining districts, and they were drawing near the once famous gold quarries on the way to Cajamarca:

> "Rocks rich in gems, and mountains big with mines,
> That on the high equator ridgy rise."

**"The embassy arrived, which consisted of one of the Inca nobles and several attendants."**

Here Pizarro halted for the coming up of the rear. The air was sharp and frosty; and the soldiers, spreading their tents, lighted fires, and, huddling round them, endeavored to find some repose after their laborious march.

They had not been long in these quarters when a messenger arrived, one of those who had accompanied the Indian envoy sent by Pizarro to Atahuallpa. He informed the general that the road was free from enemies, and that an embassy from the Inca was on its way to the Castilian camp. Pizarro now sent back to quicken the march of the rear, as he was unwilling that the Peruvian envoy should find him with his present diminished numbers. The rest of the army were not far distant, and not long after reached the encampment.

In a short time the Indian embassy also arrived, which consisted of one of the Inca nobles and several attendants, bringing a welcome present of llamas to the Spanish commander. The Peruvian bore also the greetings of his master, who wished to know when the Spaniards would arrive at Cajamarca, that he might provide suitable refreshments for them. Pizarro learned that the Inca had left Huamachuco, and was now lying with a small force in the neighborhood of Cajamarca, at a place celebrated for its natural springs of warm water. The Peruvian was an intelligent person, and the Spanish commander gathered from him many particulars respecting the late contests which had distracted the empire.

As the envoy vaunted in lofty terms the military prowess and resources of his sovereign, Pizarro thought it politic to show that it had no power to overawe him. He expressed his satisfaction at the triumphs of Atahuallpa, who, he acknowledged, had raised himself high in the rank of Indian warriors. But he was an inferior, he added with more policy than politeness, to the monarch who ruled over the white men, as the petty curacas of the country were inferior to him. This was evident from the ease with which a few Spaniards had overrun this great continent, subduing one nation after another that had offered resistance to their arms. He had been led by the fame of Atahuallpa to visit his dominions and to offer him his services in his wars, and if he were received by the Inca in the same friendly spirit with which he came, he was willing, for the aid he could render him, to postpone awhile his passage across the country to the opposite seas. The Indian, according to the Castilian accounts, listened with awe to this strain of glorification from the Spanish commander. Yet it is possible that the envoy was a better diplomatist than they imagined, and that he understood it was only the game of brag at which he was playing with his more civilized antagonist.

On the succeeding morning, at an early hour, the troops were again on their march, and for two days were occupied in threading the airy defiles of the Cordilleras. Soon after beginning their descent on the eastern side, another emissary arrived from the Inca, bearing a message of similar import to the preceding, and a present, in like manner, of Peruvian sheep. This was the same noble that had visited Pizarro in the valley. He now came in more state, quaffing *chicha*—the fermented juice of the maize—from golden goblets borne by his attendants, which sparkled in the eyes of the rapacious adventurers.

While he was in the camp, the Indian messenger, originally sent by Pizarro to the Inca, returned, and no sooner did he behold the Peruvian, and the honorable reception which he met with from the Spaniards, than he was filled with wrath, which would have vented itself in personal violence but for the interposition of the bystanders. It was hard, he said, that this Peruvian dog should be thus courteously treated, when he himself had nearly lost his life on a similar mission among his countrymen. On reaching the Inca's camp he had been refused admission to his presence, on the ground that he was keeping a fast and could not be seen. They had paid no respect to his assertion that he came as an envoy from the white men, and would probably not have suffered him to escape with life, if he had not assured them that any violence offered to him would be retaliated in full measure on the persons of the Peruvian envoys now in the Spanish quarters. There was no doubt, he continued, of the hostile intentions of Atahuallpa; for he was surrounded with a powerful army, strongly encamped about a league from Cajamarca, while that city was entirely evacuated by its inhabitants.

To all this the Inca's envoy coolly replied that Pizarro's messenger might have reckoned on such a reception as he had found, since he seemed to have taken with him no credentials of his mission. As to the Inca's fast, that was true; and although he would doubtless have seen the messenger had he known there was one from the strangers, yet it was not safe to disturb him at these solemn seasons, when engaged in his religious duties. The troops by whom he was surrounded were not numerous, considering that the Inca was at that time carrying on an important war; and as to Cajamarca, it was abandoned by the inhabitants in order to make room for the white men, who were so soon to occupy it.

This explanation, however plausible, did not altogether satisfy the general; for he had too deep a conviction of the cunning of Atahuallpa, whose intentions towards the Spaniards he had long greatly distrusted. As he proposed, however, to keep on friendly relations with the monarch for the present, it was obviously not his cue to manifest suspicion. Affecting, therefore, to give full credit to the explanation of the envoy, he dismissed him with reiterated assurances of speedily presenting himself before the Inca.

The descent of the sierra, though the Andes are less precipitous on their eastern side than towards the west, was attended with difficulties almost equal to those of the upward march; and the Spaniards felt no little satisfaction when, on the seventh day, they arrived in view of the valley of Cajamarca, which, enameled with all the beauties of cultivation, lay unrolled like a rich and variegated carpet of verdure, in strong contrast with the dark forms of the Andes that rose up everywhere around it. The valley is of an oval shape, extending about five leagues in length by three in breadth. It was inhabited by a population of a superior character to any which the Spaniards had met on the other side of the mountains, as was argued by the superior style of their attire and the greater cleanliness and comfort visible both in their persons and dwellings. As far as the eye could reach, the level tract exhibited the show of a diligent and thrifty husbandry. A broad river rolled through the meadows, supplying facilities for copious irrigation by means of the usual canals and subterraneous aqueducts. The land, intersected by verdant hedgerows, was checkered with patches of various cultivation; for the soil was rich, and the climate, if less stimulating than that of the sultry regions of the coast, was more favorable to the hardy products of the temperate latitudes. Below the adventurers, with its white houses glittering in the sun, lay the little city of Cajamarca, like a sparkling gem on the dark skirts of the sierra. At the distance of about a league farther, across the valley, might be seen columns of vapor rising up towards the heavens, indicating the place of the famous hot baths, much frequented by the Peruvian princes. And here, too, was a spectacle less grateful to the eyes of the Spaniards; for along the slope of the hills a white cloud of pavilions was seen covering the ground, as thick as snowflakes, for the space, apparently, of several miles. "It filled us all with amazement," exclaims one of the Conquerors, "to behold the Indians occupying so proud a position! So many tents, so well appointed, as were never seen in the Indies till now! The spectacle caused something like confusion and even fear in the stoutest bosom. But it was too late to turn back, or to betray the least sign of weakness, since the natives in our own company would, in such case, have been the first to rise upon us. So, with as bold a countenance

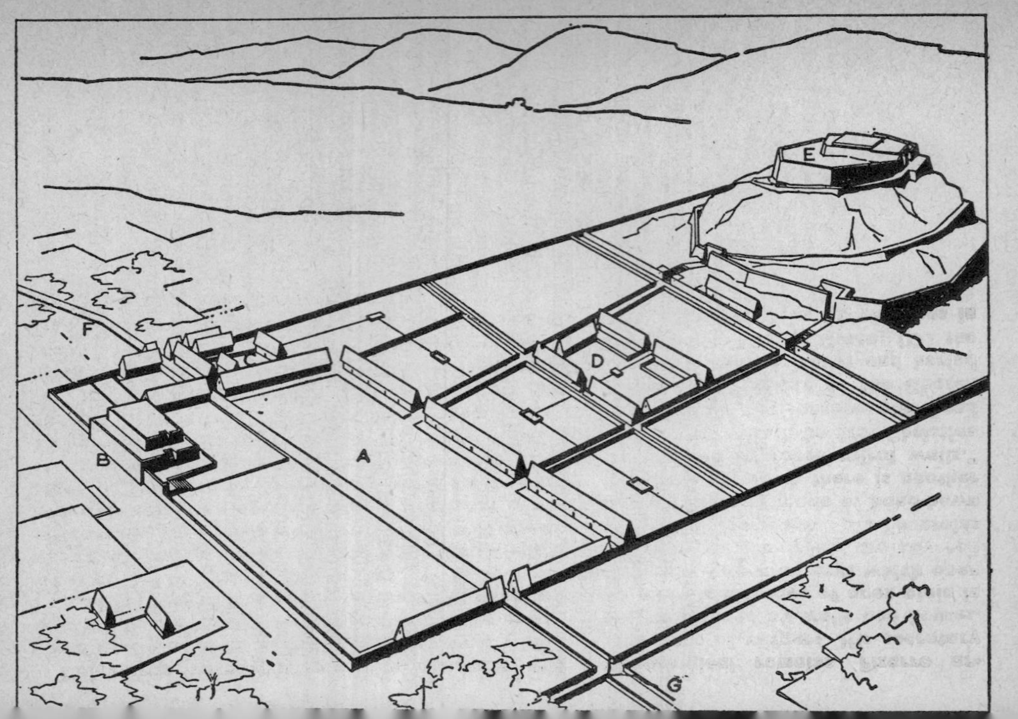

E
F
B
A
D
G

Cajamarca reconstructed from accounts and archaeological remains. Pizarro arrived at Cajamarca on Friday, November 15, 1532, at the hour of vespers. His secretary wrote: "In the middle of the town there is a great square surrounded by walls and houses. . . . It is situated in a valley between the mountains, and there is a league of open plain in front of it. The plaza is larger than any in Spain and entered by two gateways which open upon the streets. The houses are more than 200 paces in length, and the roofs are covered with straw. . . . Their walls are of very well-cut stone . . . with doorways. . . . Fountains of water are in an open court. . . . In front of the plaza is a fortress made of hand-hewn stone; a staircase leads from the plaza to the fort. . . . Above the town there is another fort, the greater part of which is hewn out of rock, surrounded by three spiral walls." (A) the Great Plaza; (B) the interior fortress where Pizarro later raised the first Christian church; (C) the Inca's quarters, a one-room house, which was later the ransom room (and the only part still intact); (D) the place of the Aclla-huasi—the house of the Chosen Women; (E) the fortress, where Pedro de Candia mounted his small falconet and hurled shot and shell upon the Inca; (F) the royal road of the Incas which led to Cuzco; (G) the Inca road from the north, by which Pizarro and his army entered to take up positions in the three large houses facing the plaza.

as we could, after coolly surveying the ground, we prepared for our entrance into Cajamarca."

What were the feelings of the Peruvian monarch we are not informed, when he gazed on the martial cavalcade of the Christians, as, with banners streaming, and bright panoplies glistening in the rays of the evening sun, it emerged from the dark depths of the sierra and advanced in hostile array over the fair domain which, until this period, had never been trodden by other foot than that of the red man. It might be, as several of the reports had stated, that the Inca had purposely decoyed the adventurers into the heart of his populous empire, that he might envelop them with his legions and the more easily become master of their property and persons. Or was it from a natural feeling of curiosity, and relying on their professions of friendship, that he had thus allowed them, without any attempt at resistance, to come into his presence? At all events, he could hardly have felt such confidence in himself as not to look with apprehension, mingled with awe, on the mysterious strangers, who, coming from an unknown world and possessed of such wonderful gifts, had made their way across mountain and valleys in spite of every obstacle which man and nature had opposed to them.

Pizarro meanwhile, forming his little corps into three divisions, now moved forward, at a more measured pace, and in order of battle, down the slopes that led towards the Indian city. As he drew near, no one came out to welcome him; and he rode through the streets without meeting with a living thing, or hearing a sound, except the echoes, sent back from the deserted dwellings, or the tramp of the soldiery.

It was a place of considerable size, containing about ten thousand inhabitants, somewhat more, probably, than the population assembled at this day within the walls of the modern city of Cajamarca. The houses, for the most part, were built of clay, hardened in the sun; the roofs thatched or of timber. Some of the more ambitious dwellings were of hewn stone; and there was a convent in the place, occupied by the Virgins of the Sun, and a temple dedicated to the same tutelar deity, which last was hidden in the deep embowering shades of a grove on the skirts of the city. On the quarter towards the Indian camp was a square—if square it might be called, which was almost triangular in form—of an immense size, surrounded by low buildings. These consisted of capacious halls, with wide doors or openings communicating with the square. They were probably intended as a sort of barracks for the Inca's soldiers. At the end of the *plaza*, looking towards the country, was a fortress of stone, with a stairway leading from the city, and a private entrance from the adjoining suburbs. There was still another fortress on the rising ground which commanded the town, built of hewn stone and encompassed by three circular walls—or rather one and the same wall, which wound up spirally around it. It was a place of great strength, and the workmanship showed a better knowledge of masonry, and gave a higher impression of the architectural science of the people, than anything the Spaniards had yet seen.

It was late in the afternoon of the fifteenth of November, 1532, when the Conquerors entered the city of Cajamarca. The weather, which had been fair during the day, now threatened a storm, and some rain mingled with hail—for it was unusually cold—began to fall. Pizarro, however, was so anxious to ascertain the dispositions of the Inca that he determined to send an embassy at once to his quarters. He selected for this Hernando de Soto with fifteen horse, and, after his departure, conceiving that the number was too small in case of any unfriendly demonstrations by the Indians, he ordered his brother Hernando to follow with twenty additional troopers. This captain and one other of his party have left us an account of the excursion.

Between the city and the imperial camp was a causeway, built in a substantial manner across the meadowland that intervened. Over this the cavalry galloped at a rapid pace, and before they had gone a league they came in front of the Peruvian encampment, where it spread along the gentle slope of the mountains. The lances of the warriors were fixed in the ground before their tents, and the Indian soldiers were loitering without, gazing with silent astonishment at the Christian cavalcade, as with clangor of arms and shrill blast of trumpet it swept by, like some fearful apparition on the wings of the wind.

The party soon came to a broad but shallow stream, which, winding through the meadow, formed a defense for the Inca's position. Across it was a wooden bridge; but the cavaliers, distrusting its strength, preferred to dash through the waters, and without difficulty gained the opposite bank. A battalion of Indian warriors was drawn up under arms on the farther side of the bridge, but they offered no molestation to the Spaniards; and these latter had strict orders from Pizarro—scarcely necessary in their present circumstances—to treat the natives with courtesy. One of the Indians pointed out the quarter occupied by the Inca.

It was an open courtyard, with a light building or pleasure house in the center, having galleries running round it, and

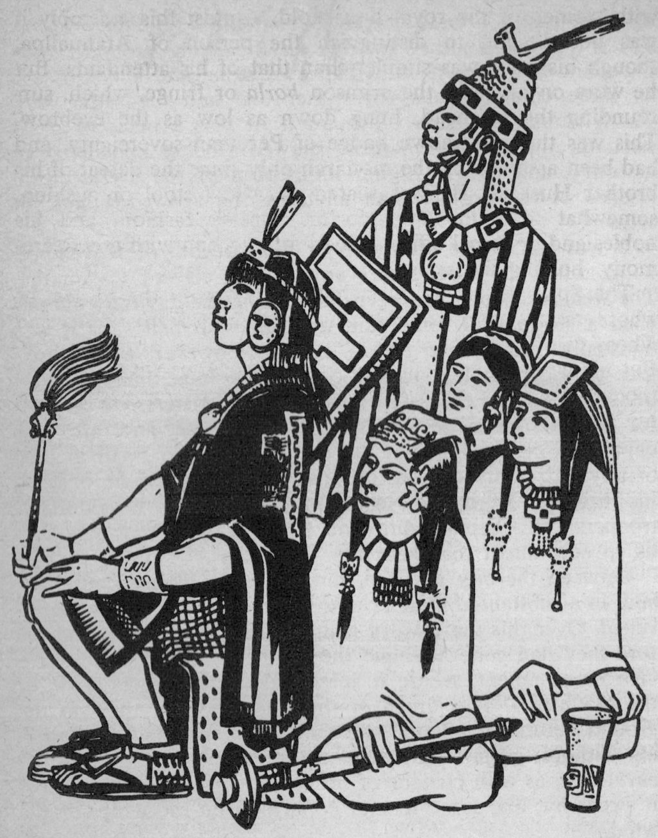

"Atahuallpa . . . was seated on a low stool . . . and his nobles and principal officers stood around him, with great ceremony."

opening in the rear on a garden. The walls were covered with a shining plaster, both white and colored, and in the area before the edifice was seen a spacious tank or reservoir of stone, fed by aqueducts that supplied it with both warm and cold water. A basin of hewn stone—it may be of a more recent construction—still bears, on the spot, the name of the "Inca's bath." The court was filled with Indian nobles, dressed in gaily ornamented attire, in attendance on the monarch, and with women of the royal household. Amidst this assembly it was not difficult to distinguish the person of Atahuallpa, though his dress was simpler than that of his attendants. But he wore on his head the crimson *borla* or fringe, which, surrounding the forehead, hung down as low as the eyebrow. This was the well-known badge of Peruvian sovereignty, and had been assumed by the monarch only since the defeat of his brother Huascar. He was seated on a low stool or cushion, somewhat after the Morisco or Turkish fashion, and his nobles and principal officers stood around him with great ceremony, holding the stations suited to their rank.

The Spaniards gazed with much interest on the prince, of whose cruelty and cunning they had heard so much, and whose valor had secured to him the possession of the empire. But his countenance exhibited neither the fierce passions nor the sagacity which had been ascribed to him; and though in his bearing he showed a gravity and a calm consciousness of authority well becoming a king, he seemed to discharge all expression from his features, and to discover only the apathy so characteristic of the American races. On the present occasion this must have been in part, at least, assumed. For it is impossible that the Indian prince should not have contemplated with curious interest a spectacle so strange, and in some respects appalling, as that of these mysterious strangers, for which no previous description could have prepared him.

Hernando Pizarro and Soto, with two or three only of their followers, slowly rode up in front of the Inca; and the former, making a respectful obeisance, but without dismounting, informed Atahuallpa that he came as an ambassador from his brother, the commander of the white men, to acquaint the monarch with their arrival in his city of Cajamarca. They were the subjects of a mighty prince across the waters, and had come, he said, drawn thither by the report of his great victories, to offer their services, and to impart to him the doctrines of the true faith which they professed; and he brought an invitation from the general to Atahuallpa that the latter would be pleased to visit the Spaniards in their present quarters.

To all this the Inca answered not a word; nor did he make even a sign of acknowledgment that he comprehended it; though it was translated for him by Felipillo, one of the interpreters already noticed. He remained silent, with his eyes fastened on the ground; but one of his nobles, standing by his side, answered, "It is well." This was an embarrassing situation for the Spaniards, who seemed to be as far from ascertaining the real disposition of the Peruvian monarch towards themselves as when the mountains were between them.

In a courteous and respectful manner, Hernando Pizarro again broke the silence by requesting the Inca to speak to them himself and to inform them what was his pleasure. To this Atahuallpa condescended to reply, while a faint smile passed over his features, "Tell your captain that I am keeping a fast, which will end to-morrow morning. I will then visit him, with my chieftains. In the meantime, let him occupy the public buildings on the square, and no other, till I come, when I will order what shall be done."

Soto, one of the party present at this interview, as before noticed, was the best mounted and perhaps the best rider in Pizarro's troop. Observing that Atahuallpa looked with some interest on the fiery steed that stood before him, champing the bit and pawing the ground with the natural impatience of a warhorse, the Spaniard gave him the rein, and, striking his iron heel into his side, dashed furiously over the plain, then, wheeling him round and round, displayed all the beautiful movements of his charger and his own excellent horsemanship. Suddenly checking him in full career, he brought the animal almost on his haunches, so near the person of the Inca that some of the foam that flecked his horse's sides was thrown on the royal garments. But Atahuallpa maintained the same marble composure as before, though several of his soldiers, whom De Soto passed in the course, were so much disconcerted by it that they drew back in manifest terror—an act of timidity for which they paid dearly *if*, as the Spaniards assert, Atahuallpa caused them to be put to death that same evening for betraying such unworthy weakness to the strangers.

Refreshments were now offered by the royal attendants to the Spaniards, which they declined, being unwilling to dismount. They did not refuse, however, to quaff the sparkling chicha from golden vases of extraordinary size, presented to them by the dark-eyed beauties of the harem. Taking then a respectful leave of the Inca, the cavaliers rode back to Cajamarca, with many moody speculations on what they had seen: on the state and opulence of the Indian monarch; on the strength of his military array, their excellent appointments, and the apparent discipline in their ranks—all arguing a much higher degree of civilization, and consequently of power, than anything they had witnessed in the lower regions of the country. As they contrasted all this with their own diminutive force, too far advanced, as they now were, for succor to reach them, they felt they had done rashly in throwing themselves into the midst of so formidable an empire, and were filled with gloomy forebodings of the result. Their comrades in the camp soon caught the infectious spirit of despondency, which was not lessened as night came on, and they beheld the watch fires of the Peruvians lighting up the sides of the mountains and glittering in the darkness, "as thick," says one who saw them, "as the stars of heaven."

Yet there was one bosom in that little host which was not touched with the feeling either of fear or dejection. That was Pizarro's, who secretly rejoiced that he had now brought matters to the issue for which he had so long panted. He saw the necessity of kindling a similar feeling in his followers, or all would be lost. Without unfolding his plans, he went round among his men, beseeching them not to show faint hearts at the crisis, when they stood face to face with the foe whom they had been so long seeking. "They were to rely on themselves, and on that Providence which had carried them safe through so many fearful trials. It would not now desert them; and if numbers, however great, were on the side of their enemy, it mattered little, when the arm of Heaven was on theirs." The Spanish cavalier acted under the combined influence of chivalrous adventure and religious zeal. The latter was the more effective in the hour of peril; and Pizarro, who understood well the characters he had to deal with, by presenting the enterprise as a crusade, kindled the dying embers of enthusiasm in the bosoms of his followers, and restored their faltering courage.

He then summoned a council of his officers, to consider the plan of operations, or rather to propose to them the extraordinary plan on which he had himself decided. This was to lay an ambuscade for the Inca and take him prisoner in the face of his whole army! It was a project full of peril—bordering, as it might well seem, on desperation. But the circumstances of the Spaniards were desperate. Whichever way they turned, they were menaced by the most appalling dangers; and better was it bravely to confront the danger than weakly to shrink from it, when there was no avenue for escape.

To fly was now too late. Whither could they fly? At the first signal of retreat, the whole army of the Inca would be upon them. Their movements would be anticipated by a foe far better acquainted with the intricacies of the sierra than themselves; the passes would be occupied, and they would be hemmed in on all sides; while the mere fact of this retrograde movement would diminish their confidence and with it their effective strength, while it doubled that of their enemy.

Yet to remain long inactive in their present position seemed almost equally perilous. Even supposing that Atahuallpa should entertain friendly feelings towards the Christians, they could not depend on the continuance of such feelings. Familiarity with the white men would soon destroy the idea of anything supernatural, or even superior, in their natures. He would feel contempt for their diminutive numbers. Their horses, their arms and showy appointments would be an attractive bait in the eye of the barbaric monarch, and when conscious that he had the power to crush their possessors, he would not be slow in finding a pretext for it. A sufficient one had already occurred in the high-handed measures of the Conquerors on their march through his dominions.

But what reason had they to flatter themselves that the Inca cherished such a disposition towards them? He was a crafty and unscrupulous prince, and, if the accounts they had repeatedly received on their march were true, had ever regarded the coming of the Spaniards with an evil eye. It was scarcely possible he should do otherwise. His soft messages had only been intended to decoy them across the mountains, where, with the aid of his warriors, he might readily overpower them. They were entangled in the toils which the cunning monarch had spread for them.

Their only remedy, then, was to turn the Inca's arts against himself; to take him, if possible, in his own snare. There was no time to be lost; for any day might bring back the victorious legions who had recently won his battles at the south, and thus make the odds against the Spaniards far greater than now.

Yet to encounter Atahuallpa in the open field would be attended with great hazard; and, even if victorious, there would be little probability that the person of the Inca, of so much importance, would fall into their hands. The invitation he had so unsuspiciously accepted to visit them in their quarters afforded the best means for securing this desirable prize. Nor was the enterprise so desperate, considering the great advantages afforded by the character and weapons of the invaders and the unexpectedness of the assault. The mere circumstance of acting on a concerted plan would alone make a small number more than a match for a much larger one. But it was not necessary to admit the whole of the Indian force into the city before the attack; and the person of the Inca once secured, his followers, astounded by so strange an event, were they few or many, would have no heart for further resistance; and with the Inca once in his power, Pizarro might dictate laws to the empire.

In this daring project of the Spanish chief it was easy to see that he had the brilliant exploit of Cortés in his mind when he carried off the Aztec monarch in his capital. But that was not by violence—at least not by open violence—and it received the sanction, compulsory though it were, of the monarch himself. It was also true that the results in that case did not altogether justify a repetition of the experiment, since the people rose in a body to sacrifice both the prince and his kidnapers. Yet this was owing, in part at least, to the indiscretion of the latter. The experiment in the outset was perfectly successful; and could Pizarro once become master of the person of Atahuallpa, he trusted to his own discretion for the rest. It would at least extricate him from his present critical position, by placing in his power an inestimable guarantee for his safety; and if he could not make his own terms with the Inca at once, the arrival of reinforcements from home would, in all probability, soon enable him to do so.

Pizarro having concerted his plans for the following day, the council broke up, and the chief occupied himself with providing for the security of the camp during the night. The approaches to the town were defended; sentinels were posted at different points, especially on the summit of the fortress, where they were to observe the position of the enemy and to report any movement that menaced the tranquillity of the night. After these precautions, the Spanish commander and his followers withdrew to their appointed quarters—but not to sleep. At least, sleep must have come late to those who were aware of the decisive plan for the morrow; that morrow which was to be the crisis of their fate—to crown their ambitious schemes with full success, or consign them to irretrievable ruin!

# ◆ CHAPTER FIVE ◆

DESPERATE PLAN OF PIZARRO—ATAHUALLPA VISITS

THE SPANIARDS—HORRIBLE

MASSACRE—THE INCA A PRISONER—

CONDUCT OF THE CONQUERORS—

SPLENDID PROMISES OF THE INCA—

DEATH OF HUASCAR

(1532)

The clouds of the evening had passed away, and the sun rose bright on the following morning, the most memorable epoch in the annals of Peru. It was Saturday, the sixteenth of November, 1532. The loud cry of the trumpet called the Spaniards to arms with the first streak of dawn; and Pizarro, briefly acquainting them with the plan of the assault, made the necessary dispositions.

The *plaza,* as mentioned in the preceding chapter, was defended on its three sides by low ranges of buildings, consisting of spacious halls with wide doors or vomitories opening into the square. In these halls he stationed his cavalry in two divisions, one under his brother Hernando, the other under De Soto. The infantry he placed in another of the buildings, reserving twenty chosen men to act with himself as occasion might require. Pedro de Candia, with a few soldiers and the artillery—comprehending under this imposing name two small pieces of ordnance, called falconets—he established in the fortress. All received orders to wait at their posts till the arrival of the Inca. After his entrance into the great square, they were still to remain under cover, withdrawn from observation, till the signal was given by the discharge of a gun, when they were to cry their war cries, to rush out in a body from their covert, and, putting the Peruvians to the sword, bear off the person of the Inca. The arrangement of the immense halls, opening on a level with the *plaza,* seemed to be contrived on purpose for a *coup de théâtre.* Pizarro particularly inculcated order and implicit obedience, that in the hurry of the moment there should be no confusion. Everything depended on their acting with concert, coolness, and celerity.

The chief next saw that their arms were in good order, and that the breastplates of their horses were garnished with bells, to add by their noise to the consternation of the Indians. Refreshments were also liberally provided, that the troops should be in condition for the conflict. These arrangements being completed, mass was performed with great solemnity by the ecclesiastics who attended the expedition; the God of Battles was invoked to spread his shield over the soldiers who were fighting to extend the empire of the Cross; and all joined with enthusiasm in the chant, *"Exsurge, Domine,"* "Rise, O Lord! and judge thine own cause." One might have supposed them a company of martyrs about to lay down their lives in defense of their faith, instead of a licentious band of adventurers meditating one of the most atrocious acts of perfidy on the record of history! Yet, whatever were the vices of the Castilian cavalier, hypocrisy was not among the number. He felt that he was battling for the Cross, and under this conviction, exalted as it was at such a moment as this into the predominant impulse, he was blind to the baser motives which mingled with the enterprise. With feelings thus kindled to a flame of religious ardor, the soldiers of Pizarro looked forward with renovated spirits to the coming conflict; and the chieftain saw with satisfaction that in the hour of trial his men would be true to their leader and themselves.

It was late in the day before any movement was visible in the Peruvian camp, where much preparation was making to approach the Christian quarters with due state and ceremony. A message was received from Atahuallpa, informing the Spanish commander that he should come with his warriors fully armed, in the same manner as the Spaniards had come to his quarters the night preceding. This was not an agreeable intimation to Pizarro, though he had no reason, probably, to expect the contrary. But to object might imply distrust, or perhaps disclose, in some measure, his own designs. He expressed his satisfaction, therefore, at the intelligence, assuring the Inca that, come as he would, he would be received by him as a friend and brother.

It was noon before the Indian procession was on its march, when it was seen occupying the great causeway for a long extent. In front came a large body of attendants, whose office seemed to be to sweep away every particle of rubbish from the road. High above the crowd appeared the Inca, borne on the shoulders of his principal nobles, while others of the same rank marched by the sides of his litter, displaying such a dazzling show of ornaments on their persons that, in the language of one of the Conquerors, "they blazed like the sun." But the greater part of the Inca's forces mustered along the fields that lined the road, and were spread over the broad meadows as far as the eye could reach.

When the royal procession had arrived within half a mile of the city, it came to a halt; and Pizarro saw with surprise that Atahuallpa was preparing to pitch his tents, as if to encamp there. A messenger soon after arrived, informing the Spaniards that the Inca would occupy his present station the ensuing night, and enter the city on the following morning.

This intelligence greatly disturbed Pizarro, who had shared in the general impatience of his men at the tardy movements of the Peruvians. The troops had been under arms since daylight, the cavalry mounted, and the infantry at their post, waiting in silence the coming of the Inca. A profound stillness reigned throughout the town, broken only at intervals by the cry of the sentinel from the summit of the fortress, as he proclaimed the movements of the Indian army. Nothing, Pizarro well knew, was so trying to the soldier as prolonged suspense in a critical situation like the present, and he feared lest his ardor might evaporate, and be succeeded by that nervous feeling natural to the bravest soul at such a crisis, and which, if not fear, is near akin to it. He returned an answer, therefore, to Atahuallpa, deprecating his change of purpose, and adding that he had provided everything for his entertainment, and expected him that night to sup with him.

This message turned the Inca from his purpose; and, striking his tents again, he resumed his march, first advising the general that he should leave the greater part of his warriors behind, and enter the place with only a few of them, and without arms, as he preferred to pass the night at Cajamarca. At the same time he ordered accommodations to be provided for himself and his retinue in one of the large stone buildings, called, from a serpent sculptured on the walls, "the House of the Serpent." No tidings could have been more grateful to the Spaniards. It seemed as if the Indian monarch was eager to rush into the snare that had been spread for him! The fanatical cavalier could not fail to discern in it the immediate finger of Providence.

It is difficult to account for this wavering conduct of Atahuallpa, so different from the bold and decided character which history ascribes to him. There is no doubt that he made his visit to the white men in perfect good faith; though Pizarro was probably right in conjecturing that this amiable disposition stood on a very precarious footing. There is as little reason to suppose that he distrusted the sincerity of the strangers, or he would not thus unnecessarily have proposed to visit them unarmed. His original purpose of coming with all his force was doubtless to display his royal state, and perhaps, also, to show greater respect for the Spaniards; but when he consented to accept their hospitality and pass the night in their quarters, he was willing to dispense with a great part of his armed soldiery and visit them in a manner that implied entire confidence in their good faith. He was too absolute in his own empire easily to suspect; and he probably could not comprehend the audacity with which a few men, like those now assembled at Cajamarca, meditated an assault on a powerful monarch in the midst of his victorious army. He did not know the character of the Spaniard.

It was not long before sunset when the van of the royal procession entered the gates of the city. First came some hundreds of the menials, employed to clear the path of every obstacle, and singing songs of triumph as they came, "which in our ears," says one of the Conquerors, "sounded like the songs of hell!" Then followed other bodies of different ranks, and dressed in different liveries. Some wore a showy stuff, checkered white and red, like the squares of a chessboard. Others were clad in pure white, bearing hammers or maces of silver or copper; and the guards, together with those in immediate attendance on the prince, were distinguished by a rich azure livery and a profusion of gay ornaments, while the large pendants attached to the ears indicated the Peruvian noble.

Elevated high above his vassals came the Inca Atahuallpa, borne on an open litter, on which was a sort of throne made of massive gold of inestimable value. The palanquin was lined with the richly colored plumes of tropical birds, and studded with shining plates of gold and silver. The monarch's attire was much richer than on the preceding evening. Round his neck was suspended a collar of emeralds of uncommon size and brilliancy. His short hair was decorated with golden ornaments, and the imperial *borla* encircled his temples. The bearing of the Inca was sedate and dignified; and from his lofty station he looked down on the multitudes below with an air of composure, like one accustomed to command.

As the leading files of the procession entered the great square, larger, says an old chronicler, than any square in

Spain, they opened to the right and left for the royal retinue to pass. Everything was conducted with admirable order. The monarch was permitted to traverse the *plaza* in silence, and not a Spaniard was to be seen. When some five or six thousand of his people had entered the place, Atahuallpa halted and, turning round with an inquiring look, demanded, "Where are the strangers?"

At this moment Fray Vicente de Valverde, a Dominican friar, Pizarro's chaplain, and afterwards Bishop of Cuzco, came forward with his breviary, or, as other accounts say, a Bible, in one hand, and a crucifix in the other, and, approaching the Inca, told him that he came by order of his commander to expound to him the doctrines of the true faith, for which purpose the Spaniards had come from a great distance to his country. The friar then explained, as clearly as he could, the mysterious doctrine of the Trinity, and, ascending high in his account, began with the creation of man, thence passed to his fall, to his subsequent redemption by Jesus Christ, to the crucifixion an dthe ascension, when the Saviour left the Apostle Peter as his Vicegerent upon earth. This power had been transmitted to the successors of the apostle, good and wise men, who, under the title of Popes, held authority over all powers and potentates on earth. One of the last of these Popes had commissioned the Spanish emperor, the most mighty monarch in the world, to conquer and convert the natives in this Western Hemisphere; and his general, Francisco Pizarro, had now come to execute this important mission. The friar concluded with beseeching the Peruvian monarch to receive him kindly, to abjure the errors of his own faith, and embrace that of the Christians now proffered to him, the only one by which he could hope for salvation; and, furthermore, to acknowledge himself a tributary of the Emperor Charles the Fifth, who, in that event, would aid and protect him as his loyal vassal.

Whether Atahuallpa possessed himself of every link in the curious chain of argument by which the monk connected Pizarro with St. Peter may be doubted. It is certain, however, that he must have had very incorrect notions of the Trinity, if, as Garcilasso states, the interpreter Felipillo explained it by saying that "the Christians believed in three Gods and one God, and that made four." But there is no doubt he perfectly comprehended that the drift of the discourse was to persuade him to resign his scepter and acknowledge the supremacy of another.

The eyes of the Indian monarch flashed fire, and his dark brow grew darker, as he replied, "I will be no man's tributary.

I am greater than any prince upon earth. Your emperor may be a great prince; I do not doubt it, when I see that he has sent his subjects so far across the waters; and I am willing to hold him as a brother. As for the Pope of whom you speak, he must be crazy to talk of giving away countries which do not belong to him. For my faith," he continued, "I will not change it. Your own God, as you say, was put to death by the very men whom he created. But mine," he concluded, pointing to his Deity—then, alas! sinking in glory behind the mountains—"my God still lives in the heavens and looks down on his children."

He then demanded of Valverde by what authority he had said these things. The friar pointed to the book which he held as his authority. Atahuallpa, taking it, turned over the pages a moment, then, as the insult he had received probably flashed across his mind, he threw it down with vehemence, and exclaimed, "Tell your comrades that they shall give me an account of their doings in my land. I will not go from here till they have made me full satisfaction for all the wrongs they have committed."

The friar, greatly scandalized by the indignity offered to the sacred volume, stayed only to pick it up, and, hastening to Pizarro, informed him of what had been done, exclaiming, at the same time, "Do you not see that while we stand here wasting our breath in talking with this dog, full of pride as he is, the fields are filling with Indians? Set on at once; I absolve you." Pizarro saw that the hour had come. He waved a white scarf in the air, the appointed signal. The fatal gun was fired from the fortress. Then, springing into the square, the Spanish captain and his followers shouted the old war cry of "Santiago and at them!" It was answered by the battle cry of every Spaniard in the city as, rushing from the avenues of the great halls in which they were concealed, they poured into the *plaza*, horse and foot, each in his own dark column, and threw themselves into the midst of the Indian crowd. The latter, taken by surprise, stunned by the report of artillery and muskets, the echoes of which reverberated like thunder from the surrounding buildings, and blinded by the smoke which rolled in sulphurous volumes along the square, were seized with a panic. They knew not whither to fly for refuge from the coming ruin. Nobles and commoners—all were trampled down under the fierce charge of the cavalry, who dealt their blows, right and left, without sparing; while their swords, flashing through the thick gloom, carried dismay into the hearts of the wretched natives, who now for the first time saw the horse and his rider in all their terrors. They made no resistance—as, indeed, they had no weapons with which to make it. Every avenue to escape was closed, for the entrance to the square was choked up with the dead bodies of men who had perished in vain efforts to fly; and such was the agony of the survivors under the terrible pressure of their assailants, that a large body of Indians, by their convulsive struggles, burst through the wall of stone and dried clay which formed part of the boundary of the *plaza!* It fell, leaving an opening of more than a hundred paces, through which multitudes now found their way into the country, still hotly pursued by the cavalry, who, leaping the fallen rubbish, hung on the rear of the fugitives, striking them down in all directions.

Meanwhile the fight, or rather massacre, continued hot around the Inca, whose person was the great object of the assault. His faithful nobles, rallying about him, threw themselves in the way of the assailants, and strove, by tearing them from their saddles, or at least by offering their own bosoms as a mark for their vengeance, to shield their beloved master. It is said by some authorities that they carried weapons concealed under their clothes. If so, it availed them little, as it is not pretended that they used them. But the most timid animal will defend itself when at bay. That the Indians did not do so in the present instance is proof that they had no weapons to use. Yet they still continued to force back the cavaliers, clinging to their horses with dying grasp, and, as one was cut down, another taking the place of his fallen comrade with a loyalty truly affecting.

The Indian monarch, stunned and bewildered, saw his faithful subjects falling around him without fully comprehending his situation. The litter on which he rode heaved to and fro, as the mighty press swayed backwards and forwards; and he gazed on the overwhelming ruin, like some forlorn mariner, who, tossed about in his bark by the furious elements, sees the lightning's flash and hears the thunder bursting around him with the consciousness that he can do nothing to avert his fate. At length, weary with the work of destruction, the Spaniards, as the shades of evening grew deeper, felt afraid that the royal prize might after all elude them; and some of the cavaliers made a desperate attempt to end the affray at once by taking Atahuallpa's life. But Pizarro, who was nearest his person, called out, with stentorian voice, "Let no one who values his life strike at the Inca!" and, stretching out his arm to shield him, received a wound on the hand from one of his own men—the only wound received by a Spaniard in the action.

The struggle now became fiercer than ever round the royal

litter. It reeled more and more, and at length, several of the nobles who supported it having been slain, it was overturned, and the Indian prince would have come with violence to the ground, had not his fall been broken by the efforts of Pizarro and some other of the cavaliers, who caught him in their arms. The imperial *borla* was instantly snatched from his temples by a soldier named Miguel De Estete, and the unhappy monarch, strongly secured, was removed to a neighboring building, where he was carefully guarded.

All attempt at resistance now ceased. The fate of the Inca soon spread over town and country. The charm which might have held the Peruvians together was dissolved. Every man thought only of his own safety. Even the soldiery encamped on the adjacent fields took the alarm, and, learning the fatal tidings, were seen flying in every direction before their pursuers, who in the heat of triumph showed no touch of mercy. At length night, more pitiful than man, threw her friendly mantle over the fugitives, and the scattered troops of Pizarro rallied once more at the sound of the trumpet in the bloody square of Cajamarca.

The number of slain is reported, as usual, with great discrepancy. Pizarro's secretary says two thousand natives fell. A descendant of the Incas—a safer authority than Garcilasso —swells the number to ten thousand. Truth is generally found somewhere between the extremes. The slaughter was incessant, for there was nothing to check it. That there should have been no resistance will not appear strange when we consider the fact that the wretched victims were without arms, and that their senses must have been completely overwhelmed by the strange and appalling spectacle which burst on them so unexpectedly. "What wonder was it," said an ancient Inca to a Spaniard, who repeats it—"what wonder that our countrymen lost their wits, seeing blood run like water, and the Inca, whose person we all of us adore, seized and carried off by a handful of men?" Yet, though the massacre was incessant, it was short in duration. The whole time consumed by it, the brief twilight of the tropics, did not much exceed half an hour; a short period, indeed, yet long enough to decide the fate of Peru and to subvert the dynasty of the Incas.

That night Pizarro kept his engagement with the Inca, since he had Atahuallpa to sup with him. The banquet was served in one of the halls facing the great square, which a few hours before had been the scene of slaughter, and the pavement of which was still encumbered with the dead bodies of the Inca's subjects. The captive monarch was placed next his conqueror. He seemed like one who did not yet fully comprehend the extent of his calamity. If he did, he showed an amazing fortitude. "It is the fortune of war," he said; and, if we may credit the Spaniards, he expressed his admiration of the adroitness with which they had contrived to entrap him in the midst of his own troops.[37] He added that he had been made acquainted with the progress of the white men from the hour of their landing, but that he had been led to undervalue their strength from the insignificance of their numbers. He had no doubt he should be easily able to overpower them, on their arrival at Cajamarca, by his superior strength; and as he wished to see for himself what manner of men they were, he had suffered them to cross the mountains, meaning to select such as he chose for his own service, and, getting possession of their wonderful arms and horses, put the rest to death.

That such may have been Atahuallpa's purpose is not improbable. It explains his conduct in not occupying the mountain passes, which afforded such strong points of defense against invasion. But that a prince so astute, as by the general testimony of the Conquerors he is represented to have been, should have made so impolitic a disclosure of his hidden motives, is not so probable. The intercourse with the Inca was carried on chiefly by means of the interpreter Felipillo, or *little Philip,* as he was called, from his assumed Christian name—a malicious youth, as it appears, who bore no good will to Atahuallpa, and whose interpretations were readily admitted by the Conquerors, eager to find some pretext for their bloody reprisals.

Atahuallpa, as elsewhere noticed, was at this time about thirty years of age. He was well made, and more robust than usual with his countrymen. His head was large, and his countenance might have been called handsome, but that his eyes, which were bloodshot, gave a fierce expression to his features. He was deliberate in speech, grave in manner, and towards his own people stern even to severity; though with the Spaniards he showed himself affable, sometimes even indulging in sallies of mirth.

Pizarro paid every attention to his royal captive, and endeavored to lighten, if he could not dispel, the gloom which, in spite of his assumed equanimity, hung over the monarch's brow. He besought him not to be cast down by his reverses, for his lot had only been that of every prince who had resisted the white men. They had come into the country to proclaim the gospel, the religion of Jesus Christ; and it was no wonder they had prevailed, when His shield was over them. Heaven had permitted that Atahuallpa's pride should be humbled, because of his hostile intentions towards the Spaniards and the insult he had offered to the sacred volume. But he bade the Inca take courage and confide in him, for the Spaniards were a generous race, warring only against those who made war on them, and showing grace to all who submitted! Atahuallpa may have thought the massacre of that day an indifferent commentary on this vaunted lenity.

Before retiring for the night, Pizarro briefly addressed his troops on their present situation. When he had ascertained that not a man was wounded, he bade them offer up thanksgivings to Providence for so great a miracle; without its care, they could never have prevailed so easily over the host of their enemies; and he trusted their lives had been reserved for still greater things. But, if they would succeed, they had much to do for themselves. They were in the heart of a powerful kingdom, encompassed by foes deeply attached to their own sovereign. They must be ever on their guard, therefore, and be prepared at any hour to be roused from their slumbers by the call of the trumpet. Having then posted his sentinels, placed a strong guard over the apartment of Atahuallpa, and taken all the precautions of a careful commander, Pizarro withdrew to repose; and if he could really feel that in the bloody scenes of the past day he had been fighting only the good fight of the Cross, he doubtless slept sounder than on the night preceding the seizure of the Inca.

On the following morning, the first commands of the Spanish chief were to have the city cleaned of its impurities; and the prisoners, of whom there were many in the camp, were employed to remove the dead and give them decent burial. His next care was to dispatch a body of about thirty horse to the quarters lately occupied by Atahuallpa at the baths, to take possession of the spoil, and disperse the remnant of the Peruvian forces which still hung about the place.

Before noon, the party which he had detached on this service returned with a large troop of Indians, men and women, among the latter of whom were many of the wives and attendants of the Inca. The Spaniards had met with no resistance; since the Peruvian warriors, though so superior in number, excellent in appointments, and consisting mostly of able-bodied young men—for the greater part of the veteran forces were with the Inca's generals at the south—lost all heart from the moment of their sovereign's captivity. There was no leader to take his place; for they recognized no authority but that of the Child of the Sun, and they seemed to be held by a sort of invisible charm near the place of his confinement; while they gazed with superstitious awe on the white men who could achieve so audacious an enterprise.

The number of Indian prisoners was so great that some of the Conquerors were for putting them all to death, or at least cutting off their hands, to disable them from acts of violence and to strike terror into their countrymen. The proposition, doubtless, came from the lowest and most ferocious of the soldiery. But that it should have been made at all shows what materials entered into the composition of Pizarro's company. The chief rejected it at once, as no less impolitic than inhuman, and dismissed the Indians to their several homes, with the assurance that none should be harmed who did not offer resistance to the white men. A sufficient number, however, were retained to wait on the Conquerors, who were so well provided in this respect that the most common soldier was attended by a retinue of menials that would have better suited the establishment of a noble.

The Spaniards had found immense droves of llamas under the care of the shepherds in the neighborhood of the baths, destined for the consumption of the court. Many of them were now suffered to roam abroad among their native mountains, though Pizarro caused a considerable number to be reserved for the use of the army. And this was no small quantity, if, as one of the Conquerors says, a hundred and fifty of the Peruvian sheep were frequently slaughtered in a day. Indeed, the Spaniards were so improvident in their destruction of these animals that in a few years the superb flocks, nurtured with so much care by the Peruvian government, had almost disappeared from the land.

The party sent to pillage the Inca's pleasure house brought back a rich booty in gold and silver, consisting chiefly of plate for the royal table, which greatly astonished the Spaniards by their size and weight. These, as well as some large emeralds obtained there, together with the precious spoils found on the bodies of the Indian nobles who had perished in the massacre, were placed in safe custody, to be hereafter divided. In the city of Cajamarca the troops also found magazines stored with goods, both cotton and woolen, far superior to any they had seen, for fineness of texture and the skill with which the various colors were blended. They were piled from the floors to the very roofs of the buildings, and in such quantity that, after every soldier had provided himself with what he desired, it made no sensible diminution of the whole amount.

Pizarro would now gladly have directed his march on the Peruvian capital. But the distance was great, and his force was small. This must have been still further crippled by the guard required for the Inca, and the chief feared to involve

himself deeper in a hostile empire so populous and powerful,
with a prize so precious in his keeping. With much anxiety,
therefore, he looked for reinforcements from the colonies;
and he dispatched a courier to San Miguel, to inform the
Spaniards there of his recent successes, and to ascertain if
there had been any arrival from Panamá. Meanwhile he employed his men in making Cajamarca a more suitable residence for a Christian host, by erecting a church, or perhaps
appropriating some Indian edifice to this use, in which mass

**"He told Pizarro that if he would set him free, he would en-
gage to cover the floor of the apartment on which they stood
with gold. . . . As the Inca received no answer, he said . . .
that he would not merely cover the floor, but would fill the room
with gold as high as he could reach."**

was regularly performed by the Dominican fathers with great solemnity. The dilapidated walls of the city were also restored in a more substantial manner than before, and every vestige was soon effaced of the hurricane that had so recently swept over it.

It was not long before Atahuallpa discovered, amidst all the show of religious zeal in his Conquerors, a lurking appetite more potent in most of their bosoms than either religion or ambition. This was the love of gold. He determined to avail himself of it to procure his own freedom. The critical posture of his affairs made it important that this should not be long delayed. His brother Huascar, ever since his defeat, had been detained as a prisoner, subject to the victor's orders. He was now at Andamarca, at no great distance from Cajamarca; and Atahuallpa feared, with good reason, that, when his own imprisonment was known, Huascar would find it easy to corrupt his guards, make his escape, and put himself at the head of the contested empire without a rival to dispute it.

In the hope, therefore, to effect his purpose of appealing to the avarice of his keepers, he one day told Pizarro that if he would set him free he would engage to cover the floor of the apartment on which they stood with gold. Those present listened with an incredulous smile; and as the Inca received no answer, he said, with some emphasis, that "he would not merely cover the floor, but would fill the room with gold as high as he could reach"; and, standing on tiptoe, he stretched out his hand against the wall. All stared with amazement; while they regarded it as the insane boast of a man too eager to procure his liberty to weigh the meaning of his words. Yet Pizarro was sorely perplexed. As he had advanced into the country, much that he had seen, and all that he had heard, had confirmed the dazzling reports first received of the riches of Peru. Atahuallpa himself had given him the most glowing picture of the wealth of the capital, where the roofs of the temples were plated with gold, while the walls were hung with tapestry and the floors inlaid with tiles of the same precious metal. There must be some foundation for all this. At all events, it was safe to accede to the Inca's proposition, since by so doing he could collect at once all the gold at his disposal, and thus prevent its being purloined or secreted by the natives. He therefore acquiesced in Atahuallpa's offer, and, drawing a red line along the wall at the height which the Inca had indicated, he caused the terms of the proposal to be duly recorded by the notary. The apartment was about seventeen feet broad, by twenty-two feet long, and the line round the walls was nine feet from the floor.[38] This space was to be filled with gold; but it was understood that the gold was not to be melted down into ingots, but to retain the original form of the articles into which it was manufactured, that the Inca might have the benefit of the space which they occupied. He further agreed to fill an adjoining room of smaller dimensions twice full with silver, in like manner; and he demanded two months to accomplish all this.

No sooner was this arrangement made than the Inca dispatched couriers to Cuzco and the other principal places in the kingdom, with orders that the gold ornaments and utensils should be removed from the royal palaces, and from the temples and other public buildings, and transported without loss of time to Cajamarca. Meanwhile he continued to live in the Spanish quarters, treated with the respect due to his rank, and enjoying all the freedom that was compatible with the security of his person. Though not permitted to go abroad, his limbs were unshackled, and he had the range of his own apartments under the zealous surveillance of a guard, who knew too well the value of the royal captive to be remiss. He was allowed the society of his favorite wives, and Pizarro took care that his domestic privacy should not be violated. His subjects had free access to their sovereign, and every day he received visits from the Indian nobles, who came to bring presents and offer condolence to their unfortunate master. On such occasions the most potent of these great vassals never ventured into his presence without first stripping off their sandals and bearing a load on their backs in token of reverence. The Spaniards gazed with curious eyes on these acts of homage, or rather of slavish submission, on the one side, and on the air of perfect indifference with which they were received, as a matter of course, on the other; and they conceived high ideas of the character of a prince who, even in his present helpless condition, could inspire such feelings of awe in his subjects. The royal levee was so well attended, and such devotion was shown by his vassals to the captive monarch, as did not fail, in the end, to excite some feelings of distrust in his keepers.

Pizarro did not neglect the opportunity afforded him of communicating the truths of revelation to his prisoner, and both he and his chaplain, Father Valverde, labored in the same good work. Atahuallpa listened with composure and apparent attention. But nothing ssemed to move him so much as the argument with which the military polemic closed his discourse—that it could not be the true God whom Atahuallpa worshiped, since he had suffered him to fall into the hands of his enemies. The unhappy monarch assented to the force of this, acknowledging that his Deity had indeed deserted him in his utmost need.

Yet his conduct towards his brother Huascar at this time too clearly proves that, whatever respect he may have shown for the teachers, the doctrines of Christianity had made little impression on his heart. No sooner had Huascar been informed of the capture of his rival, and of the large ransom he had offered for his deliverance, than, as the latter had foreseen, he made every effort to regain his liberty, and sent, or attempted to send, a message to the Spanish commander, that he would pay a much larger ransom than that promised by Atahuallpa, who, never having dwelt in Cuzco, was ignorant of the quantity of treasure there, and where it was deposited.

Intelligence of all this was secretly communicated to Atahuallpa by the persons who had his brother in charge; and his jealousy, thus roused, was further heightened by Pizarro's declaration that he intended to have Huascar brought to Cajamarca, where he would himself examine into the controversy and determine which of the two had the better title to the scepter of the Incas. Pizarro perceived, from the first, the advantages of a competition which would enable him, by throwing his sword into the scale he preferred, to give it a preponderance. The party who held the scepter by his nomination would henceforth be a tool in his hands, with which to work his pleasure more effectually than he could well do in his own name. It was the game, as every reader knows, played by Edward the First in the affairs of Scotland, and by many a monarch both before and since; and though their examples may not have been familiar to the unlettered soldier, Pizarro was too quick in his perceptions to require, in this matter at least, the teachings of history.

Atahuallpa was much alarmed by the Spanish commander's determination to have the suit between the rival candidates brought before him; for he feared that, independently of the merits of the case, the decision would be likely to go in favor of Huascar, whose mild and ductile temper would make him a convenient instrument in the hands of his conquerors. Without further hesitation, he determined to remove this cause of jealousy forever, by the death of his brother.

His orders were immediately executed, and the unhappy prince was drowned, as was commonly reported, in the river of Andamarca, declaring with his dying breath that the white men would avenge his murder, and that his rival would not long survive him. Thus perished the unfortunate Huascar, the legitimate heir of the throne of the Incas, in the very morning of life and the commencement of his reign; a reign, however, which had been long enough to call forth the display of many excellent and amiable qualities, though his nature was too gentle to cope with the bold and fiercer temper of his brother. Such is the portrait we have of him from the Indian and Castilian chroniclers; though the former, it should be added, were the kinsmen of Huascar, and the latter certainly bore no good will to Atahuallpa.

That prince received the tidings of Huascar's death with every mark of surprise and indignation. He immediately sent for Pizarro, and communicated the event to him with expressions of the deepest sorrow. The Spanish commander refused, at first, to credit the unwelcome news, and bluntly told the Inca that his brother could not be dead, and that he should be answerable for his life. To this Atahuallpa replied by renewed assurances of the fact, adding that the deed had been perpetrated, without his privity, by Huascar's keepers, fearful that he might take advantage of the troubles of the country to make his escape. Pizarro, on making further inquiries, found that the report of his death was but too true. That it should have been brought about by Atahuallpa's officers without his express command would only show that by so doing they had probably anticipated their master's wishes. The crime, which assumes in our eyes a deeper dye from the relation of the parties, had not the same estimation among the Incas, in whose multitudinous families the bonds of brotherhood must have sat loosely—much too loosely to restrain the arm of the despot from sweeping away any obstacle that lay in his path.

## ✌ CHAPTER SIX ✌

GOLD ARRIVES FOR THE RANSOM—VISIT TO

PACHACAMAC—DEMOLITION OF THE IDOL—

THE INCA'S FAVORITE GENERAL—THE INCA'S

LIFE IN CONFINEMENT—

ENVOYS' CONDUCT IN CUZCO—

ARRIVAL OF ALMAGRO

(1533)

Several weeks had now passed since Atahuallpa's emissaries had been dispatched for the gold and silver that were to furnish his ransom to the Spaniards. But the distances were great, and the returns came in slowly. They consisted, for the most part, of massive pieces of plate, some of which weighed two or three *arrobas*—a Spanish weight of twenty-five pounds. On some days, articles of the value of thirty or forty thousand *pesos de oro* were brought in, and, occasionally, of the value of fifty or even sixty thousand *pesos*. The greedy eyes of the Conquerors gloated on the shining heaps of treasure, which were transported on the shoulders of the Indian porters, and, after being carefully registered, were placed in safe deposit under a strong guard. They now began to believe that the magnificent promises of the Inca would be fulfilled. But as their avarice was sharpened by the ravishing display of wealth such as they had hardly dared to imagine, they became more craving and impatient. They made no allowance for the distance and the difficulties of the way, and loudly inveighed against the tardiness with which the royal commands were executed. They even suspected Atahuallpa of devising this scheme only to gain a pretext for communicating with his subjects in distant places, and of proceeding as dilatorily as possible, in order to secure time for the execution of his plans.

262

**"The greedy eyes of the Conquerors gloated on the shining heaps of treasure, which were transported on the shoulders of the Indian porters, and, after being carefully registered, were placed in safe deposit under a strong guard."**

Rumors of a rising among the Peruvians were circulated, and the Spaniards were in apprehension of some general and sudden assault on their quarters. Their new acquisitions gave them additional cause for solicitude: like a miser, they trembled in the midst of their treasures.

Pizarro reported to his captive the rumors that were in circulation among the soldiers, naming, as one of the places pointed out for the rendezvous of the Indians, the neighboring city of Huamachuco. Atahuallpa listened with undisguised astonishment, and indignantly repelled the charge, as false from beginning to end. "No one of my subjects," said he, "would dare to appear in arms, or to raise his finger, without my orders. You have me," he continued, "in your power. Is not my life at your disposal? And what better security can you have for my fidelity?" He then represented to the Spanish commander that the distances of many of the places were very great; that to Cuzco, the capital, although a message might be sent by post, through a succession of couriers, in five days from Cajamarca, it would require weeks for a porter

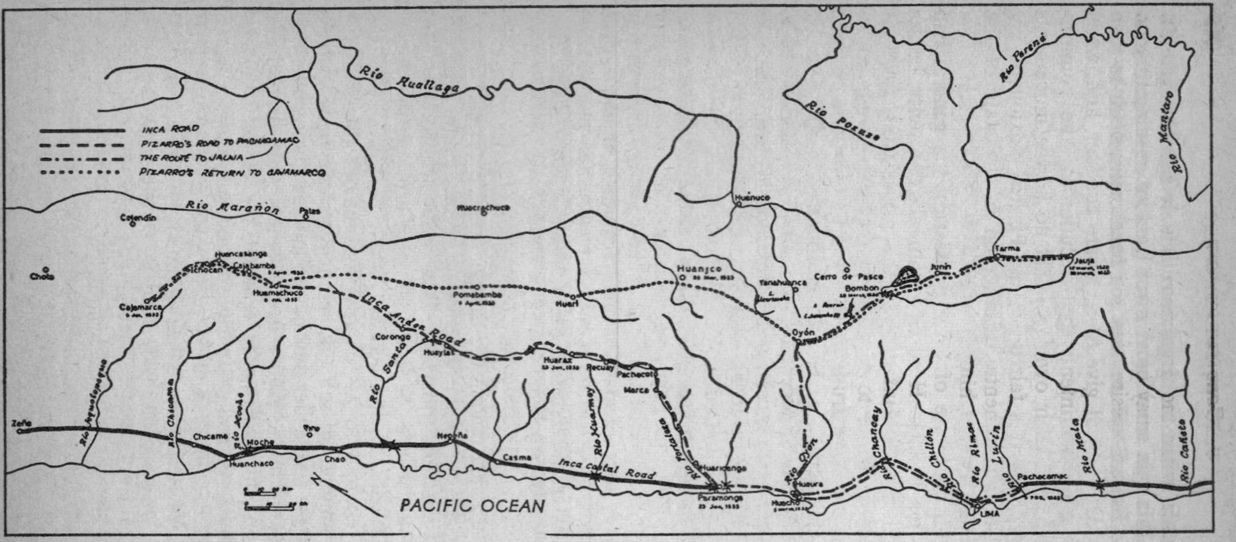


The cental portion of the Inca empire, showing the route of Hernando Pizarro, Gonzalo Pizarro, and "twenty others" to the shrine of Pachacamac. It was a thousand-mile journey entirely through enemy "Inca" territory. Hernando Pizarro left Cajamarca January 5, 1533, and returned April 7, 1533.

to travel over the same ground with a heavy load on his back. "But, that you may be satisfied I am proceeding in good faith," he added, "I desire you will send some of your own people to Cuzco. I will give them a safe conduct, and, when there, they can superintend the execution of the commission, and see with their own eyes that no hostile movements are intended." It was a fair offer; and Pizarro, anxious to get more precise and authentic information of the state of the country, gladly availed himself of it.

Before the departure of these emissaries, the general had dispatched his brother Hernando with about twenty horses and a small body of infantry to the neighboring town of Huamachuco, in order to reconnoiter the country and ascertain if there was any truth in the report of an armed force having assembled there. Hernando found everything quiet, and met with a kind reception from the natives. But before leaving the place he received further orders from his brother to continue his march to Pachacamac, a town situated on the coast, at least a hundred leagues distant from Cajamarca. It was consecrated as the seat of the great temple of the deity of that name, whom the Peruvians worshiped as the Creator of the world. It is said that they found there altars raised to this god, on their first occupation of the country; and such was the veneration in which he was held by the natives, that the Incas, instead of attempting to abolish his worship, deemed it more prudent to sanction it conjointly with that of their own deity, the Sun. Side by side the two temples rose on the heights that overlooked the city of Pachacamac, and prospered in the offerings of their respective votaries. "It was a cunning arrangement," says an ancient writer, "by which the great enemy of man secured to himself a double harvest of souls."

But the temple of Pachacamac continued to maintain its ascendency; and the oracles delivered from its dark and mysterious shrine were held in no less repute among the natives of *Tawantinsuyu* (or "the four quarters of the world," as Peru under the Incas was called) than the oracles of Delphi obtained among the Greeks. Pilgrimages were made to the hallowed spot from the most distant regions, and the city of Pachacamac became among the Peruvians what Mecca was among the Mahometans, or Cholula with the people of Anahuac. The shrine of the deity, enriched by the tributes of the pilgrims, gradually became one of the most opulent in the land; and Atahuallpa, anxious to collect his ransom as speedily as possible, urged Pizarro to send a detachment in that direction, to secure the treasures before they could be secreted by the priests of the temple.

It was a journey of considerable difficulty. Two-thirds of the route lay along the tableland of the Cordilleras, intersected occasionally by crests of the mountain range that imposed no slight impediment to their progress. Fortunately, much of the way they had the benefit of the great road to Cuzco; and "nothing in Christendom," exclaims Hernando Pizarro, "equals the magnificence of this road across the sierra." In some places the rocky ridges were so precipitous that steps were cut in them for the travelers, and though the sides were protected by heavy stone balustrades or parapets, it was with the greatest difficulty that the horses were enabled to scale them. The road was frequently crossed by streams, over which bridges of wood and sometimes of stone were thrown; though occasionally, along the declivities of the mountains, the waters swept down in such furious torrents that the only method of passing them was by the swinging bridges of osier, of which till now the Spaniards had had little experience. They were secured on either bank to heavy buttresses of stone. But as they were originally designed for nothing heavier than the foot passenger and the llama, and as they had something exceedingly fragile in their appearance, the Spaniards hesitated to venture on them with their horses. Experience, however, soon showed they were capable of bearing a much greater weight; and though the traveler, made giddy by the vibration of the long avenue, looked with a reeling brain into the torrent that was tumbling at the depth of a hundred feet or more below him, the whole of the cavalry effected their passage without an accident. At these bridges, it may be remarked, they found persons stationed whose business it was to collect toll for the government from all travelers.

The Spaniards were amazed by the number as well as magnitude of the flocks of llamas which they saw browsing on the stunted herbage that grows in the elevated regions of the Andes. Sometimes they were gathered in enclosures, but more usually were roaming at large under the conduct of their Indian shepherds; and the Conquerors now learned, for the first time, that these animals were tended with as much care, and their migrations as nicely regulated, as those of the vast flocks of merinos in their own country.

The tableland and its declivities were thickly sprinkled with hamlets and towns, some of them of considerable size; and the country in every direction bore the marks of a thrifty husbandry. Fields of Indian corn were to be seen in all its different stages, from the green and tender ear to the yellow ripeness of harvest time. As they descended into the valleys and deep ravines that divided the crests of the Cordilleras, they were surrounded by the vegetation of a warmer climate, which delighted the eye with the gay livery of a thousand bright colors and intoxicated the senses with its perfumes. Everywhere the natural capacities of the soil were stimulated by a minute system of irrigation, which drew the fertilizing moisture from every stream and rivulet that rolled down the declivities of the Andes; while the terraced sides of the mountains were clothed with gardens and orchards that teemed with fruits of various latitudes. The Spaniards could not sufficiently admire the industry with which the natives had availed themselves of the bounty of Nature, or had supplied the deficiency where she had dealt with a more parsimonious hand.

Whether from the commands of the Inca, or from the awe which their achievements had spread throughout the land, the Conquerors were received, in every place through which they passed, with hospitable kindness. Lodgings were provided for them, with ample refreshments from the well-stored magazines distributed at intervals along the route. In many of the towns the inhabitants came out to welcome them with singing and dancing, and when they resumed their march, a number of able-bodied porters were furnished to carry forward their baggage.

At length, after some weeks of travel, severe even with all these appliances, Hernando Pizarro arrived before the city of Pachacamac. It was a place of considerable population, and the edifices were, many of them, substantially built. The temple of the tutelar deity consisted of a vast stone building, or rather pile of buildings, which, clustering around a conical hill, had the air of a fortress rather than a religious establishment. But though the walls were of stone, the roof was composed of a light thatch, as usual in countries where rain seldom or never falls, and where defense, consequently, is wanted chiefly against the rays of the sun.

Presenting himself at the lower entrance of the temple, Hernando Pizarro was refused admittance by the guardians of the portal. But exclaiming that "he had come too far to be stayed by the arm of an Indian priest," he forced his way into the passage, and, followed by his men, wound up the gallery which led to an area on the summit of the mount, at one end of which stood a sort of chapel. This was the sanctuary of the dread deity. The door was garnished with ornaments of crystal and with turquoises and bits of coral. Here again the Indians would have dissuaded Pizarro from violating the consecrated precincts, when at that moment the shock

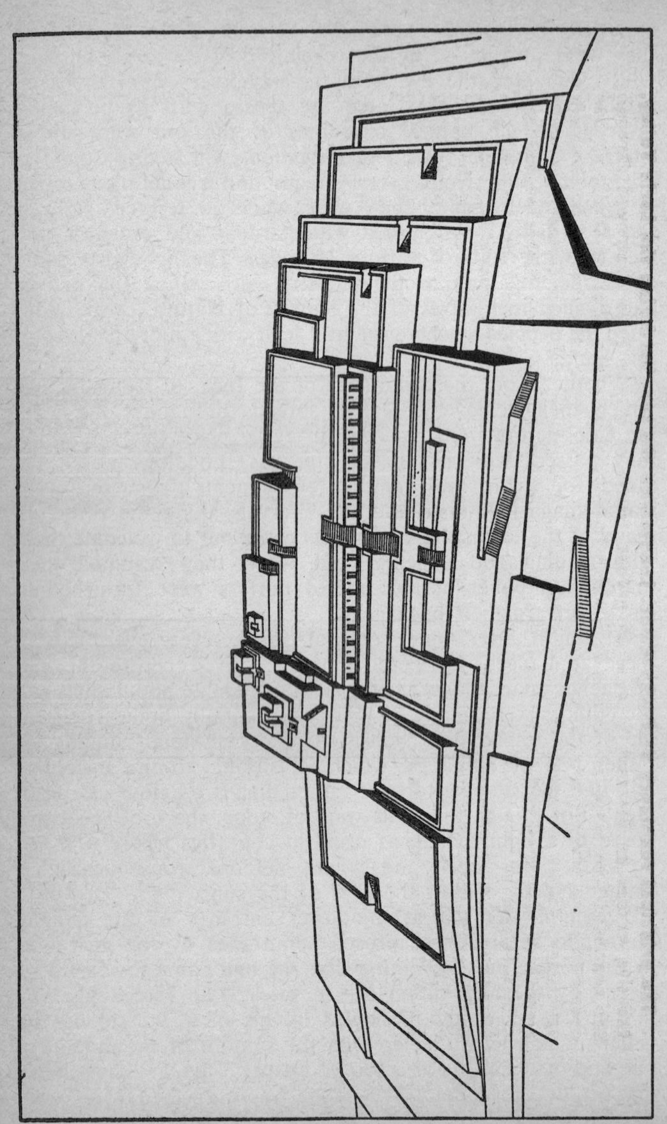

The principal sanctuary at Pachacamac. Located on the sea, bordering the Lurin Valley, the site covers an immense amount of ground. Most of it has been destroyed through the centuries. The name "Pachacamac," which is Inca, means "the Creator God"; no one seems to know what it was called before the Incas took it over after 1450 A.D. The main sanctuary is built of rectangular adobe blocks, held together with mud cement; the walls were once plastered and painted, and parts of it still preserved show flights of pelicans drawn in violent colors. At the very pinnacle of the truncated pyramid was the oracle. Hernando Pizarro entered Pachacamac with twenty soldiers on February 5, 1533. The scribe wrote, "This Pachacamac is very large. Adjoining the sanctuary there is a House of the Sun, well built, with five surrounding walls. There are houses with terrace roofs as in Spain. The town appears to be very old."

"Hernando Pizarro was refused admittance by the guardians of the portal. But, exclaiming that 'he had come too far to be stayed by the arm of an Indian priest,' he forced his way into the passage."

of an earthquake, that made the ancient walls tremble to their foundation, so alarmed the natives, both those of Pizarro's own company and the people of the place, that they fled in dismay, nothing doubting that their incensed deity would bury the invaders under the ruins or consume them with his lightnings. But no such terror found its way into the breasts of the Conquerors, who felt that here, at least, they were fighting the good fight of the Faith.

Tearing open the door, Pizarro and his party entered. But instead of a hall blazing, as they had fondly imagined, with gold and precious stones, offerings of the worshipers of Pachacamac, they found themselves in a small and obscure apartment, or rather den, from the floor and sides of which steamed up the most offensive odors—like those of a slaughterhouse. It was the place of sacrifice. A few pieces of gold and some emeralds were discovered on the ground, and as their eyes became accommodated to the darkness, they discerned in the most retired corner of the room the figure of the deity. It was an uncouth monster, made of wood, with the head resembling that of a man. This was the god through whose lips Satan had breathed forth the far-famed oracles which had deluded his Indian votaries!

Tearing the idol from its recess, the indignant Spaniards dragged it into the open air, and there broke it into a hundred fragments. The place was then purified, and a large cross, made of stone and plaster, was erected on the spot. In a few years the walls of the temple were pulled down by the Spanish settlers, who found there a convenient quarry for their own edifices. But the cross still remained spreading its broad arms over the ruins. It stood where it was planted in the very heart of the stronghold of heathendom; and while all was in ruins around it, it proclaimed the permanent triumphs of the Faith.

The simple natives, finding that Heaven had no bolts in store for the Conquerors, and that their god had no power to prevent the profanation of his shrine, came in gradually and tendered their homage to the strangers, whom they now regarded with feelings of superstitious awe. Pizarro profited by this temper to wean them, if possible, from their idolatry; and though no preacher himself, as he tells us, he delivered a discourse as edifying, doubtless, as could be expected from the mouth of a soldier; and, in conclusion, he taught them the sign of the cross, as an inestimable talisman to secure them against the future machinations of the devil.

But the Spanish commander was not so absorbed in his spiritual labors as not to have an eye to those temporal concerns for which he had been sent to this quarter. He now found, to his chagrin, that he had come somewhat too late, and that the priests of Pachacamac, being advised of his mission, had secured much the greater part of the gold and decamped with it before his arrival. A quantity was afterwards discovered buried in the grounds adjoining. Still, the amount obtained was considerable, falling little short of eighty thousand castellanos, a sum which once would have been deemed a compensation for greater fatigues than they had encountered. But the Spaniards had become familiar with gold; and their imaginations, kindled by the romantic adventures in which they had of late been engaged, indulged in visions which all the gold of Peru would scarcely have realized.

One prize, however, Hernando obtained by his expedition, which went far to console him for the loss of his treasure. While at Pachacamac, he learned that the Indian commander Calicuchima lay with a large force in the neighborhood of Jauja, a town of some strength at a considerable distance among the mountains. This man, who was nearly related to Atahuallpa, was his most experienced general, and together

"The road across the mountains presented greater difficulties than those on the former march. To add to the troubles of the cavalry, the shoes of their horses were worn out."

with Quizquiz, now at Cuzco, had achieved those victories at the south which placed the Inca on the throne. From his birth, his talents, and his large experience, he was accounted second to no subject in the kingdom. Pizarro was aware of the importance of securing his person. Finding that the Indian noble declined to meet him on his return, he determined to march at once on Jauja and take the chief in his own quarters. Such a scheme, considering the enormous disparity of numbers, might seem desperate even for Spaniards. But success had given them such confidence that they hardly condescended to calculate chances.

The road across the mountains presented greater difficulties than those on the former march. To add to the troubles of the cavalry, the shoes of their horses were worn out, and their hoofs suffered severely on the rough and stony ground. There was no iron at hand, nothing but gold and silver. In the present emegency they turned even those to account; and Pizarro caused the horses of the whole troop to be shod with silver. The work was done by the Indian smiths, and it answered so well that in this precious material they found a substitute for iron during the remainder of the march.

Jauja was a large and populous place, though we shall hardly credit the assertion of the Conquerors that a hundred thousand persons assembled habitually in the great square of the city. The Peruvian commander was encamped, it was said, with an army of five-and-thirty thousand men, at only a few miles' distance from the town. With some difficulty he was persuaded to an interview with Pizarro. The latter addressed him courteously, and urged his return with him to the Castilian quarters in Cajamarca, representing it as the command of the Inca. Ever since the capture of his master, Calicuchima had remained uncertain what course to take. The capture of the Inca in this sudden and mysterious manner by a race of beings who seemed to have dropped from the clouds, and that too in the very hour of his triumph, had entirely bewildered the Peruvian chief. He had concerted no plan for the rescue of Atahuallpa, nor, indeed, did he know whether any such movement would be acceptable to him. He now acquiesced in his commands, and was willing, at all events, to have a personal interview with his sovereign. Pizarro gained his end without being obliged to strike a single blow to effect it. The barbarian, when brought into contact with the white man, would seem to have been rebuked by his superior genius, in the same manner as the wild animal of the forest is said to quail before the steady glance of the hunter.

Calicuchima came attended by a numerous retinue. He was

borne in his sedan on the shoulders of his vassals, and, as he accompanied the Spaniards on their return through the country, received everywhere from the inhabitants the homage paid only to the favorite of a monarch. Yet all this pomp vanished on his entering the presence of the Inca, whom he approached with his feet bare, while a light burden, which he had taken from one the attendants, was laid on his back. As he drew near, the old warrior, raising his hands to heaven, exclaimed, "Would that I had been here!—this would not then have happened"; then, kneeling down, he kissed the hands and feet of his royal master and bathed them with his tears. Atahuallpa, on his part, betrayed not the least emotion, and showed no other sign of satisfaction at the presence of his favorite counselor than by simply bidding him welcome. The cold demeanor of the monarch contrasted strangely with the loyal sensibility of the subject.

The rank of the Inca placed him at an immeasurable distance above the proudest of his vassals; and the Spaniards had repeated occasion to admire the ascendency which, even in his present fallen fortunes, he maintained over his people, and the awe with which they approached him. Pedro Pizarro records an interview, at which he was present, between Atahuallpa and one of his great nobles, who had obtained leave to visit some remote part of the country on condition of returning by a certain day. He was detained somewhat beyond the appointed time, and on entering the presence with a small propitiatory gift for his sovereign his knees shook so violently that it seemed, says the chronicler, as if he would have fallen to the ground. His master, however, received him kindly, and dismissed him without a word of rebuke.

Atahuallpa in his confinement continued to receive the same respectful treatment from the Spaniards as hitherto. They taught him to play with dice, and the more intricate game of chess, in which the royal captive became expert, and loved to beguile with it the tedious hours of his imprisonment. Towards his own people he maintained as far as possible his wonted state and ceremonial. He was attended by his wives and the girls of his harem, who, as was customary, waited on him at table and discharged the other menial offices about his person. A body of Indian nobles were stationed in the antechamber, but never entered the presence unbidden; and when they did enter it, they submitted to the same humiliating ceremonies imposed on the greatest of his subjects. The service of his table was gold and silver plate. His dress, which he often changed, was composed of the wool of the vicuña wrought into mantles, so fine that it had the appearance of silk. He sometimes exchanged these for a robe made of the skins of bats, as soft and sleek as velvet. Round his head he wore the *llautu,* a woolen turban or shawl of the most delicate texture, wreathed in folds of various bright colors; and he still continued to encircle his temples with the *borla,* the crimson threads of which, mingled with gold, descended so as partly to conceal his eyes. The image of royalty had charms for him when its substance had departed. No garment or utensil that had once belonged to the Peruvian sovereign could ever be used by another. When he laid it aside, it was carefully deposited in a chest kept for the purpose, and afterwards burned. It would have been sacrilege to apply to vulgar uses that which had been consecrated by the touch of the Inca.

Not long after the arrival of the party from Pachacamac, in the latter part of May, the three emissaries returned from Cuzco. They had been very successful in their mission. Owing to the Inca's order, and the awe which the white men now inspired throughout the country, the Spaniards had everywhere met with a kind reception. They had been carried on the shoulders of the natives in the *hamacas,* or litters, of the country; and as they had traveled all the way to the capital on the great imperial road, along which relays of Indian carriers were established at stated intervals, they performed this journey of more than six hundred miles, not only without inconvenience, but with the most luxurious ease. They passed through many populous towns, and always found the simple natives disposed to venerate them as beings of a superior nature. In Cuzco they were received with public festivities, were sumptuously lodged, and had every want anticipated by the obsequious devotion of the inhabitants.

Their accounts of the capital confirmed all that Pizarro had before heard of the wealth and population of the city. Though they had remained more than a week in this place, the emissaries had not seen the whole of it. The great temple of the Sun they found literally covered with plates of gold. They had entered the interior and beheld the royal mummies, seated each in his gold-embossed chair and in robes profusely covered with ornaments. The Spaniards had the grace to respect these, as they had been previously enjoined by the Inca; but they required that the plates which garnished the walls should be all removed. The Peruvians most reluctantly acquiesced in the commands of their sovereign to desecrate the national temple, which every inhabitant of the city regarded with peculiar pride and veneration. With less reluctance they assisted the Conquerors in stripping the ornaments from some of the other edifices, where the gold, however, being mixed with a large proportion of alloy, was of much less value.

The number of plates they tore from the temple of the Sun was seven hundred; and though of no great thickness, probably, they are compared in size to the lid of a chest ten or twelve inches wide. A cornice of pure gold encircled the edifice, but so strongly set in the stone that it fortunately defied the efforts of the spoilers. The Spaniards complained of the want of alacrity shown by the Indians in the work of destruction, and said that there were other parts of the city containing buildings rich in gold and silver which they had not been allowed to see. In truth, their mission, which at best was a most ungrateful one, had been rendered doubly annoying by the manner in which they had executed it. The emissaries were men of a very low stamp, and puffed up by the honors conceded to them by the natives, they looked on themselves as entitled to these, and contemned the poor Indians as a race immeasurably beneath the European. They not only showed the most disgusting rapacity, but treated the highest nobles with wanton insolence. They even went so far, it is said, as to violate the privacy of the convents, and to outrage the religious sentiments of the Peruvians by their scandalous amours with the Virgins of the Sun. The people of Cuzco were so exasperated that they would have laid violent hands on them, but for their habitual reverence for the Inca, in whose name the Spaniards had come there. As it was, the Indians collected as much gold as was necessary to satisfy their unworthy visitors, and got rid of them as speedily as possible. It was a great mistake in Pizarro to send such men. There were persons, even in his company, who, as other occasions showed, had some sense of self-respect, if not respect for the natives.

The messengers brought with them, besides silver, full two hundred *cargas* or loads of gold. This was an important accession to the contributions of Atahuallpa; and although the treasure was still considerably below the mark prescribed, the monarch saw with satisfaction the time drawing nearer for the completion of his ransom.

Not long before this, an event had occurred which changed the condition of the Spaniards and had an unfavorable influence on the fortunes of the Inca. This was the arrival of Almagro at Cajamarca with a strong reinforcement. That chief had succeeded, after great efforts, in equipping three vessels and assembling a body of one hundred and fifty men, with which he sailed from Panamá the latter part of the preceding year. On his voyage he was joined by a small additional force from Nicaragua, so that his whole strength amounted to one hundred and fifty foot and fifty horse, well provided with the munitions of war. His vessels were steered by the old pilot Ruiz; but, after making the Bay of St. Matthew, he crept slowly along the coast, baffled as usual by winds and currents, and experiencing all the hardships incident to that protracted navigation. From some cause or other, he was not so fortunate as to obtain tidings of Pizarro; and so disheartened were his followers, most of whom were raw adventurers, that when arrived at Puerto Viejo they proposed to abandon the expedition and return at once to Panamá. Fortunately, one of the little squadron which Almagro had sent forward to Tumbes brought intelligence of Pizarro and of the colony he had planted at San Miguel. Cheered by the tidings, the cavalier resumed his voyage, and succeeded at length, towards the close of December, 1532, in bringing his whole party safe to the Spanish settlement.

He there received the account of Pizarro's march across the mountains, his seizure of the Inca, and, soon afterwards, of the enormous ransom offered for his liberation. Almagro and his companions listened with undisguised amazement to this account of his associate, and of a change in his fortunes so rapid and wonderful that it seemed little less than magic. At the same time, he received a caution from some of the colonists not to trust himself in the power of Pizarro, who was known to bear him no good will.

Not long after Almagro's arrival at San Miguel, advices were sent of it to Cajamarca, and a private note from his secretary Perez informed Pizarro that his associate had come with no purpose of co-operating with him, but with the intention to establish an independent government. Both of the Spanish captains seem to have been surrounded by mean and turbulent spirits, who sought to embroil them with each other, trusting, doubtless, to find their own account in the rupture. For once, however, their malicious machinations failed.

Pizarro was overjoyed at the arrival of so considerable a reinforcement, which would enable him to push his fortunes as he had desired and go forward with the conquest of the country. He laid little stress on the secretary's communication, since, whatever might have been Almagro's original purpose, Pizarro knew that the richness of the vein he had now opened in the land would be certain to secure his co-operation in working it. He had the magnanimity, therefore—for there is something magnanimous in being able to stifle the suggestions of a petty rivalry in obedience to sound policy—to send at once to his ancient comrade, and invite him, with many assurances of friendship, to Cajamarca. Almagro, who was of a frank and careless nature, received the communication in the spirit in which it was made, and, after some necessary delay, directed his march into the interior. But before leaving San Miguel, having become acquainted with the treacherous conduct of his secretary, he recompensed his treason by hanging him on the spot.

Almagro reached Cajamarca about the middle of February, 1533. The soldiers of Pizarro came out to welcome their countrymen, and the two captains embraced each other with every mark of cordial satisfaction. All past differences were buried in oblivion, and they seemed only prepared to aid one another in following up the brilliant career now opened to them in the conquest of an empire.

There was one person in Cajamarca on whom this arrival of the Spaniards produced a very different impression from that made on their own countrymen. This was the Inca Atahuallpa. He saw in the newcomers only a new swarm of locusts to devour his unhappy country; and he felt that, with his enemies thus multiplying around him, the chances were diminished of recovering his freedom, or of maintaining it if recovered. A little circumstance, insignificant in itself, but magnified by superstition into something formidable, occurred at this time to cast an additional gloom over his situation.

A remarkable appearance, somewhat of the nature of a meteor, or it may have been a comet, was seen in the heavens by some soldiers and pointed out to Atahuallpa. He gazed on it with fixed attention for some minutes, and then exclaimed, with a dejected air, that "a similar sign had been seen in the skies a short time before the death of his father Huayna Capac." From this day a sadness seemed to take possession of him, as he looked with doubt and undefined dread to the future. Thus it is that in seasons of danger the mind, like the senses, becomes morbidly acute in its perceptions, and the least departure from the regular course of nature, that would have passed unheeded in ordinary times, to the superstitious eye seems pregnant with meaning, as in some way or other connected with the destiny of the individual.

# ꛳ CHAPTER SEVEN ꛾

IMMENSE AMOUNT OF TREASURE—ITS DIVISION

AMONG THE TROOPS—RUMORS OF A

RISING—TRIAL OF THE INCA—HIS

EXECUTION—REFLECTIONS

(1533)

The arrival of Almagro produced a considerable change in Pizarro's prospects, since it enabled him to resume active operations and push forward his conquests in the interior. The only obstacle in his way was the Inca's ransom, and the Spaniards had patiently waited till the return of the emissaries from Cuzco swelled the treasure to a large amount, though still below the stipulated limit. But now their avarice got the better of their forbearance, and they called loudly for the immediate division of the gold. To wait longer would only be to invite the assault of their enemies, allured by a bait so attractive. While the treasure remained uncounted, no man knew its value, nor what was to be his own portion. It was better to distribute it at once, and let everyone possess and defend his own. Several, moreover, were now disposed to return home and take their share of the gold with them, where they could place it in safety. But these were few; while much the larger part were only anxious to leave their present quarters and march at once to Cuzco. More gold, they thought, awaited them in that capital than they could get here by prolonging their stay; while every hour was precious, to prevent the inhabitants from secreting their treasures, of which design they had already given indication.

Pizarro was especially moved by the last consideration; and he felt that without the capital he could not hope to become master of the empire. Without further delay, the division of the treasure was agreed upon.

Yet, before making this, it was necessary to reduce the

whole to ingots of a uniform standard, for the spoil was composed of an infinite variety of articles, in which the gold was of very different degrees of purity. These articles consisted of goblets, ewers, salvers, vases of every shape and size, ornaments and utensils for the temples of the royal palaces, tiles and plates for the decoration of the public edifices, curious imitations of different plants and animals. Among the plants, the most beautiful was the Indian corn, in which the golden ear was sheathed in its broad leaves of silver, from which hung a rich tassel of threads of the same precious metal. A fountain was also much admired, which sent up a sparkling jet of gold, while birds and animals of the same material played in the waters at its base. The delicacy of the workmanship of some of these, and the beauty and ingenuity of the de-

"Hernando Pizarro looked upon Almagro as coming to defraud his brother. . . . Instead of exchanging the cordial greeting proffered by Almagro . . . the arrogant cavalier held back in sullen silence."

sign, attracted the admiration of better judges than the rude Conquerors of Peru.

Before breaking up these specimens of Indian art, it was determined to send a quantity, which should be deducted from the royal fifth, to the emperor. It would serve as a sample of the ingenuity of the natives, and would show him the value of his conquests. A number of the most beautiful articles was selected, of the value of a hundred thousand ducats, and Hernando Pizarro was appointed to be the bearer of them to Spain. He was to obtain an audience of Charles, and at the same time that he laid the treasures before him he was to give an account of the proceedings of the Conquerors, and to seek a further augmentation of their powers and dignities.

No man in the army was better qualified for this mission, by his address and knowledge of affairs, than Hernando Pizarro; no one would be so likely to urge his suit with effect at the haughty Castilian court. But other reasons influenced the selection of him at the present juncture.

His former jealousy of Almagro still rankled in his bosom, and he had beheld that chief's arrival at the camp with feelings of disgust, which he did not care to conceal. He looked on him as coming to share the spoils of victory and defraud his brother of his legitimate honors. Instead of exchanging the cordial greeting proffered by Almagro at their first interview, the arrogant cavalier held back in sullen silence. His brother Francisco was greatly displeased at conduct which threatened to renew their ancient feud, and he induced Hernando to accompany him to Almagro's quarters and make some acknowledgment of his uncourteous behavior. But, notwithstanding this show of reconciliation, the general thought the present a favorable opportunity to remove his brother from the scene of operations, where his factious spirit more than counterbalanced his eminent services.

The business of melting down the plate was entrusted to the Indian goldsmiths, who were thus required to undo the work of their own hands. They toiled day and night, but such was the quantity to be recast that it consumed a full month. When the whole was reduced to bars of a uniform standard, they were nicely weighed under the superintendence of the royal inspectors. The total amount of the gold was found to be one million three hundred and twenty-six thousand five hundred and thirty-nine *pesos de oro*, which, allowing for the greater value of money in the sixteenth century, would be equivalent, probably, at the present time, to near *three millions and a half of pounds sterling*, or somewhat less than *fifteen millions and a half of dollars.* The quantity of silver was estimated at fifty-one thousand six hundred and ten marks. History affords no parallel of such a booty—and that, too, in the most convertible form, in ready money, as it were —having fallen to the lot of a little band of military adventurers, like the Conquerors of Peru.[39] The great object of the Spanish expeditions in the New World was gold. It is remarkable that their success should have been so complete. Had they taken the track of the English, the French, or the Dutch, on the shores of the northern continent, how different would have been the result! It is equally worthy of remark that the wealth thus suddenly acquired, by diverting them from the slow but surer and more permanent sources of national prosperity, has in the end glided from their grasp and left them among the poorest of the nations of Christendom.

A new difficulty now arose in respect to the division of the treasure. Almagro's followers claimed to be admitted to a share of it; which, as they equaled and, indeed, somewhat exceeded in number Pizarro's company, would reduce the gains of these last very materially. "We were not here, it is true," said Almagro's soldiers to their comrades, "at the seizure of the Inca, but we have taken our turn in mounting guard over him since his capture, have helped you to defend your treasures, and now give you the means of going forward and securing your conquests. It is a common cause," they urged, "in which all are equally embarked, and the gains should be shared equally between us."

But this way of viewing the matter was not at all palatable to Pizarro's company, who alleged that Atahuallpa's contract had been made exclusively with them; that they had seized the Inca, had secured the ransom, had incurred, in short, all the risk of the enterprise, and were not now disposed to share the fruits of it with everyone who came after them. There was much force, it could not be denied, in this reasoning, and it was finally settled between the leaders that Almagro's followers should resign their pretensions for a stipulated sum of no great amount, and look to the career now opened to them for carving out their fortunes for themselves.

This delicate affair being thus harmoniously adjusted, Pizarro prepared, with all solemnity, for a division of the imperial spoil. The troops were called together in the great square, and the Spanish commander, "with the fear of God before his eyes," says the record, "invoked the assistance of Heaven to do the work before him conscientiously and justly." The appeal may seem somewhat out of place at the distribution of spoil so unrighteously acquired; yet in truth, considering the magnitude of the treasure, and the power assumed by Pizarro to distribute it according to the respective deserts of the individuals, there were few acts of his life involving a heavier responsibility. On his present decision might be said to hang the future fortunes of each one of his followers—poverty or independence during the remainder of his days.

The royal fifth was first deducted, including the remittance already sent to Spain. The share appropriated by Pizarro amounted to fifty-seven thousand two hundred and twenty-two pesos of gold, and two thousand three hundred and fifty marks of silver. He had besides this the great chair or throne of the Inca, of solid gold, and valued at twenty-five thousand *pesos de oro*. To his brother Hernando were paid thirty-one thousand and eighty pesos of gold, and two thousand three hundred and fifty marks of silver. De Soto received seventeen thousand seven hundred and forty pesos of gold, and seven hundred and twenty-four marks of silver. Most of the remaining cavalry, sixty in number, received each eight thousand eight hundred and eighty pesos of gold, and three hundred and sixty-two marks of silver, though some had more, and a few considerably less. The infantry mustered in all one hundred and five men. Almost one-fifth of them were allowed, each, four thousand four hundred and forty pesos of gold and one hundred and eighty marks of silver, half of the compensation of the troopers. The remainder received one-fourth part less; though here again there were exceptions, and some were obliged to content themselves with a much smaller share of the spoil.

The new church of San Francisco, the first Christian temple in Peru, was endowed with two thousand two hundred and twenty pesos of gold. The amount assigned to Almagro's company was not excessive, if it was not more than twenty thousand pesos; and that reserved for the colonists of San Miguel, which amounted only to fifteen thousand pesos, was unaccountably small. There were among them certain soldiers who, at an early period of the expedition, as the reader may remember, abandoned the march and returned to San Miguel. These, certainly, had little claim to be remembered in the division of booty. But the greater part of the colony consisted of invalids, men whose health had been broken by their previous hardships, but who still, with a stout and willing heart, did good service in their military post on the seacoast. On what grounds they had forfeited their claims to a more ample remuneration it is not easy to explain.

Nothing is said, in the partition, of Almagro himself, who, by the terms of the original contract, might claim an equal share of the spoil with his associate. As little notice is taken of Luque, the remaining partner. Luque himself was, indeed, no longer to be benefited by worldly treasure. He had died a short time before Almagro's departure from Panamá; too soon to learn the full success of the enterprise, which, but for his exertions, must have failed; too soon to become acquainted with the achievements and the crimes of Pizarro. But the licentiate Espinosa, whom he represented, and who, it appears, had advanced the funds for the expedition, was still living at St. Domingo, and Luque's pretensions were explicitly transferred to him. Yet it is unsafe to pronounce, at this distance of time, on the authority of mere negative testimony; and it must be admitted to form a strong presumption in favor of Pizarro's general equity in the distribution, that no complaint of it has reached us from any of the parties present, nor from contemporary chroniclers.

The division of the ransom being completed by the Spaniards, there seemed to be no further obstacle to their resuming active operations and commencing the march to Cuzco. But what was to be done with Atahuallpa? In the determination of this question, whatever was expedient was just. To liberate him would be to set at large the very man who might prove their most dangerous enemy—one whose birth and royal station would rally round him the whole nation, place all the machinery of government at his control, and all its resources—one, in short, whose bare word might concentrate all the energies of his people against the Spaniards, and thus delay for a long period, if not wholly defeat, the conquest of the country. Yet to hold him in captivity was attended with scarcely less difficulty, since to guard so important a prize would require such a division of their force as must greatly cripple its strength, and how could they expect, by any vigilance, to secure their prisoner against rescue in the perilous passes of the mountains?

The Inca himself now loudly demanded his freedom. The proposed amount of the ransom had, indeed, not been fully paid. It may be doubted whether it ever would have been, considering the embarrassments thrown in the way by the guardians of the temples, who seemed disposed to secrete the treasures rather than despoil these sacred depositories to satisfy the cupidity of the strangers. It was unlucky, too, for the Indian monarch that much of the gold, and that of the best quality, consisted of flat plates or tiles, which, however valuable, lay in a compact form that did little towards swelling the heap. But an immense amount had been already realized, and it would have been a still greater one, the Inca might allege, but for the impatience of the Spaniards. At all events, it was a magnificent ransom, such as was never paid by prince or potentate before.

These considerations Atahuallpa urged on several of the cavaliers, and especially on Hernando de Soto, who was on terms of more familiarity with him than Pizarro. De Soto reported Atahuallpa's demands to his leader; but the latter evaded a direct reply. He did not disclose the dark purposes over which his mind was brooding. Not long afterwards he caused the notary to prepare an instrument in which he fully

"The Inca himself now loudly demanded his freedom."

acquitted the Inca of further obligation in respect to the ransom. This he commanded to be publicly proclaimed in the camp, while at the same time he openly declared that the safety of the Spaniards required that the Inca should be detained in confinement until they were strengthened by additional reinforcements.

Meanwhile the old rumors of a meditated attack by the natives began to be current among the soldiers. They were repeated from one to another, gaining something by every repetition. An immense army, it was reported, was mustering at Quito, the land of Atahuallpa's birth, and thirty thousand

Caribs were on their way to support it. The Caribs were distributed by the early Spaniards rather indiscriminately over the different parts of America, being invested with peculiar horrors as a race of cannibals.

It was not easy to trace the origin of these rumors. There was in the camp a considerable number of Indians who belonged to the party of Huascar and who were, of course, hostile to Atahuallpa. But his worst enemy was Felipillo, the interpreter from Tumbes, already mentioned in these pages. This youth had conceived a passion for, or, as some say, had been detected in an intrigue with, one of the royal concubines. The circumstance had reached the ears of Atahuallpa, who felt himself deeply outraged by it. "That such an insult should have been offered by so base a person was an indignity," he said, "more difficult to bear than his imprisonment"; and he told Pizarro "that, by the Peruvian law, it could be expiated, not by the criminal's own death alone, but by that of his whole family and kindred." But Felipillo was too important to the Spaniards to be dealt with so summarily; nor did they probably attach such consequence to an offense which, if report be true, they had countenanced by their own example. Felipillo, however, soon learned the state of the Inca's feelings towards himself, and from that moment he regarded him with deadly hatred. Unfortunately his malignant temper found ready means for its indulgence.

The rumors of a rising among the natives pointed to Atahuallpa as the author of it. Calicuchima was examined on the subject, but avowed his entire ignorance of any such design, which he pronounced a malicious slander. Pizarro next laid the matter before the Inca himself, repeating to him the stories in circulation with the air of one who believed them. "What treason is this," said the general, "that you have meditated against me—me, who have ever treated you with honor, confiding in your words, as in those of a brother?" "You jest," replied the Inca, who perhaps did not feel the weight of this confidence; "you are always jesting with me. How could I or my people think of conspiring against men so valiant as the Spaniards? Do not jest with me thus, I beseech you." "This," continues Pizarro's secretary, "he said in the most composed and natural manner, smiling all the while to dissemble his falsehood, so that we were all amazed to find such cunning in a barbarian."

But it was not with cunning, but with the consciousness of innocence, as the event afterwards proved, that Atahuallpa thus spoke to Pizarro. He readily discerned, however, the causes, perhaps the consequences, of the accusation. He saw a dark gulf opening beneath his feet; and he was surrounded by strangers, on none of whom he could lean for counsel or protection. The life of the captive monarch is usually short; and Atahuallpa might have learned the truth of this, when he thought of Huascar. Bitterly did he now lament the absence of Hernando Pizarro, for, strange as it may seem, the haughty spirit of this cavalier had been touched by the condition of the royal prisoner, and he had treated him with a deference which won for him the peculiar regard and confidence of the Indian. Yet the latter lost no time in endeavoring to efface the general's suspicions and to establish his own innocence. "Am I not," said he to Pizarro, "a poor captive in your hands? How could I harbor the designs you impute to me, when I should be the first victim of the outbreak? And you little know my people, if you think that such a movement would be made without my orders; when the very birds in my dominions," said he, with somewhat of an hyperbole, "would scarcely venture to fly contrary to my will."

But these protestations of innocence had little effect on the troops, among whom the story of a general rising of the natives continued to gain credit every hour. A large force, it was said, was already gathered at Huamachuco, not a hundred miles from the camp, and their assault might be hourly expected. The treasure which the Spaniards had acquired afforded a tempting prize, and their own alarm was increased by the apprehension of losing it. The patrols were doubled. The horses were kept saddled and bridled. The soldiers slept on their arms; Pizarro went the rounds regularly to see that every sentinel was on his post. The little army, in short, was in a state of preparation for instant attack.

Men suffering from fear are not likely to be too scrupulous as to the means of removing the cause of it. Murmurs, mingled with gloomy menaces, were now heard against the Inca, the author of these machinations. Many began to demand his life, as necessary to the safety of the army. Among these the most vehement were Almagro and his followers. They had not witnessed the seizure of Atahuallpa. They had no sympathy with him in his fallen state. They regarded him only as an encumbrance, and their desire now was to push their fortunes in the country, since they had got so little of the gold of Cajamarca. They were supported by Riquelme, the treasurer, and by the rest of the royal officers. These men had been left at San Miguel by Pizarro, who did not care to have such official spies on his movements. But they had come to the camp with Almagro, and they loudly demanded the Inca's death, as indispensable to the tranquillity of the country and the interests of the crown.

To these dark suggestions Pizarro turned—or seemed to turn—an unwilling ear, showing visible reluctance to proceed to extreme measures with his prisoner. There were some few, and among others Hernando de Soto, who supported him in these views, and who regarded such measures as not at all justified by the evidence of Atahuallpa's guilt. In this state of things, the Spanish commander determined to send a small detachment to Huamachuco, to reconnoiter the country and ascertain what ground there was for the rumors of an insurrection. De Soto was placed at the head of the expedition, which, as the distance was not great, would occupy but a few days.

After that cavalier's departure, the agitation among the soldiers, instead of diminishing, increased to such a degree that Pizarro, unable to resist their importunities, consented to bring Atahuallpa to instant trial. It was but decent, and certainly safer, to have the forms of a trial. A court was organized, over which the two captains, Pizarro and Almagro, were to preside as judges. An attorney general was named to prosecute for the crown, and counsel was assigned to the prisoner.

The charges preferred against the Inca, drawn up in the form of interrogatories, were twelve in number. The most important were that he had usurped the crown and assassinated his brother Huascar; that he had squandered the public revenues since the conquest of the country by the Spaniards, and lavished them on his kindred and his minions; that he was guilty of idolatry, and of adulterous practices, indulging openly in a plurality of wives; finally, that he had attempted to excite an insurrection against the Spaniards.

These charges, most of which had reference to national usages, or to the personal relations of the Inca, over which the Spanish conquerors had clearly no jurisdiction, are so absurd that they might well provoke a smile, did they not excite a deeper feeling. The last of the charges was the only one of moment in such a trial; and the weakness of this may be inferred from the care taken to bolster it up with the others. The mere specification of the articles must have been sufficient to show that the doom of the Inca was already scaled.

A number of Indian witnesses were examined, and their testimony, filtrated through the interpretation of Felipillo, received, it is said, when necessary, a very different coloring from that of the original. The examination was soon ended, and "a warm discussion," as we are assured by one of Pizarro's own secretaries, "took place in respect to the probable good or evil that would result from the death of Atahuallpa." It was a question of expediency. He was found guilty—whether of all the crimes alleged we are not informed—and he was sentenced to be burnt alive in the great square of Cajamarca. The sentence was to be carried into execution that very night. They were not even to wait for the return of De Soto, when the information he would bring would go far to establish the truth or the falsehood of the reports respecting the insurrection of the natives. It was desirable to obtain the countenance of Father Valverde to these proceedings, and a copy of the judgment was submitted to the friar for his signature, which he gave without hesitation, declaring that, "in his opinion, the Inca, at all events, deserved death."

Yet there were some few in that martial conclave who resisted these high-handed measures. They considered them as a poor requital of all the favors bestowed on them by the Inca, who hitherto had received at their hands nothing but wrong. They objected to the evidence as wholly insufficient; and they denied the authority of such a tribunal to sit in judgment on a sovereign prince in the heart of his own dominions. If he were to be tried, he should be sent to Spain, and his cause brought before the emperor, who alone had power to determine it.

But the great majority—and they were ten to one—overruled these objections, by declaring there was no doubt of Atahuallpa's guilt, and they were willing to assume the responsibility of his punishment. A full account of the proceedings would be sent to Castile, and the emperor should be informed who were the loyal servants of the crown, and who were its enemies. The dispute ran so high that for a time it menaced an open and violent rupture; till, at length, convinced that resistance was fruitless, the weaker party, silenced, but not satisfied, contented themselves with entering a written protest against these proceedings, which would leave an indelible stain on the names of all concerned in them.

When the sentence was communicated to the Inca, he was greatly overcome by it. He had, indeed, for some time, looked to such an issue as probable, and had been heard to intimate as much to those about him. But the probability of such an event is very different from its certainty—and that, too, so sudden and speedy. For a moment, the overwhelming conviction of it unmanned him, and he exclaimed, with tears in his eyes, "What have I done, or my children, that I should meet such a fate? And from your hands, too," said he, addressing Pizarro; "you, who have met with friendship and kindness from my people, with whom I have shared my treasures, who have received nothing but benefits from my hands!" In the most piteous tones, he then implored that his life might be spared, promising any guarantee that might be required for the safety of every Spaniard in the army—promising double the ransom he had already paid, if time were only given him to obtain it.

An eyewitness assures us that Pizarro was visibly affected as he turned away from the Inca, to whose appeal he had no power to listen in opposition to the voice of the army and to his own sense of what was due to the security of the country. Atahuallpa, finding he had no power to turn his Conqueror from his purpose, recovered his habitual self-possession, and from that moment submitted himself to his fate with the courage of an Indian warrior.

The doom of the Inca was proclaimed by sound of trumpet in the great square of Cajamarca; and, two hours after sunset, the Spanish soldiery assembled by torchlight in the *plaza* to witness the execution of the sentence. It was on the twenty-ninth of August, 1533. Atahuallpa was led out chained hand and foot—for he had been kept in irons ever since the great excitement had prevailed in the army respecting an assault. Father Vicente de Valverde was at his side, striving to administer consolation, and, if possible, to persuade him at this last hour to abjure his superstition to embrace the religion of his Conquerors. He was willing to save the soul of his victim from the terrible expiration in the next world to which he had so cheerfully consigned his mortal part in this.

During Atahuallpa's confinement, the friar had repeatedly expounded to him the Christian doctrines, and the Indian monarch discovered much acuteness in apprehending the discourse of his teacher. But it had not carried conviction to his mind, and though he listened with patience, he had shown no disposition to renounce the faith of his fathers. The Dominican made a last appeal to him in this solemn hour; and when Atahuallpa was bound to the stake, with the fagots that were to kindle his funeral pile lying around him, Valverde, holding up the cross, besought him to embrace it and be baptized, promising that, by so doing, the painful death to which he had been sentenced should be commuted for the milder form of the *garrote*—a mode of punishment by strangulation, used for criminals in Spain.

The unhappy monarch asked if this were really so, and on its being confirmed by Pizarro he consented to abjure his own religion and receive baptism. The ceremony was performed by Father Valverde, and the new convert received the name of Juan de Atahuallpa—the name of Juan being conferred

**"Recovering his stoical bearing, which for a moment had been shaken, Atahuallpa submitted himself calmly to his fate."**

in honor of John the Baptist, on whose day the event took place.

Atahuallpa expressed a desire that his remains might be transported to Quito, the place of his birth, to be preserved with those of his maternal ancestors. Then, turning to Pizarro, as a last request, he implored him to take compassion on his young children and receive them under his protection. Was there no other one in that dark company who stood grimly around him, to whom he could look for the protection of his offspring? Perhaps he thought there was no other so competent to afford it, and that the wishes so solemnly expressed in that hour might meet with respect even from his Conqueror. Then, recovering his stoical bearing, which for a moment had been shaken, he submitted himself calmly to his fate—while the Spaniards, gathering around, muttered their *credos* for the salvation of his soul! Thus by death of a vile malefactor perished the last of the Incas!

I have already spoken of the person and the qualities of Atahuallpa. He had a handsome countenance, though with an expression somewhat too fierce to be pleasing. His frame was muscular and well-proportioned; his air commanding; and his deportment in the Spanish quarters had a degree of refinement, the more interesting that it was touched with melancholy. He is accused of having been cruel in his wars and bloody in his revenge. It may be true, but the pencil of an enemy would be likely to overcharge the shadows of the portrait. He is allowed to have been bold, high-minded, and liberal. All agree that he showed singular penetration and quickness of perception. His exploits as a warrior had placed his valor beyond dispute. The best homage to it is the reluctance shown by the Spaniards to restore him to freedom. They dreaded him as an enemy, and they had done him too many wrongs to think that he could be their friend. Yet his conduct towards them from the first had been most friendly; and they repaid it with imprisonment, robbery, and death.

The body of the Inca remained on the place of execution through the night. The following morning it was removed to the Church of San Francisco, where his funeral obsequies were performed with great solemnity. Pizarro and the principal cavaliers went into mourning, and the troops listened with devout attention to the service of the dead from the lips of Father Valverde. The ceremony was interrupted by the sound of loud cries and wailing, as of many voices, at the doors of the church. These were suddenly thrown open, and a number of Indian women, the wives and sisters of the deceased, rushing up the great aisle, surrounded the corpse. This was not the way, they cried, to celebrate the funeral rites of an Inca; and they declared their intention to sacrifice themselves on his tomb and bear him company to the land of spirits. The audience, outraged by this frantic behavior, told the intruders that Atahuallpa had died in the faith of a Christian, and that the God of the Christians abhorred such sacrifices. They then caused the women to be excluded from the church, and several, retiring to their own quarters, laid violent hands on themselves, in the vain hope of accompanying their beloved lord to the bright mansions of the Sun.

Atahuallpa's remains, notwithstanding his request, were laid in the cemetery of San Francisco. But from thence, as is reported, after the Spaniards left Cajamarca, they were secretly removed and carried, as he had desired, to Quito. The colonists of a later time supposed that some treasures might have been buried with the body. But, on excavating the ground, neither treasure nor remains were to be discovered.

A day or two after these tragic events, Hernando de Soto returned from his excursion. Great was his astonishment and indignation at learning what had been done in his absence. He sought out Pizarro at once, and found him, says the chronicler, "with a great felt hat, by way of mourning, slouched over his eyes," and in his dress and demeanor exhibiting all the show of sorrow. "You have acted rashly," said De Soto to him bluntly; "Atahuallpa had been basely slandered. There was no enemy at Huamachuco; no rising among the natives. I have met with nothing on the road but demonstrations of good will, and all is quiet. If it was necessary to bring the Inca to trial, he should have been taken to Castile and judged by the emperor. I would have pledged myself to see him safe on board the vessel." Pizarro confessed that he had been precipitate, and said that he had been deceived by Riquelme, Valverde, and the others. These charges soon reached the ears of the treasurer and the Dominican, who, in their turn, exculpated themselves, and upbraided Pizarro to his face, as the only one responsible for the deed. The dispute ran high; and the parties were heard by the bystanders to give one another the lie! This vulgar squabble among the leaders, so soon after the event, is the best commentary of the iniquity of their own proceedings and the innocence of the Inca.

The treatment of Atahuallpa, from first to last, forms undoubtedly one of the darkest chapters in Spanish colonial history. There may have been massacres perpetrated on a more extended scale, and the executions accompanied with a greater refinement of cruelty. But the bloodstained annals of the Conquest afford no such example of coldhearted and systematic persecution, not of an enemy, but of one whose whole deportment had been that of a friend and a benefactor.

From the hour that Pizarro and his followers had entered within the sphere of Atahuallpa's influence, the hand of friendship had been extended to them by the natives. Their first act, on crossing the mountains, was to kidnap the monarch and massacre his people. The seizure of his person might be vindicated, by those who considered the end as justifying the means, on the ground that it was indispensable to secure the triumphs of the Cross. But no such apology can be urged for the massacre of the unarmed and helpless population—as wanton as it was wicked.

The long confinement of the Inca had been used by the Conquerors to wring from him his treasures with the hard grip of avarice. During the whole of this dismal period he had conducted himself with singular generosity and good faith. He had opened a free passage for the Spaniards through every part of his empire, and had furnished every facility for the execution of their plans. When these were accomplished, and he remained an encumbrance on their hands, notwithstanding their engagement, expressed or implied, to release him—and Pizarro, as we have seen, by a formal act acquitted his captive of any further obligation on the score of the ransom—he was arraigned before a mock tribunal, and, under pretenses equally false and frivolous, was condemned to an excruciating death. From first to last, the policy of the Spanish conquerors towards their unhappy victim is stamped with barbarity and fraud.

It is not easy to acquit Pizarro of being in a great degree responsible for this policy. His partisans have labored to show that it was forced on him by the necessity of the case, and that in the death of the Inca, especially, he yielded reluctantly to the importunities of others. But, weak as is this apology, the historian who has the means of comparing the various testimony of the period will come to a different conclusion. To him it will appear that Pizarro had probably long felt the removal of Atahuallpa to be essential to the success of his enterprise. He foresaw the odium that would be incurred by the death of his royal captive without sufficient grounds; while he labored to establish these, he still shrank from the responsibility of the deed, and preferred to perpetrate it in obedience to the suggestions of others, rather than his own. Like many an unprincipled politician, he wished to reap the benefit of a bad act and let others bear the blame of it.

Almagro and his followers were reported by Pizarro's secretaries to have first insisted on the Inca's death. They were loudly supported by the treasurer and the royal officers, who considered it as indispensable to the interests of the crown; and, finally, the rumors of a conspiracy raised the same cry among the soldiers, and Pizarro, with all his tenderness for his prisoner, could not refuse to bring him to trial. The form of a trial was necessary to give an appearance of fairness to the proceedings. That it was only form is evident from the indecent haste with which it was conducted—the examination of evidence, the sentence, and the execution being all on the same day. The multiplication of the charges, designed to place the guilt on the accused on the strongest ground, had, from their very number, the opposite effect, proving only the determination to convict him. If Pizarro had felt the reluctance to his conviction which he pretended, why did he send De Soto, Atahuallpa's best friend, away, when the inquiry was to be instituted? Why was the sentence so summarily executed, as not to afford opportunity, by that cavalier's return, of disproving the truth of the principal charges—the only one, in fact, with which the Spaniards had any concern? The solemn farce of mourning and deep sorrow affected by Pizarro, who by these honors to the dead would intimate the sincere regard he had entertained for the living, was too thin a veil to impose on the most credulous.

It is not intended by these reflections to exculpate the rest of the army, and especially its officers, from their share in the infamy of the transaction. But Pizarro, as commander of the army, was mainly responsible for its measures. For he was not a man to allow his own authority to be wrested from his grasp, or to yield timidly to the impulses of others. He did not even yield to his own. His whole career shows him, whether for good or for evil, to have acted with a cool and calculating policy.

A story has been often repeated which refers the motives of Pizarro's conduct, in some degree at least, to personal resentment. The Inca had requested one of the Spanish soldiers to write the name of God on his nail. This the monarch showed to several of his guards successively, and, as they read it, and each pronounced the same word, the sagacious mind of the barbarian was delighted with what seemed to him little short of a miracle—to which the science of his own nation afforded no analogy. On showing the writing to Pizarro, that chief remained silent; and the Inca, finding he could not read, conceived a contempt for the commander who was even less informed than his soldiers. This he did not wholly conceal, and Pizarro, aware of the cause of it, neither forgot nor forgave it. The anecdote is reported not on the highest authority. It may be true; but it is unnecessary to look for the motives of Pizarro's conduct in personal pique, when so many proofs are to be discerned of a dark and deliberate policy.

Yet the arts of the Spanish chieftain failed to reconcile his countrymen to the atrocity of his proceedings. It is singular to observe the difference between the tone assumed by the first chroniclers of the transaction, while it was yet fresh, and that of those who wrote when the lapse of a few years had shown the tendency of public opinion. The first boldly avow the deed as demanded by expediency, if not necessity; while they deal in no measured terms of reproach with the character of their unfortunate victim. The latter, on the other hand, while they extenuate the errors of the Inca and do justice to his good faith, are unreserved in their condemnation of the Conquerors, on whose conduct, they say, Heaven set the seal of its own reprobation, by bringing them all to an untimely and miserable end. The sentence of contemporaries has been fully ratified by that of posterity; and the persecution of Atahuallpa is regarded with justice as having left a stain, never to be effaced, on the Spanish arms in the New World.

DISORDERS IN PERU—MARCH TO CUZCO—

ENCOUNTER WITH THE NATIVES—

CALICUCHIMA BURNT—ARRIVAL IN

CUZCO—DESCRIPTION OF THE CITY—

TREASURE FOUND THERE

(1533–1534)

The Inca of Peru was its sovereign in a peculiar sense. He received an obedience from his vassals more implicit than that of any despot; for his authority reached to the most secret conduct—to the thoughts of the individual. He was reverenced as more than a human. He was not merely the head of the state, but the point to which all its institutions converged as to a common center—the keystone of the political fabric which must fall to pieces by its own weight when that was withdrawn. So it fared on the death of Atahuallpa. His death not only left the throne vacant, without any certain successor, but the manner of it announced to the Peruvian people that a hand stronger than that of their Incas had now seized the scepter, and that the dynasty of the Children of the Sun had passed away forever.

The natural consequences of such a conviction followed. The beautiful order of the ancient institutions was broken up, as the authority which controlled it was withdrawn. The Indians broke out into greater excesses from the uncommon restraint to which they had been before subjected. Villages were burnt, temples and palaces were plundered, and the gold they contained was scattered or secreted. Gold and silver acquired an importance in the eyes of the Peruvian, when he saw the importance attached to them by his conquerors. The precious metals, which before served only for purposes of state or religious decoration, were now hoarded up and buried in caves and forests. The gold and silver concealed by the natives were affirmed greatly to exceed in quantity that which fell into the hands of the Spaniards.[40] The remote provinces now shook off their allegiance to the Incas. Their great captains, at the head of distant armies, set up for themselves. Ruminawi, a commander on the borders of Quito, sought to detach that kingdom from the Peruvian empire and to reassert its ancient independence. The country, in short, was in that state in which old things are passing away and the new order of things has not yet been established. It was in a state of revolution.

The authors of the revolution, Pizarro and his followers, remained meanwhile at Cajamarca. But the first step of the Spanish commander was to name a successor to Atahuallpa. It would be easy to govern under the venerated authority to which the homage of the Indians had been so long paid; and it was not difficult to find a successor. The true heir to the crown was a second son of Huayna Capac, named Manco, a legitimate brother of the unfortunate Huascar. But Pizarro had too little knowledge of the dispositions of this prince; and he made no scruple to prefer a brother of Atahuallpa, and to present him to the Indian nobles as their future Inca. We know nothing of the character of the young Toparca, who probably resigned himself without reluctance to a destiny which, however humiliating in some points of view, was more exalted than he could have hoped to obtain in the regular course of events. The ceremonies attending a Peruvian coronation were observed as well as time would allow; the brows of the young Inca were encircled with the imperial *borla* by the hands of his conqueror, and he received the homage of his Indian vassals. They were the less reluctant to pay it, as most of those in the camp belonged to the faction of Quito.

All thoughts were now eagerly turned towards Cuzco, of which the most glowing accounts were circulated among the soldiers, and whose temples and royal palaces were represented as blazing with gold and silver. With imaginations thus excited, Pizarro and his entire company, amounting to almost five hundred men, of whom nearly a third, probably, were cavalry, took their departure early in September from Cajamarca—a place ever memorable as the theater of some of the most strange and sanguinary scenes recorded in history. All set forward in high spirits—the soldiers of Pizarro from the expectation of doubling their present riches, and Almagro's followers from the prospect of sharing equally in the spoil with "the first conquerors." The young Inca and the old chief Calicuchima accompanied the march in their litters, attended by a numerous retinue of vassals, and moving in as much state and ceremony as if in the possession of real power.

Their course lay along the great road of the Incas, which stretched across the elevated regions of the Cordilleras, all the way to Cuzco. It was of nearly a uniform breadth, though constructed with different degrees of care, according to the ground. Sometimes it crossed smooth and level valleys, which offered of themselves little impediment to the traveler; at other times it followed the course of a mountain stream that flowed round the base of some beetling cliff, leaving small space for the foothold; at others, again, where the sierra was so precipitous that it seemed to preclude all farther progress, the road, accommodated to the natural sinuosities of the ground, wound round the heights which it would have been impossible to scale directly.

But, although managed with great address, it was a formidable passage for the cavalry. The mountain was hewn into steps, but the rocky ledges cut up the hoofs of the horses; and though the troopers dismounted and led them by the bridle, they suffered severely in their efforts to keep their footing. The road was constructed for man and the light-footed llama; and the only heavy beast of burden at all suited to it was the sagacious and sure-footed mule, with which the Spanish adventurers were not then provided. It was a singular chance that Spain was the land of the mule; and thus the country was speedily supplied with the very animal which seems to have been created for the difficult passes of the Cordilleras.

Another obstacle, often occurring, was the deep torrents that rushed down in fury from the Andes. They were traversed by the hanging bridges of osier, whose frail materials were after a time broken up by the heavy tread of the cavalry, and the holes made in them added materially to the dangers of the passage. On such occasions the Spaniards contrived to work their way across the rivers on rafts, swimming their horses by the bridle.

All along the route they found posthouses for the accommodation of the royal couriers, established at regular intervals; and magazines of grain and other commodities, provided in the principal towns for the Indian armies. The Spaniards profited by the prudent forecast of the Peruvian government.

Passing through several hamlets and towns of some note, the principal of which were Huamachuco and Huanuco, Pizarro, after a tedious march, came in sight of the rich valley of Jauja. The march, though tedious, had been attended with little suffering, except in crossing the bristling crests of the Cordilleras, which occasionally obstructed their path—a rough setting to the beautiful valleys that lay scattered like gems along this elevated region. In the mountain passes they found some inconvenience from the cold, since, to move more quickly, they had disencumbered themselves of all superfluous baggage, and were even unprovided with tents. The bleak winds of the mountains penetrated the thick harness of the soldiers; but the poor Indians, more scantily clothed, and accustomed to a tropical climate, suffered most severely. The Spaniard seemed to have a hardihood of body, as of soul, that rendered him almost indifferent to climate.

On the march they had not been molested by enemies. But more than once they had seen vestiges of them in smoking hamlets and ruined bridges. Reports, from time to time, had reached Pizarro of warriors on his track; and small bodies of Indians were occasionally seen like dusky clouds on the verge of the horizon, which vanished as the Spaniards approached. On reaching Jauja, however, these clouds gathered into one dark mass of warriors, which formed on the opposite bank of the river that flowed through the valley.

The Spaniards advanced to the stream, which, swollen by the melting of the snows, was now of considerable width, though not deep. The bridge had been destroyed; but the Conquerors, without hesitation, dashing boldly in, advanced, swimming and wading, as they best could, to the opposite bank. The Indians, disconcerted by this decided movement, as they had relied on their watery defenses, took to flight after letting off an impotent volley of missiles. Fear gave wings to the fugitives; but the horse and his rider were swifter, and the victorious pursuers took bloody vengeance on their enemy for having dared even to meditate resistance.

Jauja was a considerable town. It was the place already noticed as having been visited by Hernando Pizarro. It was seated in the midst of a verdant valley, fertilized by a thousand little rills, which the thrifty Indian husbandmen drew from the parent river that rolled sluggishly through the meadows. There were several capacious buildings of rough stone in the town, and a temple of some note in the times of the Incas. But the strong arm of Father Valverde and his countrymen soon tumbled the heathen deities from their pride of place, and established in their stead the sacred effigies of the Virgin and Child.

Here Pizarro proposed to halt for some days, and to found a Spanish colony. It was a favorable position, he thought, for holding the Indian mountaineers in check, while at the same time it afforded an easy communication with the seacoast. Meanwhile he determined to send forward De Soto, with a detachment of sixty horse, to reconnoiter the country in advance, and to restore the bridges where demolished by the enemy.

That active cavalier set forward at once, but found considerable impediments to his progress. The traces of an enemy became more frequent as he advanced. The villages were burnt, the bridges destroyed, and heavy rocks and trees strewed in the path to impede the march of the cavalry. As he drew near to Vilcas, once an important place, though now effaced from the map, he had a sharp encounter with the natives in a mountain defile, which cost him the lives of two or three troopers. The loss was light; but any loss was felt by the Spaniards, so little accustomed as they had been of late to resistance.

Still pressing forward, the Spanish captain crossed the river Abancay and the broad waters of the Apurimac; and as he drew near the sierra of Vilcaconga, he learned that a considerable body of Indians lay in wait for him in the dangerous passes of the mountains. The sierra was several leagues from Cuzco; and the cavalier, desirous to reach the farther side of it before nightfall, incautiously pushed on his wearied horses. When he was fairly entangled in its rocky defiles, a multitude of armed warriors, springing, as it seemed, from every cavern and thicket of the sierra, filled the air with their war cries

**"When De Soto was fairly entangled in the rocky defiles, a multitude of armed warriors, springing, as it seemed, from every cavern and thicket of the sierra, filled the air with their war cries."**

and rushed down, like one of their own mountain torrents, on the invaders, as they were painfully toiling up the steeps. Men and horses were overturned in the fury of the assault, and the foremost files, rolling back on those below, spread ruin and consternation in their ranks. De Soto in vain endeavored to restore order, and, if possible, to charge the assailants. The horses were blinded and maddened by the missiles, while the desperate natives, clinging to their legs, strove to prevent their ascent up the rocky pathway. De Soto saw that, unless he gained a level ground which opened at some distance before him, all must be lost. Cheering on his men with the old battle cry that always went to the heart of a Spaniard, he struck his spurs deep into the sides of his wearied charger, and, gallantly supported by his troop, broke through the dark array of warriors, and, shaking them off to the right and left, at length succeeded in placing himself on the broad level.

Here both parties paused, as if by mutual consent, for a few moments. A little stream ran through the plain, at which the Spaniards watered their horses; [41] and the animals having recovered wind, De Soto and his men made a desperate charge on their assailants. The undaunted Indians sustained the shock with firmness; and the result of the combat was still doubtful, when the shades of evening, falling thicker around them, separated the combatants.

Both parties then withdrew from the field, taking up their respective stations within bowshot of each other, so that the voices of the warriors on either side could be distinctly heard in the stillness of the night. But very different were the reflections of the two hosts. The Indians, exulting in their temporary triumph, looked with confidence to the morrow to complete it. The Spaniards, on the other hand, were proportionately discouraged. They were not prepared for this spirit of resistance in an enemy hitherto so tame. Several cavaliers had fallen—one of them by a blow from a Peruvian battle-ax, which clove his head to the chin, attesting the power of the weapon and of the arm that used it. Several horses, too, had been killed; and the loss of these was almost as severely felt as that of their riders, considering the great cost and difficulty of transporting them to these distant regions. Few either of the men or horses had escaped without wounds, and the Indian allies had suffered still more severely.

It seemed probable, from the pertinacity and a certain order maintained in the assault, that it was directed by some leader of military experience—perhaps the Indian commander Quizquiz, who was said to be hanging round the environs of Cuzco with a considerable force.

Notwithstanding the reasonable cause of apprehension for the morrow, De Soto, like a stout-hearted cavalier as he was, strove to keep up the spirits of his followers. If they had beaten off the enemy when their horses were jaded and their own strength nearly exhausted, how much easier it would be to come off victorious when both were restored by a night's rest! And he told them to "trust in the Almighty, who would never desert His faithful followers in their extremity." The event justified De Soto's confidence in this reasonable succor.

From time to time, on his march, he had sent advices to Pizarro of the menacing state of the country, till his commander, becoming seriously alarmed, was apprehensive that the cavalier might be overpowered by the superior numbers of the enemy. He accordingly detached Almagro, with nearly all the remaining horse, to his support—unencumbered by infantry, that he might move the faster. That efficient leader advanced by forced marches, stimulated by the tidings which met him on the road, and was so fortunate as to reach the foot of the sierra of Vilcaconga the very night of the engagement.

There, hearing of the encounter, he pushed forward without halting, though his horses were spent with travel. The night was exceedingly dark, and Almagro, afraid of stumbling on the enemy's bivouac, and desirous to give De Soto information of his approach, commanded his trumpets to sound, till the notes, winding through the defiles of the mountains, broke the slumbers of his countrymen, sounding like blithest music in their ears. They quickly replied with their own bugles, and soon had the satisfaction to embrace their deliverers.

Great was the dismay of the Peruvian host when the morning light discovered the fresh reinforcement of the ranks of the Spaniards. There was no use in contending with an enemy who gathered strength from the conflict, and who seemed to multiply his numbers at will. Without further attempt to renew the fight, they availed themselves of a thick fog, which hung over the lower slopes of the hills, to effect their retreat, and left the passes open to the invaders. The two cavaliers then continued their march until they extricated their forces from the sierra, when, taking up a secure position, they proposed to await there the arrival of Pizarro.

The commander in chief, meanwhile, lay at Jauja, where he was greatly disturbed by the rumors which reached him of the state of the country. His enterprise, thus far, had gone forward so smoothly that he was no better prepared than his lieutenant to meet with resistance from the natives. He did not seem to comprehend that the mildest nature might at last be roused by oppression, and that the massacre of their Inca, whom they regarded with such awful veneration, would be likely, if anything could do it, to wake them from their apathy.

The tidings which he now received of the retreat of the Peruvians were most welcome; and he caused mass to be said, and thanksgivings to be offered up to Heaven, "which had shown itself thus favorable to the Christians throughout this mighty enterprise." The Spaniard was ever a Crusader. He was in the sixteenth century what *Coeur de Lion* and his brave knights were in the twelfth, with this difference: the cavalier of that day fought for the Cross and for glory, while gold and the Cross were the watchwords of the Spaniard. The spirit of chivalry had waned somewhat before the spirit of trade; but the fire of religious enthusiasm still burned as bright under the quilted mail of the American Conqueror as it did of yore under the iron panoply of the soldier of Palestine.

It seemed probable that some man of authority had organized, or at least countenanced, this resistance of the natives; and suspicion fell on the captive chief Calicuchima, who was accused of maintaining a secret correspondence with his confederate Quizquiz. Pizarro waited on the Indian noble and, charging him with the conspiracy, reproached him, as he had formerly done his royal master, with ingratitude towards the Spaniards, who had dealt with him so liberally. He concluded by the assurance that, if he did not cause the Peruvians to lay down their arms and tender their submission at once, he should be burned alive so soon as they reached Almagro's quarters.

The Indian chief listened to the terrible menace with the utmost composure. He denied having had any communication with his countrymen, and said that, in his present state of confinement at least, he could have no power to bring them to submission. He then remained doggedly silent, and Pizarro did not press the matter further. But he placed a strong guard over his prisoner, and caused him to be put in irons. It was an ominous proceeding, and had been the precursor of the death of Atahuallpa.

Before quitting Jauja, a misfortune befell the Spaniards in the death of their creature, the young Inca Toparca. Suspicion, of course, fell on Calicuchima, now selected as the scapegoat for all the offenses of his nation. It was a disappointment to Pizarro, who hoped to find a convenient shelter for his future proceedings under this shadow of royalty.

The general considered it most prudent not to hazard the

"Father Valverde accompanied the Peruvian chieftain to the stake. . . . But his arguments fell on a stony heart. In the midst of his tortures, Calicuchima showed the characteristic courage of the American Indian . . . and he died with his last breath invoking the name of Pachacamac."

loss of his treasures by taking them on the march, and he accordingly left them at Jauja under guard of forty soldiers, who remained there in garrison. No event of importance occurred on the road, and Pizarro having effected a junction with Almagro, their united forces soon entered the vale of Xaquixahuana, about fives leagues from Cuzco. This was one of those bright spots, so often found embosomed amidst the Andes, the more beautiful from contrast with the savage character of the scenery around it. A river flowed through the valley, affording the means of irrigating the soil and clothing it in perpetual verdure; and the rich and flowering vegetation spread out like a cultivated garden. The beauty of the place and its delicious coolness commended it as a residence of the Peruvian nobles, and the sides of the hills were dotted with their villas, which afforded them a grateful retreat in the heats of summer. Yet the center of the valley was disfigured by a quagmire of some extent, occasioned by the frequent overflowing of the waters; but the industry of the Indian architects had constructed a solid causeway, faced with heavy stone, and connected with the great road, which traversed the whole breadth of the morass.[42]

In this valley Pizarro halted for several days, while he refreshed his troops from the well-stored magazines of the Incas. His first act was to bring Calicuchima to trial—if trial that could be called, where sentence may be said to have gone hand in hand with accusation. We are not informed of the nature of the evidence. It was sufficient to satisfy the Spanish captains of the chieftain's guilt. Nor is it at all incredible that Calicuchima should have secretly encouraged a movement among the people, designed to secure his country's freedom and his own. He was condemned to be burned alive on the spot. "Some thought it a hard measure," says Herrera; "but those who are governed by reasons of state policy are apt to shut their eyes against everything else." Why this cruel mode of execution was so often adopted by the Spanish Conquerors is not obvious; unless it was that the Indian was an infidel, and fire, from ancient date, seems to have been considered the fitting doom of the infidel, as the type of that inextinguishable flame which awaited him in the regions of the damned.

Father Valverde accompanied the Peruvian chieftain to the stake. He seems always to have been present at this dreary moment, anxious to profit by it, if possible, to work the conversion of the victim. He painted in gloomy colors the dreadful doom of the unbeliever, to whom the waters of baptism could alone secure the ineffable glories of paradise. It does not appear that he promised any commutation of punishment

in this world. But his arguments fell on a stony heart, and
the chief coldly replied, he "did not understand the religion
of the white men." He might be pardoned for not comprehending the beauty of a faith which, as it would seem, had
borne so bitter fruits to him. In the midst of his tortures he
showed the characteristic courage of the American Indian,
whose power of endurance triumphs over the power of persecution in his enemies, and he died with his last breath invoking the name of Pachacamac. His own followers brought the
fagots to feed the flames that consumed him.

Soon after this tragic event, Pizarro was surprised by a
visit from a Peruvian noble, who came in great state, attended
by a numerous and showy retinue. It was the young prince
Manco II, brother of the unfortunate Huascar, and the rightful successor to the crown. Being brought before the Spanish commander, he announced his pretensions to the throne
and claimed the protection of the strangers. It is said he had
meditated resisting them by arms, and had encouraged the
assaults made on them on their march, but finding resistance
ineffectual, he had taken this politic course, greatly to the
displeasure of his more resolute nobles. However this may be,
Pizarro listened to his application with singular contentment,
for he saw in this new scion of the true royal stock a more
effectual instrument for his purposes than he could have found
in the family of Quito, with whom the Peruvians had but little sympathy. He received the young man, therefore, with
great cordiality, and did not hesitate to assure him that he
had been sent into the country by his master, the Castilian
sovereign, in order to vindicate the claims of Huascar to the
crown, and to punish the usurpation of his rival.

Taking with him the Indian prince, Pizarro now resumed
his march. It was interrupted for a few hours by a party of
the natives, who lay in wait for him in the neighboring sierra.
A sharp skirmish ensued, in which the Indians behaved with
great spirit and inflicted some little injury on the Spaniards;
but the latter at length, shaking them off, made good their
passage through the defile, and the enemy did not care to follow them into the open country.

It was late in the afternoon when the Conquerors came in
sight of Cuzco. The descending sun was streaming his broad
rays full on the imperial city, where many an altar was dedicated to his worship. The low ranges of buildings, showing in
his beams like so many lines of silvery light, filled up the
bosom of the valley and the lower slopes of the mountains,
whose shadowy forms hung darkly over the fair city, as if to
shield it from the menaced profanation. It was so late that

Pizarro resolved to defer his entrance till the following morning.

That night vigilant guard was kept in the camp, and the soldiers slept on their arms. But it passed away without annoyance from the enemy; and early on the following day, November 15, 1533, Pizarro prepared for his entrance into the Peruvian capital.[43]

The little army was formed into three divisions, of which the center, or "battle," as it was called, was led by the general. The suburbs were thronged with a countless multitude of the natives, who had flocked from the city and the surrounding country to witness the showy and, to them, startling pageant. All looked with eager curiosity on the strangers, the fame of whose terrible exploits had spread to the remotest parts of the empire. They gazed with astonishment on their dazzling arms and fair complexions, which seemed to proclaim them the true Children of the Sun; and they listened with feelings of mysterious dread as the trumpet sent forth its prolonged notes through the streets of the capital, and the solid ground shook under the heavy tramp of the cavalry.

The Spanish commander rode directly up the great square. It was surrounded by low piles of buildings, among which were several palaces of the Incas. One of these, erected by Huayna Capac, was surmounted by a tower, while the ground floor was occupied by one or more immense halls, like those described in Cajamarca, where the Peruvian nobles held their *fêtes* in stormy weather. These buildings afforded convenient barracks for the troops, though during the first few weeks they remained under their tents in the open *plaza*, with their horses picketed by their side, ready to repulse any insurrection of the inhabitants.

The capital of the Incas, though falling short of the *El Dorado* which had engaged their credulous fancies, astonished the Spaniards by the beauty of its edifices, the length and regularity of its streets, and the good order and appearance of comfort, even luxury, visible in its numerous population. It far surpassed all they had yet seen in the New World. The population of the city is computed by one of the Conquerors at two hundred thousand inhabitants, and that of the suburbs at as many more. This account is not confirmed, as far as I have seen, by any other writer. But, however it may be exaggerated, it is certain that Cuzco was the metropolis of a great empire, the residence of the court and the chief nobility; frequented by the most skillful mechanics and artisans of every description, who found a demand for their ingenuity in the royal precincts; while the place was garrisoned by a nu-

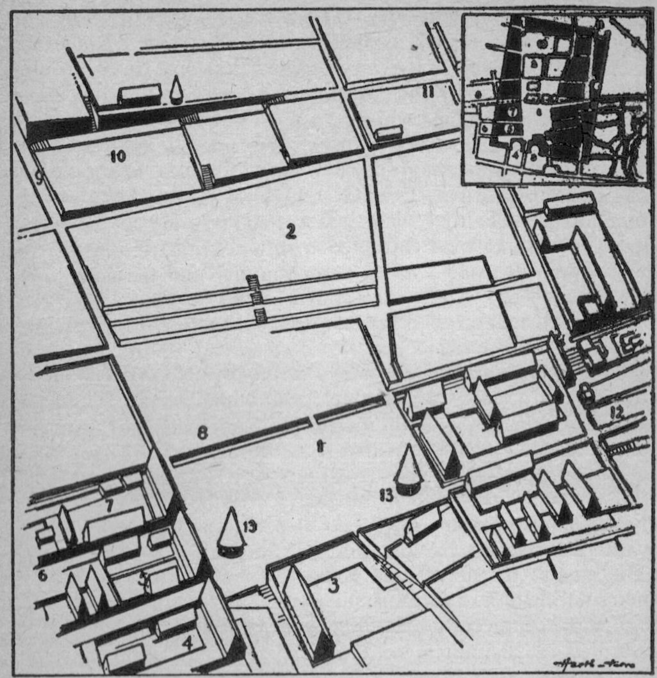

The center of Cuzco, the capital of the Incas, at an altitude of 11,007 feet. Francisco Pizarro entered Cuzco on November 15, 1533. There are no contemporary accounts of this entry or any description of the city. Later, in 1538, Pedro de Cieza de Leon wrote: "Cuzco . . . surrounded by mountains . . . stands on the banks of two streams. From the large square . . . the four royal roads lead out to all the points of the empire. . . . The stream which flows through the city has its bridges for passing from one side to the other. . . . It has fine streets except that they are narrow. The houses are built of stone finely joined. . . . Roofs are of straw." (1) Huayka-pata (Joy Square), the principal plaza, out of which all roads of the empire lead; (2) Cusi-pata, the secondary plaza, reached by flights of stairs; (3) the temple of Viracocha (the site of which is now occupied by the Cathedral of Cuzco); (4) Hatun-Cancha, the palace of Topa Inca; (5) Aclla-huasi, the House of the Chosen Women; (6) the road to the south, to Colla-suyu; (7) Amaru-cancha, a temple whose walls were covered with carved stone snakes (on the site of which the church of the Jesuits now stands; (8) the Huatanay River, which was canalized, "with bridges to pass merous soldiery, and was the resort, finally, of emigrants from the most distant provinces. The quarters whence this motley population came were indicated by their peculiar dress, and especially their headgear, so rarely found at all on the American Indian, which, with its variegated colors, gave a picturesque effect to the groups and masses in the streets. The habitual order and decorum maintained in this multifarious assembly showed the excellent police of the capital, where the only sounds that disturbed the repose of the Spaniards were the noises of feasting and dancing, which the natives, with happy insensibility, constantly prolonged to a late hour of the night.

The edifices of the better sort—and they were very numerous—were of stone, or faced with stone. Among the principal were the royal residences, as each sovereign built a new palace for himself, covering, though low, a large extent of ground. The walls were sometimes stained or painted with gaudy tints, and the gates, we are assured, were sometimes of colored marble. "In the delicacy of the stonework," says another of the Conquerors, "the natives far excelled the Spaniards, though the roofs of their dwellings, instead of tiles, were only of thatch, but put together with the nicest art." The sunny climate of Cuzco did not require a very substantial material for defense against the weather.

The most important building was the fortress, planted on a solid rock that rose boldly over the city. It was built of hewn stone, so finely wrought that it was impossible to detect the line of junction between the blocks; and the approaches to it were defended by three semicircular parapets, composed of such heavy masses of rock that it bore resemblance to the kind of work known to architects as the Cyclopean. The fortress was raised to a height rare in Peruvian architecture; and from the summit of the tower the eye of the spectator ranged over a magnificent prospect, in which the wild features of the mountain scenery, rocks, woods, and waterfalls, were mingled with the rich verdure of the valley, and the shining city filling up the foreground—all blended in sweet harmony under the deep azure of a tropical sky.

---

from one side to the other." (9) The beginning of the road to the west, Cunti-suyu; (10) residence area for governors of the realm, now the site of the convent and church of San Francisco; (11) the road to the north, which went to and beyond Quito; (12) the road to the eastern montana, which led to Pisac, Ollantaytambo, etc.; (13) the round, straw-roofed structures are known as Suntur-huasi.

The streets were long and narrow. They were arranged with perfect regularity, crossing one another at right angles; and from the great square diverged four principal streets connecting with the highroads of the empire. The square itself, and many parts of the city, were paved with a fine pebble. Through the heart of the capital ran a river of pure water, if it might not be rather termed a canal, the banks or sides of which, for the distance of twenty leagues, were faced with stone. Across this stream, bridges, constructed of similar broad flags, were thrown at intervals, so as to afford an easy communication between the different quarters of the capital.

The most sumptuous edifice in Cuzco in the times of the Incas was undoubtedly the great temple dedicated to the Sun, which, studded with gold plates, as already noticed, was surrounded by convents and dormitories for the priests, with their gardens and broad parterres sparkling with gold. The exterior ornaments had been already removed by the Conquerors—all but the frieze of gold, which, embedded in the stones, still encircled the principal building. It is probable that the tales of wealth so greedily circulated among the Spaniards greatly exceeded the truth. If they did not, the natives must have been very successful in concealing their treasures from the invaders. Yet much still remained, not only in the great House of the Sun, but in the inferior temples which swarmed in the capital.

Pizarro, on entering Cuzco, had issued an order forbidding any soldier to offer violence to the dwellings of the inhabitants. But the palaces were numerous, and the troops lost no time in plundering them of their contents, as well as in despoiling the religious edifices. The interior decorations supplied them with considerable booty. They stripped off the jewels and rich ornaments that garnished the royal mummies in the temple of Curicancha. Indignant at the concealment of their treasures, they put the inhabitants, in some instances, to the torture, and endeavored to extort from them a confession of their hiding places. They invaded the repose of the sepulchers, in which the Peruvians often deposited their valuable effects, and compelled the grave to give up its dead. No place was left unexplored by the rapacious Conquerors; and they occasionally stumbled on a mine of wealth that rewarded their labors.

In a cavern near the city they found a number of vases of pure gold, richly embossed with the figures of serpents, locusts, and other animals. Among the spoil were four golden llamas and ten or twelve statues of women, some of gold, others of silver, "which merely to see," says one of the Con-

querors, with some *naïveté,* "was truly a great satisfaction."
The gold was probably thin, for the figures were all as large as
life; and several of them, being reserved for the royal fifth,
were not recast, but sent in their original form to Spain. The
magazines were stored with curious commodities: richly tinted
robes of cotton and featherwork, gold sandals, and slippers of
the same material for the women, and dresses composed entirely of beads of gold. The grain and other articles of food,
with which the magazines were filled, were held in contempt
by the Conquerors, intent only on gratifying their lust for
gold. The time came when the grain would have been of far
more value.

Yet the amount of treasure in the capital did not equal the
sanguine expectations that had been formed by the Spaniards.
But the deficiency was supplied by the plunder which they had
collected at various places on their march. In one place, for
example, they met with ten planks or bars of solid silver, each
piece being twenty feet in length, one foot in breadth, and two
or three inches thick. They were intended to decorate the
dwelling of an Inca noble.

The whole mass of treasure was brought into a common
heap, as in Cajamarca; and after some of the finer specimens had been deducted for the crown, the remainder was
delivered to the Indian goldsmiths to be melted down into
ingots of a uniform standard. The division of the spoil was
made on the same principle as before. There were four hundred and eighty soldiers, including the garrison of Jauja, who
were each to receive a share, that of the cavalry being double
that of the infantry. The amount of booty is stated variously
by those present at the division of it. According to some, it
considerably exceeded the ransom of Atahuallpa. Others state
it as less. Pedro Pizarro says that each horseman got six thousand *pesos de oro,* and each one of the infantry half that sum;
though the same discrimination was made by Pizarro as before, in respect to the rank of the parties and their relative
services. But Sancho, the royal notary, and secretary of the
commander, estimates the whole amount as far less—not exceeding five hundred and eight thousand and two hundred
*pesos de oro,* and two hundred and fifteen thousand marks of
silver. In the absence of the official returns, it is impossible
to determine which is correct. But Sancho's narrative is coun-
tersigned, it may be remembered, by Pizarro and the royal
treasurer Riquelme, and doubtless, therefore, shows the actual
amount for which the Conquerors accounted to the crown.

Whichever statement we receive, the sum, combined with
that obtained at Cajamarca, might well have satisfied the crav-

ings of the most avaricious. The sudden influx of so much wealth, and that, too, in so transferable a form, among a party of reckless adventurers little accustomed to the possession of money, had its natural effect. It supplied them with the means of gaming, so strong and common a passion with the Spaniards that it may be considered a national vice. Fortunes were lost and won in a single day, sufficient to render the proprietors independent for life; and many a desperate gamester, by an unlucky throw of the dice or turn of the cards, saw himself stripped in a few hours of the fruits of years of toil, and obliged to begin over again the business of rapine. Among these, one in the cavalry service is mentioned, named Leguizano, who had received as his share of the booty the image of the Sun, which, raised on a plate of burnished gold, spread over the walls in a recess of the great temple, and which, for some reason or other—perhaps because of its superior fineness—was not recast like the other ornaments. This rich prize the spendthrift lost in a single night; whence it came to be a proverb in Spain, *Juega el Sol antes que amanezca,* "He plays away the Sun before sunrise."

The effect of such a surfeit of the precious metals was instantly felt on prices. The most ordinary articles were only to be had for exorbitant sums. A quire of paper was sold for ten *pesos de oro;* a bottle of wine, for sixty; a sword, for forty or fifty; a cloak, for a hundred—sometimes more; a pair of shoes cost thirty or forty *pesos de oro,* and a good horse could not be had for less than twenty-five hundred. Some brought a still higher price. Every article rose in value, as gold and silver, the representatives of all, declined. Gold and silver, in short, seemed to be the only things in Cuzco that were not wealth. Yet there were some few wise enough to return contented with their present gains to their native country. Here their riches brought them consideration and competence, and while they excited the envy of their countrymen, stimulated them to seek their own fortunes in the like path of adventure.

# ❧ CHAPTER NINE ❧

NEW INCA CROWNED—MUNICIPAL REGULATIONS—

TERRIBLE MARCH OF ALVARADO—INTERVIEW

WITH PIZARRO—FOUNDATION OF LIMA—

HERNANDO PIZARRO REACHES SPAIN—

SENSATION AT COURT—FEUDS OF

ALMAGRO AND THE PIZARROS

## (1534–1535)

The first care of the Spanish general, after the division of the booty, was to place Manco II on the throne, and to obtain for him the recognition of his countrymen. He, accordingly, presented the young prince to them as their future sovereign, the legitimate son of Huayna Capac, and the true heir of the Peruvian scepter. The annunciation was received with enthusiasm by the people, attached to the memory of his illustrious father, and pleased that they were still to have a monarch rule over them of the ancient line of Cuzco.

Everything was done to maintain the illusion with the Indian population. The ceremonies of a coronation were studiously observed. The young prince kept the prescribed fasts and vigils; and on the appointed day the nobles and the people, with the whole Spanish soldiery, assembled in the great square of Cuzco to witness the concluding ceremony. Mass was publicly performed by Father Valverde, and the Inca Manco II received the fringed diadem of Peru, not from the hand of the high priest of his nation, but from his conqueror, Pizarro. The Indian lords then tendered their obeisance in the customary form; after which the royal notary read aloud the instrument asserting the supremacy of the Castilian crown, and requiring the homage of all present to its authority. This address was explained by an interpreter, and the ceremony of homage was performed by each one of the parties waving the royal banner of Castile twice or thrice with his hands. Manco II then pledged the Spanish commander in a golden goblet of the sparkling *chicha*,[44] and, the latter having cordially embraced the new monarch, the trumpets announced the conclusion of the ceremony. But it was not the note of triumph, but of humiliation; for it proclaimed that the armed foot of the stranger was in the halls of the Peruvian Incas; that the ceremony of coronation was a miserable pageant; that their prince himself was but a puppet in the hands of his conqueror; and that the glory of the Children of the Sun had departed forever!

Yet the people readily yielded the illusion, and seemed willing to accept this image of their ancient independence. The accession of the young monarch was greeted by all the usual *fêtes* and rejoicings. The mummies of his royal ancestors, with such ornaments as were still left to them, were paraded in the great square. They were attended each by his own numerous retinue, who performed all the menial offices, as if the object of them were alive and could feel their import. Each ghostly form took its seat at the banquet table—now, alas! stripped of the magnificent service with which it was wont to blaze at these high festivals—and the guests drank deep to the illustrious dead. Dancing succeeded the carousal, and the festivities, prolonged to a later hour, were continued night after night by the giddy population, as if their Conquerors had not been entrenched in the capital!—What a contrast to the Aztecs in the conquest of Mexico!

Pizarro's next concern was to organize a municipal government for Cuzco, like those in the cities of the parent country. Two *alcaldes* were appointed and eight *regidores,* among which last functionaries were his brothers Gonzalo and Juan. The oaths of office were administered with great solemnity, on the twenty-fourth of March, 1534, in presence both of Spaniards and Peruvians, in the public square; as if the general were willing by this ceremony to intimate to the latter that, while they retained the semblance of their ancient institutions, the real power was henceforth vested in their conquerors. He invited Spaniards to settle in the place by liberal grants of lands and houses, for which means were afforded by the numerous palaces and public buildings of the Incas; and many a cavalier who had been too poor in his own country to find a place to rest in, now saw himself the proprietor of a spacious mansion that might have entertained the retinue of a prince. From this time, says an old chronicler, Pizarro, who had hitherto been distinguished by his military title of "Captain-

General," was addressed by that of "Governor." Both had been bestowed on him by the royal grant.

Nor did the chief neglect the interests of religion. Father Valverde, whose nomination as Bishop of Cuzco not long afterwards received the Papal sanction, prepared to enter on the duties of his office. A place was selected for the cathedral of his diocese, facing the *plaza*. A spacious monastery subsequently rose on the ruins of the gorgeous House of the Sun; its walls were constructed of the ancient stones; the altar was raised on the spot where shone the bright image of the Peruvian deity, and the cloisters of the Indian temple were trodden by the friars of St. Dominic. To make the metamorphosis more complete, the House of the Virgins of the Sun was replaced by a Roman Catholic Nunnery. Christian churches and monasteries gradually supplanted the ancient edifices, and such of the latter as were suffered to remain, despoiled of their heathen insignia, were placed under the protection of the Cross.

"The fathers of . . . the Order of Mercy and other missionaries now busied themselves in the good work of conversion."

The Fathers of St. Dominic, the Brethren of the Order of Mercy, and other missionaries, now busied themselves in the good work of conversion. We have seen that Pizarro was required by the crown to bring out a certain number of these holy men in his own vessels; and every succeeding vessel brought an additional reinforcement of ecclesiastics. They were not all like the Bishop of Cuzco, with hearts so seared by fanaticism as to be closed against sympathy with the unfortunate natives. They were, many of them, men of singular humility, who followed in the track of the conqueror to scatter the seeds of spiritual truth and, with disinterested zeal, devoted themselves to the propagation of the gospel. Thus did their pious labors prove them the true soldiers of the Cross, and show that the object so ostentatiously avowed of carrying its banner among the heathen nations was not an empty vaunt.

The effort to Christianize the heathen is an honorable characteristic of the Spanish conquests. The Puritan, with equal religious zeal, did comparatively little for the conversion of the Indian, content, as it would seem, with having secured to himself the inestimable privilege of worshiping God in his own way. Other adventurers who have occupied the New World have often had too little regard for religion themselves to be very solicitous about spreading it among the savages. But the Spanish missionary, from first to last, has shown a keen interest in the spiritual welfare of the natives. Under his auspices, churches on a magnificent scale have been erected, schools for elementary instruction founded, and every rational means taken to spread the knowledge of religious truth, while he has carried his solitary mission into remote and almost inaccessible regions, or gathered his Indian disciples into communities, like the good Las Casas in Cumaná, or the Jesuits in California and Paraguay. At all times the courageous ecclesiastic has been ready to lift his voice against the cruelty of the conqueror and the no less wasting cupidity of the colonist; and when his remonstrances, as was too often the case, have proved unavailing, he has still followed to bind up the brokenhearted, to teach the poor Indian resignation under his lot, and light up his dark intellect with the revelation of a holier and happier existence. In reviewing the bloodstained records of Spanish colonial history, it is but fair, and at the same time cheering, to reflect that the same nation which sent forth the hardhearted conqueror from its bosom, sent forth the missionary to do the work of beneficence and spread the light of Christian civilization over the farthest regions of the New World.

While the governor, as we are henceforth to style him, lay

at Cuzco, he received repeated accounts of a considerable force in the neighborhood, under the command of Atahuallpa's officer, Quizquiz. He accordingly detached Almagro, with a small body of horse and a large native force under the Inca Manco II, to disperse the enemy, and, if possible, to capture the leader. Manco was the more ready to take part in the expedition, as the hostile Indians were soldiers of Quito, who, with their commander, bore no good will to himself.

Almagro, moving with characteristic rapidity, was not long in coming up with the Indian chieftain. Several sharp encounters followed, as the army of Quito fell back on Jauja, near which a general engagement decided the fate of the war by the total discomfiture of the natives. Quizquiz fled to the elevated plains of Quito, where he still held out with undaunted spirit against a Spanish force in that quarter, till at length his own soldiers, wearied by these long and ineffectual hostilities, massacred their commander in cold blood. Thus fell the last of the two great officers of Atahuallpa, who, if their nation had been animated by a spirit equal to their own, might long have successfully maintained their soil against the invader.

Some time before this occurrence, the Spanish governor, while in Cuzco, received tidings of an event much more alarming to him than any Indian hostilities. This was the arrival on the coast of a strong Spanish force, under the command of Don Pedro de Alvarado, the gallant officer who had served under Cortés with such renown in the war of Mexico.[45] That cavalier, after forming a brilliant alliance in Spain, to which he was entitled by his birth and military rank, had returned to his government of Guatemala, where his avarice had been roused by the magnificent reports he daily received of Pizarro's conquests. These conquests, he learned, had been confined to Peru; while the northern kingdom of Quito, the ancient residence of Atahuallpa, and, no doubt, the principal depository of his treasures, yet remained untouched. Affecting to consider this country as falling without the governor's jurisdiction, he immediately turned a large fleet, which he had intended for the Spice Islands, in the direction of South America; and in March, 1534, he landed in the Bay of Caraques, with five hundred followers, of whom half were mounted, and all admirably provided with arms and ammunition. It was the best-equipped and most formidable array that had yet appeared in the Southern seas.

Although manifestly an invasion of the territory conceded to Pizarro by the crown, the reckless cavalier determined to march at once on Quito. With the assistance of an Indian guide, he proposed to take the direct route across the mountains, a passage of exceeding difficulty, even at the most favorable season.

After crossing the Rio Daule, Alvarado's guide deserted him, so that he was soon entangled in the intricate mazes of the sierra; and as he rose higher and higher into the regions of winter, he became surrounded with ice and snow, for which his men, taken from the warm countries of Guatemala, were but ill prepared. As the cold grew more intense, many of them were so benumbed that it was with difficulty they could proceed. The infantry, compelled to make exertions, fared best. Many of the troopers were frozen stiff in their saddles. The Indians, still more sensible to the cold, perished by hundreds. As the Spaniards huddled round their wretched bivouacs, with such scanty fuel as they could glean, and almost without food, they waited in gloomy silence the approach of morning. Yet the morning light, which gleamed coldly on the cheerless waste, brought no joy to them. It only revealed more clearly the extent of their wretchedness. Still struggling on through the winding Puertos Nevados, or Snowy Passes, their track was dismally marked by fragments of dress, broken harness, golden ornaments, and other valuables plundered on their march—by the dead bodies of men, or by those, less fortunate, who were left to die alone in the wilderness. As for the horses, their carcasses were not suffered long to cumber the ground, as they were quickly seized and devoured half raw by the starving soldiers, who, like the famished condors now hovering in troops above their heads, greedily banqueted on the most offensive offal to satisfy the gnawings of hunger.

Alvarado, anxious to secure the booty which had fallen into his hands at an earlier part of his march, encouraged every man to take what gold he wanted from the common heap, reserving only the royal fifth. But they only answered, with a ghastly smile of derision, "that food was the only gold for them." Yet in this extremity, which might seem to have dissolved the very ties of nature, there are some affecting instances recorded of self-devotion—of comrades who lost their lives in assisting others, and of parents and husbands (for some of the cavaliers were accompanied by their wives) who, instead of seeking their own safety, chose to remain and perish in the snows with the objects of their love.

To add to their distress, the air was filled for several days with thick clouds of earthy particles and cinders, which blinded the men and made respiration exceedingly difficult. This phenomenon, it seems probable, was caused by an eruption of the distant Cotopaxi, which, about twelve leagues southeast of Quito, rears its colossal and perfectly symmetrical cone far above the limits of eternal snow—the most beautiful and the most terrible of the American volcanoes. At the time of Alvarado's expedition it was in a state of eruption, the earliest instance of the kind on record, though doubtless not the earliest. Since that period it has been in frequent commotion, sending up its sheets of flame to the height of half a mile, spouting forth cataracts of lava that have overwhelmed towns and villages in their career, and shaking the earth with subterraneous thunders, that, at the distance of more than a hundred leagues, sounded like the reports of artillery! Alvarado's followers, unacquainted with the cause of the phenomenon, as they wandered over tracts buried in snow—the sight of which was strange to them—in an atmosphere laden with ashes, became bewildered by this confusion of the elements, which Nature seemed to have contrived purposely for their destruction. Some of these men were soldiers of Cortés, steeled by many a painful march and many a sharp encounter with the Aztecs. But this war of the elements, they now confessed, was mightier than all.

At length, Alvarado, after sufferings which even the most hardy, probably, could have endured but a few days longer, emerged from the Snowy Pass, and came on the elevated tableland which spreads out at the height of more than nine thousand feet above the ocean, in the neighborhood of Riobamba. But one-fourth of his gallant army had been left to feed the condor in the wilderness, besides the greater part, at least two thousand, of his Indian auxiliaries. A great number of his horses, too, had perished; and the men and horses that escaped were all of them more or less injured by the cold and the extremity of suffering. Such was the terrible passage of the Puertos Nevados, which I have only briefly noticed as an episode to the Peruvian conquest, but the account of which, in all its details, though it occupied but a few weeks in duration, would give one a better idea of the difficulties encountered by the Spanish cavaliers than volumes of ordinary narrative.

As Alvarado, after halting some time to restore his exhausted troops, began his march across the broad plateau, he was astonished by seeing the prints of horses' hoofs on the soil. Spaniards, then, had been there before him, and, after all his toil and suffering, others had forestalled him in the enterprise against Quito! It is necessary to say a few words in explanation of this.

When Pizarro quitted Cajamarca, being sensible of the growing importance of San Miguel, the only port of entry then in the country, he dispatched a person in whom he had great confidence to take charge of it. This person was Sebastian Benalcazar, a cavalier who afterwards placed his name in the first rank of the South American conquerors for courage, capacity—and cruelty. But this cavalier had hardly reached his government, when, like Alvarado, he received such accounts of the riches of Quito that he determined, with the force at his command, though without orders, to undertake its reduction.

At the head of about a hundred and forty soldiers, horse and foot, and a stout body of Indian auxiliaries, he marched up the broad range of the Andes, to where it spreads out into the tableland of Quito, by a road safer and more expeditious than that taken by Alvarado. On the plains of Riobamba he encountered the Indian general Ruminawi. Several engagements followed, with doubtful success, when, in the end, science prevailed where courage was well matched, and the victorious Benalcazar planted the standard of Castile on the ancient towers of Atahuallpa. The city, in honor of his general, Francisco Pizarro, he named San Francisco del Quito. But great was his mortification on finding that either the stories of its riches had been fabricated, or that these riches were secreted by the natives. The city was all that he gained by his victories—the shell without the pearl of price which gave it its value. While swallowing his chagrin as he best could, the Spanish captain received tidings of the approach of his superior, Almagro.

No sooner had the news of Alvarado's expedition reached Cuzco than Almagro left the place with a small force for San Miguel, proposing to strengthen himself by reinforcement from that quarter, and to march at once against the invaders. Greatly was he astonished, on his arrival in that city, to learn the departure of its commander. Doubting the loyalty of his motives, Almagro, with the buoyancy of spirit which belongs to youth, though in truth somewhat enfeebled by the infirmities of age, did not hesitate to follow Benalcazar at once across the mountains.

With his wonted energy, the intrepid veteran, overcoming all the difficulties of his march, in a few weeks placed himself and his little company on the lofty plains which spread around the Indian city of Riobamba; though in his progress he had more than one hot encounter with the natives, whose courage and perseverance formed a contrast sufficiently striking to the apathy of the Peruvians. But the fire only slumbered in the bosom of the Peruvian. His hour had not yet come.

At Riobamba, Almagro was soon joined by the commander

of San Miguel, who disclaimed, perhaps sincerely, any disloyal intent in his unauthorized expedition. Thus reinforced, the Spanish captain coolly awaited the coming of Alvarado. The forces of the latter, though in a less serviceable condition, were much superior in number and appointments to those of his rival. As they confronted each other on the broad plains of Riobamba, it seemed probable that a fierce struggle must immediately follow, and the natives of the country have the satisfaction to see their wrongs avenged by the very hands that inflicted them. But it was Almagro's policy to avoid such an issue.

Negotiations were set on foot, in which each party stated his claims to the country. Meanwhile Alvarado's men mingled freely with their countrymen in the opposite army, and heard there such magnificent reports of the wealth and wonders of Cuzco that many of them were inclined to change their present service for that of Pizarro. Their own leader, too, satisfied that Quito held out no recompense worth the sacrifices he had made, and was like to make by insisting on his claim, became now more sensible of the rashness of a course which must doubtless incur the censure of his sovereign. In this temper, it was not difficult for them to effect an adjustment of difficulties; and it was agreed, as the basis of it, that the governor should pay one hundred thousand *pesos de oro* to Alvarado, in consideration of which the latter was to resign to him his fleet, his forces, and all his stories and munitions. His vessels, great and small, amounted to twelve in number, and the sum he received, though large, did not cover his expenses. This treaty being settled, Alvarado proposed, before leaving the country, to have an interview with Pizarro.

The governor, meanwhile, had quitted the Peruvian capital for the seacoast, from his desire to repel any invasion that might be attempted in that direction by Alvarado, with whose real movements he was still unacquainted. He left Cuzco in charge of his brother Juan, a cavalier whose manners were such as, he thought, would be likely to gain the good will of the native population. Pizarro also left ninety of his troops, as the garrison of the capital and the nucleus of his future colony. Then, taking the Inca Manco with him, he proceeded as far as Jauja. At this place he was entertained by the Indian prince with the exhibition of a great national hunt—such as has been already described in these pages—in which immense numbers of wild animals were slaughtered, and the vicuñas, and other races of Peruvian sheep, which roam over the mountains, driven into enclosures and relieved of their delicate fleeces.

The Spanish governor then proceeded to Pachacamac, where he received the grateful intelligence of the accommodation of Alvarado; and not long afterwards he was visited by that cavalier himself, previously to his embarkation.

The meeting was conducted with courtesy, and a show, at least, of good will on both sides, as there was no longer real cause for jealousy between the parties; and each, as may be imagined, looked on the other with no little interest, as having achieved such distinction in the bold path of adventure. In this comparison, Alvarado had somewhat the advantage; for Pizarro, though of commanding presence, had not the brilliant exterior, the free and joyous manner, which, no less than his fresh complexion and sunny locks, had won for the conqueror of Guatemala, in his campaigns against the Aztecs, the *sobriquet* of *Tonatiuh,* or "Child of the Sun."

Blithe were the revels that now rang through the ancient city of Pachacamac; where, instead of songs, and of the sacrifices so often seen there in honor of the Indian deity, the walls echoed to the noise of tourneys and Moorish tilts of reeds, with which the martial adventurers loved to recall the sports of their native land. When these were concluded, Alvarado re-embarked for his government of Guatemala, where his restless spirit soon involved him in other enterprises that cut short his adventurous career. His expedition to Peru was eminently characteristic of the man. It was founded in injustice, conducted with rashness, and ended in disaster.

The reduction of Peru might now be considered as, in a manner, accomplished. Some barbarous tribes in the interior, it is true, still held out, and Alonso de Alvarado, a prudent and able officer, was employed to bring them into subjection. Benalcazar was still at Quito, of which he was subsequently appointed governor by the crown. There he was laying deeper the foundation of Spanish power, while he advanced the line of conquest still higher towards the north. But Cuzco, the ancient capital of the Indian monarchy, had submitted. The armies of Atahuallpa had been beaten and scattered. The empire of the Incas was dissolved, and the prince who now wore the Peruvian diadem was but the shadow of a king, who held his commission from his conqueror.

The first act of the governor was to determine on the site of the future capital of this vast colonial empire. Cuzco, withdrawn among the mountains, was altogether too far removed from the seacoast for a commercial people. The little settlement of San Miguel lay too far to the north. It was desirable to select some more central position, which could be easily found in one of the fruitful valleys that bordered the Pacific.

was . . . . City of the Kings. . . . But the Castilian name . . . was supplanted by that of Lima."

Such was that of Pachacamac, which Pizarro now occupied. But, on further examination, he preferred the neighboring valley of Rimac, which lay to the north, and which took its name, signifying in the Quechua tongue "one who speaks," from a celebrated idol, whose shrine was much frequented by the Indians for the oracles it delivered. Through the valley flowed a broad stream, which, like a great artery, was made, as usual, by the natives, to supply a thousand finer veins that meandered through the beautiful meadows.

On this river Pizarro fixed the site of his new capital, at somewhat less than two leagues' distance from its mouth, which expanded into a commodious haven for the commerce that the prophetic eye of the founder saw would one day— and no very distant one—float on its waters. The central situation of the spot recommended it as a suitable residence for the Peruvian viceroy, whence he might hold easy communication with the different parts of the country and keep vigilant watch over his Indian vassals. The climate was delightful and, though only twelve degrees south of the line, was so far tempered by the cool breezes that generally blow from the Pacific, or from the opposite quarter down the frozen sides of the Cordilleras, that the heat was less than in corresponding latitudes on the continent. It never rained on the coast; but this dryness was corrected by a vaporous cloud, which, through the summer months, hung like a curtain over the valley, sheltering it from the rays of a tropical sun, and imperceptibly distilling a refreshing moisture that clothed the fields in the brightest verdure.

The name bestowed on the infant capital was *Ciudad de los Reyes*, or City of the Kings, in honor of the day, being the sixth of January, 1535—the festival of Epiphany—when it was said to have been founded, or more probably when its site was determined, as its actual foundation seems to have been twelve days later. But the Castilian name ceased to be used even within the first generation, and was supplanted by that of Lima, into which the original Indian name of Rimac was corrupted by the Spaniards.

The city was laid out on a very regular plan. The streets were to be much wider than usual in Spanish towns, and perfectly straight, crossing one another at right angles, and so far asunder as to afford ample space for gardens to the dwellings, and for public squares. It was arranged in a triangular form, having the river for its base, the waters of which were to be carried, by means of stone conduits, through all the principal streets, affording facilities for irrigating the grounds around the houses.

No sooner had the governor decided on the site and on the plan of the city than he commenced operations with characteristic energy. The Indians were collected from a distance of more than a hundred miles to aid in the work. The Spaniards applied themselves with vigor to the task, under the eye of their chief. The sword was exchanged for the tool of the artisan. The camp was converted into a hive of diligent laborers; and the sounds of war were succeeded by the peaceful hum of a busy population. The *plaza,* which was extensive, was to be surrounded by the cathedral, the palace of the viceroy, that of the municipality, and other public buildings; and their foundations were laid on a scale and with a solidity which defied the assaults of time, and, in some instances, even the more formidable shock of earthquakes, which, at different periods, have laid portions of the fair capital in ruins.

While these events were going on, Almagro, the marshal, as he is usually termed by chroniclers of the time, had gone to Cuzco, whither he was sent by Pizarro to take command of that capital. He received also instructions to undertake, either by himself or by his captains, the conquest of the countries towards the south, forming part of Chile. Almagro, since his arrival at Cajamarca, had seemed willing to smother his ancient feelings of resentment towards his associate, or at least to conceal the expressions of them, and had consented to take command under him in obedience to the royal mandate. He had even, in his despatches, the magnanimity to make honorable mention of Pizarro, as one anxious to promote the interests of the crown. Yet he did not so far trust his companion as to neglect the precaution of sending a confidential agent to represent his own services, when Hernando Pizarro undertook his mission to the mother country.

That cavalier, after touching at St. Domingo, had arrived without accident at Seville in January, 1534. Besides the royal fifth, he took with him gold to the value of half a million of *pesos,* together with a large quantity of silver, the property of private adventurers, some of whom, satisfied with their gains, had returned to Spain in the same vessel with himself. The customhouse was filled with solid ingots, and with vases of different forms, imitations of animals, flowers, fountains, and other objects, executed with more or less skill, and all of pure gold, to the astonishment of the spectators, who flocked from the neighboring country to gaze on these marvelous productions of Indian art. Most of the manufactured articles were the property of the crown; and Hernando Pizarro, after a short stay at Seville, selected some of the most gorgeous specimens, and crossed the country to Calatayud, where the emperor was holding the Cortes of Aragon.

Hernando was instantly admitted to the royal presence, and obtained a gracious audience. He was more conversant with courts than either of his brothers, and his manners, when in situations that imposed a restraint on the natural arrogance of his temper, were graceful and even attractive. In a respectful tone, he now recited the stirring adventures of his brother and his little troop of followers, the fatigues they had endured, the difficulties they had overcome, their capture of the Peruvian Inca, and his magnificent ransom. He had not to tell of the massacre of the unfortunate prince, for that tragic event, which had occurred since his departure from the country, was still unknown to him. The cavalier expatiated on the productiveness of the soil, and on the civilization of the people, evinced by their proficiency in various mechanic arts; in proof of which he displayed the manufactures of wool and cotton and the rich ornaments of gold and silver. The monarch's eyes sparkled with delight as he gazed on these last. He was too sagacious not to appreciate the advantages of a conquest which secured to him a country so rich in agricultural resources. But the returns from these must necessarily be gradual and long deferred; and he may be excused for listening with still greater satisfaction to Pizarro's tales of its mineral stores; for his ambitious projects had drained the imperial treasury, and he saw in the golden tide thus unexpectedly poured in upon him the immediate means of replenishing it.

Charles made no difficulty, therefore, in granting the petitions of the fortunate adventurer. All the previous grants to Francisco Pizarro and his associates were confirmed in the fullest manner; and the boundaries of the governor's jurisdiction were extended seventy leagues farther towards the south. Nor did Almagro's services, this time, go unrequited. He was empowered to discover and occupy the country for the distance of two hundred leagues, beginning at the southern limit of Pizarro's territory. Charles, in still further proof of his satisfaction, was graciously pleased to address a letter to the two commanders, in which he complimented them on their prowess and thanked them for their services. This act of justice to Almagro would have been highly honorable to Hernando Pizarro, considering the unfriendly relations in which they stood to each other, had it not been made necessary by the presence of the marshal's own agents at court, who, as already noticed, stood ready to supply any deficiency in the statements of the emissary.

In this display of the royal bounty, the envoy, as will readily be believed, did not go without his reward. He was lodged as an attendant of the court; was made a knight of Santiago, the most prized of the chivalric orders in Spain; was empowered to equip an armament, and to take command of it; and the royal officers at Seville were required to aid him in his views and facilitate his embarkation for the Indies.

The arrival of Hernando Pizarro in the country, and the reports spread by him and his followers, created a sensation among the Spaniards such as had not been felt since the first voyage of Columbus. The discovery of the New World had filled the minds of men with indefinite expectations of wealth, of which almost every succeeding expedition had proved the fallacy. The conquest of Mexico, though calling forth general admiration as a brilliant and wonderful exploit, had as yet failed to produce those golden results which had been so fondly anticipated. The splendid promises held out by Francisco Pizarro on his recent visit to Spain had not revived the confidence of his countrymen, made incredulous by repeated disappointment. All that they were assured of was the difficulties of the enterprise; and their distrust of its results was sufficiently shown by the small number of followers, and those only of the most desperate stamp, who were willing to take their chance in the adventure.

But now these promises were realized. It was no longer the golden reports that they were to trust, but the gold itself, which was displayed in such profusion before them. All eyes were now turned towards the West. The broken spendthrift saw in it the quarter where he was to repair his fortunes as speedily as he had ruined them. The merchant, instead of seeking the precious commodities of the East, looked in the opposite direction, and counted on far higher gains, where the most common articles of life commanded such exorbitant prices. The cavalier, eager to win both gold and glory at the point of his lance, thought to find a fair field for his prowess on the mountain plains of the Andes. Hernando Pizarro found that his brother had judged rightly in allowing as many of his company as chose to return home, confident that the display of their wealth would draw ten to his banner for every one that quitted it.

In a short time that cavalier saw himself at the head of one of the most numerous and well-appointed armaments, probably, that had left the shores of Spain since the great fleet of Ovando, in the time of Ferdinand and Isabella. It was scarcely more fortunate than this. Hardly had Hernando put to sea when a violent tempest fell on the squadron and compelled him to return to port and refit. At length he crossed the ocean, and reached the little harbor of Nombre de Dios in safety. But no preparations had been made for his coming, and as he was detained here some time before he could pass the mountains, his company suffered greatly from scarcity of food. In their extremity, the most unwholesome articles were greedily devoured, and many a cavalier spent his little savings to procure himself a miserable subsistence. Disease, as usual, trod closely in the track of famine, and numbers of the unfortunate adventurers, sinking under the unaccustomed heats of the climate, perished on the very threshold of discovery.

It was the tale so often repeated in the history of Spanish enterprise. A few, more lucky than the rest, stumbled on some unexpected prize, and hundreds, attracted by their success, pressed forward in the same path. But the rich spoil which lay on the surface had been already swept away by the first comers, and those who followed were to win their treasure by long-protracted and painful exertion. Broken in spirit and in fortune, many returned in disgust to their native shores, while others remained where they were, to die in despair. They thought to dig for gold; but they dug only their graves.

Yet it fared not thus with all Pizarro's company. Many of them, crossing the Isthmus with him to Panamá, came in time to Peru, where, in the desperate chances of its revolutionary struggles, some few arrived at posts of profit and distinction. Among those who first reached the Peruvian shore was an emissary sent by Almagro's agent to inform him of the important grant made to him by the crown. The tidings reached him just as he was making his entry into Cuzco, where he was received with all respect by Juan and Gonzalo Pizarro, who, in obedience to their brother's command, instantly resigned the government of the capital into the marshal's hands. But Almagro was greatly elated on finding himself now placed by his sovereign in a command that made him independent of the mán who had so deeply wronged him; and he intimated that in the exercise of his present authority he acknowledged no superior. In this lordly humor he was confirmed by several of his followers, who insisted that Cuzco fell to the south of the territory ceded to Pizarro, and consequently came within that now granted to the marshal. Among these followers were several of Alvarado's men, who, though of better condition than the soldiers of Pizarro, were under much worse discipline, and had acquired, indeed, a spirit of unbridled license under that unscrupulous chief. They now evinced little concern for the native population of Cuzco, and, not content with the public edifices, seized on the dwellings of individuals, where it suited their convenience, appropriating their contents without ceremony—showing as little respect, in short, for person or property as if the place had been taken by storm.

While these events were passing in the ancient Peruvian capital, the governor was still at Lima, where he was greatly disturbed by the accounts he received of the new honors conferred on his associate. He did not know that his own jurisdiction had been extended seventy leagues farther to the south, and he entertained the same suspicion with Almagro, that the capital of the Incas did not rightfully come within his present limits. He saw all the mischief likely to result from this opulent city falling into the hands of his rival, who would thus have an almost indefinite means of gratifying his own cupidity and that of his followers. He felt that, under the present circumstances, it was not safe to allow Almagro to anticipate the possession of power to which, as yet, he had no legitimate right; for the dispatches containing the warrant for it still remained with Hernando Pizarro, at Panamá, and all that had reached Peru was a copy of a garbled extract.

Without loss of time, therefore, he sent instructions to Cuzco for his brothers to resume the government, while he defended the measure to Almagro on the ground that when he should hereafter receive his credentials it would be unbecoming to be found already in possession of the post. He concluded by urging him to go forward without delay in his expedition to the south.

But neither the marshal nor his friends were pleased with the idea of so soon relinquishing the authority which they now considered as his right. The Pizarros, on the other hand, were pertinacious in reclaiming it. The dispute grew warmer and warmer. Each party had its supporters; the city was split into factions; and the municipality, the soldiers, and even the Indian population, took sides in the struggle for power. Matters were proceeding to extremity, menacing the capital with violence and bloodshed, when Pizarro himself appeared among them.

On receiving tidings of the fatal consequences of his mandates, he had posted in all haste to Cuzco, where he was greeted with undisguised joy by the natives, as well as by the more temperate Spaniards, anxious to avert the impending storm. The governor's first interview was with Almagro, whom he embraced with a seeming cordiality in his manner, and, without any show of resentment, inquired into the cause of the present disturbances. To this the marshal replied by throwing the blame on Pizarro's brothers; but although the governor reprimanded them with some asperity for their violence, it was soon evident that his sympathies were on their side, and the dangers of a feud between the two associates seemed greater than ever. Happily, it was postponed by the intervention of some common friends, who showed more discretion than their leaders. With their aid a reconciliation was at length effected, on the grounds substantially of their ancient compact.

It was agreed that their friendship should be maintained inviolate; and, by a stipulation that reflects no great credit on the parties, it was provided that neither should malign nor disparage the other, especially in their dispatches to the emperor, and that neither should hold communication with the government without the knowledge of his confederate; lastly, that both the expeditures and the profits of future discovery should be shared equally by the associates. The wrath of Heaven was invoked by the most solemn imprecations on the head of whichever should violate this compact, and the Almighty was implored to visit the offender with loss of property and of life in this world, and with eternal perdition in that to come! The parties further bound themselves to the observance of this contract by a solemn oath taken on the sacrament, as it was held in the hands of Father Bartolomé de Segovia, who concluded the ceremony by performing mass. The whole proceeding, and the articles of agreement, were carefully recorded by the notary, in an instrument bearing date June 12, 1535, and attested by a long list of witnesses.

Thus did these two ancient comrades, after trampling on the ties of friendship and honor, hope to knit themselves to each other by the holy bands of religion. That it should have been necessary to resort to so extraordinary a measure might have furnished them with the best proof of its inefficacy.

Not long after this accommodation of their differences, the marshal raised his standard for Chile; and numbers, won by his popular manners and by his liberal largesses—liberal to prodigality—eagerly joined in the enterprise, which they fondly trusted would lead even to greater riches than they had found in Peru. Two Indians, Paullu Inca,[46] a brother of the Inca Manco II, and the Villac Umu, the high priest of the nation, were sent in advance, with three Spaniards, to prepare the way for the little army. A detachment of a hundred and fifty men, under an officer named Saavedra, next followed. Almagro remained behind to collect further recruits; but before his levies were completed he began his march, feeling himself insecure, with his diminished strength, in the neighborhood of Pizarro! The remainder of his forces, when mustered, were to follow him.

Thus relieved of the presence of his rival, the governor returned without further delay to the coast, to resume his labors in the settlement of the country. Besides the principal city of "The Kings," he established others along the Pacific, destined to become hereafter the flourishing marts of commerce. The most important of these, in honor of his birthplace, he named Trujillo, planting it on a site already indicated by Almagro. He made also numerous *repartimientos* both of lands and Indians among his followers, in the usual manner of the Spanish Conquerors; though here the ignorance of the real resources of the country led to very different results from what he had intended, as the territory smallest in extent not unfrequently, from the hidden treasures in its bosom, turned out greatest in value.

But nothing claimed so much of Pizarro's care as the rising metropolis of Lima; and so eagerly did he press forward the work, and so well was he seconded by the multitude of laborers at his command, that he had the satisfaction to see his young capital, with its stately edifices and its pomp of gardens, rapidly advancing towards completion. It is pleasing to contemplate the softer features in the character of the rude soldier, as he was thus occupied with healing up the ravages of war, and laying broad the foundations of an empire more civilized than that which he had overthrown. This peaceful occupation formed a contrast to the life of incessant turmoil in which he had been hitherto engaged. It seemed, too, better suited to his own advancing age, which naturally invited to repose. And, if we may trust his chroniclers, there was no part of his career in which he took greater satisfaction. It is certain there is no part which has been viewed with greater satisfaction by posterity; and, amidst the woe and desolation which Pizarro and his followers brought on the devoted land of the Incas, Lima, the beautiful City of the Kings, still survives as the most glorious work of his creation, the fairest gem on the shores of the Pacific.

# ✿ CHAPTER TEN ✿

ESCAPE OF THE INCA—RETURN OF HERNANDO

PIZARRO—RISING OF THE PERUVIANS—

SIEGE AND BURNING OF CUZCO—

DISTRESSES OF THE SPANIARDS—

STORMING OF THE FORTRESS—PIZARRO'S

DISMAY—THE INCA RAISES

THE SIEGE

## (1535–1536)

While the absence of his rival Almagro relieved Pizarro from all immediate disquietude from that quarter, his authority was menaced in another, where he had least expected it. This was from the native population of the country. Hitherto the Peruvians had shown only a tame and submissive temper, that inspired their conquerors with too much contempt to leave room for apprehension. They had passively acquiesced in the usurpation of the invaders—had seen one monarch butchered, another placed on the vacant throne, their temples despoiled of their treasures, their capital and country appropriated and parceled out among the Spaniards, but, with the exception of an occasional skirmish in the mountain passes, not a blow had been struck in defense of their rights. Yet this was the warlike nation which had spread its conquests over so large a part of the continent!

In his career, Pizarro, though he scrupled at nothing to effect his object, had not usually countenanced such superfluous acts of cruelty as had too often stained the arms of his countrymen in other parts of the continent, and which in the course of a few years had exterminated nearly a whole population in Hispaniola. He had struck one astounding blow, by the seizure of Atahuallpa; and he seemed willing to rely on this to strike terror into the natives. He even affected some respect for the institutions of the country, and had replaced the monarch he had murdered by another of the legitimate line. Yet this was but a pretext. The kingdom had experienced a revolution of the most decisive kind. Its ancient institutions were subverted. Its heaven-descended aristocracy was leveled almost to the condition of the peasant. The people became the serfs of the Conquerors. Their dwellings in the capital—at least, after the arrival of Alvarado's officers—were seized and appropriated. The temples were turned into stables; the royal residences into barracks for the troops. The sanctity of the religious houses was violated. Thousands of matrons and maidens, who, however erroneous their faith, lived in chaste seclusion in the conventual establishments, were now turned abroad and became the prey of a licentious soldiery. A favorite wife of the young Inca was debauched by the Castilian officers. The Inca, himself treated with contemptuous indifference, found that he was a poor dependent, if not a tool, in the hands of his conquerors.

Yet Manco II was a man of a lofty spirit and a courageous heart; such a one as might have challenged comparison with the bravest of his ancestors in the prouder days of the empire. Stung to the quick by the humiliations to which he was exposed, he repeatedly urged Pizarro to restore him to the real exercise of power, as well as to the show of it. But Pizarro evaded a request so incompatible with his own ambitious schemes, or, indeed, with the policy of Spain, and the young Inca and his nobles were left to brood over their injuries in secret and await patiently the hour of vengeance.

The dissensions among the Spaniards themselves seemed to afford a favorable opportunity for this. The Peruvian chiefs held many conferences together on the subject, and the high priest Villac Umu urged the necessity of a rising so soon as Almagro had withdrawn his forces from the city. It would then be comparatively easy, by assaulting the invaders on their several posts, scattered as they were over the country, to overpower them by superior numbers, and shake off their detested yoke before the arrival of fresh reinforcements should rivet it forever on the necks of his countrymen. A plan for a general rising was formed, and it was in conformity to it that the priest was selected by the Inca to bear Almagro company on the march, that he might secure the co-operation of the natives in the country, and then secretly return—as in fact he did—to take a part in the insurrection.

To carry their plans into effect, it became necessary that Manco II should leave the city and present himself among his people. He found no difficulty in withdrawing from Cuzco, where his presence was scarcely heeded by the Spaniards, as his nominal power was held in little deference by the haughty and confident Conquerors. But in the capital there was a body of Indian allies more jealous of his movements. These were from the tribe of the Cañaris, a warlike race of the north, too recently reduced by the Incas to have much sympathy with them or their institutions. There were about a thousand of this people in the place, and as they had conceived some suspicion of the Inca's purposes, they kept an eye on his movements and speedily reported his absence to Juan Pizarro.

That cavalier, at the head of a small body of horse, instantly marched in pursuit of the fugitive, whom he was so fortunate as to discover in a thicket of reeds, in which he had sought to conceal himself, at no great distance from the city. Manco was arrested, brought back a prisoner to Cuzco, and placed under a strong guard in the fortress. The conspiracy seemed now at an end; and nothing was left to the unfortunate Peruvians but to bewail their ruined hopes, and to give utterance to their disappointment in doleful ballads, which rehearsed the captivity of their Inca and the downfall of his royal house.

While these things were in progress, Hernando Pizarro returned to Ciudad de los Reyes, bearing with him the royal commission for the extension of his brother's powers, as well as those conceded in Almagro. The envoy also brought the royal patent conferring on Francisco Pizarro the title of *Marques de los Atavillos*—a province in Peru. Thus was the fortunate adventurer placed in the ranks of the proud aristocracy of Castile, few of whose members could boast—if they had the courage to boast—their elevation from so humble an origin, as still fewer could justify it by a show of greater services to the crown.

The new marquis resolved not to forward the commission at present to the marshal, whom he designed to engage still deeper in the conquest of Chile, that his attention might be diverted from Cuzco, which, however, his brother assured him, now fell, without doubt, within the newly extended limits of his own territory. To make more sure of this important prize, he dispatched Hernando to take the government of the capital into his own hands, as the one of his brothers on whose talent and practical experience he placed greatest reliance.

Hernando, notwithstanding his arrogant bearing towards his countrymen, had ever manifested a more than ordinary sympathy with the Indians. He had been the friend of Atahuallpa —to such a degree, indeed, that it was said, if he had been in the camp at the time, the fate of that unhappy monarch would probably have been averted. He now showed a similar friendly disposition towards his successor, Manco II. He caused the Peruvian prince to be liberated from confinement, and gradually admitted him to some intimacy with himself. The crafty Indian availed himself of his freedom to mature his plans for the rising, but with so much caution that no suspicion of them crossed the mind of Hernando. Secrecy and silence are characteristic of the American, almost as invariably as the peculiar color of his skin. Manco II disclosed to his conqueror the existence of several heaps of treasure and the places where they had been secreted; and when he had thus won his confidence, he stimulated his cupidity still further by an account of a statue of pure gold of his father Huayna Capac, which the wily Peruvian requested leave to bring from a secret cave in which it was deposited, among the neighboring Andes. Herando, blinded by his avarice, consented to the Inca's departure.

He sent with him two Spanish soldiers, less as a guard than to aid him in the object of his expedition. A week elapsed, and yet he did not return, nor were there any tidings to be gathered of him. Hernando now saw his error, especially as his own suspicions were confirmed by the unfavorable reports of his Indian allies. Without further delay, he dispatched his brother Juan, at the head of sixty horse, in quest of the Peruvian prince, with orders to bring him back once more a prisoner to his capital.

That cavalier, with his well-armed troops, soon traversed the environs of Cuzco without discovering any vestige of the fugitive. The country was remarkably silent and deserted, until, as he approached the mountain range that hems in the valley of Yucay, about six leagues from the city, he was met by the two Spaniards who had accompanied Manco II. They informed Pizarro that it was only at the point of the sword he could recover the Inca, for the country was all in arms, and the Peruvian chief at its head was preparing to march on the capital. Yet he had offered no violence to their persons, but had allowed them to return in safety.

The Spanish captain found this story fully confirmed when he arrived at the river Yucay, on the opposite bank of which were drawn up the Indian battalions to the number of many thousand men, who, with their young monarch at their head, prepared to dispute his passage. It seemed that they could not feel their position sufficiently strong without placing a river, as usual, between them and their enemy. The Spaniards were not checked by this obstacle. The stream, though deep, was narrow; and plunging in, they swam their horses boldly across, amidst a tempest of stones and arrows that rattled thick as hail on their harness, finding occasionally some crevice or vulnerable point—although the wounds thus received only goaded them to more desperate efforts. The barbarians fell back as the cavaliers made good their landing; but, without allowing the latter time to form, they returned with a spirit which they had hitherto seldom displayed, and enveloped them on all sides with their greatly superior numbers. The fight now raged fiercely. Many of the Indians were armed with lances headed with copper tempered almost to the hardness of steel, and with huge maces and battle-axes of the same metal. Their defensive armor also was in many respects excellent, consisting of stout doublets of quilted cotton, shields covered with skins, and casques richly ornamented with gold and jewels, or sometimes made like those of the Mexicans, in the fantastic shape of the heads of wild animals, garnished with rows of teeth that grinned horribly above the visage of the warrior. The whole army wore an aspect of martial ferocity, under the control of much higher military discipline than the Spaniards had before seen in the country.

The little band of cavaliers, shaken by the fury of the Indian assault, were thrown at first into some disorder; but at length, cheering on one another with the old war cry of "Santiago!" they formed in solid column and charged boldly into the thick of the enemy. The latter, incapable of withstanding the shock, gave way, or were trampled down under the feet of the horses, or pierced by the lances of the riders. Yet their flight was conducted with some order; and they turned at intervals, to let off a volley of arrows or to deal furious blows with their poleaxes and war clubs. They fought as if conscious that they were under the eye of their Inca.

It was evening before they had entirely quitted the level ground and withdrawn into the fastnesses of the lofty range of hills which belt round the beautiful valley of Yucay. Juan Pizarro and his little troop encamped on the level at the base of the mountains. He had gained a victory, as usual, over immense odds; but he had never seen a field so well disputed, and his victory had cost him the lives of several men and horses, while many more had been wounded and were nearly disabled by the fatigues of the day. But he trusted the severe lesson he had inflicted on the enemy, whose slaughter was great, would crush the spirit of resistance. He was deceived.

The following morning, great was his dismay to see the passes of the mountains filled up with dark lines of warriors, stretching as far as the eye could penetrate into the depths of the sierra, while dense masses of the enemy were gathered like thunderclouds along the slopes and summits, as if ready to pour down in fury on the assailants. The ground, altogether unfavorable to the maneuvers of cavalry, gave every advantage to the Peruvians, who rolled down huge rocks from their elevated position, and sent off incessant showers of missiles on the heads of the Spaniards. Juan Pizarro did not care to entangle himself farther in the perilous defile; and, though he repeatedly charged the enemy and drove them back with considerable loss, the second night found him with men and horses wearied and wounded, and as little advanced in the object of his expedition as on the preceding evening. From this embarrassing position, after a day or two more spent in unprofitable hostilities, he was surprised by a summons from his brother to return with all expedition to Cuzco, which was now besieged by the enemy!

Without delay he began his retreat, recrossed the valley, the recent scene of slaughter, swam the river Yucay, and, by a rapid countermarch, closely followed by the victorious Indians, who celebrated their success with songs or rather yells of triumph, he arrived before nightfall in sight of the capital.

But very different was the sight which there met his eyes from what he had beheld on leaving it a few days before. The extensive environs, as far as the eye could reach, were occupied by a mighty host, which an indefinite computation swelled to the number of two hundred thousand warriors. The dusky lines of the Indian battalions stretched out to the very verge of the mountains; while, all around, the eye saw only the crests of waving banners of chieftains, mingled with rich panoplies of featherwork, which reminded some few who had served under Cortés of the military costume of the Aztecs. Above all rose a forest of long lances and battle-axes edged with copper, which, tossed to and fro in wild confusion, glittered in the rays of the setting sun, like light playing on the surface of a dark and troubled ocean. It was the first time that the Spaniards had beheld an Indian army in all its terrors— such an army as the Incas led to battle when the banner of the Sun was borne triumphant over the land.

Yet the bold hearts of the cavaliers, if for a moment dismayed by the sight, soon gathered courage as they closed up their files and prepared to open a way for themselves through the beleaguering host. But the enemy seemed to shun the encounter, and, falling back at their approach, left a free entrance into the capital. The Peruvians were probably not unwilling to draw as many victims as they could into the toils, conscious that the greater the number the sooner they would become sensible to the approaches of famine.

Hernando Pizarro greeted his brother with no little satisfaction; for he brought an important addition to his force, which now, when all were united, did not exceed two hundred, horse and foot, besides a thousand Indian auxiliaries; an insignificant number, in comparison with the countless multitudes that were swarming at the gates. That night was passed by the Spaniards with feelings of the deepest anxiety, as they looked forward with natural apprehension to the morrow. It was early in February, 1536, when the siege of Cuzco commenced—a siege memorable as calling out the most heroic displays of Indian and European valor, and bringing the two races into deadlier conflict with each other than had yet occurred in the conquest of Peru.

The numbers of the enemy seemed no less formidable during the night than by the light of day: far and wide their watch fires were to be seen gleaming over valley and hilltop, as thickly scattered, says an eyewitness, as "the stars of heaven in a cloudless night." Before these fires had become pale in the light of the morning, the Spaniards were roused by the hideous clamor of conch, trumpet, and atabal, mingled with the fierce war cries of the barbarians, as they let off volleys of missiles of every description, most of which fell harmless within the city. But others did more serious execution. These were burning arrows, and red-hot stones wrapped in cotton that had been steeped in some bituminous substance; which, scattering long trains of light through the air, fell on the roofs of the buildings and speedily set them on fire. These roofs, even of the better sort of edifices, were uniformly of thatch, and were ignited as easily as tinder. In a moment the flames burst forth from the most opposite quarters of the city. They quickly communicated to the woodwork in the interior of the buildings, and broad sheets of flame mingled with smoke rose up towards the heavens, throwing a fearful glare over every object. The rarefied atmosphere heightened the previous impetuosity of the wind, which fanning the rising flames, they rapidly spread from dwelling to dwelling, till the whole fiery mass, swayed to and fro by the tempest, surged and roared with the fury of a volcano. The heat became intense, and clouds of smoke, gathering in a dark pall over the city, produced a sense of suffocation and almost blindness in those quarters where it was driven by the winds.

The Spaniards were encamped in the great square, partly under awnings, and partly in the hall of the Inca Viracocha, on the ground since covered by the cathedral. Three times in the course of that dreadful day the roof of the building was on fire; but, although no efforts were made to extinguish it, the flames went out without doing much injury. This miracle was ascribed to the Blessed Virgin, who was distinctly seen by several of the Christian combatants hovering over the spot on which was to be raised the temple dedicated to her worship.

Fortunately, the open space around Hernando's little company separated them from the immediate scene of conflagration. It afforded a means of preservation similar to that employed by the American hunter who endeavors to surround himself with a belt of wasted land when overtaken by a conflagration in the prairies. All day the fire continued to rage, and at night the effect was even more appalling; for by the lurid flames the unfortunate Spaniards could read the consternation depicted in each other's ghastly countenances; while in the suburbs, along the slopes of the surrounding hills might be seen the throng of besiegers, gazing with fiendish exultation on the work of destruction. High above the town, to the north, rose the gray fortress, which now showed ruddy in the glare, looking grimly down on the ruins of the fair city which it was no longer able to protect; and in the distance were to be discerned the shadowy forms of the Andes, soaring up in solitary grandeur into the regions of eternal silence, far beyond the wild tumult that raged so fearfully at their base.

Such was the extent of the city that it was several days before the fury of the fire was spent. Tower and temple, hut, palace, and hall, went down before it. Fortunately, among the buildings that escaped were the magnificent House of the Sun and the neighboring Convent of the Virgins. Their insulated position afforded the means, of which the Indians from motives of piety were willing to avail themselves, for their preservation. Full one-half of the capital, so long the chosen seat of Western civilization, the pride of the Incas, and the bright abode of their tutelar deity, was laid in ashes by the hands of his own children. It was some consolation for them to reflect that it burned over the heads of its conquerors—their trophy and their tomb!

During the long period of the conflagration the Spaniards made no attempt to extinguish the flames. Such an attempt would have availed nothing. Yet they did not tamely submit to the assault of the enemy, and they sallied forth from time to time to repel them. But the fallen timbers and scattered rubbish of the houses presented serious impediments to the movements of horse; and when these were partially cleared away by the efforts of the infantry and the Indian allies, the

Peruvians planted stakes and threw barricades across the path, which proved equally embarrassing. To remove them was a work of time and no little danger, as the pioneers were exposed to the whole brunt of the enemy's archery, and the aim of the Peruvian was sure. When at length the obstacles were cleared away and a free course was opened to the cavalry, they rushed with irresistible impetuosity on their foes, who, falling back in confusion, were cut to pieces by the riders or pierced through with their lances. The slaughter on these occasions was great; but the Indians, nothing disheartened, usually returned with renewed courage to the attack, and while fresh reinforcements met the Spaniards in front, others, lying in ambush among the ruins, threw the troops into disorder by assailing them on the flanks. The Peruvians were expert both with bow and sling; and these encounters, notwithstanding the superiority of their arms, cost the Spaniards more lives than in their crippled condition they could afford to spare—a loss poorly compensated by that of tenfold the number of the enemy. One weapon, peculiar to South American warfare, was used with some effect by the Peruvians. This was the *lasso*—a long rope with a noose at the end, which they adroitly threw over the rider, or entangled with it the legs of his horse, so as to bring them both to the ground. More than one Spaniard fell into the hands of the enemy by this expedient.

Thus harassed, sleeping on their arms, with their horses picketed by their side, ready for action at any and every hour, the Spaniards had no rest by night or by day. To add to their troubles, the fortress, which overlooked the city and completely commanded the great square in which they were quartered, had been so feebly garrisoned in their false sense of security that on the approach of the Peruvians it had been abandoned without a blow in its defense. It was now occupied by a strong body of the enemy, who from his elevated position sent down showers of missiles from time to time, which added greatly to the annoyance of the besieged. Bitterly did their captain now repent the improvident security which had led him to neglect a post so important.[47]

Their distresses were still further aggravated by the rumors which continually reached their ears of the state of the country. The rising, it was said, was general throughout the land; the Spaniards living on their insulated plantations had all been massacred; Lima and Trujillo and the principal cities were besieged and must soon fall into the enemy's hands; the Peruvians were in possession of the passes, and all communications were cut off, so that no relief was to be expected from their countrymen on the coast. Such were the dismal stories (which, however exaggerated, had too much foundation in fact) that now found their way into the city from the camp of the besiegers. And, to give greater credit to the rumors, eight or ten human heads were rolled into the *plaza,* in whose bloodstained visages the Spaniards recognized with horror the lineaments of their companions who they knew had been dwelling in solitude on their estates!

Overcome by these horrors, many were for abandoning the place at once, as no longer tenable, and for opening a passage for themselves to the coast with their own good swords. There was a daring in the enterprise which had a charm for the adventurous spirit of the Castilian. Better, they said, to perish in a manly struggle for life than to die thus ignominiously, pent up like foxes in their holes to be suffocated by the hunter!

But the Pizarros, De Rojas, and some others of the principal cavaliers refused to acquiesce in a measure which, they said, must cover them with dishonor. Cuzco had been the great prize for which they had contended; it was the ancient seat of empire, and, though now in ashes, would again rise from its ruins as glorious as before. All eyes would be turned on them as its defenders, and their failure, by giving confidence to the enemy, might decide the fate of their countrymen throughout the land. They were placed in that post as the post of honor, and better it be to die there than to desert it.

There seemed, indeed, no alternative; for every avenue to escape was cut off by an enemy who had perfect knowledge of the country and possession of all its passes. But this state of things could not last long. The Indian could not, in the long run, contend with the white man. The spirit of insurrection would die out of itself. The great army would melt away, unaccustomed as the natives were to the privations incident to a protracted campaign. Reinforcements would be daily coming in from the colonies; and if the Castilians would be but true to themselves for a season, they would be relieved by their own countrymen, who would never suffer them to die like outcasts among the mountains.

The cheering words and courageous bearing of the cavaliers went to the hearts of their followers; for the soul of the Spaniards readily responded to the call of honor, if not of humanity. All now agreed to stand by their leader to the last. But if they would remain longer in their present position, it was absolutely necessary to dislodge the enemy from the fortress; and before venturing on this dangerous service, Hernando Pizarro resolved to strike such a blow as should intimidate the besiegers from further attempts to molest his present quarters.

He communicated his plan of attack to his officers; and forming his little troop into three divisions, he placed them under command of his brother Gonzalo, of Gabriel de Rojas, an officer in whom he reposed great confidence, and of Hernan Ponce de Leon. The Indian pioneers were sent forward to clear away the rubbish, and the several divisions moved simultaneously up the principal avenues towards the camp of the besiegers. Such stragglers as they met in their way were easily cut to pieces, and the three bodies, bursting impetuously on the disordered lines of the Peruvians, took them completely by surprise. For some moments there was little resistance, and the slaughter was terrible. But the Indians gradually rallied, and, coming into something like order, returned to the fight with the courage of men who had long been familiar with danger. They fought hand to hand with their copper-headed war clubs and poleaxes, while a storm of darts, stones, and arrows rained on the well-defended bodies of the Christians.

The barbarians showed more discipline than was to have been expected; for which, it is said, they were indebted to some Spanish prisoners, from several of whom the Inca, having generously spared their lives, took occasional lessons in the art of war. The Peruvians had also learned to manage with some degree of skill the weapons of their conquerors; and they were seen armed with bucklers, helmets, and swords of European workmanship, and even, in a few instances, mounted on the horses which they had taken from the white men. The young Inca, in particular, accoutered in the European fashion, rode a war horse, which he managed with considerable address, and, with a long lance in his hand, led on his followers to the attack. This readiness to adopt the superior arms and tactics of the Conquerors intimates a higher civilization than that which belonged to the Aztec, who, in his long collision with the Spaniards, was never so far divested of his terror of the horse as to venture to mount him.

But a few days or weeks of training were not enough to give familiarity with weapons, still less with tactics, so unlike those to which the Peruvians had been hitherto accustomed. The fight on the present occasion, though hotly contested, was not of long duration. After a gallant struggle, in which the natives threw themselves fearlessly on the horsemen, endeavoring to tear them from their saddles, they were obliged to give way before the repeated shock of their charges. Many were trampled under foot, others cut down by the Spanish broadswords, while the arquebusiers, supporting the cavalry, kept up a running fire that did terrible execution on the flanks and rear of the fugitives. At length, sated with slaughter, and trusting that the chastisement he had inflicted on the enemy would secure him from further annoyance for the present, the Castilian general drew back his forces to their quarters in the capital.

His next step was the recovery of the citadel Sacsahuamán. It was an enterprise of danger. The fortress, which overlooked the northern section of the city, stood high on a rocky eminence, so steep as to be inaccessible on this quarter, where it was defended only by a single wall. Towards the open country it was more easy of approach; but there it was protected by two semicircular walls, each about twelve hundred feet in length, and of great thickness. They were built of massive stones, or rather rocks, put together without cement, so as to form a kind of rustic-work. The level of the ground between these lines of defense was raised up so as to enable the garrison to discharge their arrows at the assailants while their own persons were protected by the parapet. Within the interior wall was the fortress, consisting of three strong towers, one of great height, which, with a smaller one, was now held by the enemy, under the command of an Inca noble, a warrior of well-tried valor, prepared to defend it to the last extremity.

The perilous enterprise was entrusted by Hernando Pizarro to his brother Juan, a cavalier in whose bosom burned the adventurous spirit of a knight-errant of romance. As the fortress was to be approached through the mountain passes, it became necessary to divert the enemy's attention to another quarter. A little while before sunset, Juan Pizarro left the city with a picked corps of horsemen and took a direction opposite to that of the fortress, that the besieging army might suppose the object was a foraging expedition. But, secretly countermarching in the night, he fortunately found the passes undefended, and arrived before the outer wall of the fortress without giving the alarm to the garrison.

The entrance was through a narrow opening in the center of the rampart; but this was now closed up with heavy stones, that seemed to form one solid work with the rest of the masonry. It was an affair of time to dislodge these huge masses in such a manner as not to rouse the garrison. The Indian nations, who rarely attacked in the night, were not sufficiently acquainted with the art of war even to provide against surprise by posting sentinels. When the task was accomplished,

Juan Pizarro and his gallant troop rode through the gateway and advanced towards the second parapet.

But their movements had not been conducted so secretly as to escape notice, and they now found the interior court swarming with warriors, who, as the Spaniards drew near, let off clouds of missiles that compelled them to come to a halt. Juan Pizarro, aware that no time was to be lost, ordered one-half of his corps to dismount, and, putting himself at their head, prepared to make a breach as before in the fortifications. He had been wounded some days previously in the jaw, so that, finding his helmet caused him pain, he rashly dispensed with it, and trusted for protection to his buckler. Leading on his men, he encouraged them in the work of demolition, in the face of such a storm of stones, javelins, and arrows as might have made the stoutest heart shrink from encountering it. The good mail of the Spaniards did not always protect them; but others took the place of such as fell, until a breach was made, and the cavalry, pouring in, rode down all who opposed them.

The parapet was now abandoned, and the Indians, hurrying with disorderly flight across the enclosure, took refuge on a kind of platform or terrace, commanded by the principal tower. Here, rallying, they shot off fresh volleys of missiles against the Spaniards, while the garrison in the fortress hurled down fragments of rock and timber on their heads. Juan Pizarro, still among the foremost, sprang forward on the terrace, cheering on his men by his voice and example; but at this moment he was struck by a large stone on the head, not then protected by his buckler, and was stretched on the ground. The dauntless chief still continued to animate his followers by his voice, till the terrace was carried and its miserable defenders were put to the sword. His sufferings were then too much for him, and he was removed to the town below, where, notwithstanding every exertion to save him, he survived the injury but a fortnight, and died in great agony. To say that he was a Pizarro is enough to attest his claim to valor. But it is his praise that his valor was tempered by courtesy. His own nature appeared mild by contrast with the haughty temper of his brothers, and his manners made him a favorite of the army. He had served in the conquest of Peru from the first, and no name on the roll of its conquerors is less tarnished by the reproach of cruelty or stands higher in all the attributes of a true and valiant knight.

Though deeply sensible to his brother's disaster, Hernando Pizarro saw that no time was to be lost in profiting by the advantages already gained. Committing the charge of the town to Gonzalo, he put himself at the head of the assailants and laid vigorous siege to the fortresses. One surrendered after a short resistance. The other and more formidable of the two still held out under the brave Inca noble who commanded it. He was a man of an athletic frame, and might be seen striding along the battlements, armed with a Spanish buckler and cuirass, and in his hand wielding a formidable mace, garnished with points or knobs of copper. With this terrible weapon he struck down all who attempted to force a passage into the fortress. Some of his own followers who proposed a surrender he is said to have slain with his own hand. Hernando prepared to carry the place by escalade. Ladders were planted against the walls, but no sooner did a Spaniard gain the topmost round than he was hurled to the ground by the strong arm of the Indian warrior. His activity was equal to his strength; and he seemed to be at every point the moment that his presence was needed.

. The Spanish commander was filled with admiration at this display of valor; for he could admire valor even in an enemy. He gave orders that the chief should not be injured, but be taken alive, if possible. This was not easy. At length, numerous ladders having been planted against the tower, the Spaniards scaled it on several quarters at the same time, and leaping into the place, overpowered the few combatants who still made a show of resistance. But the Inca chieftain was not to be taken; and, finding further resistance ineffectual, he sprang to the edge of the battlements, and, casting away his war club, wrapped his mantle around him, and threw himself headlong from the summit. He died like an ancient Roman. He had struck his last stroke for the freedom of his country, and he scorned to survive her dishonor. The Castilian commander left a small force in garrison to secure his conquest, and returned in triumph to his quarters.

Week after week rolled away, and no relief came to the beleaguered Spaniards. They had long since begun to feel the approaches of famine. Fortunately, they were provided with water from the streams which flowed through the city. But though they had well husbanded their resources, their provisions were exhausted, and they had for some time depended on such scanty supplies of grain as they could gather from the ruined magazines and dwellings, mostly consumed by the fire, or from the produce of some successful foray. This latter resource was attended with no little difficulty, for every expedition led to a fierce encounter with the enemy, which usually cost the lives of several Spaniards and inflicted a much heavier injury on the Indian allies. Yet it was at least one good result of such loss that it left fewer to provide for. But the whole number of the besieged was so small that any loss greatly increased the difficulties of defense by the remainder.

As months passed away without bringing any tidings of their countrymen, their minds were haunted with still gloomier apprehensions as to their fate. They well knew that the governor would make every effort to rescue them from their desperate condition. That he had not succeeded in this, made it probable that his own situation was no better than theirs, or perhaps he and his followers had already fallen victims to the fury of the insurgents. It was a dismal thought that they alone were left in the land, far from all human succor, to perish miserably by the hands of the barbarians among the mountains.

Yet the actual state of things, though gloomy in the extreme, was not quite so desperate as their imaginations had painted it. The insurrection, it is true, had been general throughout the country, at least that portion of it occupied by the Spaniards. It had been so well concerted that it broke out almost simultaneously, and the Conquerors who were living in careless security on their estates had been massacred to the number of several hundreds. An Indian force had sat down before Jauja, and a considerable army had occupied the valley of Rimac and laid siege to Lima. But the country around that capital was of an open, level character, very favorable to the action of cavalry. Pizarro no sooner saw himself menaced by the hostile array than he sent such a force against the Peruvians as speedily put them to flight; and, following up his advantage, he inflicted on them such a severe chastisement that, although they still continued to hover in the distance and cut off his communications with the interior, they did not care to trust themselves on the other side of the Rimac.

The accounts that the Spanish commander now received of the state of the country filled him with the most serious alarm. He was particularly solicitous for the fate of the garrison at Cuzco, and he made repeated efforts to relieve that capital. Four several detachments, amounting to more than four hundred men in all, half of them cavalry, were sent by him at different times, under some of his bravest officers. But none of them reached their place of destination. The wily natives permitted them to march into the interior of the country until they were fairly entangled in the passes of the Cordilleras. They then enveloped them with greatly superior numbers, and, occupying the heights, showered down their fatal missiles on the heads of the Spaniards, or crushed them under the weight of fragments of rock which they rolled on them from the mountains. In some instances the whole detachment was cut off to a man. In others, a few stragglers only survived to return and tell the bloody tale to their countrymen at Lima.

Pizarro was now filled with consternation. He had the most dismal forebodings of the fate of the Spaniards dispersed throughout the country, and even doubted the possibility of maintaining his own foothold in it without assistance from abroad. He dispatched a vessel to the neighboring colonists at Trujillo, urging them to abandon the place, with all their effects, and to repair to him in Lima. The measure was, fortunately, not adopted. Many of his men were for availing themselves of the vessels which rode at anchor in the port to make their escape from the country at once and take refuge in Panamá. Pizarro would not hearken to so dastardly a counsel, which involved the desertion of the brave men in the interior who still looked to him for protection. He cut off the hopes of these timid spirits by dispatching all the vessels then in port on a very different mission. He sent letters by them to the governors of Panamá, Nicaragua, Guatemala, and Mexico, representing the gloomy state of his affairs, and invoking their aid. His epistle to Alvarado, then established at Guatemala, has been preserved. He conjures him by every sentiment of honor and patriotism to come to his assistance, and this before it is too late. Without assistance, the Spaniards can no longer maintain their footing in Peru, and that great empire will be lost to the Castilian crown. He finally engages to share with him such conquests as they may make with their united arms. Such concessions to the very man whose absence from the country, but a few months before, Pizarro would have been willing to secure at almost any price, are sufficient evidence of the extremity of his distress. The succors thus earnestly solicited arrived in time, not to quell the Indian insurrection, but to aid him in a struggle quite as formidable with his own countrymen.

It was now August. More than five months had elapsed since the commencement of the siege of Cuzco, yet the Peruvian legions still lay encamped around the city. The siege had been protracted much beyond what was usual in Indian warfare, and showed the resolution of the natives to exterminate the white men. But the Peruvians themselves had for some time been straitened by the want of provisions. It was no easy matter to feed so numerous a host; and the obvious resource of the magazines of grain, so providently prepared by the Incas, did them but little service, since their contents had been more prodigally used, and even dissipated, by the Spaniards, on their first occupation of the country. The season for plant-

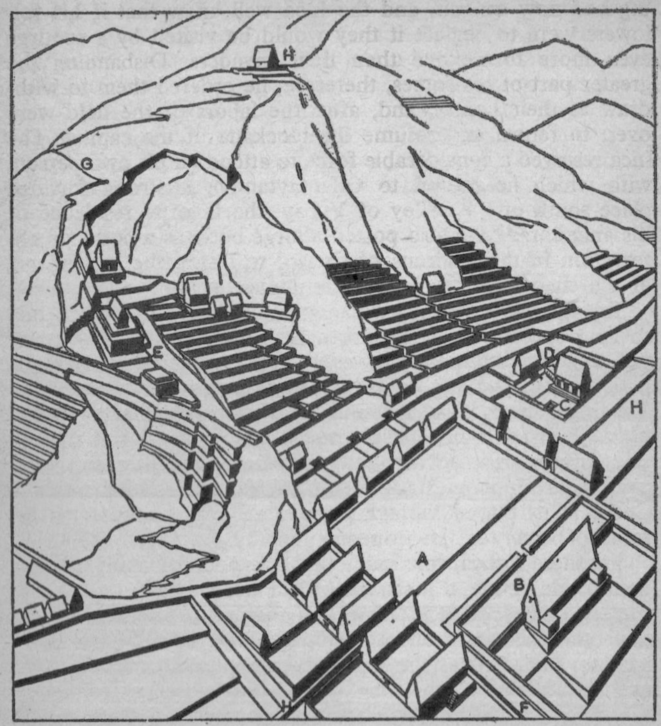

The fortress, city, and terraces of Ollantaytambo. This famous site is thirty miles northwest of Cuzco on the Urubamba River, the site of many battles between Spaniard and Inca, after the 1534 conquest. Ollantaytambo guarded the road to the eastern jungles (the Incas had no route corresponding to the one that now runs along the Urubamba River). Work on the fortress was in progress when the Spaniards arrived. Later, in 1537, Manco II again began work on the fortress but was put to flight by the Spaniards. The terraces were cut into the living rock, and the fortress still stands more or less intact. The original Inca houses of the village are still occupied and give a good idea of the Kancha form of house complex. (A) Plaza of Petitions; (B) a particularly well-built palace, where Gonzalo Pizarro wished to place a church after the fall of the city; (C) the house of the three doors; (D) the baths of the Chosen Women, which contained a beautiful fountain carved out of the living rock; (E) the fortress, built on precipitous hills with well-laid walls; (F) the defense wall and the sally port and road to the top of the ing had now arrived, and the Inca well knew that if his followers were to neglect it they would be visited by a scourge even more formidable than their invaders. Disbanding the greater part of his forces, therefore, he ordered them to withdraw to their homes, and, after the labors of the field were over, to return and resume the blockade of the capital. The Inca reserved a considerable force to attend on his own person, with which he retired to Ollantaytambo, a strong fortified place south of the valley of Yucay, the favorite residence of his ancestors.[48] He also posted a large body as a corps of observation in the environs of Cuzco, to watch the movements of the enemy and to intercept supplies.

The Spaniards beheld with joy the mighty host which had so long encompassed the city now melting away. They were not slow in profiting by the circumstance, and Hernando Pizarro took advantage of the temporary absence to send out foraging parties to scour the country and bring back supplies to his famishing soldiers. In this he was so successful that on one occasion no less than two thousand head of llama were swept away from the Indian plantations and brought safely to Cuzco. This placed the army above all apprehensions on the score of want for the present.

Yet these forays were made with the point of the lance, and many a desperate contest ensued, in which the best blood of the Spanish chivalry was shed. The contests, indeed, were not confined to large bodies of troops, but skirmishes took place between smaller parties, which sometimes took the form of personal combats. Nor were the parties so unequally matched as might have been supposed in these single rencontres; and the Peruvian warrior, with his sling, his bow, and his *lasso*, proved no contemptible antagonist for the mailed horseman, whom he sometimes even ventured to encounter, hand to hand, with his formidable battle-ax. The ground around Cuzco became a battlefield, like the *vega* of Granada, in which Christian and pagan displayed the characteristics of their peculiar warfare; and many a deed of heroism was performed, which wanted only the song of the minstrel to shed around it a glory like that which rested on the last days of the Moslem of Spain.

But Hernando Pizarro was not content to act wholly on the defensive; and he meditated a bold stroke by which at

---

mountain; (G) the Inti-huatana, a carved stone sundial called "the Hitching Place of the Sun"; (H) the road to the larger village and to Cuzco.

once to put an end to the war. This was the capture of Manco II, whom he hoped to surprise in his quarters at Tambo.

For this service he selected about eighty of his best-mounted cavalry, with a small body of foot, and, making a large detour through the less frequented mountain defiles, he arrived before Ollantaytambo without alarm to the enemy. He found the place more strongly fortified than he had imagined. The palace, or rather fortress, of the Incas stood on a lofty eminence, the steep sides of which, on the quarter where the Spaniards approached, were cut into terraces, defended by strong walls of stone and sunburnt brick. The place was impregnable on this side. On the opposite, it looked toward the Yucay, and the ground descended by a gradual declivity towards the plain through which rolled its deep but narrow current. This was the quarter on which to make the assault.

Crossing the stream without much difficulty, the Spanish commander advanced up the smooth glacis with as little noise as possible. The morning light had hardly broken on the mountains; and Pizarro, as he drew near the outer defenses, which, as in the fortress of Cuzco, consisted of a stone parapet of great strength drawn round the enclosure, moved quickly forward, confident that the garrison were still buried in sleep. But thousands of eyes were upon him; and as the Spaniards came within bowshot, a multitude of dark forms suddenly rose above the rampart, while the Inca, with his lance in hand, was seen on horseback in the enclosure, directing the operations of his troops. At the same moment the air was darkened with innumerable missiles, stones, javelins, and arrows, which fell like a hurricane on the troops, and the mountains rang to the wild war whoop of the enemy. The Spaniards, taken by surprise, and many of them sorely wounded, were staggered; and though they quickly rallied, and made two attempts to renew the assault, they were at length obliged to fall back, unable to endure the violence of the storm. To add to their confusion, the lower level in their rear was flooded by the waters, which the natives, by opening the sluices, had diverted from the bed of the river, so that their position was no longer tenable. A council of war was then held, and it was decided to abandon the attack as desperate, and to retreat in as good order as possible.

The day had been consumed in these ineffectual operations; and Hernando, under cover of the friendly darkness, sent forward his infantry and baggage, taking command of the center himself and trusting the rear to his brother Gonzalo. The river was happily recrossed without accident, although the Indians,

"The victorious foe still hung on the rear of the discomfited cavaliers. . . . It was the last triumph of the Inca."

now confident in their strength, rushed out of their defenses and followed up the retreating Spaniards, whom they annoyed with repeated discharges of arrows. More than once they pressed so closely on the fugitives that Gonzalo and his chivalry were compelled to turn and make one of those desperate charges that effectually punished their audacity and stayed the tide of pursuit. Yet the victorious foe still hung on the rear of the discomfited cavaliers, till they had emerged from the mountain passes and come within sight of the blackened walls of the capital. It was the last triumph of the Inca.

# Civil Wars of the Conquerors [1]

*[The following is the editor's rewritten versions of Books IV
and V of Prescott's* The Conquest of Peru, *which are concerned with the civil wars. This account includes a description
of events in the years following the point at which Prescott
concluded his narrative.]*

The civil wars waged between the conquerors over the carcass
of in the Inca Empire had begun even before the revolt of Inca
Manco II. The seeds of it, in fact, were planted as early as 1533
and they germinated while the conquest of Peru was in progress.
At the very moment of the triumph, while Atahuallpa writhed
in chains and the gold of his empire was being melted down
into ingots, Francisco Pizarro was at loggerheads with Diego
de Almagro.

Because Almagro was not present at the actual seizure of
the Inca, Hernando Pizarro, the proudest of the Pizarro clan,
opined that Almagro should not receive his full share of
Atahuallpa's ransom. Hot words were spilled between the two
partners in rapine in that sulphurous room where the gold
was being melted down; and with this the wars began.

Hernando Pizarro could take full credit for being the pri-
mary cause of the quarrel; Francisco gave ear to him too
often. Hernando was not an easy man to understand, and he
cannot be passed off in a sentence. In the strange genealogy
of the Pizarro family, with one father and three mothers,
Hernando alone was legitimate. Born in 1501 (he was twenty
years younger than Francisco), Hernando was, more than
any of the other three, a real warrior; Charles V had himself
created him a captain on one of Europe's battlefields. When
he arrived in Peru at the age of thirty-two, he was literate,
able to pen a good letter or report, equally at home either at
Court or on the battlefield—and contemptuous of those with
lesser gifts. Hernando called Almagro "the Blinkard," since
he had lost an eye to an Indian arrow while searching out the
"Kingdom of Gold," and thought of him only as a plodding
bringer of supplies; so toward him he maintained an arrogant
and overbearing attitude. On the other hand, he showed rare

humanity toward the Indians and uncommon courage, for, as will be remembered, he led twenty men on the first expedition through the land, nine hundred miles down the valleys to the coast and there with an effrontery out of proportion to the numbers he had, destroyed the sacred huaca of the great temple of Pachacamac. Hernando Pizarro also published the first report [2] on the nature of the Inca Empire, and when he was chosen to bring the raped gold to Spain, Atahuallpa burst into tears at his departure.

The king, although astonished and pleased at the arrival of the *Santa Maria del Campo* at Sevilla on January 9, 1534,[3] bringing the immense treasure of gold and silver bullion—squired by the gaudy person of Hernando Pizarro to explain the incredible story of it all—still did not close his eyes to the danger of eventual civil war.[4] Being made aware of the differences between Pizarro and Almagro, the king consented to give the latter the title of "adelantado" and his own "kingdom"; it was to be called Nueva Toledo and was to lie immediately south of Pizarro's fief of Peru. Although the boundary between the two was clearly defined, the royal geographer could be excused for not knowing in this raw land precisely where one was to begin and the other to end.

Each of the two claimants, Pizarro and Almagro, claimed Cuzco, which then was the real prize. Francisco Pizarro, in his persuasive manner, urged Almagro to press an exploration into his new realm, that vast unknown land of Nueva Toledo which took in part of Bolivia, and Argentina and the whole of Chile, stretching endlessly down to Antarctica. Leaving Cuzco as a point to be settled later, Almagro set off with a well-armed expedition—with hosts of Indians—down the royal Inca road. Despite the fact that they followed the well-laid highway, the sufferings of men and beasts in the sharp cold heights, at times well above 14,000 feet, were indeed horrible. When they reached the "kingdom," the harsh, rainless, desert coast of Chile offered nothing; and when, after several months they reached the end of the Inca coastal road at the fortress called Paucamarca, they were 35 degree's south latitude, the farthest extension of the Inca Empire; beyond lay the fierce Araucanos, with whom even the well-trained Inca warriors refused to make war. Fighting with climate and hunger, Almagro's men felt that they had been purposely tricked into taking this two-thousand-mile march into the antipodes to put them off from what they believed to be their legitimate fief—Cuzco and the land about it. On the return journey the "men of Chile," as they were henceforth to be called, were sustained in their march by the thought of revenge. The "men of Chile" arrived, it will be remembered, near to the environs of Cuzco to see with their own eyes what they had heard by rumor—the war of Manco II against Cuzco and the Spaniards there under command of Hernando Pizarro.

For some reason, Manco II trusted Almagro, presumably because he was not present physically during the murder of Atahuallpa; yet assuredly most of the "men of Chile" had been as much part of the conquest of the Inca realm as those under the command of Pizarro. Whatever the historical merits of preference, Almagro did enter into negotiations with Manco II. Whether the nature of these talks was that Manco II would break off the siege of Cuzco in return for recognition of his Neo-Inca empire, or whether the warriors of the Inca were dismayed by the arrival of this body of troops (for they had heretofore prevented any great number of troops from reaching Cuzco during the siege), they broke off the siege. Whatever the logic for the action, the siege of Cuzco was over.

Now Spaniard faced Spaniard; they tried parley. Hernando Pizarro, who had commanded this epical defense of Cuzco, rode off toward Urcos, the headquarters of Almagro, some twenty miles from the capital. Almagro made his position plain: even though the whole of Peru was up in arms and Manco II threatened the Spaniard's very existence, Cuzco was his and he proposed to have it. A truce was arranged, but Hernando Pizarro began to strengthen Cuzco against attack, while a relieving force, originally dispatched to fight the Indians, would now be used to secure Cuzco for the Pizarros.

Under cover of darkness on a stormy night, April 8, 1537, Almagro's superior force invested the city; he laid siege to an Inca building which housed the Pizarros. Unable to assault it without great loss of life, they burned the roof—and the Pizarros, forced out of the building, were captured and put in chains.

Almagro was now master of Cuzco. He sent out his troops to prevent reinforcements from reaching Cuzco (this he did with little loss of life on July 12, 1537, adding greatly to his forces) and sent out another part of his force against Manco II, who, knowing now that all Spaniards were enemies, had again renewed his attacks.

The Spaniards were now as witless as the Peruvians once were. In the beginning of the conquest many tribes of the Inca—since there was no racial unity among them—sided with the Spaniards against the Incas; now the Spaniards were so blinded by their own victories that they fought each other, while on the periphery a huge host of well-armed warriors of Manco II watchfully waited to see the Spaniards eliminate each other. Although Francisco Pizarro had received reinforcements from his cousin Hernán Cortés in faraway Mexico, his force was not sufficient to undertake a battle against Cuzco. So in Lima he frothed and fumed, just as his own brothers frothed and fumed in chains at Cuzco.

Rodrigo de Orgoñez, who was the operational general, urged Almagro to strike off the heads of the Pizarros, who were in his power: ". . . that while they lived his life would never be safe, for a Pizarro," he said, "was never known to forget an injury and that which they had received from Almagro was too deep for them to forgive."

Almagro refused, perhaps because there was still a residue in his simple soul of that old camaraderie he held for Francisco Pizarro. But Orgoñez had not drunk so much of the milk of human kindness. A native of Oropesa, Spain, and trained in battle in the Italian wars, he had held the rank of ensign under the Constable of Bourbon during the fight and the sack of Rome. His heart was steeled to human suffering; he was a professional soldier, prompt, fearless, and exacting. To him the dictates of strategy demanded that the Pizarros lose their heads. It was unfortunate for Almagro that he did not lend his ear to that advice. He spared the heads of the Pizarros, but in the end he lost his own.

There were enough men of sense left in Peru to see that reconciliations between the two factions must be essayed. Almagro, who already planned to have his own seaport to supply "his capital," Cuzco, had moved down to Chincha, a lovely valley on the southern coast of Peru. He renamed it "Almagro" and was busily engaged in making it into a usable port. A conference was then called at Mala. The first condition of it was that the brothers Pizarro should be released; and so, over the loud protests of his captains, Almagro allowed Gonzalo and Hernando Pizarro their freedom. Then on November 13, 1537, Francisco Pizarro and Almagro met in the small valley just south of Lima, at the two-storied Inca tambo by the Mala River.

The antagonists faced each other. A friar, judged to be impartial, was there to act as referee, but meanwhile, known or unknown to Francisco, his brothers had placed soldiers in the canebrakes, hoping to ambush Almagro. The heat of words between the two grew so great that the friar remarked, "It seems to me, gentlemen, that you have come here more to quarrel than anything else."

Back and forth went the accusations, until a soldier posted there by Almagro began a song of warning:

> "Time it is, Caballero,
> Time it is for you to flee. . . ."

Which Almagro did, jumping from the second story, eluding the ambush and riding with his followers all night toward Chincha.

After that everything went against him. His enemies, with Hernando Pizarro at the head, seized the guarded Andean passes by stratagem and on the morning of April 26, 1538, took up battle positions at Salinas outside of Cuzco. Almagro, too ill to ride, was carried to the battle site on a litter. Indians lined the hills on both sides of the valley and looked down on the amphitheater of incipient carnage. Hernando Pizarro's arquebusiers were supplied with a new type of bullet recently brought from Flanders. It was so cast that the bullet, when it emerged from the piece, divided into two parts connected by a small chain and rushed down the battlefield cutting men and pikes like a scythe. The battle lasted two hours; within that time two hundred men lay dead on the field, and those who did not have the good luck to die were horribly dispatched by the Indians.

On July 8, 1538, Hernando Pizarro sentenced Almagro to death with the words, "Your doom is inevitable and you must prepare to meet it."

"Almagro was a man of strong passions," wrote Prescott, "and not too well used to control them. . . . No commander was ever more beloved by his soldiers. His generosity was carried to prodigality. . . . He was a good soldier, careful and judicious. . . . His body was covered with scars of his battles."

And—"A man of short stature," said Pedro de Cieza, the soldier-historian, "ugly features but of great courage and endurance. A great part of the discovery of these kingdoms was due to him. . . . He was of such humble parentage that it may be said of him that his lineage began and ended with himself. . . . He died at the age of sixty-three years." So perished Almagro.

Free of rivals to claim the "Kingdom of Peru," and with the "men of Chile" reduced to penury and deprived of their estates, Hernando Pizarro, in the name of his brother the Marqués Francisco Pizarro, began to rid himself of possible rivals. Pedro de Valdivia [5] was sent to Chile to follow up the explorations of Almagro. Pedro de Candia, a "man of Gallo," the same who first walked ashore in 1527, was allowed to take an expedition into the montaña east of Peru; it was a heroic but disastrous undertaking. Gonzalo Pizarro, named governor of Quito, went there and later set out from his realm to the east, to Upper Amazonia, to search for the spice called "cinnamon" which was said to be found in the land beyond Quito.

On one bright Quito morning in 1540 he set out with a vast concourse of knights, foot soldiers, Indians, pigs, and a number of Indian women. He would not return until 1542; Orellana, his second-in-command, was to abandon him, stating: "Having eaten our shoes and saddles boiled with certain herbs, we set out to reach the kingdom of the Amazons." [6] Those and other expeditions having been sent off, and finding it good, Hernando Pizarro (who now seemed to rule Peru rather than his brother) prepared to sail to Spain and justify his conduct, bringing to the king a vast amount of accumulated gold—the king's fifth—thus hoping to use the gold as leverage. On the way to Panamá he heard that the king, highly disapproving of his conduct in usurping the power of the crown to try and condemn, had issued a warrant for his arrest; he avoided it by sailing up to the port of Huatulco, recently built by Cortés on the Isthmus of Tehuantepec. From there he transported the gold overland to Vera Cruz, now a lively port of Spanish commerce, and sailed secretly to Spain.

The king was delighted to see the gold, but not Hernando Pizarro. He reached Spain in July, 1539, and it was not until 1541 that he had his first audience with Charles V. It was to be his last. He was never tried formally for the murder of Almagro, but confined to the fortress of Medina del Campo, there to remain for 21 years and 3 days.[7] Not too confined, though; he had time to make love to one Isabel Mercado, who left him two sons, and then to assuage his "loneliness" he had Francisca, the daughter of his brother Francisco by Inés Yupanqui Huaylas, who had been the granddaughter of Huayna Capac. He married her in 1552, when he was fifty-one and she eighteen; in all, she lived with him nineteen years in prison. First the crown placed an embargo on all his property—for Hernando was immensely rich. Later he recovered it, and upon being released from his confinement, and surrounded by five children, he began to lay down his "line." *"Dinero es Don Caballero"* ("Money is a gentleman"). So went the adage when Hernando Pizarro purchased his titles. His son became the Marqués de la Conquista—could anyone claim it more than he, having leveled the Inca Empire and married the granddaughter of the last great Inca? Thereafter all his sons became gentlemen of quality. The imposing arms are still to be seen at the seigniorial house of the Marqués de la Conquista in Trujillo, Spain.

Hernando Pizarro died there in 1580 at the age of eighty years.

His brother Francisco, the first Marqués, had not such good fortune. Hernando's last warning to his brother on departing Peru in 1539 was, "Beware of the men of Chile." It was a good warning. The "men of Chile" wandered the streets of Lima, without employment, money, or estates, landless and desperate. Well installed in his palace as governor of Peru, captain general of the realm and entered on the lists of the nobility as Marqués de Pizarro (although he still could not make more than a rubric beside his name), he remained the governor. In 1541 he was awaiting the arrival of Vaca de Castro, a gentleman being sent out by the king of Spain to look into the affairs of Peru. He awaited him in confidence. But on Sunday, June 26, 1541, twenty "men of Chile," desperate beyond measure and wanting to strike before the arrival of the king's councilor who would confirm Pizarro in his offices, met in the house of Diego Almagro.

Diego, known as "Almagro the Lad," was a young man of twenty. He was the only son of Almagro; his mother was a Panamá Indian. An earnest young man but lacking, naturally, experience in war, he was the symbol of the "men of Chile"; he was to be used to place them again in power. On that Sunday, when the guard was small, the conspirators assaulted Pizarro in his palace. Having dispatched the first resistance, they broke into Pizarro's room, and he hardly had time to put on his cuirass. Still, there he stood, at sixty-nine years of age, white flowing beard, tall and spare as Don Quixote. Sword in hand, he held off six of his attackers, giving as good as he received. The leader of the "men of Chile" suddenly grabbed one of his own men and pushed him up into Pizarro's sword; before the Marqués could extricate his weapon they leaped upon him and stabbed him in the neck.

"Jesus," he said, and sank down in a pool of blood; he scarcely had time to trace a cross on it before another blow dispatched him.

The "men of Chile" now secured possession of Lima. Messages were sent to all other cities to announce what had taken place and demand that all within Peru acknowledge Diego Almagro "the Lad" as governor of Peru. Since Gonzalo Pizarro had disappeared in the Amazon, and Hernando Pizarro was held in Spain, there was little opposition; even Pedro de Candia, the old companion of Pizarro, had turned against his faction since he had been falsely accused by Hernando of plotting against him. So he now turned his talents, which were prodigious enough, to the side of Almagro the

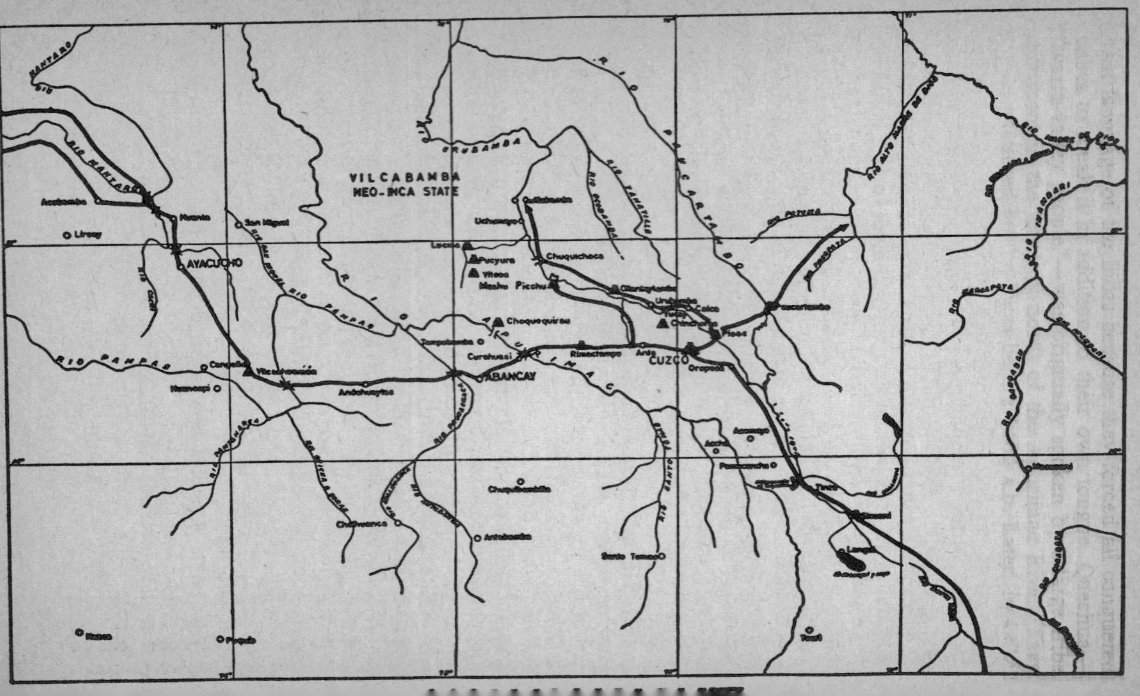

VILCABAMBA
NEO-INCA STATE
RIO MANTARO
RIO URUBAMBA
RIO YANATILLO
RIO OCOBAMBA
RIO PAUCARTAMBO
RIO PAMPAS
RIO APURIMAC
RIO SANTO TOMAS
AYACUCHO
ABANCAY
CUZCO
Acobamba
Huanta
Liray
San Miguel
Lucma
Pucyura
Vitcos
Machu Picchu
Choquequirau
Ollantaytambo
Urubamba
Yucay
Calca
Chinchero
Pisac
Paucartambo
Uchuroyo
Chuquichaca
Tambobamba
Curahuasi
Rimactampu
Anta
Oropesa
Carapata
Vilcashuamán
Huancapi
Andahuaylas
Chuquibambilla
Chilhuanuca
Antabamba
Santo Tomas
Accha
Acomayo
Pampacancha
Tinta
Itabo
Puquio
Tisco
Santo Tomas

Vilcabamba, the last redoubt of the Neo-Inca state, included in its area the royal road of the Incas and its laterals. The Inca road that ran north toward Amazonia passed behind Ollantaytambo and, a short distance beyond, was carried across the suspension bridge of Chuquichaca, which figures so prominently in this history.

Lad. Most of those within Peru joined the victor, except Alonso de Álvarado—brother of one of the principal conquerors of Mexico—who withdrew with two hundred men and awaited the king's emissary.

Vaca de Castro had expected, as a member of the Royal Council and bearing the king's seal, to be received in a manner befitting his age and position. Instead he learned at Buenaventura, where his ship touched for supples, that Pizarro was dead and Peru again torn by dissension. He was not a military man, yet he acted with boldness; he moved up to Quito and was there joined by Benalcazar, that wonderful old warrior. He it was who had conquered Quito and marched through Colombia not many years before to vanquish the Chibchas at the very edge of their lake of Guatavita, that same lake which became the El Dorado of legend. It is said of Benalcazar that more than three quarters of his life was a question mark; still he was a bold captain, an efficient, predatory sort of man, one who took no more notice of a thousand armed Indians than he would a handful of flies. When he gave notice that he was for Vaca de Castro and the king, all those who were not committed to Almagro and the "men of Chile" rallied to his cause. The second battle of the civil wars was building up.

The spring of 1542 found the two armies taking up their positions for battle. Since Almagro could use all the gold and silver without thought of turning over the required king's fifth, the armaments he was preparing were formidable. Pedro de Candia, with the aid of a regiment of Indians, cast huge bronze cannons in Cuzco; out of a primitive forge he made sixteen large pieces and eight smaller ones "of such good quality," said an old solder who had fought in the Italian wars, "that they could have vied with those from the workshops of Milan." Helmets, swords, cuirasses, were all made in Cuzco by the same "Greek," that worthy but not overly bright Pedro de Candia. There was good reason for Almagro radiating confidence upon seeing his army. Vaca de Castro had perforce to drag his ordnance up the sides of the Andes, while Almagro need only roll his along the intermontane valleys to the site of battle. Moreover, Manco II, who was building up his forces behind the redoubt of Vilcabamba—which no Spaniard had dared enter—promised to aid him with Indian warriors; he even delivered up to him guns, spearmen, shields, and horses, which he had captured during the long siege of Cuzco in 1537. When Almagro the Lad viewed all this, his face was radiant; "they could have formed," said an old conquistador, "a beautiful park of artillery and would have made a brave show even in the citadel of Burgos." While Almagro, then, built up strength in Cuzco, the armies of Vaca de Castro were assembling at Huamanga (Ayacucho).

The city had been founded in 1540 by Francisco Pizarro as a protection against the raids of Indian warriors whose sally-port from their own mountain citadel lay close to the Inca highway. At 8,500 feet Ayacucho had a climate of eternal spring; it attracted many a conquistador and was destined to be the third city of Peru. In 1542 it was a garrison. Soldiers swarmed into it as both sides made final preparations for battle. Vaca de Castro, deficient in ordnance, had more men and was superior in arquebusiers; he also had Francisco de Carvajal.

Carvajal made his first formal appearance at this Battle of Chupas. Tall and robust, a *pícaro* of high degree, he had been born in 1468 at a village called Ragana near Arévalo. Of good education, he entered military service under the great captain Gonzalvo de Córdoba. He was a soldier for forty years and had seen action in all the great battles. At the sack of Rome in 1527, he was intelligent enough not to encumber himself with unwieldy booty; he took the archives of a lawyer, who gave him so great a ransom for it that he was enabled to go to Mexico with his wife, Catalina Leyton, herself of a noble Portuguese family.

In 1536 he was sent by the viceroy of Mexico, Antonio de Mendoza, with a company of soldiers to aid Pizarro, then fighting against the uprising of Manco II and his warriors. Arriving too late to take part in this action, he was assigned to settle the lands of Charcas in Bolivia. The murder of Pizarro and the challenge of Almagro brought this old war horse out from domestic pasture.

"The time was now approaching," wrote Pedro de Cieza de León,[8] "when the hills of Chupas would be sprinkled with the blood of men who were born in Spain, to bear witness in future times that the weeds and stunted bushes growing on them are seedlings sprung from Spanish elements." On Saturday, September 16, 1542, the forces of Vaca de Castro moved out to Chupas, where the "men of Chile" were in position. Chupas was, or better is, a field a half-mile in width, a little longer in length, a flattened portion of a mountain spur; it is at 9,500 feet altitude and twelve miles south of Ayacucho. The hills were soon covered with Indians out to see the fun and slaughter; they were divided, as in a football game, between those who favored one side or the other. In both camps, the Spaniards had their *pallas,* women of rank, Indian mistresses "who acted," said one historian, "as proxies to their lawful wives in Spain."

The artillery of Pedro de Candia was well placed, and the small army of Almagro's 550 men well armed and well mounted. It was a formidable array. Since the field of battle was confined and Carvajal, the old master, in charge of the infantry, did not like looking down the muzzles of the artillery, he moved off his arquebusiers to the right flank. It was well he did so, for the balls of those cannons were sent careering down the narrow aisle of battle, knocking down horses and carrying away the heads of Vaca de Castro's army as if they were tenpins. Under this the army wavered. In stepped Carvajal seventy-five years of age and as gross as Falstaff: "Forward, good cavaliers . . . advance without fear. . . . Look at me, how fat I am, yet I go forward. . . ." To give substance to his words, he took off his cuirass and helmet—and with that they moved forward. Now finding cover, Carvajal dodged behind the hills, but he was set upon by Inca warriors sent, as promised, by Manco II; these he put to flight and then, setting his arquebusiers in position, began to pick off the *artilleros* of Pedro de Candia. The field was a melee of men and horses, but Candia, seeing the source of the danger to his artillery soldiers, turned his weapons to fire at the hills. The salvo went wild of the mark. At that moment Almagro the Lad rode up, and believing that Candia had betrayed him called out, "Traitor, why have you sold me?" and ran the old Greek through with a lance. With the ordnance unmanned, the battle went against the "men of Chile." Soon it was a slaughter; those that could took off, including Captain Diego Méndez, who with six others fled with Manco II's warriors and found refuge in the secret capital of the Neo-Inca state. Those who had not the fortune to die "were killed," said one who was present, "by the Indians and the Negroes and until darkness put an end to it the victors were busy gathering up horses and booty and also the Indian girls, who were what the soldiers were most eager about in those times."

Almagro the Lad and all his principal captains were executed.

Vaca de Castro, having acquitted himself well, moved down to Lima and prepared to hand over his office to the first viceroy of Peru, who, he had been notified in a royal writ. was en route. The last battle had scarcely been fought, when another, and this more dangerous, was in the making. It began out of the "New Laws."

The king of Spain, appalled by the cruelty of his captains in the "newfounde world" and even more by the depopulation of his realms by the manner in which some of the Spaniards treated the Indians, gave heed to the reports which came to the royal council. One of the most persistent crusaders for firm laws to deal with the Spaniard in the new world was Bartolomé de Las Casas, Bishop of Chiapas, a priest of good family. While Las Casas padded his figures of the number of Indians wantonly and uselessly exterminated, still there was much substance to all he said, and the royal council sat down to hear him out.

Unfortunately, Las Casas compromised a generous cause by the very intensity he brought to it. The "New Laws" as framed were unworkable in that vast wild land, where men were out of reach of immediate supervision. These laws were primarily concerned with conserving the natives. The Indians were declared free from slavery and vassals of the crown; colonists could no longer have grants, "commanderies of Indians," nor work them under slave conditions. Those Indian slaves belonging to religious orders or crown officials were to be given up. Those who had them, i.e., the original conquistadors, could retain theirs, but on their death the Indians were to be released; land and Indians could not be inherited. The effect of the "New Laws" on the Spaniards can be imagined. There were not enough of them, they said, to work the land; the Indians were wont to work communal land, communally; they had a ritual work rhythm which was not the way of the white man. They had no concept of the cash-nexus, nor had they the "wants" of the Spaniard. Since they had no desires, as the Spaniard had, there was no need for them to work unless forced to do so; even though Las Casas inconsistently urged Negro slavery as an answer to the objections of labor shortage, this would not answer the immediate problem of compliance with the "New Laws."

The conquistadors who had suffered the tortures of Tantalus fighting, conquering, settling the new lands, loudly demanded to see "the clause in Adam's will which allowed the king of Spain to deprive them of their natural rights." Francisco de Carvajal, wise in the ways of the world, aware what storms would be provoked by the "New Laws," tried to leave the country; he sold all his property, put it into bullion, reached Lima, and tried to induce the Council of Lima to allow his departure, but just as one could not come from Spain without official leave, in like manner one could not quit America without license. Vaca de Castro, with experience in Peru, sympathized with the settlers and actually urged that Carvajal be allowed to go to Spain to plead their cause before the king. He was gainsaid by the arrival of the new viceroy.

Blasco Núñez Vela, a knight of Avila, was handsome, brave,

and—obtuse. He was scarcely the man to handle so volatile a matter as the application of the "New Laws," for when approached by sober-minded citizens, who begged him to consider some alleviation of them, he replied haughtily: "I have come not to tamper with the laws nor to discuss their merits, but to execute them," and showed that he intended to do so by imprisoning his predecessor Vaca de Castro on suspicion of sympathy with the settlers. That poor man, albeit a member of the royal council, was arrested on his arrival in Spain and held a prisoner in the fortress of Arévalo for twelve years until the tardy tribunals of Spanish justice found a judgment in his favor. Then, at last, he was released and reinstated in his honors and dignities and took his seat anew in the royal council.

The new viceroy should have known what he was in for, because no sooner had he been received in the manner in which the king himself would have been, he discovered on his table a notice, pinned there with a dagger: "Each man knows what he has and does not give up his property to another; one may attempt it but he will lose his life in the meanwhile." And that was the leitmotif of the dirge which played over the land; as for the musical director of this dance of death, the settlers almost to a voice agreed on a single conductor—Gonzalo Pizarro.

Gonzalo, the last of the brothers of doom, had emerged from his amazing journey to the land of cinnamon to find all that he had known changed: his brother the marqués dead, Hernando in a Spanish prison, his own property seized, and the hated "men of Chile" in power. He offered his services to Vaca de Castro, but they were refused, so in high dudgeon he went off to the only estates left him, in Charcas in Bolivia. But now with the proclamation of the "New Laws," he became the champion of the resistance. He had the support of the redoubtable Francisco de Carvajal, who said, "I tried to leave this country when I saw what was approaching, and permission to do so was denied me. I was very unwilling to put my hands into the warp of this cloth [i.e., armed opposition to viceroy and king], but now that things are as they are, I promise to be the principal weaver."

On the pretense that he would carry the war to Manco II, who in this interval of the civil wars was allowed free movement, Gonzalo Pizarro was named by all the magistrate of the land and captain against the Inca; when this was proclaimed, "soldiers," said the historian Pedro de Cieza de León, "arrived from all parts well armed with arquebuses and powder, eager that rumors should be converted into war, that they might emerge from the poverty caused by peace."

Gonzalo had then no intention of seeking out Manco II, for he already secretly knew of his death. He was arming instead to oust the viceroy and place himself in his stead as governor of Perú. Now, while all the first settlers in Peru were against the "New Laws," they were not all of one opinion that the best means of accomplishing their purpose was a physical assault on the viceroy, who, after all, was vice-king; it meant open rebellion. Carvajal silenced the opposition, and Gonzalo prepared to move on to Lima with his newly assembled army. Hearing this, the viceroy was aghast. "Am I to be told," he exclaimed, "that Charles, our Lord, who is feared in all the provinces of Europe and to whom the Turk, master of the East, dares not show himself hostile, should be disobeyed by a bastard who refuses to comply with the Laws?"

The bastard did and could. Gonzalo Pizarro entered Lima on October 28, 1544, and the viceroy fled with such loyal troops as he could muster. Carvajal ordered the judges to acknowledge Pizarro as governor. They refused, and he ordered them to be hanged outside of town. Carvajal was so witty at the preliminaries to the execution that "the three found it quite a pleasure to be hanged by him." Then, since the viceroy was now attempting to invade Lima again, Pizarro set off in pursuit.

The forces of Pizarro met those of the viceroy at Añaquito, outside of Quito. Since the brave but obtuse viceroy was no match in battle with the "bastard" and since his army was heavily outnumbered, he lost two hundred men, killed within an hour, and he himself was knocked off his horse. One of Gonzalo's soldiers struck off his head, which much grieved Gonzalo, who, enraged by it, hanged the soldier and gave the viceroy an honorable burial, he himself being the principal mourner. Thus ended the third battle of the civil wars, on January 18, 1546.

Gonzalo Pizarro was now the undisputed master of Peru. From Quito to the most northern confines of Chile the whole country acknowledged his authority. His fleet rode triumphant on the Pacific and gave him the command of every city; Admiral Hinojosa had secured for him Panamá, the principal key of communications with Europe; his forces were on excellent footing; and with the tide of wealth that flowed in from the mines of Potosí, he was supplied with the resources of a European monarch. Gonzalo Pizarro now played the part of king; he extended his hand to be kissed, he used the plural

". . . we are not pleased"; his dress was sumptuous, he was attended by a bodyguard, he dined in public with no less than a hundred people in attendance. Through all of this his mentor Francisco de Carvajal, who viewed it from the side lines in obvious amusement, but whose own tastes remained simple, said:

"Why don't you declare yourself king? In fact, you have already done so: you have raised arms against the viceroy and killed him in battle. What favor or what mercy can you expect from the crown? You have gone too far to either halt or recede. You *must* go boldly on, proclaim yourself king, marry a *coya*, a direct descendant of the wives of the Incas, unite the two races so that they may henceforth repose in quiet under a common scepter. Long live King Gonzalo!"

Pizarro was never able to take this final step. The very boldness of Carvajal's advice—given partly in irony, partly in earnest—he never accepted. What would defeat him in the end was not an enemy who came on the pinions of eagles but one who was trained in the double subtleties of dialects; these would take the place of ordnance and pikes. His nemesis was a bishop, and he moved just as a bishop on a chessboard moved—obliquely.

Pedro de La Gasca was already on his way when most of these events were in progress. Charles V, Holy Roman Emperor, made, admittedly, mistakes; but he seldom made the same mistake twice. He soon knew from reports that Nuñez Vela was too proud to negotiate or to bring the raw conquistadors under the aegis of his rule; a man who was a grandee of Spain, who numbered among his family twelve bishops and four popes and who began his prayers "Mother of God, our cousin . . ." was going to make no headway.

Pedro de la Gasca was no soldier. Although his ancestry was as pure as virgin water, he had seen enough of the world to know that dissimulation can be used as a technique in human relations and that speech was perfected to hide one's true thoughts. He had studied law and theology at Salamanca and carried out delicate negotiations in Africa; moreover, he was a member of the Council of the Spanish Inquisition, where one's dialectic conceits were sharpened by prying. Frail in body, long in years, confessedly ignorant of military affairs—La Gasca offset these defects by a subtle intellect that plied an "infinite tongue." Finally, he was well endowed with the world's goods and thus impervious to bribery. To his king, on the notice of his appointment he said:

"Sire, this enterprise seems to me troublesome and dangerous, but since men are condemned to death at the moment of their birth . . . and since Your Majesty commands me, I feel I must obey without question or excuse." [9]

La Gasca knew what he was about. He asked for and received plenary authority, something that Spain has never given before or since. He was given a quire of royal decrees signed in blank to be filled in at his discretion. Apart from that, when he sailed he had nothing but a groom to attend him! There were neither arms nor bodyguards. When he arrived in Panamá in July, 1546, his presence soon began to be felt; the rumors percolated down to Peru; Pizarro's comment was, "I do not trust priests and saintly men. They have no place in Peru, where there is too much gold."

And as always Pizarro heard what he wanted to hear rather than the substance of reality. "Do not drown yourself in shallow water," wrote his trusted aide from Panamá, "claim what you will, for La Gasca comes with a quire of blank decrees from the king. . . . Because of this you can request what you will and it will be confirmed. . . . You should ask to be nominated viceroy of Peru for life, duke over twenty thousand vassals in whatsoever part of Peru you wish; Francisco de Carvajal should be made Marqués de los Cañaris . . .[10] and all the rest of us should have permanent slave grants. . . . From what I already know of La Gasca, he is anxious to return to Spain, where they are reserving for him the archbishopric of Sevilla." How easily La Gasca dissimulated! Meanwhile his letters from Panamá were sent all over Peru. He advised all who were committed to Pizarro to uncommit themselves; he came in the king's name to pardon—but as for those who refused, their lives would be forfeit. Priests and friars became the bearers of these messages.

Pizarro's governor in Quito warned him that a Franciscan friar had been taking letters from La Gasca to various municipalities, "which arouses my ire," and he advised Pizarro to toss La Gasca into the sea. Still another reported that he had confiscated a whole pile of "crafty letters which are like hidden poison designed to kill men." Then it was announced that La Gasca was sending his personal emissary, Hernández Paniagua,[11] to Peru to bring proposals and letters to Gonzalo Pizarro. When he arrived in Peru, the agents of Pizarro trussed him up. From Lima the man who would be king wrote: "Let him not come here. . . . For me there is no brother or friend where the execution of my plans is concerned, and do not let La Gasca think I am going to be deceived by words." Pizarro was now arming in earnest; he could boast that he had 1,800 pieces of ordnance, 700 arquebuses (not counting those in the hands of his large army), 1,700 helmets, 250 suits of mail, 1,000 horses, and 5,000 men.

He ordered a scorched-earth policy, and all along the desert shore in those oases which held the towns his agents reported that as far north as Tumbes they had destroyed all the tambos and sent away the llamas and the women. Further instructions followed from Gonzalo: "I want not a single word nor a single Indian to fall into La Gasca's hands; I have taken all wheat, fowls, llamas, and now I want you to induce all the Indians on the coast to rebel . . . and when the enemy arrives see that not a mule or a llama remains alive behind. . . ."

All this was in vain. La Gasca induced Pizarro's entire fleet with all their crew to come over to the king's side, and desertions in the north, beyond the long arm of Francisco de Carvajal, were wholesale. At that moment Pizarro lost something of his sureness, so he gave audience to the little friar who carried a message from La Gasca. As this Hernández Paniagua was a cousin to the Archbishop of Lima, he could not be dealt with summarily; still Pizarro threatened, "I will send for Carvajal so that you shall make his acquaintance."

"I would not, sir, wish for that particularly. . . . Let us consider that I have already met him."

After a long examination the friar made inquiry as to the precise nature of their terms.

"We do not want pardon for what we have done," said Gonzalo Pizarro.

"What, then, do your Lordships wish?"

"Approbation."

The friar noted all this down, then as he was being led out to return to La Gasca with his answer, he was stopped at the door.

"Give him this as my reply, and there is nothing more to be said about it: tell him I will die governing."

Gonzalo Pizarro was to have his wish.

He was to "die governing," for La Gasca was assembling a formidable force at Tumbes; famous captains came from all sections of South America to bring their troops. In a letter dated from Tumbes August 11, 1547, he informed his king, Charles V, of his vast military preparations. The various captains took diverse routes; one column traveled along the coast, and another took the royal Inca road in the Andes. All this to deceive Gonzalo Pizarro as to the point of attack. By the end of November, 1547, all the armies had converged into one at Jauja in the central Andes. It was then that they heard that another battle, number four of the civil wars, had been fought.

This time Gonzalo Pizarro had followed Francisco de Carvajal's counsel. He had abandoned Lima on the coast as untenable and had taken up headquarters at Cuzco; there, it was felt, he had a better chance to use his troops. In the meanwhile Diego Centeno, an ally of La Gasca, had put a large force of more than a thousand well-armed men in the rear of Pizarro's position, at a point at the end of Lake Titicaca, to prevent his escape from Peru into Chile. Pizarro moved to destroy the threat.

The Battle of Huarina was fought on marshy ground at the southern end of Lake Titicaca, not far from the great ruins of Tiahuanaco. Centeno's troops outnumbered those of Pizarro two to one; he thought his victory assured. A Spaniard who knew Centeno described him in this manner: "He was a native of Ciudad Rodrigo, Spain. He was a gentleman, not very tall; he had a fair skin, pleasant countenance with a red beard. Of noble condition, he was not very liberal as regards his own estates, but expended that of the king with largesse."

Centeno had eluded Carvajal for years, having been chased all over the Andes. Now he thought that the time for settling those debts was at hand. Gonzalo Pizarro himself commanded the cavalry, riding into the field superbly accoutered in slashed crimson velvet over his shining mail, mounted on a high-mettled charger also laid out with gaudy caparisons. On the drab gray puna he was as conspicuous as a parrot. "Lucifer" Carvajal, who put small stock in strutting like a popinjay, wore soiled armor and a surcoat of greenish color which blended well with the ground. His four hundred arquebusiers were similarly attired; they were encumbered with two or three loaded blunderbusses apiece, which they complainingly carried into position. Carvajal waited; he had no intention of walking into an enemy force twice the size of his own. Centeno's men, knowing now that they faced the devil incarnate— the demon of the Andes, old Carvajal himself—hesitated. Seeing this, Carvajal dispatched several of his better marksmen within range to fire at them and goad them into action. The stratagem worked, and Centeno's troops ran across the high, cold, treeless puna into the massed riflemen. The bullets were whistling past the corpulent body of Carvajal, but in giant strides he marched up and down the line:

"Hold your fire, my lads—wait it out."

Then when the charging enemy was within a hundred paces, he gave the order to fire. It was a tempest of fire and shell. One hundred men and horses died in the first volley, and before they could recover, Carvajal's men took up the second and then the third of the blunderbusses they had carried loaded into the field. Although the cavalry troop of Gonzalo Pizarro was badly pummeled, his defeat was turned into victory as old Carvajal now took on the enemy cavalry. More than half of Centeno's troops were killed. It was the most fatal battle yet found in the civil wars. As Gonzalo Pizarro rode his jaded horse over the battlefield of Huarina, strewn with corpses, he gazed down in wonder. He kept crossing himself as he rode:

"Jesus, what a victory!"

It was however, to be his last. This was not at first apparent, for that victory gave him a mistaken confidence about his chances against the formidable hosts pushing toward him for final battle.

Carvajal now took up his pen against La Gasca. In a letter dated December 29, 1547, from Cuzco, he asked La Gasca, "Where in Holy Writ do you find it permissible to proclaim with your fox's conscience that the king has given you the right to give battle to our governor?" And did La Gasca hope, by continuing to send his letters, to cause defections before battle? Carvajal told him it was a waste of time to send further messages with those knavish priests, "for on arrival I hanged two of them." Finally: "May the Lord preserve your revered personality by permitting through His most holy clemency that your sins should bring you into my hands."

Had any other than La Gasca received such a notice from Carvajal he would have quit the field of battle. However, he merely made a marginal note on the letter, "He tries to make me seem odious"—and he ordered the whole army to advance.

This was the most dangerous moment of the crusade. They had reached the great Apurimac canyon and river; across it on the other side were the troops of Pizarro. To prevent La Gasca from crossing, all four of the great suspension cable bridges of the Apurimac built by the Incas had been cut; the thick cables wound from cabuya fiber could be seen lying in the turbulent waters of the river. Among La Gasca's troops were many of the old conquistadors who had fought back and forth across the land. These scouted out the best place to rehang a bridge; Indians nearby, whose age-old duty it was to weave and replace the huge suspension cables of the bridge each year, were assembled and put to work. Then carrying on their shoulders these immense cables—two hundred feet long and as thick as a man's body—the Indians under cover of darkness brought them into place at Cotapampa, one of the sites where the bridge had been destroyed. The masonry at the ends of the bridges was still intact, and on this were secured the cables from which would hang the flooring. La Gasca reported that "we were so careful that the enemy would never discover exactly where we were or what we were doing"—so careful, yet Francisco de Carvajal knew from his scouts what was occurring: "News has reached me at Cuzco of the enemy's approach across the river Apurimac by means of a suspension bridge that they have constructed at the pass of Cotapampa."

Gonzalo Pizarro did not act decisively; when he sent three Cañari Indians and some Spaniards to cut the cables, it was too late. La Gasca's troops commanded both sides of the bridgehead, and the army was pouring over to the other side. On April 5, 1548, Pizarro, fully realizing his disaster, ordered 300 of his troops and 700 of his Cañari Indians to attack the bridge. They were too few and too late; they were routed.

The next day, on the plains of Xaquixahuana, the troops of both sides were set up for formal battle. The vast oval plain is in good part a quagmire, since several streams pour down from the overlooking heights into the plain, and the river that drains it performs its task badly; over and across it as the most direct route from Cuzco the Incas had built an eight-foot-high causeway eight miles long. Pizarro, who could have chosen his own field of battle, for some unaccountable reason put his back to the swamps; in front of him was the army of La Gasca—300 pikemen, 400 arquebusiers, 18 large cannon, hundreds of fine cavalry bearing aloft on their pikes the royal standard. Pizarro even allowed them to gain possession of a hill overlooking the field; and from the top of it, four mortars which they had hauled up with the aid of hundreds of Indians were already firing and throwing his troops into confusion.

It was when La Gasca ordered his arquebusiers into action and there was scattered firing that a series of strange events took place which showed that La Gasca—and his letters—had been tactically right. Pizarro's men, in twos and threes, suddenly threw away their arms and rushed to La Gasca's line. Then the desertion became general. Captain Garcilasso de la Vega [12] (who claimed he had been held on Pizarro's side against his will) came over with a hundred men; the army was melting in front of the enemy's eyes. On a small knoll where he had placed himself to direct, as he thought, the fire of his arquebusiers, Francisco de Carvajal sat on his horse "Boscanillo," laughing at the contretemps which would bring him to the headman's axe. Very much alive at eighty years of age, he who had fought at Pavia, Rome, and throughout Peru, festooning the unfruited trees of Peru with the bodies of men who had the ill luck to run counter to his wishes, Carvajal sat their laughing with all his might. Above the sound of battle he sang in a deep basso:

> "O mother, my hairs
> one by one they fly away
> in the air
> O poor mother, my hairs!"

Yet when he saw Gonzalo Pizarro drop his lance and slowly ride over to La Gasca, he felt that the time had come to take off. But his horse floundered in the marshes and he was soon set upon, pulled off his old horse, and, with arms pinioned, brought in as prisoner. Gonzalo Pizarro marched up to La Gasca with the hauteur of a conqueror; he even asked and was granted permission "to make a survey of his enemy's position." Then La Gasca cut him down. He was to be beheaded at once, for "while Gonzalo Pizarro lived there would be no assurance of peace in the country." They dragged in Carvajal, and he was, reported La Gasca, "surrounded by a hostile crowd who had been ill-treated by him and who wanted to kill him there and then." Carvajal said "he would prefer to be killed that way and begged me to allow it. . . ." It was not allowed. He was to die, of course, but he must die with all the proper formalities. The crowd still kept up a clamor for him and would have pulled him apart had they not been stayed by Diego Centeño. Carvajal straightened out his Falstaffian attire, looked at his champion, and even attempted to bend his leg in deference.

"To whom," he asked mock-heroically, "am I indebted to for this protection?"

"Do you not know me?" answered Centeno in bewilderment. "You have pursued me all these years over the Andes for more than three thousand leagues."

"Oh, yes," replied Carvajal, as if he had to jog his memory. "I crave your pardon; it is so long since I have seen anything but your fleeing ass, I have fully forgotten your face."

On the morrow, April 10, 1548, Gonzalo Pizarro, still a fine-looking man at forty-two years of age, was beheaded. His head was sent to hang in a cage in Lima; his home in Cuzco was destroyed and the earth about it salted. La Gasca showed superb humane feeling at the execution: "My generals insisted that he should be drawn and quartered, but I demurred out of respect for the late marqués, his brother. . . ."

The drawing and quartering were to be reserved for Carvajal. Various people called on him in the last hours; one, a well-placed knight, proffered his aid because Carvajal had once spared his life. He inquired whether there was anything he might do.

"Well, what service can you offer me? Can you set me free?"

"No."

"Then you can do nothing. If I spared your life, it was probably because I did not think it worth while."

The padre who was assigned to attend his soul had never found one so obdurate; he asked him if he had anything to confess besides the three hundred men he admitted having dispatched.

"No, little friar, there is nothing on my conscience except"—the friar thought he had broken the barrier—"except that I owe a half-real to a shopkeeper in Sevilla."

Still the padre would not give up; all the way down to the place of execution he begged Carvajal to pray for his soul. At last, driven to desperation, he said: "I beg of you to say at least one paternoster."

"All right, little padre, to please you then, 'paternoster.'"

Down went the axe, and then the great hulk of Carvajal was torn, quartered into four sections, and these were hung like so much butchered beef at the four entrances into Cuzco.

The civil wars had ended. And with their cessation, La Gasca asked in a letter to his king, from Lima, dated September, 1548, that a viceroy be named, "as there is nothing I would desire so much as to return to my native country." The king named Antonio de Mendoza, the former viceroy of Mexico, but he died within a few months of arrival; another was named, and yet another. When this last arrived and took office, he was faced with a task as great as the civil wars. He had to put down, somehow, the last of the Incas, who, holding out in the redoubt of the massif of Vilcabamba, had been growing in power and daring during the years.

### The Death of Manco II and the Last Years of the Neo-Inca Empire

Inca Manco II had learned much after the failure of his warriors to take Cuzco either by envelopment or by frontal attack. Although his troops totaled 80,000 or more and the defenders consisted of only 130 Spaniards, only half of them mounted (and less than 5,000 Cañari Indians, who because of their hatred of the Incas threw in their lot with the Spaniards), still they were not able to effect a victory. After a series of other defeats in the Urubamba valley after they were forced to give up the fortress of Ollantaytambo, the Inca retired to an intricate mountain area, difficult of access. It lay, roughly shaped as a triangle, between the rivers Apurimac, Urubamba, and Vilcamayu, the last flowing into the jungles.

This great masif of Vilcabamba, highly auriferous, with mountains of great height, also had sloping eastward many long, warm valleys. It was also in contact with the jungle areas. There Inca Manco II made common cause with the Antis who lived in the jungle, for they all had one object: their common passion and common hatred for the Spaniard. After Manco II's defeat at Ollantaytambo, in which the Spaniards succeeded in capturing his son, the Inca heir-apparent, and some of his principal wives and much booty, he moved into the prepared positions and fortresses within Vilcabamba.

History allows no precise idea of the extent of the area or the number of cities or even the whereabouts of the capital of the Neo-Inca state. It has never been seen by anyone who could report it, and although Hiram Bingham proclaimed that he had found it, during which time he discovered Machu Picchu, this we now know is not true.[13]

Within that sanctuary Manco II built up his strength between 1537 and the battle of Chupas (1545). He had horses (he rode himself) who had been trained by the Spaniards, he had guns, ordnance, spears, and armor that he had captured in his battles; his men were taught how to fire and repair arquebuses. He had so much that he even offered to send troops to fight on the side of Almagro the Lad at the battle of Chupas, where in fact his warriors saw action. So closely was Manco II cooperating with the "men of Chile" that on their defeat seven of them whose lives were forfeit sought and were given sanctuary at Vilcabamba. During the five years that the "seven" lived there, they set up forges, made swords and horseshoes, repaired guns—and even taught the Indians chess, checkers, bowling, and quoits. Soon they initiated them in the principles of Spanish attack; they perfected their guerrilla warfare, and as one of their sally ports lay across the Apurimac close to the royal road, they were able to keep up a steady flow of supplies by waylaying the Spanish caravans moving between Cuzco and Jauja.

The Spaniards were powerless to prevent the attacks or to gain entrance into this sanctuary until, in a raid upon a Spanish caravan moving along the Inca road toward Cuzco, the Indians found among the booty copies of the "New Laws." These proclaimed, as we know, a new code in which the Spanish settlers had to renounce their commanderies of Indians and put an end to compulsory personal service. It seemed to the Inca that there was now a chance to have peace with honor. He selected Gómez Pérez, one of the renegade Spaniards, as his "ambassador"; with an escort of twelve Indians he contacted the viceroy.

Nuñez Vela was delighted at this turn of events, and even though Gonzalo Pizarro threatened him, he offered the Inca full consideration; as to the renegade Spaniards, by this act they "wrote for themselves a pardon for all things past. . . ." But before any of this good will could be put to the test, Gonzalo Pizarro moved out of Cuzco toward Lima and the viceroy was in full flight. This determined Manco II to move against Cuzco, as his spies told him it was lightly held; he moved with a large force of warriors, destroying all houses in the path. They came within eighteen miles of Cuzco. Diego Maldonado "the Rich," distressed that Pizarro should have taken most of the horses, rallied those that remained, saying: "There is no fortress for resisting the fury of the Indians equal to Spaniards on horseback," and went out to attack. Had the Inca's warriors shown more determination they might have retaken Cuzco, but once again they were routed.

Within Vilcabamba there followed a dispute between the Spaniards and the Inca. There are many versions of the story: Garcilasso de la Vega (although five years old at the time of the occurrence) said that he had his from the chiefs and nobles present (there were none); the reliable soldier-historian Pedro de Cieza de León said that he had the whole of it from Friar Ortún Sánchez, "who, being in charge of Paullu Inca, brother of Manco II, heard all the history; Titu Cusi Yupanqui, son of Manco II, although then aged twelve, related it to a friar, for he was there at the time. There was an Indian woman named Bamba, "and the Spaniards present were Diego Mendez, Francisco Barba, Gómez Pérez, Cornejo, Monroy and two others . . . who had been with my father for several years." The dispute arose over a game of bowls; there was a quarrel over the marking of the score, and Mendez struck the Inca full on the head with a bowling ball. (In all probability the Spaniards were in touch with Cuzco and had been offered freedom, pardon, and reward for disposing of the Inca.) The boy said that the Spaniards then stabbed him, for they always went armed; Titu escaped. They moved to get out of the city, but at that moment the Inca's captain, Rimachi Yupanqui, arrived with numerous well-armed Antis. These transfixed the Spaniards with their spears, and later burned them in the Christian manner. None escaped.

Manco II survived for three days. "Before he died he sent for me," said Titu Cusi, "and all his captains. . . ." His eldest son, Sayri Tupac, then still a minor, was to be the Inca. However, since he had been reared only by women who lived at Vilcabamba, he had acquired no appetite for warfare; Peru remained relatively quiet for the next ten years.

In 1555 the viceroy sent Juan de Betanzos,[14] who later married Atahuallpa's daughter, in an embassy to visit Sayri Tupac. The ambassadors met the Inca at the hanging bridge of Chuquichaca; when they painted a glowing picture of the outside world, the Inca, despite the entreaties of his captains, went over to the Spaniards. He was carried to Lima in a litter with full panoply of regal power, lodged in one of the refurbished Inca palaces at Cuzco, and publicly given the Inca fringe. He married a *coya* and took up his abode in the Yucay valley. A few years later he was poisoned by his own people. Then Titu Cusi (the younger son, the same who at twelve years of age saw his father killed by the Spaniards) was acknowledged Lord Inca of the kingdoms of Peru.

Titu Cusi was as belligerent as his father, Manco II. The raids increased, and any attempt on the part of the Spaniard to penetrate the citadel of Vilcabamba was frustrated. The Inca rode horseback, attacked, and then disappeared. All attempts at direct military action availing nothing, the viceroy of Peru, Francisco de Toledo, remembering the methods of La Gasca, thought that someone could enter Vilcabamba alone, without soldiers, and induce the Inca to come out.

Diego Rodríguez, who had come to Peru in 1552, too late to take part in the mass conversions of the Indians, too late to be ceremoniously pulled apart by their savagery and thus acquire that martyrdom which was the key to eternal life, eagerly took up the offer. More important to his immortality was his contribution to the history of the last days of the Incas, for he wrote a memoir which, thanks to the perception of Alexander von Humboldt, was preserved and eventually published: [15]

"I left Cuzco on the eighth of April, 1565, after having received letters from Judge Matienzos directed to the Inca, Titu Cusi Yupanqui . . . with leave to make an entrance"; he first went to Ollantaytambo (the Inca fortress located on the Urubamba River before Machu Picchu), set off to the pass of Panticalla (once fortified by the Incas), and then struck off to the hanging bridge of Chuquichaca. It had been removed. As there was no other way to cross the turbulent Urubamba River, he continued down to the province of Amaibamba, the warm humid *montaña* where the Incas raised coca, the leaves of which yielded cocaine. There he made a fire and displayed a cross; and as spies already knew he was en route, it was not long before the Inca warriors appeared on the other bank of the river. On the fifth of May, "ten captains came . . . richly dressed with diadems of plumes and lance in hand . . . wearing *masks.* . . . Asked if he had the audacity to come to speak to the Inca, he replied in the affirmative, and they pulled him across in an *oroya,* a basket suspended from a rope. He now followed an Inca road into the interior of the Neo-Inca state; the warriors who accompanied him put him under constant threat: "Let us kill this little bearded one to avenge ourselves on the Castilians."

Three days later he had reached Lucuma, located halfway between the Urubamba and Apurimac rivers. There he wrote another letter to the Inca telling him of his peaceful mission. This was sent by a *chasqui.* To show the distance of the Inca capital—which no white man had ever seen and departed from alive—the reply of the Inca came days later by a *chasqui* who "covered 40 leagues (i.e., 125 miles) in two days"; by May 12 he had reached Vitcos. This was the place where the seven Spaniards had killed the Inca; their heads—in Spanish fashion—were still exposed. Days later, near this region, preparations were made for the reception of the Inca so that he might parley with Friar Diego. The details of the ritual are most valuable, for they show how much these Indians retained of the old forms in their citadel of Vilcabamba thirty-two years after the Lord Inca Atahuallpa was murdered.

Elaborate arrangements were made: entrenchments and fortifications of spiked treetops were prepared; the road over which the Inca was to pass was swept clean; and an amphitheater was made of red clay "by three hundred Indians of the surrounding country." Warriors were all about, drawn up with lances ready, when *chasquis* ran up to announce the Inca's approach. Then his escort of nobles, followed by the Lord Inca Titu Cusi Yupanqui. "He wore a headdress of plumes of many colors, a silver plate ornament on his chest, a golden shield in one hand, and a lance all of gold. He wore garters of feathers, and fastened to them were small wooden bells. On his head a diadem, around his neck another. In one hand he held a gilded dagger and he came in a mask of several colors." The Inca made obeisance to the Sun, followed by the *orejones*—those nobles who had extended earlobes with gold disks in them, who were richly dressed in plumes, gold and silver; they came forward and made a *mucha* to both Sun and Inca. The Villac Umu, chief priest, began by saying: "Child of the Sun thou art, the child of the day." Hundreds of warriors surrounded the Inca; ". . . *all wore masks of different colors, which they put before their faces.*" There were many famed captains; one called Cusi Puma came forward with fifty archers, Anti tribesmen from the Vilcamayu jungle areas, who now were allied to the Inca. The number of warriors about the Inca doubtless showed the great number he still commanded within the sanctuary of Vilcabamba.

The friar, being called forward, doffed his biretta, made a speech, and gave presents such as a case of comfits, four drinking glasses—for the Incas, having none, valued them highly—a few pounds of pearls and crystals, and knives for his captains; in turn the Inca presented him with two baskets of peanuts and a parrot.

"Titu Cusi," he wrote, "was a man forty years old, of middle height, with marks of smallpox on his face. His mien was rather severe and manly. He wore a shirt of blue damask [obtained from raiding Spanish caravans] and a mantle of vicuña cloth. He is served on silver and there are also twenty or thirty fairly good-looking women waiting behind him." Later the friar attended a meeting of the Inca's council, where the captains were unmasked. At night there was detailed a guard of a hundred armed warriors; flutes and drums were played at each change of the watch. On the morrow Friar Diego presented the letters of the viceroy and explained through an interpreter (a cholo), who came with shield and sword, high-crowned Spanish hat, Spanish dress, and a very old Spanish cloak. He promised that if the Inca would come out of the fastness of Vilcabamba and live in Cuzco, he would have a grant of several villages and an income of $15,000 yearly. If the Inca did not accept this at once, war, relentless war, would be waged upon him, for the *entries into their land were no longer secret.*

The friar was as near to immortality as he would ever be at that moment. The chiefs stood up, raising their daggers in defiance, and one named "Chinchero" came close enough to stab him, but since he received no order from the Inca, he returned to his seat. Next day the friar went further: he asked how many of the captains present were Christians, and a number of them indicating that they had received "the word," he opened up in a primitive homily that soon, he said, set some of them to weeping; that set off the Inca's rage.

"No one, since the death of my father, killed by you Christians, dares to mention the name of Jesus Christ in this land. . . . I should have you killed."

"No better time, my Lord," he retorted, "than to die at present."

This storm passed; to show that "natural men" respect the idea of sanctuary they sent him to eat "a sheep of Castile, many fowls and partridges and other food which their country produces." Still the friar would not let go. The next day he accused the Inca of all the deaths perpetrated in the land; the Inca countered that he could have killed many more, that the images from the churches he had destroyed "were here and well guarded"; besides, his people had more liberty than the Spaniards (which was certainly true). Then the little friar, continuing to crowd his good fortune, said that the Inca was a bastard and that he was usurping the Incaship. The Inca replied that in his land and in his customs there were no bastards; Manco II had had a principal wife, a *coya*, but he had had other wives; and when a son was not available from the principal wife, then sons of the others succeeded to leadership. Moreover, he was high priest "in what he called spiritual things." He, Titu Cusi, was in posession, all recognized him, so that none should form any ideas of driving a wedge between them; in addition, he found all white men deceptive, "all who come try to deceive me."

That night they put on a war dance, there marched up six hundred or more Anti Indians, all with bows and arrows, clubs, and axes; they threatened to kill all the Spaniards that appeared and the Inca said close to the ear of Friar Diego, "I will order my wild Indians to eat them all . . . and all the Indians of Peru will rise at my order," whereupon an Anti chieftain shoved his painted face into the little friar's brown cowl, a face made more hideous since the nose was pierced and the teeth filed—and threatened to eat him raw. Others came up and shouted to the Inca, "What are you doing talking to this little bearded one who is trying to deceive you? We should eat him at once."

Friar Diego shivered in ecstasy.

The next day they returned to negotiation. What were the Inca's final terms? First, Titu Cusi objected to the stipulation that he allow the Spaniards to come into his sanctuary and set up a city. This was the oblique entering wedge, of course. He wanted the following: that the Spanish crown should give estates to all his captains who had served him; that the Indians taken from his *ayllus*, the communal lands, should be returned to him and not to be subject to work-service for the Spaniard; that if the friars entered to teach their religion, his nobles the *orejones* should continue to enjoy the "liberties and privileges" of people of noble birth; that his son Titu should be married in Cuzco to his niece (Doña Beatriz, a great-granddaughter of the Lord Inca Huayna Capac, who had died in 1527); that the Spanish crown should provide him with $15,000 the year. If this was done, the Inca undertook to come peacefully from Vilcabamba and settle near to Huamanga (one must note that this was on the quickest and easiest route to Vilcabamba) or Cuzco, "whichever locality he liked best." The friar agreed "in principle" and said he would send out these proposals to Cuzco.

Then, working the old and tried system of the oblique approach, Friar Diego suggested that the Inca, to show his good faith, should allow him to set up a small chapel and preach the word of Christ and should consent to be baptized. The Inca consented; he was baptized Diego, taking his name from the padre.

As matters were proceeding, it much looked as if the friar would never find martyrdom, so he suggested that thirty of the Inca's captains go out bearing the Inca's proposal to Cuzco, to see how well they would be treated. As for himself, he would remain behind as hostage to answer for their safe return. This was agreed to. They calculated it would take the men six days to get to Cuzco from where they were then and five to return; they would rendezvous at the famous bridge of Chuquichaca. If the men did not return in the stipulated time, the little friar would be hanged. The given time elapsed and there was no news; guards then surrounded the hut of Friar Diego, a gallows was put up, and the Incas quickly assembled Anti warriors and two thousand of their chosen men; they were to attack all frontier posts on his order. But on the twentieth of May the news came that the captains had reached Cuzco and had been well received; there was a spontaneous celebration and "they played on their drums and trumpets in a great feast."

The Inca let it be known that he would march to the bridge of Chuquichaca and meet the judge being sent out from Cuzco for a final parley. At this the friar slipped out and erected a huge cross above the temporary daïs of the Inca, and no one seemed to object—until on the twenty-fifth of May the Lord Yamqui Mayta arrived from Vilcabamba with a hundred of his captains and many warriors. After making obeisance to the Sun and Inca, he saw the cross. He was furious. "Why had the Inca consented to have the cross planted in their land, seeing that it had never been set up in the time of Inca Manco his father?" He averred that it was only a prelude to a plot for his death. The Inca silenced him. Three days later, on the twenty-eighth of May, they set out for the bridge, which had been put up again. When they arrived they found on the other side of the river, standing close to the bridge, Judge Matienzos [16] in his robe of office, 30 Spaniards, 20 arquebusiers, rifles fused and ready, 10 Negroes and 150 Cañari Indians (who seemed to have thrown in their lot permanently with the Spaniard). The two groups stood facing each other across the raging torrent of the Urubamba, while the bridge of Chuquichaca swayed in the wind; no one from either side seemed willing to move across it without ample guarantee. The Inca's captains were cautious. They brought up three hundred cloaks and breeches of Spaniards whom they had killed and stripped, and shouted to the astonished judge that if there was treachery at this meeting, their cloaks would join the pile.

At last the Inca was induced to go across the bridge alone. His captains tried to restrain him, but there by his elbow was his gray eminence the little friar, who worked his dialectics. Once he faced Matienzos, mutual accusations flowed from both sides; the Spaniard complained of the thirty years of war and terror, the destructions and the burnings; the Inca reminded him how the Spaniards had captured him as a boy with his mother at Ollantaytambo, how they had kept them both in prison, chained like dogs, until they revealed the whereabouts of buried gold, and of the wars waged upon his father Manco II, who, after giving refuge to seven Spaniards, had been killed by them.

Finally Judge Matienzos agreed to all of the Inca's terms, except that he must come to Cuzco at once. The Inca demurred, saying that his capital was "60 leagues" (i.e., 180 miles) from there and things could not be effected "so quickly." Moreover, he would have to confer with his council. The little friar, at the moment of triumph (he had been promised the office of *Defensor de todos los Indios* if he succeeded—or if killed in martyrdom, 5,000 masses and a place in the heavens), "passed backwards and forwards," he said, "four or five times"—over that swaying suspension bridge—to ascertain when the Inca would resume the conference. Neither side would give way. The Inca then ordered the bridge cut again, and the thick cables of the Chuquichaca dropped once more into the river.

And so Friar Diego sadly departed with those of Cuzco, having gained neither one triumph nor the other.

The next year, 1566, another friar, Marcos García, decided to give it another try; he communicated his "holy impulse to the worthy father, prior of the Agustinos at Cuzco," and being given leave, set off but did not know what route to take; inquiry from the Indians elicited the reply that "entry into Vilcabamba was so difficult that he had best desist, unless he had the wings of a bird." Still he persisted; he made contact with Titu Cusi's Indians, who lent him ear, and later even allowed him to build a church at Puquira, which is at the headwaters of the Vilcabamba River. He had gotten into the Inca citadel.

The Inca's priests made his life a series of little hells, nor did he make it less by planting "crosses in the land and in the forests"; he was soon joined by another, Friar Diego Ortiz, a man of equal purpose, so they requested the Inca to let them enter his capital at Vilcabamba. They started toward it, but never reached it.

At this time Titu Cusi fell ill. The padres had it that while celebrating some festival he overdrank, as the Indians always did when ritual drunkenness was *de rigueur,* and he contracted pneumonia. One look at him and Friar Ortiz knew he was doomed; he commended his soul to God, at the same time imploring a miracle, for if it was granted he would make great headway among them, and if he did not . . . It was not granted. At the moment the Inca was declared dead, Quispi, an attendant, asked him why his God had not cured the Inca, seeing He was so all-powerful, and receiving no positive answer, struck him. "The friar," says the historian,[17] "knocked down on his knees, offered the other cheek to smite. . . ." Instead the Indian pulled the friar's head back by his beard, sank a *tumi* knife into his throat, and pushed a rope through the hole until it came out of his mouth; with this device they dragged the padre to his doom. "He suffered unheard-of martyrdom. . . . The blessed father took it all smiling with his eyes raised to heaven."

The final obsequies of the Inca were related to some Spaniard who later set it down. The place of burial was never seen; it was, they said, at Pitcos, "on a high mountain which commanded the whole view of the province of Vilcabamba, here . . . an extensive level place with very sumptuous and majestic buildings erected with great skill and art, all the lintels and doors as well . . . being of marble." This is doubtless an exaggeration, since no one has ever seen it, but as the Inca had occupied the land for a hundred years before the conquest and the Neo-Inca state had endured for thirty-five years (that is, from 1536 until 1572, there must have been interestingly constructed buildings upon it.[18]

While all this was transpiring, another embassy was on its way to Titu Cusi to agree to his terms. Naturally, they did not know what had happened; and so, walking into ambush, they were set upon and killed.

Tupac Amaru, another son of Manco II, was now Inca. His only distinction is that he was the last. He prepared for war in the best way he knew, though he had apparently little appetite for the battle which he knew must now come. He had it from his spies in Cuzco (all the mistresses and domestics in that city kept him well supplied with valuable information).

That after the death of the ambassador, Cuzco was arming. Some of the most prominent citizens of Cuzco volunteered their services—Alonso de Meza, who had shared Atahuallpa's ransom; Mancio Sierra de Leguisamo, that one of the early settlers of Cuzco in 1534 whose gambling of his share of the booty had created a pun (he had married an Inca *palla,* Doña Beatriz, the one whom Titu Cusi had meant for his own son); Martín Hurtado, a warrior of great renown, famed mostly for his escape on three occasions from the long arm of Francisco de Carvajal; and many others.

The army, divided into three groups, moved to all the three known entries into the Vilcabamba massif-fortress. Captain Gaspar de Sotelo plugged up the gap at Curahuasi, the place from which the warriors were wont to emerge to attack the caravans on the Inca highway; another force went down the Urubamba to the area about the famous bridge of Chuquichaca; another group continued down to the right, west bank of the Urubamba into the *montaña.* They found the Inca Tupac Amaru at the bridge, having just been to the "House of the Sun" (perhaps at Machu Picchu); someone detailed to destroy the rope bridge forgot it—and the Spaniards poured across. After a short, sharp struggle the Inca retreated precipitately—not toward the mountain fastness of Vilcabamba, but into the jungle toward the Vilcamayu River into the Manaries country. The Spaniards were in such close pursuit that they had no supplies, so they were delighted to find herds of cattle, sheep, and llamas (which gives some idea of the extent of the Neo-Inca economy). Pressing on, they found the Inca and many of his warriors supported by the Anti Indians in the act of going down the river on balsa rafts.

Tupac Amaru and his principal chiefs and wives were marched off to Cuzco; the common Indians were forcibly made to settle in a city named San Francisco de la Victoria de Vilcabamba, at the headwaters of the river of the same name. This is the "Vilcabamba" which appears on the maps; the location of the last capital of the Inca, the real Vilcabamba, is still unknown.

So in 1572 they brought in Tupac Amaru, the last Inca, "dressed in a mantle and doublet of crimson velvet, his shoes made of wool of the country in several colors, his crown, the *mascapachu,* the royal insignia on his head and chained by the neck to all his captains. They were pulled in before the viceroy, Francisco de Toledo.

"After his Excellency had felt the pleasure of conquest," he ordered them all chained to the walls of Colkampata in Upper Cuzco. In three days a court of justice, hastily convened, ordered death by hanging for all the Inca *orejones* or captains. Tupac Amaru was to be beheaded. This being decided, the town crier announced the sentence, but "three died in the public streets and two at the foot of the gallows because they had been tortured in prison until they were dying." However, they were hanged just the same so that the majesty of the law would be upheld.[19]

The execution of the sentence of the Inca took a few days longer, since he had to be taught and catechized and then rebaptized. He was converted by two padres who worked on the matter day and night, for they were, remembered the historian, "so great adepts in their offices that they fed the Inca the holy spirit, as if with a spoon."

All those who had long memories in Cuzco, those who remembered all the hundreds they had seen brought to justice— the garrotings, hangings, eye-gougings, beheadings—were of one voice; this was the most memorable execution they had ever seen. It was superb theater. As the church bells of the cathedral rang out, the Inca was escorted from his prison by four hundred armed Cañari Indians; two monks were on hand to give his soul solace. Before he reached the gallows the Inca was allowed to see his wife torn apart before his eyes; four "beautiful and high-mettled" horses had ropes harnessed to the four extremities of the little Inca *coya,* and as they all pulled at the same time in different directions "the deed was soon done. . . ."

No doubt after this Tupac Amaru found some consolation in religion. The two fathers "remained with the Inca, comforting his soul with holy preparation." The city was packed, the great square which in the Incas' time was called Huaykapata and now Plaza Mayor, was jam-packed; Indians rubbed shoulders with conquistadors, pícaros with noblemen. Windows, roofs, churches, were dark with spectators. "Why, if an orange had been thrown," said one, "it could not have reached the ground, so closely were people confined."

A Cañari Indian was to be executioner. When he raised the enormous knife a marvelous thing happened: as if a signal had been given, there rose from all the Indian voices a long prolonged note of grief. "There was not a Spaniard there," said one, "who failed to show his feelings."

Tupac Amaru spoke well and simply. His course having run its way, he merited death. He besought all those present who had children to punish them, not curse them, for once when he had angered his mother, she had put a malediction on him by telling him he would end by being put to death. At this there was much consternation among his father-confessors.

They interrupted his death speech; even the archbishop showed his pain. The people whistled at the padres for spoiling the concourse of the execution. Still the padres rebuked the Inca: his death was not due to his mother's curse but to the will of God. They were appalled to think that after all that concentrated catechizing for three days and three nights he, Tupac Amaru, would say so unchristian a thing; so "they easily convinced him and he repented of what he had said" and asked their forgiveness. So he went on with his grave small speech. Then he stepped forward to put his head on the block. The director of the execution, he who had arranged the protocol of each event, was aghast at these proceedings; it really was not done. The padres had no respect for the formalities of the moment. The crowd now was uneasy; and to make it worse, suddenly, with much shoving and shouldering, Friar Agustín de la Coruña, Bishop of Popayán, one of the famous Augustine friars who were the first to enter Mexico, and twelve others made their way before the viceroy. They fell on their knees, besought his mercy, insisted that Tupac Amaru, as king in his own right, could only be tried by his peer—the king of Spain. The viceroy refused to listen and ordered the Inca's head cut off at once. It fell at one blow.

As the Cañari Indian held the head up by its long hair, sprinkling the whole of the gentlemen who had ringside seats with royal Inca blood, the church bells of the cathedral began to peal, to be joined a moment later by those of all the other churches throughout Cuzco.

So in 1572 perished Tupac Amaru, the last of the Incas.

The conquest of Peru was now complete, and his Indians passed under the yoke of peace.

# Notes on the Text

1 Garcilasso de la Vega, surnamed (by himself) "Inca," was born in Cuzco in 1539. He was of the "new race" encouraged by Spain; his father was a conquistador, his mother the niece of the Lord Inca Huayna Capac (d. 1527). Garcilasso's early life was spent in the "school for nobles" in Cuzco. At home he learned the fables and spoken history of the Incas. At nineteen years of age he left Peru for Spain; he never returned. After seeing service in the Spanish army he settled in Cordova. There in his old age, with failing memory making a selection of personal and general history "sicklied o'er with the pale cast of thought," he wrote his *Royal Commentaries—Comentarios Reales de los Incas.* The first of the volumes dealt with Inca history, the second with the Spanish conquest. His avowed purpose in writing these books was to glorify the Inca past, styling them for a sophisticated European audience. In marshaling his recollections he depended on those of his Peruvian friends who confirmed this or that; he also made full use of chronicles already published. The *Royal Commentaries* were denied license in Spain; they appeared in Lisbon in 1609, after which their circulation was forbidden in Hispanic America. The *Commentaries* were widely esteemed and read; they appeared in English in 1688.

The "Inca" began the vogue of the "noble savage," the theme having much appeal in France. Rousseau used it to fashion therefrom his theories of primitive society in the *Social Contract;* Marmontel (*Les Incas ou la destruction de l'empire,* Paris, 1777) and all the other subsequent writers of the "noble savage" school, including James Fenimore Cooper, stem from this original—Garcilasso de la Vega. Time has dealt harshly with him; Albert Gallatin (Jefferson's Secretary of the Treasury) said: "I have no faith in Garcilasso . . . he is both a plagiarist and a romancer." The modern school of archaeological historians dismisses him; his accounts of Inca history and religion are considered entirely unreliable. Prescott was not blind to his unreliabilities. "His writings are an emanation from an Indian mind." Garcilasso's writings—like any overpopular work—suffer from reaction.

2 "We may reasonably conclude that there existed in [Peru]

. . . a race advanced in civilization before the time of the Incas. . . ." This sentence shows that Prescott was well aware that the Incas were not, as they claimed, the bringers of culture, before whose advent all was chaos and void. When Prescott wrote, the archaeology of Peru as art and history scarcely existed. Archaeology had not yet revealed the reality of these pre-Inca civilizations. Many of the cultures which were conquered and absorbed into the Inca system were consistently purged of their racial memory by a sort of selective distortion of history.

The Peruvians had weaving and agriculture on the coast of Peru before 3000 B.C.; Chavín, the first dominant culture, appears about 1000 B.C. (both coastal and Andean); Paracas, mostly known by the wide range of its weavings, appears about 400 B.C. and continues into Period III. By this time there were the Mochicas (400–1000 A.D.), a tribal coastal empire, very advanced in all respects; and in southern Peru there were the Nazcas, equally advanced. At the same time the Andean culture of Tiahuanaco (500–900 A.D.), the remains of which are found about Lake Titicaca, came into full flower, grew, and invaded the coast, leaving along almost its entire length their religious cult of the "weeping god." Later the Chimú (1000–1463 A.D.) absorbed the Mochica and became a rival coastal empire; meanwhile the area around the valley of Rimac (Lima) was a *cordon sanitaire* between the Chimú and the aggressive cultures of the southern tribes under the leadership of Lord Inca Chuquimancu. The Incas began their coastal invasions as early as 1350 and continued until, by 1476, they dominated the three Perus—mountain, coast, and a fringe of the jungle.

[3] The farthest penetration was at the river Maule, 35° S.; an Inca fortress there was called Puru-Marca (near present-day Concepción).

[4] This is the *pucará* (fortress) of Sacsahuamán. It was begun by the Inca Pachacuti after 1440 to replace a smaller *pucará;* it was part of the rebuilding of Cuzco after the attack by the Chancas. Sacsahuamán was more than eighty years in the building; it was 1,600 feet in length, composed of three imposing tiers, one atop another, and forty salients for crossfire; there are upwards of 100,000 immense stones such as Prescott describes. More than 20,000 Indians were engaged annually in its construction, and it was finished about 1520, seventeen years before the coming of the Spaniards. Like the Maginot Line, of late memory, it was of no use in defense.

[5] The tambos (or *tampus*) were set along the entire length of the road, a day's journey apart. The distance varied between

four and twenty miles, depending on the nature of the terrain. Tambos varied in size and importance; the "royal" tambo was reserved for the upper classes; all were maintained by the Indians living in the vicinity.

6 The Inca empire at its height stretched from the Angas-mayu River in Colombia (1° N.) to Puru-Marca, Chile (35° S.), a distance of 3,250 linear miles. Along the entire length of the Inca empire are still found the remains of tambos, Sun temples, *pucará* fortresses, administrative centers, population centers. The Inca empire then was almost four times as vast as the Egyptian, which at the height of its Middle Kingdom covered only 625 linear miles. The remains of Inca structures are so many that no calculation of their number has ever been attempted.

7 The "opulence" was not exaggerated by Prescott; the complaint from the discouragists was that Prescott's Indians were "operatic" and "his accounts" of gold ornaments "highly colored." Archaeology has turned up during the last century evidence of an opulence not even dreamed of by Prescott; and thus archaeology has confirmed his descriptions.

8 The nobility of Peru was headed by the Lord Inca, who claimed lineal descent from the sun; his principal wife was a *coya* (queen); in addition he had a large harem, the numerous offspring of which formed a royal *ayllu*. From the members of the Lord Inca's family were chosen the principal administrators.

The *Koraka* classes were of the lower nobility; they were allowed to have their ears pierced and enlarged and were "Big Ears" (*Pakoyoc*). A *Hono-Koraka* was chief of 10,000 Indians; *Pika-waranka Koraka,* chief of 5,000; and so down to the lowest official, *konka-kamayoc,* who was responsible for ten people—in short, a "straw boss." At the base of the social pyramid was the *puric*—an able-bodied tax-paying Indian. For every 10,000 there were 1,331 officials.

9 The four great provinces or quarters were called *suyu;* together they made up *Tawantin-suyu,* the four quarters of the world. This was the name of the Inca empire. The *suyus* lay roughly in the four cardinal directions: *Anti-suyu* was all of the land east of the Andes, including the mountains and the jungle; *Colla-suyu* (taken from the tribal name of the Collas, who lived around Lake Titicaca) embraced all the land south of Cuzco, extended down to Chile, and took in Bolivia and Argentina; the western area, *Cunti-suyu,* extended from Cuzco to the Pacific; and the last was *Chinchay-suyu* (named after the lake now called Junín) and the Chinchay, a tribe to the north. This enormous quarter included everything north of

Cuzco as far as Quito. Each *suyu* or quarter was ruled by a governor, *apu,* related by blood ties to the Lord Inca.

[10] The quipu (Khipo-knot) was a mnemonic device; as its name implies, the knot was a "memory factor"; it consisted of a principal cord from which hung a series of strings that were knotted by the composer of the quipu. In principle it worked like the Chinese abacus. The quipus were used for recording numbers in a decimal system; zero was indicated by leaving an empty space. The *quipu-kamayoc* were a trained class of readers, and each quipu had to be transmitted with a verbal message to indicate what was being counted; without this the quipus were meaningless strings. The quipu has been extensively studied. As a memory aid it was used in reciting time, genealogies, narrative verse.

[11] The Incas built over 10,000 miles of all-weather roads; these ranged from sea level to 17,160 feet, the highest road known. The Andean Royal Road, *Capac Ñan,* was 3,250 miles in length, running from Angasmayu to Chile; it varied in width from 8 to 36 feet; the road was stone-laid in wet country, fashioned into causeways when crossing bogs, and well laid in cities such as Cuzco, but generally it was unsurfaced. It needed no surfacing, since it was for foot traffic and llamas. Climbing mountains, the roads were stepped. The coastal road was 2,520 miles in length from Tumbes in the North to Chile; it had a consistent 24-foot width along its entire distance and was not surfaced, but along its sides yard-high walls of stone or adobe were erected to guide and keep soldiers and llama caravans from wandering and also to keep out the heavy drift of sand. In addition to these there were wonderfully engineered lateral roads, binding coastal and mountain roads into a highway system. Interested readers may wish to consult *Highway of the Sun* (Victor W. von Hagen) London: Victor Gollancz, Ltd., 1955. New York: Duell, Sloan & Pearce, Inc.

[12] The courier-*chasqui* system was pre-Inca, having been extensively used by the Chimú coastal empire. All that Prescott here takes from the early chroniclers has been confirmed. The *chasqui,* a complex relay (each runner running his top speed for only one to two miles) could and did send messages from Quito to Cuzco, a distance of 1,250 miles, in five days! Along the roads the *chasqui* stations—*o'kla*—were placed about two miles apart. In many parts of Peru they are still to be seen. Two *chasquis* waited at each station on a 24-hour basis and were changed every other day. The system was so efficient that the Spanish government maintained it until 1824. In remote parts of Peru *chasquis* are still employed.

[13] Quichua, or *Quechua,* as it is now written, was the domi-

nant language of the Incas because they forced all conquered tribes to speak it in addition to their own tongue. Quechua—"warm-valley people"—was originally spoken by a large tribe dominant in the territory north of the Apurimac River. They were conquered by the Incas before 1400 A.D. Later, in 1438, the Lord Inca Pachacuti—"Earth-Shaker"—made Quechua the official language. The question arises, What did the people of the Inca speak before they spoke Quechua? As a language Quechua is more closely related to Aymará (spoken by those who live about Titicaca and in Bolivia) than to any other. It still remains a living language and is spoken by millions of Indians, cholos, and whites; variants of it are used in Colombia, Ecuador, Argentina, and Chile.

[14] Curicancha = "Golden Enclosure."

[15] For each month there was a particular festival. These were:

| Gregorian months | Peruvian months | Translation |
| --- | --- | --- |
| December | Kapaj Raymi | The Principal Festival |
| January | Juchuy Pokoy | The Small Ripening |
| February | Jatun Pokoy | The Great Ripening |
| March | Paukar Waray | The Garment of Flowers |
| April | Ayriway | Dance of the Young Maize |
| May | Aymuray | Song of the Harvest |
| June | Inti Raymi | Festival of the Sun |
| July | Anta Situwa | Earthly Purification |
| August | Kapaj Situwa | General Purification |
| September | Koya Raymi | Festival of the Queen |
| October | Uma Raymi | Festival of the Water |
| November | Ayamark'a | Procession of the Dead |

(From Luis E. Valcárcel, "The Andean Calendar," in *Handbook of South American Indians*, Vol. 2, pp. 471–76. Washington, 1946.)

[16] Historical events were chanted by "rememberers," who, using the quipu knot-record to aid them, told of the stirring events of each Inca's reign. This form of remembered history appears very often in other, completely unrelated cultures. The Druids had court bards; Richard Coeur de Lion employed a *versificator regis* to chant rhymed chronicles of his deeds; and a similar system was regularly employed by the Greeks.

[17] Coca (Quechua *cuca*) is as old as Peru. The delicate tealike leaves are still used by Indians and cholos from Colombia to Argentina. It is of the greatest antiquity; the methods of using it—the lime stick, the woolen bag in which to carry the coca leaf found in pre-Inca graves—suggest that it pre-

dated the Incas by two thousand years or more. Coca is cultivated in the lush rain-soaked montaña on the eastern slopes of the Andes. The Indians make a quid of it, which they hold inside the cheek; lime or ash is added to quicken the process of leaf disintegration. The daily consumption of the alkaloid cocaine derived from the coca leaf is 300 to 400 milligrams; its effect seems to be to dull the senses, making the chewer immune to hunger, thirst, and cold. The virtues of the drug and the problems raised by addiction to it have been argued over for centuries.

[18] There are four species of these cameloids: the vicuña and the guanaco (the two original and still wild species); and the hybrids, the llama and the alpaca. The primitive camel which appeared in the Eocene period—mostly in what is now Nebraska—is related to the primitive vicuña and guanaco. Groups of these protocameloids made their way over the land route then connecting Outer Asia and Alaska and evolved into the camel; the other primitive groups migrated southward and became the vicuña and the guanaco. The modern camel and the modern llama have traits in common (particularly their social symbiosis with man). The camel grows to a weight of two thousand pounds; the llama seldom exceeds five hundred.

[19] Prescott was the first to see and note the similarities and dissimilarities of Aztec and Inca history: both tribes were glebeless, both came out of the harsh lands of the mountains. The people of the Inca appeared about 1100 A.D.; their imperial system of expansion under the Incas began in 1200 and continued until 1534, when they were conquered by the Spaniards. The Aztecs entered the Mexican lakes in 1168; in 1325 they began to build their capital city, Tenochtitlan; they maintained their rule through elected "Speakers" from this date until 1521, when they fell to the legions of Hernán Cortés. The Aztecs did not constitute an empire in the same sense as the Incas, who effectively held land, under their administrators, 3,250 miles in length, and whose architectural style was imposed on their realm throughout its length and breadth.

[20] The system of *mitimaes*, population transference of peoples, consolidated Inca conquests. The Aztecs also made their conquests, which eventuated in their holding about half of what is now Mexico; however, they had no system of absorption, and they were never able to transform domination into dominion. Mexico was a tribute state. The Incas' milder, but excessively paternal state resulted in effective security—producing, however, a groveling dependence and thus a regulated

life which allowed little freedom of choice. The Aztecs gave their people a full run of individuality, and their capital, Tenochtitlan, had few counterparts in the matter of luxury in all prehistoric America. Although Mexico had nothing like the physical obstacles to communication that faced the Incas, their system of communication was infinitely inferior both on sea and on land. The Mexicans were land-bound; the Incas, after they broke through to the coast, utilized the knowledge of balsas and supplemented land traffic with coastal sea traffic. There is no actual evidence of any direct communication between Peru and Mexico or Peru and Middle America; so far as history and legend are concerned, they were unaware of each other's existence. When Cortés, after he conquered Mexico, wished to develop maritime traffic with Peru, he had to create the facilities for it. The Mexicans never knew of the white potato (the dominant Andean food) or the llama until they were brought there by Hernán Cortés.

[21] The first Spaniard to be made aware of a "kingdom of gold to the south" was Pascual de Andagoya, in 1522. Nine years after the discovery of the Pacific by Vasco Núñez de Balboa, Andagoya made a voyage of exploration on the Pacific side of Panamá, about a hundred miles south to the Bay of Piñas; close by, but still unknown, was the territory of the chieftain Birú, in which, it was said, the gold kingdom lay. Henceforth "Birú" became a symbol of the land of gold; in this way Birú (Peru) got its name. The name was utterly unknown to the people living in the territory which eventually became Peru. A chieftain modeled an animal which he meant to be a llama, but which Andagoya took for a sheep. "In the land where these sheep were," he wrote, "lies the kingdom of gold . . ." In 1524, Francisco Pizarro possessed himself of Andagoya's report, and on the basis of this he raised money, built a boat, and with 112 Spaniards sailed south toward "Birú" for the first time, on May 14, 1524.

[22] This portrait of Francisco Pizarro is somewhat foreshortened, mostly because Prescott did not have all the documents before him. Much is made of illegitimacy; to those of the lower classes at that time it was the rule rather than the exception. Pizarro had much affection for his family, and many of them played an important role in the conquest. The discovery and publication of Pizarro's testament (Raul Porras Barrenechea, Paris, 1936) exhibits another Pizarro than appears in history. His children by the sister of the Inca Atahuallpa were legitimized by the Crown in 1537; his son Gonzalo (named after his brother) was made heir to his title; the administrator of his estate was to see that Gonzalo

"learn grammar and Latin"; his concern in his testament for the Indians, Negroes, and poorer conquistadors seems very real, and he attempted to come to terms with Diego Almagro in seeking a way to keep their original contract before death intervened. It was true that, unlike his brothers, he could neither read nor write; the most he could manage was a shaky rubric beside his name.

[23] Bartolomé Ruiz, a native of the Villa de Moguer in Andalusia, arrived in Panamá in the time of Núñez de Balboa (about 1513). He first piloted Francisco Pizarro in his early searches for "Birú"; later (September, 1526) he discovered the Isle of Gallo lying off the coast of Tumaco; on this island Pizarro and the "thirteen"—those who agreed to stay with him—took refuge. On the third voyage of discovery Ruiz brought Pizarro safely into Tumbes and then made the first known voyage by a European down the southern coast of Peru. He was the first to sight and describe a Peruvian balsa. In the famous *Capitulación*, in which Francisco Pizarro was given royal sanction to search for and make conquest of "Birú," Ruiz was created "Piloto Mayor de la Mar del Sur" and made an hidalgo with the right to wear the "golden spurs." He married Leonor de Esquivel and had several children by her; he died at sea while returning to Spain in 1579.

[24] Balsas should perhaps be explained, since they have entered current history through Thor Heyerdahl's famous voyage on a balsa into the Pacific. The word "balsa" is Spanish and means something that floats, particularly a raft. The word was applied both to rafts made from balsa wood and those made from reeds. The balsa tree did not grow in coastal Peru; it appears north of Tumbes, at the end of the desert, and is most abundant in Ecuador. Considerable pre-Spanish maritime traffic grew up along the Ecuadorian coast, and later, when the Incas took over, it extended southward. The balsa raft met by Bartolomé Ruiz off Manabi carried twenty people and was loaded down with thirty tons of merchandise. It was not Inca, but of Ecuador. The Incas did not fully subdue Ecuador's coast until 1476, and until then they had only a limited knowledge of the sea. Their knowledge of water transport was limited to the reed balsas used extensively on Lake Titicaca and on various parts of the coast. It is very much to be doubted whether the Incas ever made extended sea voyages.

[25] The Isle of Gallo, so called because from a distance its profile resembles a cock's comb, lies offshore within the Rada de Tumaco, at precisely 2° north latitude. It is less than five miles in circumference, lowland tropical on one side and

on the other—which the editor of this book found in 1947 to be the refuge of Pizarro and the "thirteen"—limestone cliffs, two hundred feet high, festooned with tropical vegetation; the crescent beach on which the drama of Pizarro's line took place lies below this rock outcrop. In the lush soil the Spaniards would have had difficulty in raising tropical crops or building houses; the heavy rain and swarms of mosquitoes must have caused much suffering. Save for a few families who live there, the Isle of Gallo is as it was in 1527.

[26] The Isle of Puná lies in the Río Guayas estuary, 2° 30′ south latitude, on the Gulf of Jambelí. It is low-lying and tropical. Culturally the Indians were related to the Huancavilcas tribes which centered on Guayaquil. They had several large settlements at the time of the Spanish conquest, and recent archaeological investigations show that they were well advanced in stoneworking. They raised corn and yucca but mostly concerned themselves with fishing and trading; and as Puná lay on the main coastal trade routes, they were also considered to be pirates. War and commerce so enriched them with gold and other metals that most of the conquistadors were impressed with their prosperity. They carried on traditional warfare with the inhabitants of Tumbes and were famed for their ferocity. The friar Vicente de Valverde, who was involved in the fall of the Inca Atahuallpa at Cajamarca, was captured and eaten by the Puná Indians.

[27] It is highly unlikely that either bananas or coconuts were included, since these are not native to the Americas. The banana was introduced into the West Indies by Tomás Berlanga about 1529; coconuts were brought to the Americas from the Philippines. In all of the material that tombs have yielded—which provides a graphic or plastic description of what the native ate—there is no example of either banana or coconut. This offers further evidence that they were not known to the inhabitants of the Americas until the arrival of the white man.

[28] Pedro de Candia ("the Greek") was born at Candia on the Isle of Crete. He was one of the original "thirteen" of the Isle of Gallo—those who stood by Francisco Pizarro on the small island off Tumaco. He was the only white man, apart from Alonso de Molina and those who perished, to see Tumbes before it was destroyed in the war of contention between Atahuallpa and Huascar. Pedro de Candia participated in the capture of Atahuallpa, drew as his share of the ransom 407 marcos of silver, and was involved in all the civil wars. He shifted to the side of Almagro the Lad and was killed by him at the battle of Chupas (1542) when

treachery was suspected. His son went to the "school of nobles" in Cuzco with the "Inca" Garcilasso de la Vega.

[29] A contemporary account of Tumbes was written in 1536 by the *pícaro* Alonzo Enríquez de Guzmán. In his memoirs he says, "The great city called Tumpiz is inhabited entirely by Indians, and close to the shore is a great house belonging to the lord of the country, with walls built of adobes like bricks, very beautifully painted with many colors and varnished. I never saw anything more beautiful. The roof is straw, also painted, so that it looks more like gold. About a large temple was a garden with fruits and vegetables of the country imitated all in gold and silver. The women wore a dress large and broad like a morning gown and the chieftains went dressed in mantles and shirts and wore a thing like a turban adorned with gold and silver beads, which they call *Chaquira*. The country itself was a desert, but the Indians made it bloom by irrigation. They said they were the vassals of a great lord named Old Cuzco, who lived in the mountains, and that he had much gold and the people spent many days and nights at their drinking bouts, and it is certainly marvelous the quantity of beer-*chicha* that these Indians drink."

Tumbes was originally inhabited by the Tallanes, who spoke a language related to that of Puná and Huancavilca (Guayaquil). They are famed for their lustrous black pottery and the very striking lip and nose ornaments. The Tallanes were first conquered by the Kingdom of Chimor under Minchan-Caman, about 1450, and then later in 1463 by the Incas, who absorbed them into their empire, making Tumbes the coastal terminus of the empire.

[30] At that time (1527) magnificent Chan-Chan, capital of Chimor, was standing, and while not as opulent as it was before the Inca conquest in 1476, it was still the chief city of a vast area; more than 50,000 people lived there. Chan-Chan with its high walls and enormous Sun temples could have been seen from the sea.

[31] A salary of 725,000 maravedis sounds so imposing that its real value must be given: a maravedi was equivalent, but not in purchasing power, to one cent. Pizarro's salary was then to be $7,250 a year. To obtain an idea of its purchasing power one would have to multiply this ten times; but even so the sum was not an extraordinarily large one.

[32] Although the Spaniards called Atacames—close to the Río Cayapa—"Esmeraldas," the region contained no emeralds; historically the only emeralds which circulated all over the Americas—from Arizona to Chile—came from the region of Muzo, some distance from Bogotá in Colombia. They

were exploited by the Chibchas, who had only salt and emeralds to trade. As the Cayapa region about "Esmeraldas" in Ecuador is rich in placer gold, these people traded gold dust for emeralds. The Chibchas in highland Colombia became known as "El Dorado" even though they had no gold source, and the Cayapas known as "Esmeraldas" although they were not the source of emeralds. It is this mixing of things which caused a philosopher to call man "that intellectual maniac who unravels everything in history and tangles everything up in fact."

[33] Huayna Capac's death is variously given as 1525 and 1527. One of the most accurate chroniclers, Pedro de Cieza de León, who was in the Indies for seventeen years (1531–1548), states that Alonso de Molina and Gines were brought to him before he died (this would have been after November, 1527), and that before this the realm of Ecuador had been visited by a plague—of smallpox, some say—and this is possible, since Pizarro had contact with the coastal peoples for five years before this event.

[34] There was in the Inca system no clear line of succession. The Inca named, with the consent and advice of his council, the most competent of those sons who were born of his principal wife, the *coya*. This lack of "clear" line of succession for an heir apparent was one of the principal causes of the civil war between the two half-brothers Atahuallpa and Huascar. Various places are given for Atahuallpa's birth, but most seem to agree that it was in the North—that is, in what is now Ecuador. At the death of Huayna Capac most of his famed generals were in the North; Atahuallpa, who was present at many of his father's later battles, was well liked by the army. When, as Prescott writes, Atahuallpa was defeated in the first battle of the civil war, he was imprisoned by the Cañari at the large Inca city of Tomebamba. (This is amazing, since Huayna Capac was beloved by the Cañari, who peopled this part of the country.) When Atahuallpa escaped he ordered a massacre of those Cañari who had brought about his imprisonment. This had historical repercussions, for as soon as the Spaniards appeared the Cañari became their Indian auxiliaries. They, as will be seen, served the Spanish faithfully even during the siege of Cuzco, and their hatred of the Incas was such that they brought about the fall of the Fortress of Sacsahuamán.

[35] Zaran (now Serrán), midway between Tumbes and Batán Grande, was a large coastal administrative center controlled by the Incas; from Zaran ran a lateral road con-

necting the coastal highway with the "Royal Andean" way at Huancabamba.

[36] De Soto made the sally with forty men; it was reported in detail by Diego de Trujillo, one of the "thirteen" of the Isle of Gallo. In June, 1532, de Soto and his forty mounted soldiers entered Caxas, "a village surrounded by mountains"; it was here that they saw for the first time tangible evidence of the fabled cities of "Birú": ". . . fine edifices," wrote Trujillo, ". . . and a fortress built entirely of cut stones . . . and a wonderful road made by hand and broad enough for six men on horseback to ride abreast. . . ." It is this report by Hernando de Soto that raised the fainting hopes of Pizarro's little army.

[37] A hundred years has added little to our understanding of why Atahuallpa allowed himself to fall into so simple a trap. New historical evidence has been advanced to help understand the reason why: reports had reached Atahuallpa of the horses, and at first it was thought they were something like centaurs—man and horse being one. However, when it was found that they were two, horse and man, the man part was believed to be ineffectual when dismounted. Their guns were "fire sticks" and were thought to be thunderbolts (indeed, an Indian woman on the coast poured a libation of *chicha* down the muzzle of Pedro de Candia's piece as an "offering"); they believed that the steel swords were no more effective than a woman's weaving battens. If nothing more, it explains that, although the Spaniards reached the Pacific Ocean by 1513, and Mexico fell in 1522, and since 1524 Spaniards had been loose in Colombia, none of this intelligence reached Peru in any concrete form for the simple reason that there was no direct communication of one area with the other. There was ample indirect contact; of this there is full evidence in archaeology. What reached the Peruvians long before they saw the Spaniards were vague reports, all of which were interpreted as supernatural phenomena. The fatal mistake which Atahuallpa and all else involved in this drama made was their disbelief in the ability of the Spaniards to obtain reinforcements from the sea. To the landbound Indian the sea, except for coastal commerce, was a barrier; once an enemy was encircled on land, it was his end.

How else explain why Atahuallpa, surrounded by battle-hardened warriors, allowed a handful of men to scale the Andes and ambush him in the center of his realm. At first Atahuallpa showed amazing fortitude; he had been in a similar situation before, when he was captured at Tomebamba, and he thought to turn the tables. But when Almagro arrived with new ships and hundreds of reinforcements, the fatality of his position was impressed upon him.

[38] Atahuallpa's ransom room is still extant; it forms part of the church and hospital of Belén and it was used in 1947 (when seen by the editor) as a schoolroom. It is the only structure left of Incaic Cajamarca (if one excepts the "Baños del Inca"). The dimensions of it agree with those given by the Spaniards. The same room was seen by Alexander von Humboldt in 1802: ". . . the room is still shown in which the unfortunate Atahuallpa was confined. . . ."

[39] Atahuallpa's ransom yielded 1,326,539 pesos of pure gold; the gold averaged 22½ carats. At that time 100 gold pesos equaled 190 silver pesos. At today's value the silver of the ransom reached $8,818,876.99. Gold at the value of today ($35.02 an ounce) would bring the total gold ransom to $19,851,642.07. Thus Atahuallpa paid $28,670,519.06, but failed to ransom himself.

[40] Samuel Lothrop writes in *Inca Treasure* (1938), in the chapter "What the Spaniards Missed," that six hundred loads of gold on the way from Chile never arrived. With the premature death of Atahuallpa, 11,000 llamas loaded with gold dust disappeared close to the city of Hatun-Jauja; treasures missed by the first Spaniards were later found at Lunahuaná in the Cañete valley; 500 llamas laden with gold and silver were secreted in the Casma valley; at Curamba, Pedro Pizarro, a cousin of the conquistador, found "slabs of silver, ten in number and twenty feet in length and a thickness of three fingers . . . and for this reason," he continued, "the hidden treasures of this kingdom are many. . . ."

[41] The geography here is somewhat compressed by Prescott; the Abancay River, then called Pacha-chaca, was crossed by a large suspension bridge (which was eventually replaced by a Spanish bridge farther down the river). The Apurimac, the next valley south, has an immense canyon. The Incas placed four hanging suspension bridges across it at various points, but the greatest, and the one on the direct route to Cuzco, was the Huaca-chaca—the Holy Bridge— which crossed the river below the town of Curubamba. In the mind of the early Spaniards this bridge, 148 feet long and hanging 138 feet above the roaring Apurimac, was coexistent with Peru itself. It was the longest continuously used bridge in the Americas—1350 until 1890—it has entered the literature as the *Bridge of San Luis Rey*. On the south bank of the Apurimac was Rimac-tampu (Limatambo), a royal way station; from there the Royal Road led through a high pass at which there was an idol called Vilcaconga, where

Indians lay in ambush for Hernando de Soto. For an account of its history, size, and length, see *Highway of the Sun,* von Hagen, New York-Boston, 1955.

[42] The causeway of Anta, erected about 1350 A.D. by the Incas to span a wide-spreading quagmire, is still extant and still used. More than six feet above the flooded plains, it is twenty-four feet wide and stretches eight miles in length; it has, said a chronicler of that period, "walls on both sides so firm that they will last a long time."

[43] Cuzco is the oldest continuously inhabited city in the Americas. It was established about 1200. Various population figures are given; 100,000 seems far above the mark, but if we accept this figure, then Cuzco must have had 20,000 houses, assuming an average of five people to each house. Present-day Cuzco, although five times the size of ancient Cuzco, does not have a population of 100,000, so that 50,000 would seem to be nearer the correct figure. Mexico City, founded in 1325 A.D., had at the time of its conquest in 1521 some 90,000 inhabitants (but even this is an immense figure for the time). London had then 65,000 people, Paris 40,000. Mexico has grown with the years until the figure now has been placed as high as 1,000,000. Time, like distance, lends enchantment. Cuzco in 1534, to be within the known statistics of population, could not have had much more than 50,000 people.

[44] "Sparking *chicha*" suggests sparkling Burgundy; this it certainly was not. *Chicha* (*ak'a* in Quechua) is a gray malt-like beverage, more akin in taste and smell to stale beer. Corn was allowed to germinate, and an enzyme, diastase, converted part of the starch into the sugar maltose. This was allowed to ferment, and the "bread-beer" then became alcoholic. The longer it fermented, the stronger the brew; for daily use it was only allowed to be mildly alcoholic, but for ritual drunkenness a *chicha* of greater alcoholic strength was brewed. The only time it would have sparkled would be when tipped from a golden beaker reflecting the rays of the sun.

[45] This is the same Pedro de Alvarado, the companion of Hernán Cortés in the conquest of Mexico and later founder of Guatemala. Because of his blond hair he was called *Tonatiuh,* the "Sun," by the Aztecs. His brother, Alonso de Alvarado, who remained in Peru after this sortie, was a much-esteemed man; he was the founder of Chachapoyas.

[46] Paullu Topa Inca was the son of Huayna Capac (d. 1527) and thus the brother of Huascar and also of Manco Inca II, the one who escaped the Spaniards and set up a

neo-Inca state. Paullu sided at once with the Spaniards; he accompanied Almagro on his famous expedition to Chile in 1535, he refused to join his brother Manco Inca II in the uprising of 1536. He sided with the lost cause of Almagro's son at the Battle of Chupas (for which he earned the enmity of the Pizarros), yet he escaped the executioner's knife. After Peru settled down under the yoke of peace he took up his residence at Colkampata, under the shadows of the fortress of Sacsahuamán. He was baptized with the name of Cristóbal and then built a church to his patron saint, San Cristóbal. Both church and fragments of his "palace" are still extant. His double-purpose perfidy was rewarded by the Crown by retention of his Inca emoluments. He died in the odor of sanctity in 1549; his son was elevated to the Order of Santiago and "retired" to Spain.

[47] The plan of Manco II was to take Cuzco by siege; on April 18, 1536, the warriors converged on Cuzco on its four approaches, burned the outlying buildings, boxing the defending Spaniards—who numbered 190, of whom only 80 were mounted—and about 2,000 Cañari warriors into the center squares, driving them as a hunting party its quarry. Outside, the Indians, now learning from experience, put up an elaborate system of staked pits as defense against massed cavalry charges. Manco II's effectives numbered about 180,-000. The Inca tactics had much improved; they rained down on the hapless Cuzco garrison fire and stones from the fortress of Sacsahuamán, which overlooked the capital. They used firearms, and Manco II even commanded from a horse which he rode well. But there was traditional weakness in Inca warfare; they still retained the ritual ceremonial war—painted bodies, battle cries, conch horns, parades to overwhelm the enemy by a chaos of sound. They still attacked en masse and thus opened themselves to mass death by the cavalry squadrons; at night they ceased fighting and gave obeisance to the lunar deity; their battles were waged in a twenty-day rhythm which the Spaniards soon knew and took advantage of.

The Fortress of Sacsahuamán fell to the Spaniards on May 29, thirty-seven days after the siege had begun. This allowed the horsemen to range behind the enemy lines. In the second month they adopted what proved to be a devastating principle: they cut off the right hand of every captured Indian. This spread terror. The siege about Cuzco lasted only three months, not the nine or sixteen months given in the various histories. This is affirmed by the unpublished report of the Council of Cuzco to Charles V dated in Cuzco July 27, 1537.

[48] Tambo, or Ollantaytambo, 24 miles northeast of Cuzco, lies back of the Urubamba River. One of its sides faces the Urubamba, the other the Lares valley (the Lares were then subdued "Incas by privilege"). Ollantaytambo was a fortress; it was in the process of being completed when the Spaniards' arrival interrupted this, and massive worked stones intended for it still lie along the way from the quarry. Below there was a royal residence and a city laid out in Kancha-complex— houses placed in a rectangle with a common yard. The fortress was rebuilt in 1460 to prevent the incursion of wild tribes from the jungle Anti-suyu quarter, using the Lares valley. The old part of Ollantaytambo (see plan) is composed of a large plaza laid out like the lines of a gridiron; the fortress, arising on an acropolis, is built upon the rock outcrop, and agricultural terraces, like a flight of giant steps, were cut out of the living rock. Ollantaytambo is also the province of a popular Quechua folk legend, "The Song of Ollantay," of dubious Inca origin.

## Notes on Civil Wars of the Conquerors

[1] As the pages in *The Conquest of Peru* which deal with the civil wars total a little less than one half of the entire book, and as they do not have the importance of the first part of the narrative, the editor, in order to make it possible to issue *The Conquest of Peru* in a condensed version, has adopted the expedient of a rewritten, shortened version of this material.

[2] Hernando Pizarro wrote the report on his expedition to Pachacamac while on his way to Spain with the ransom of Atahuallpa. Although it covers the same ground as the official reports of Francisco de Xeres, who was the king's observer, it is valuable not alone because it came from the man of the highest rank in the expedition, but because it was the first. When his ships touched the island of Santo Domingo, Hernando Pizarro allowed it to be copied by the king's historiographer; it is fortunate that this was done, for the original is lost and we know it only through its appearance in *La Historia General y Natural de las Indias . . .* of

Oviedo (Chap. xv, lib. 43, published in Madrid 1851–1855).

3 Written and published anonymously, Sevilla, April, 1534, *La Conquista del Peru. . . .* The first detailed report on Peru's conquest is a work of such rarity that only one copy is known to exist (Rare Book Room—New York Public Library). Although the author is anonymous, Dr. Raul Porras, the late eminent Peruvian scholar, believes it to have been the work of Cristóbal de Mena who took part in all the phases of conquest mentioned. A facsimile copy of it was issued by the New York Public Library in 1929.

4 *The True History of the Conquest—Verdadera Relación de la Conquista del Peru. . . ,*" "true" so as to combat the other—was printed in July, 1534, and written by Francisco de Xeres. There were many versions of it, in many languages.

5 This same Pedro de Valdivia, the real conqueror and settler of Chile, wrote a fascinating eleven-page account of this epic of exploration in a letter to Hernando Pizarro. Since it lay among the La Gasca-Pizarro papers at the Huntington Library, it has never been fully published. It is dated from La Serena, Chile, September 4, 1545. The letter shows that Hernando Pizarro, even while languishing in prison, commanded respect; he begins "I have heard of your health and reputation which you enjoyed with our Caesar, the Emperor Charles V. . . . Indeed your signal services to this country as a discoverer and conqueror and founder deserve all the consideration which His Majesty may show you." Then he tells how he left Cuzco in January, 1540, and so he recounts in the bald matter-of-fact sixteenth-century manner all that befell him. This is the beginning of the history of Chile.

6 This epic journey—all of these were then epics of exploration—to the "Land of Cinnamon" in which the great Amazon was discovered is told in full in *The Discovery of the Amazon,* by José Medina (American Geographical Society Publication 17, New York, 1934).

7 These and other details of the lives and deaths of the brothers Pizarro have been published by Dr. Raul Porras in *El Testamento de Pizarro* (Paris, 1936) and in *Las Relaciones Primitivas de la Conquista del Peru* (Paris, 1937).

8 The celebrated soldier-historian who wrote eight histories of the conquest and then the civil wars in Peru; *The War of Chupas* (Hakluyt Society Publications, Second Series, xlii, Cambridge, 1918) gives all this in detail. For more on this writer see Victor Wolfgang von Hagen, *The Incas and Pedro de Cieza de León,* a newly translated version of Cieza's two Chronicles with a life and notes (University of Oklahoma

Press, Vol. 53, in *Civilizations of the American Indian* series, 1959).

[9] All of this part which deals with Pedro de La Gasca and the final battles of the civil wars has been taken from papers William Prescott never saw or had access to. The Huntington Library purchased from Messrs. Maggs Bros. in 1927 the personal papers of Pedro de La Gasca. They are in their greater part unpublished. More than three thousand folio pages, consisting of notes, diaries, letters, it is one of the most complete histories of one period preserved in one collection. The directors of the Henry E. Huntington Library allowed the editor the use of these unpublished documents for the publication of his study of Pedro de Cieza de León and has further extended permission for the use of them in this edition of Prescott. For the use of this unusual material, the editor, as in many other instances of aid from Huntington in the past, is most grateful.

[10] That the title of Marqués de los Cañaris could even be proposed for Carvajal is of historical interest. Originally Cañar, which is in Ecuador, was the tribal place of a mountain people, who, allied with the jungle headhunting Jívaros, held back the Incas' northern advance. They were conquered circa 1475 by Huayna Capac (the father of Atahuallpa and Huascar, who were to fight over the division of empire). At Tomebamba (or Tumipampa), which is now Cuenca in Ecuador, he built a large city; it became his favorite resting place on his many journeys throughout the realm. When he died there his sons began preparation for war; Atahuallpa was seized and held by the Cañaris by order of Huascar (seemingly they obeyed him as the son and legitimate heir). Atahuallpa escaped, and when he gained ascendancy he slaughtered the Cañari tribesmen. They never forgot it; they made terms with the Spaniards at once and fought as one with their legions. They helped to defend Cuzco in 1536 when it was set upon by Manco II and helped to take the fortress of Sacsahuamán. A Cañari in 1572 was given the choice job of beheading the last Inca.

[11] The report of Hernández Paniagua de Loayza's mission to Gonzalo Pizarro is contained in a twenty-six-page letter written to La Gasca dated August 1, 1547. It has never been published in full; as a word picture of Pizarro and all those about him, including Francisco de Carvajal, it is scarcely to be equaled. Vol. I, folios 235–254, La Gasca-Pizarro papers, Huntington Library, San Marino, California.

[12] This was the father of the future historian of Peru, also called Garcilasso de la Vega. The son was born in Cuzco in

1540; his mother was a niece of Huayna Capac. He passed his first years among the surviving members of the Inca royal family. He left Peru at twenty. In his old age he settled down to write, in Cordova, *Comentarios Reales*. . . . Refused license in Spain, it was published in Portugal in 1601. Written for a sophisticated European audience at the start of the baroque age, his book began the fashion of the "noble savage."

[13] In 1911, Hiram Bingham, then a young history professor at Yale, set out to find Vilcabamba, the last capital of the Incas. His early explorations were really notable; he found many of the outlying ramparts of Vilcabamba, and later a native suggested the ruins that lie about the Urubamba called Machu Picchu. Finding this marvelously placed city (even though we now know that it is bound by road to several other similarly placed cities along the high gorge of the Urubamba), unknown to Spaniards and unknown to history, Hiram Bingham believed that he had found Vilcabamba. But the bones there were mainly those of women; there were no remains of the Spaniards or their possessions, all of which were in the hands of the Incas. Machu Picchu is not Vilcabamba. Vilcabamba is still out there.

[14] Juan de Betanzos was an old conquistador who had settled in Cuzco. He had excellent opportunities of acquainting himself with Inca history and in 1551 wrote *Suma y Narración . . . de los Incas*. The manuscript lay for 300 years gathering dust in the Royal Library of El Escorial; it was finally published in 1880. Betanzos is the only historian who attempts to give a name to the people of the Inca; they were called, he said, *Capac-cuna*.

[15] The manuscript of Diego Rodríguez de Figueroa somehow came into the possession of the French Orientalist M. Eugene Jacquet who, knowing of Alexander von Humboldt's interest in South America, gave it to him in 1833 when he still lived in Paris.

[16] Matienzos was Lic. Juan de Matienzos de Peralta, Justice of the Royal Audience of Charcas, Bolivia, and Cuzco, the same who aided the viceroy, Francisco de Toledo, to put into effect the "ordenanzas" for the governing of Peru.

[17] The historian is Capitán Pedro Sarmiento de Gamboa, a gifted man, albeit reckless. While pursuing Francis Drake in 1567 in the Pacific, he discovered the Solomon Islands; he was also the inventor of several nautical instruments. Being a favorite of the viceroy, Francisco de Toledo (who twice saved him from the Inquisitors, those extractors of hidden truth), he was employed to compile a history of the

Incas, to be written so as to counteract the unfortunate impressions that the books of Las Casas had left in Europe. He traveled much in Peru, forcing all of the surviving lords to admit that the Incas were tyrannical, cruel, and oppressive; then, so that it would have the odor of truth, he had the whole of it read before forty of those Indians of "good birth" and compelled them to verify its truth. However, as often happens with things about Incas and men, the manuscript was lost on its way to Spain; it turned up, of all places, in the Library of the University at Göttingen, where in 1893 it was published by the learned Dr. Richard Pietschmann, Director of the Library. There is an English translation, *History of the Incas,* by Sir Clements Markham, with many valuable additions taken from unpublished material in the British Museum (Hakluyt Society, Cambridge, 1907).

[18] The forty-year resistance by the Neo-Inca (to 1572) was organized in the effort to escape and counter the leveling process in early colonization. The retention of the Incaship and the incorporation of many non-Quechua-speaking peoples as military allies bespeak the vital persistence of the Inca concept of the state. In what measure its highly articulated administrative system actually survived is difficult to determine. The physical mobility which characterizes other sections of Conquest Quechua life was indispensable to the survival of the Neo-Inca; their entire history may be conveniently described as a magnified and special instance of mass dispersal. Unceasing military contingencies inhibited the exercise of customary administrative faculties. All the resources of the Neo-Inca society were drawn into the struggle for survival. Hence leveling was inevitable; the fighters at the siege of Cuzco, for instance, were simultaneously food growers, and at Ollantaytambo or Viticos the traces of an administrative hierarchy are faint. The Inca ruler maintained a "court" consisting of military aides whose needs were less those of an elaborate ceremonial of caste than of soldiers in bivouac. (George Kubler, Colonial Quechua, *Handbook of South American Indians,* Vol. 2, Washington, 1946.)

[19] To show how little man is capable of immediate spiritual progress: when Hermann Göring took poison after his death sentence at the Nüremberg trials, his massive body was conveyed to the bottom of the hangman's noose meant for him, to convey the idea that even self-immolation was not enough for him to escape the majesty of the law.